To Aunt Nancy +
Uncle Joel,
Enjoy! - of course,
this is an academic
book about books, but
Mom thought you
might be interested —
— you might skip over
the introduction (pp 19-
59) — where I am
the most theoretical

Yours,
Ed.

LIBERAL EPIC

VICTORIAN LITERATURE AND CULTURE SERIES
Jerome J. McGann and Herbert F. Tucker, Editors

LIBERAL EPIC

The Victorian Practice of History from Gibbon to Churchill

EDWARD ADAMS

University of Virginia Press | Charlottesville and London

University of Virginia Press
© 2011 by the Rector and Visitors of the University of Virginia
All rights reserved
Printed in the United States of America on acid-free paper

First published 2011

1 3 5 7 9 8 6 4 2

LIBRARY OF CONGRESS CATALOGING-IN-PUBLICATION DATA

Adams, Edward, 1963–
Liberal epic : the Victorian practice of history from Gibbon to Churchill / Edward
Adams.
p.   cm. — (Victorian literature and culture series)
Includes bibliographical references and index.
ISBN 978-0-8139-3145-6 (cloth : alk. paper) — ISBN 978-0-8139-3150-0 (e-book)
1. Epic literature, English—History and criticism. 2. History in literature. 3. War
in literature. 4. Liberalism in literature. 5. Liberalism—Great Britain—
History. 6. Literature and history—Great Britain—History. I. Title.
PR468.H57A33 2011
809'.9359—dc22
2011005590

To Lucy-Jane *and* Walter

CONTENTS

ACKNOWLEDGMENTS

This book was written in splendid isolation, one of the increasingly rare benefits of the academy. I thank the generous ways of Washington and Lee University for the several summer Lenfest Grants and two sabbaticals that permitted my work. I hope my effort embodies all of the benefits and none of the limitations of that old-time luxury afforded me.

Nonetheless, such claims of solitary achievement are seldom true, and, particularly at the beginning, middle, and end of this narrative, I received considerable help. The junior faculty reading group of Lesley Wheeler, Marc Conner, Kary Smout, and Suzanne Keen (now all happily tenured—congratulations!) heartened me with their positive responses to the first chapters of this project—at a time of difficulty (the fire!), when such enthusiasm was most needed. Midway, Jay Dixon, known through our mutual friend Douglas Mao, recommended me to Thomas Gillcrist as a worthy contributor on *The History of England* for a special journal issue on Macaulay. I wish to thank Barry Tharaud for permitting its use here. At the end, the anonymous reader and Jerome McGann and Herbert Tucker at the University of Virginia Press greatly encouraged me with their detailed and generous responses. My final revisions have been firmly guided by both the spirit and the letter of their suggestions and criticisms and then carefully corrected by Colleen Romick Clark and Ellen Satrom. At the very end, my friends Stephen Cochran and John Hutson lent me a charming beach cottage (twice!) where the painful business of cutting was made (almost!) a pleasure. And long ago at Yale, before the beginning, Claude Rawson primed me to detect the subtle interworkings of style, violence, and the death wish lurking at the heart of this study.

Finally, there are two others: Suzanne, who has already been acknowledged, and John Evans. Suzanne Keen along with her husband and my friend Fran MacDonnell bore the burden of advising and listening to me all along, and, though I sought not to impose, I am sure I sometimes did. It is because of her advice that I did not submit a 300,000–word manuscript, though I still plagued UVaP (and its appropriately sharp first reader) with more than enough. Monsieur Evans has been a marvelous intellectual stimulus for many years—and many more to come. John first directed me to Churchill, and though that addition led to the most painful of this expansive manuscript's many subsequent depopulations, the sorry day that saw the removal of Lawrence of Arabia, another had to roll over and fall out.

LIBERAL EPIC

||||||||||||||||||||||||||||||||||||||||||||||||||||||||||||||||||||||||||||||||||||||||||||||||||||||||||||||||||||||||||||||||||||||||||||||||||||||||||||||||||||||

PROLOGUE

War was the chief field of heroic action, and even the history of England was chiefly the story of war. The history of the United States promised to be free from such disturbances. War counted for little, the hero for less.

—Henry Adams, *History of the United States*

Battle is unquestionably one of the most popular of all historical subjects, as something to read about.

—John Keegan, "The Historian and Battle"

In 1914, when he was nearly fifty, H. G. Wells still played elaborate war games with "toy soldiers," and even published an instructional treatise, *Little Wars* (1913), so others could play too. This indulgence represented only a small portion of his fascination with the matter of heroic warfare: "I liked especially to dream that I was a great military dictator like Cromwell, a great republican like George Washington or like Napoleon in his earlier phases. I used to fight battles whenever I went for a walk alone. . . . The citizens of Bromley . . . never [had] a suspicion of the orgies of bloodshed I once conducted there. . . . Up to 1914, I found a lively interest in playing a war game, with toy soldiers and guns" (*Experiment* 74–75). *War of the Worlds* (1898), which similarly inflicted "orgies of bloodshed" upon English towns, was written when he was thirty-two. It established his remarkable success as a writer and remains his most celebrated work—the ultimate source for many a contemporary alien war fantasy, whether on the page, screen, or video display. The year 1914 stands as a societal as well as a personal marker of a surprisingly long-delayed maturity at last gained from horrific reality, though, as he observed in his 1934 autobiography, Hitler and the German people still did not seem to have made this step forward in civilized political-economic understanding. In the wake of the Great War, which he himself first hopefully labeled the war to end war, Wells wrote one of his most spectacular and improbable successes, *The Outline of History* (1920), likewise naïvely intended as a history to end war histories, if not war itself. Wells designed his 1,200–plus-page survey to demonstrate the maturation of history into a kind of science and to educate its readers around the globe to see themselves and their world in its own broad, peaceful, progressive, and scientific terms. It pushed aside traditional content—wars, nation-states, and their various political and military heroes—to emphasize matters of evolution, technology, and the growth of global self-consciousness. Wells's narrative was the most popular expression of an ongoing effort to transform history writing that began in the nineteenth century with William Buckle, though Buckle himself rooted it in the ambitious cultural histories from Voltaire's later career. This project found its most subtle expression in the various historiographical experiments and speculations of Wells's older contemporary Henry Adams.

For all of their dedication to this effort, Adams and Wells acknowledged their personal failures and the failure of their larger cultural endeavor: Jefferson's America proved unable to get beyond the logic of war and heroism, and Adams's history itself fell back into the epic mode—expanding from a symmetrical eight-volume plan, four each for Jefferson and his heir Madison, to a lopsided nine so it could cover the War of 1812, the heroic event that exploded Jefferson's hopes, in intimate, exciting, and popularizing detail. As for Wells, there is little sign of any influence of his *Outline of History* upon either the contemporary real world (the nation-dominated and nation-riven United Nations seems to be repeating the experience of the League of Nations, against which Wells railed) or the world of historiography (now similarly dominated by heroic biographies and nationalistic histories, and still beset by a reconstituted "clash of civilizations" thesis of precisely the sort Wells was seeking to overthrow all those years ago). On the other hand, his *War of the Worlds* seems remarkably current both in terms of blockbuster film-making and of historiography. The leading academic and popular historian Niall Ferguson, in his *War of the World* (2006), plausibly claims that Wells's sci-fi classic is the key to understanding modern history.

My study presents an expansive consideration of the long history of this effort to transcend war narrative, paradoxically expressed in a series of major epic poems and histories. These narratives together form a coherent, self-conscious, but unacknowledged tradition of epic literature in the modern world. For 1914 is only one of several dates commonly assumed to mark the end of serious war epic as well as the larger culture of war out of which it grows—others include 1667 (the publication date of *Paradise Lost*, often said to have undone classicizing war epic from within), 1688, 1815, and 1851 (the year of the presumed final triumph of commercial over military competition, best expressed by the rhetoric of the Crystal Palace exhibition). Although none of these dates in fact foreclosed the writing of successful heroic narratives, the scholarly establishment has long found various excuses for dismissing those efforts, no matter how popular or critically acclaimed, and ignoring the clear evidence of this great tradition. Thus Wells continues on in this passage to accuse Winston Churchill of having a "puerile" (76) imagination that showed strange "persistence" in being fascinated by war and heroism. At the same time Wells made this charge in 1934, Churchill had begun laboring over his most ambitious epic history. It championed war's definitive place in a liberal, progressive view of history and its hero's central role in determining the outcome, even in a world supposedly dominated by the political-economic invisible hand. *Marlborough* (1938) at 2,500–plus pages clocked in at over twice the length of Wells's *Outline;* it was a major success with readers and critics; and it anticipated Churchill's even more successful post–World War II histories for which he was awarded a Nobel Prize in literature, one of only two such honors given to a historian. Moreover, it was not just a defense of heroic war history in general, but a specific apology for the Great War, the nadir of liberal confidence in the enlightenment theory of limited, restrained, legalized, and civilized warfare. That history functioned as a coded apology for Churchill's Gallipoli Campaign, one of the leading candidates for the worst battle of this worst of all possible wars, as well as a cunning preparation not only for World War II, the so-called best war ever, but for the heroic role Churchill would triumphantly assume therein.

Churchill now looms as a far larger historical and intellectual figure than Wells; his fascination with defending imperialist wars for liberal ideals points to our own struggles with this paradox. His heroic histories are being rapidly reprinted and resold, while it is Wells's largely ignored *Outline* that seems puerile in its naïve hopefulness. Nonetheless, little serious literary scholarship has attended to Churchill's epic histories. Among a spate of recent and highly politicized appreciations of his writings, none have scrutinized his place in this vigorous liberal epic tradition. Algis Valiunas's 2002 book-length analysis, *Churchill's Military Histories: A Rhetorical Study,* makes no mention of Gibbon or Macaulay, whom Churchill himself proudly identifies as his principal thematic, rhetorical, and stylistic models. In the same year, John Lukacs's *Churchill: Visionary, Statesmen, Historian* has a title that makes its hero worship plain, but whatever one might say about Churchill's histories, they are hardly visionary—representing the nostalgic tail end of a long-standing tradition. Finally, *Winston Churchill,* a third admiring book from 2002 (the events of 2001 ramped up the veneration of this liberal imperialist) by the distinguished military historian and literary theorist John Keegan, does acknowledge

Churchill's place in an epic historical tradition. It also makes plain that Churchill's heroic narratives were definitive influences upon Keegan's own influential championing of graphically violent military history of the sort Churchill himself wrote and loved. In doing so, Keegan reveals how seriously his studies of such patriotic gore in modern military history misconceived the real point of the liberal epic tradition that Churchill both inherited and perverted.

One last contribution will complete this picture. Geoffrey Best's *Churchill: A Study in Greatness* (2003) again proclaims its thoroughly heroic thesis. At 370 pages it is relatively modest in length and clearly aimed at exploiting the current and growing vogue for Churchill. (Keegan's totals an even more popularizing 196 pages.) There is, however, an enormous range up to the very long of Roy Jenkins's *Churchill* (2001) at 1,001 pages to the multivolume, many-thousand-paged immensity of the official Randolph Churchill and Martin Gilbert version. Best's study is only slightly more hero-worshipping than these last two—and not at all more than Keegan's—but has the added irony of coming from the twentieth century's foremost historian of the law of war. As I will demonstrate in detail, Churchill's histories grow out of a tradition that relied upon the legalization of warfare. They deliberately adopt the liberal epic, law-of-war-abiding style lying at the source of this genre, but then undo their inheritance and reemphasize graphic realism and the pleasures of violence for modern British readers now assumed to be so civilized that they no longer needed such training. Best, both a leading Churchill scholar and the foremost historian of the law of war, epitomizes the paradoxical drama lying at the heart of the liberal epic tradition. Best and his hero are confident that their subjects—respectively, Churchill himself and Britain's imperialist wars—have transcended the need for the restraining, civilizing efforts that originally produced them. Churchill's heroic narratives underscore two key points of my thesis: the remarkable persistence, even intensification, of epic in the modern world and its equally remarkable critical neglect. Thus my argument concludes with a full treatment of Churchill's war narratives, not Wells's experiments or Adams's speculations. It there demonstrates those heroic histories' intimate connection to a magnificent liberal epic genealogy of theme and style that goes back through Thomas Babington Macaulay to Edward Gibbon and Alexander Pope, that is, to three of the best-selling, most critically acclaimed and culturally significant texts in English literary history: *The History of England* (1848–61), *The Decline and Fall of the Roman Empire* (1776–88), and Pope's encyclopedic commentary-translation of Homer's *Iliad* (1720).

This book was composed amid the controversies surrounding the Iraq

War, a paradox-laden endeavor charged with the derivative rhetoric of a lesser Churchill and marked by the two distinctive features of all liberal epic: first, an apologetic strategy for justifying this war as a worthy exception to a general rule, as a case not of imperialist conquest but of national liberation; second, a concerted effort to limit or sanitize the public's access to graphic representations of the liberating soldier-heroes' acts of violence and domination—an effort, moreover, that has foregrounded a concern not to shock, and concealed a wish not to please. In suppressing the real violence and killing of this war, Keegan's advice, advanced in easily the most influential contemporary study of war literature, *The Face of Battle* (1976), has been resisted. During this same period, however, a counter-phenomenon, one focused upon ever more vivid simulations of graphic violence, proceeded apace—and with pleasure obeyed Keegan's call to show the true graphic terror of war. Recently, the video game industry has surpassed the film industry in sales and profits. The digitization of film, the rise of CGI effects, and the resurgence of war-spectacle films, often directly based on popular games or filmed with game spin-offs in mind, point to the video game, not film or television, as the dominant form in our popular culture. These video games have themselves flourished through ever more realistic portrayals of violent killing in the first-person shooter mode. The player becomes the hero-killer, generally in a war to save humanity from some grandiose threat of conquest. *Halo* (2001), Microsoft Corporation's first Xbox blockbuster, a spectacular success in Bill Gates's ambitious plan to transform Microsoft into a leading provider of narrative content for computers reconceived as interactive televisions, casts its player-shooter as the fearsome hero-defender against an aggressive war waged against Earth by an insectlike alien civilization marked by religious fanaticism, a race-based caste system, and political tyranny. Its sequels, *Halo II* (2004) and *Halo III* (2007), have been equally successful in purveying the thrill of saving enlightened civilization by slaughtering hordes of enemies in ever more intimate anatomical detail: there is even a reviewing term for rating success in realistically portraying this all-important matter, the "giblet" factor.

Various authorities from Jean Baudrillard to Norman Schwarzkopf have delved into the disturbing ironies of these phenomena—the way real war has become an unreal simulacrum modeled after a video game or television news; the way the long lessons of liberalism have been undone by the education in violence encoded in video games; the way those games are themselves an outgrowth of the military's strategies for making killers out of its presumably too humane American recruits. Joanna Bourke's *An Intimate History of Killing* (1999) is the most thorough history of these debates within the military establishment. Dave Grossman's deeply anxious *On Killing* (1995) presents the most detailed version of the larger debate over the now ubiquitous claim that America's youth are having their long-standing liberal conditioning not to kill or enjoy killing undone, turned from "off" to "on," in Grossman's alarming terminology. According to Grossman, the techniques exploited by video games were originally developed by a military itself made anxious by S. L. A. Marshall's notorious 1948 thesis that American soldiers often failed to fire at the enemy because of their liberal conditioning. Baudrillard argues the radical position that the reality of war has fully succumbed to the appearances of television and games. Schwarzkopf, in the vein of Keegan, has insisted on honoring the harsh reality of war by condemning the false pleasures of video representations. My study endorses neither of these heated certainties, nor does it join Grossman in assuming that liberalism ever succeeded in turning the safety "off," or that it even, finally, wanted to. It serves as an archaeology, an excavation shedding light into the depths, of the long history of this problem for liberal society, a caution against interpretations based solely upon recent developments. Dryden and Pope's poetic diction proved a sophisticated device for advancing an aestheticized simulacrum of Homeric combat long before the twentieth-century techniques of video montage; and the ethical superiority of our graphic realism over their sophisticated sanitization is not the obvious certainty (or the simple matter of ignorance) assumed by Keegan and Schwarzkopf. Pope and Dryden in England and Fénelon and Voltaire in France knowingly suppressed the illiberal appeal of Homeric violence. Their translational practices became, through the likes of Hume and Gibbon or Macaulay and Carlyle, the dominant tactic of epic and military historians who sought to limit an aggressive pleasure rather than neglected to show the true face of battle as Keegan and his followers would have it.

Thus *Masters of Doom* (2003) tells of the video designers John Romero and John Carmack, two latter-day H. G. Wellses who never grew up, have not yet proceeded from lurid science fiction to visionary world history, but have made millions for themselves and billions for their industry. These two are usually regarded as the key innovators for the first-person shooter. *Masters of Doom*'s narrative climaxes with this declaration: "Now gamers could play against spontaneous human beings—opponents who could think and strategize and scream. *We can kill each other!* 'If we get this done,' Romero said, 'this is going to be the fucking coolest game that the planet Earth has ever fucking seen in its entire history!'" (Kushner 149). My view is that even the most graphic video game falls short of Homer's detailed precision, his sublime ability to give the reader the pleasure of appreciating just how skillfully a kill can be made by one of his heroes. His epic renders killing as the essence of beautiful art—whether by hero or poet. Homer's *Iliad* was and remains the gold standard in purveying the joy of identifying with a superior killer-agent. *Halo* and *Doom* are crude by comparison—both in their construction of their heroes and in their detailing of lethal action against the anatomy of enemies' bodies. The crucial issues for serious and humane, ambitious and tradition-minded artists like Pope, Gibbon, Scott, Macaulay, and Churchill was how to retain such pleasures and how to thematize the agency of the individual, while avoiding the full immersion of themselves and their readers in the terror, sublimity, beauty, and bloodlust of either the ancient *Iliad* or the modern *Doom*. They struggled to retain this essential primal scene of the epic drama of domination, while promoting the liberal ideal of individual self-determination.

Beyond its readings of important texts as part of larger refashioning of literary history, this study asserts that the more plausible explanations of liberal epic—cultural momentum, ideological and generic compromise, hypocritical bad faith—ultimately must make room for a more disturbing insight: war epic survived and flourished, after Milton and Locke and after Wilfred Owen and John Rawls, not in spite of liberal humanism or in an uneasy truce with its attacks upon heroic warfare, but because liberalism requires the primal scene of epic, because our last great myth of individual agency cannot let go of the first great drama of heroic killing.

THE CRITICAL LANDSCAPE: LIBERAL VERSUS MODERN, NOVEL VERSUS EPIC

The literary theories of Claude Rawson, Elaine Scarry, and John Keegan permeate my argument, and, though I dispute Rawson's claim that the origins of modern epic lie in mock epic, Scarry's equation of combat killing with torture, and Keegan's humanizing explanation for the lack of horrific detail in the battle piece, their theses have guided my working assumptions and close analyses. Two more recent books highlight the principles behind my selection of texts and historical assumptions. Herbert Tucker's monumental *Epic: Britain's Heroic Muse, 1790–1910* (2008) and Simon Dentith's *Epic and Empire in the Nineteenth Century* (2006) like mine explore the persistence of epic well into eras long said to be characterized by the end of epic and the dominance of the novel. Tucker proffers an encyclopedic study of virtually all the epic poetry produced in the long nineteenth century, and Dentith focuses upon a series of texts—poems, novels, tracts, histories—that dramatize the tension between a self-consciously modern culture and a form defined by the notion of primitivism. Tucker and Dentith emerge from a long-standing critical tradition rooted in Hegel and variously restated by Lukacs, Bakhtin, and more recently Franco Moretti in *Modern Epic* (1996). This tradition characterizes epic in terms of its problematic relation to the concept of modernity. My study's foregrounding of the tension between epic and liberalism looks back to a rival Miltonic, Burkean, and Kantian intellectual heritage and results in different emphases, conclusions, and major texts. Jean-François Lyotard distinguishes two grand narratives of legitimation in the modern world: in one, "humanity [is] the hero of liberty," history is the story of the growth of national and individual freedom, and "the State receives its legitimacy not from itself but from the people" (31); in the other there reigns an impersonal ideal of totalizing scientific knowledge that is best symbolized by the German Romantic university and that, according to Lyotard, reached its illiberal nadir in 1933 with Heidegger's identification of this goal with "the 'destiny' of the German people, dubbed an 'historico-spiritual people'" (37). The former grand narrative is the template for my liberal epics, the latter for Tucker's and Dentith's modern ones—even when we study the same texts. As a result, my argument tends to focus on the problem of content, while Dentith and Tucker attend more to the question of form. Thus, too, although Moretti identifies "epic savagery" as a "phrase that describes perfectly the problem of the modern epic" (13), his Hegelian emphases lead to a privileging of savage form found in a series of monstrous epics, texts often distinctly lacking in any explicit violence, that his Darwinian taxonomy characterizes as "one-off cases, oddities, anomalies" (10), that is, revealing formal crisis points in an evolving scientific totality. In contrast, my selection privileges narratives foregrounding violent content in conjunction with the Enlightenment theme of liberty's progress. *Liberal Epic* turns to widely popular, highly acclaimed, and self-conscious epic histories, poems, and novels that struggle with a crisis very different from Moretti's, that is, the representational and ideological dilemma of their effort to celebrate both murderous heroic power and liberal self-determination.

My study's understanding of the term *liberal* thus begins with Lyotard's first grand narrative. It is liberalism in its individualist and then political dimension—liberalism epitomized in Benedetto Croce's philosophical history and then by his English disciple R. G. Collingwood—that has striven to theorize, achieve, and preserve nation-states subservient to the free will of its citizens and founded on their consent.[1] It is also the liberalism of Isaiah Berlin's negative freedom, according to which the state or society is bound to maximize the space in which individuals realize themselves apart from any positive ideal of the self imposed from above. At the same time, Berlin's influential formulation points to the crisis driving this phenomenon of liberal epic, namely, the lurking dissatisfaction with a negative formulation of individual freedom and power. Collingwood acknowledged the crisis or challenge to the modern liberal self, to "his integrity and efficacy as a moral agent in the wider sense of that term" (*Autobiography* 147), that my study locates at the origins of liberalism within this phenomenon of liberal epic. Above all, this political liberalism remains vexed and fascinated by the parallel, even competing, economic model of liberalism because it is economic liberalism that has best defined agency, but done so problematically in terms of Smith's explicitly anti-heroic "invisible hand" or, even worse, Herbert Spencer's notion of "impersonal agency." What is an ideology of individual self-determination to do when its economic other sees agency as fundamentally impersonal?[2]

Further consideration of Hegel will bring this larger dimension of my argument into contact with the specific academic debate at issue here. The military, political, and legal historian Michael Howard has succinctly argued that Hegel's thinking on matters of history, nationalism, and war derives from a Prussian tradition that never accepted the modern liberal critique of war, violence, and domination as permissible means of modern state formation and social organization:

> By the nineteenth century two very different schools of thought had developed. In Western Europe . . . it was assumed the legitimacy of the State arose from popular consent. . . . But in nineteenth-century Germany a very different analysis had been developed by Hegel and his disciples. The State . . . was created not by law but by war. Since the State was not only the highest but the sole creator of legitimacy, self-preservation was the State's first duty and the primary concern of its citizens' allegiance. As the state had come into existence through war . . . so it could only survive and express itself through war. (Howard, "Foreword" xvi)

Hegel's vision of modernity does not see epic's celebration of war, heroic agency, and violent domination as fundamentally at odds with the hopes, values, and realities of the modern world as does the liberalism of England, France, and America. Thus, the Hegelian tradition of epic criticism does not attend to the recurring paradox in modern epic texts that both seek to transcend heroic violence and desire to retain its symbolism of individual agency. Instead it stresses an alternative set of crisis points that have more to do with form, perspective, and the relation of the hero to the world: "*Marmion* not only depicts the guilty way we live now but also tells how we got that way, at a representative juncture when we traded communal wholeness . . . for the compromised terms of modern nationhood. . . . Scott had forged a nationally credible equivalent out of precisely the reluctant skepticism that made the old epic wholeness a modern impossibility" (Tucker, *Epic* 144–45). Terms such as *totality, wholeness, immanence,* and their analogs dominate this discourse with its fundamental opposition between epic's original function to portray a totality of immanent meaning as against a modern condition of fragmentation, struggle, and failure. While my study accepts the intentionally primitivist feel of Scott's heroic writings, it is more interested in those texts that actually confront and narrate war at length. Thus his epic history of *Napoleon,* which centers upon a series of set-piece battle narratives, looms large in my study, while his heroic poems, which refer to warfare but never really show much of it, do not. Indeed, Scott expressly rejected an epic classification for his heroic poems largely because they avoid war narrative: my argument attends to this basic fact, while their Hegelian concerns lead Tucker and Dentith to dispute Scott's own assertions. They pass over *The Life of Napoleon* (1828), although it was an enormous best-seller at the time, influenced the war histories of Macaulay and Carlyle, and cast itself as an epic historical heir to the histories of Gibbon and Livy. That narrative, not the heroic poems, was marked by the high style of Popeian poetic diction, by close attention to the modern laws of war, and finally by a metanarrative that looks to an ideal end of history in a world without war, hardly an end hoped for by true primitivism or Hegel.

Above all, my study privileges the civilized style of poetic diction, which it traces from Dryden and Pope to Gibbon and Macaulay and Churchill, as the key formal device for liberalizing the violent content. It is less interested in the various efforts to imitate or revive primitive ballad forms that have attracted the attention of critics of modern epic. Put another way, my working definition of epic flows out of the old distinction between *The Iliad* as the touchstone of all epic because of its concentration on war and combat and *The Odyssey* as the prototype of all romance adventure. This passage from a late eighteenth-century epic theorist, William Hayley, dramatizes my basic approach:

An Epic Poet, desirous of laying the scene of his actions in India, would be more embarrassed to find interesting Heroes than proper Divinities.—Had justice and generousity inspired and guided that English valour, which has signalized itself on the plains of Indostan; had the arms of our country been employed to deliver the native Indians from the oppressive usurpation of the Mahometan powers; such exploits would present to the Epic Muse a subject truly noble, and the mythology of the East might enrich it with the most splendid decorations. (297)

The real crisis is what to write about (ideally, a war in the cause of liberty), not how to write about it (Hayley dismisses the old bugbear regarding machinery). On the same page, Hayley reinforces his basic message by embracing Gibbon's suggestion that an epic based upon the German Odin's freedom-loving overthrow of the oppressive Roman Empire would make for a "just and splendid" epic theme, though when Wordsworth subsequently contemplated this subject, Gibbon's own language of recommendation—"immortal revenge," "martial fanaticism," "numerous swarms" (*Decline and Fall* 1: 257)—insinuates why it remained too barbaric to tempt any civilized poet seriously.

Ultimately, my study privileges epic history, which was bound up with the intellectual tradition of liberal epic poetry, but surpassed it in both popularity and critical acclaim: Wordsworth the poet, Hayley the theorist, and Gibbon the historian were all on the same page. But it was in history that the cultural effort to compose major liberal epics found its greatest success, as has long been noted but seldom studied, certainly not with attention to this phenomenon as a self-conscious tradition. My argument encompasses major texts by Hume, Gibbon, Napier, Macaulay, Carlyle, Trevelyan, and Churchill, and demonstrates their close stylistic, thematic, and cultural links to epic poetry. Still, it includes the major Romantic (Southey and Byron) and Victorian (Morris and Hardy) poets who composed epics centered on war. All these writers, historians as well as poets (and some were both), saw themselves writing heroic narratives as part of a self-conscious epic tradition. They were reviewed by contemporary critics, widely read by contemporary readers, and celebrated by subsequent literary history. In short, my decision to treat them as epic is largely unproblematic. They see themselves as part of a great tradition extending back not just to Tacitus and Thucydides, but to Vergil and Homer.

Finally, there is the problem of the novel. I accept the broad outlines of the "rise of the novel" thesis, whether in the classic formulations of Watt and Bakhtin or in the various refinements by recent authorities such as Armstrong, McKeon, and Moretti. From this perspective, *Liberal Epic* offers another refinement, a qualification of the too ready acceptance of epic's senescence. Insofar as the persistence of epic is grounded in the championing of historical struggles for tolerance, liberty, and legal constitutionalism—in heroes who fought for one or all of these ideals, such as Voltaire's Henri IV, Barlow's Washington, Southey's Joan of Arc, Hume's Alfred, Gibbon's Julian, Macaulay's William III, Adams's Jefferson, Trevelyan's Garibaldi, and Churchill's Churchill (a revealing special case)—and insofar as it presents these wars in modes designed to assuage civilized sensibilities, suppress sadistic terror, and augment masochistic pity, these texts gesture toward the increasing dominance of the novel and confess the economic, political, and social developments that accompanied and promoted that form's triumph.

On the other hand, this study maintains that this tradition corrected or rivaled the novel's core ideology, but in a subtler manner than the scholarly models have allowed. These heroic poems and histories flourished because they offered experiences and viewpoints not sufficiently promoted by the novel. Epic colored the reigning ideology of liberalism with red, as it were, making it more aggressive, more vividly agential, and more self-consciously consequential than the novel generally held itself to be. Two recent studies complement my thesis and demonstrate precisely what the epic did that the novel did not. Suzanne Keen's *Empathy and the Novel* (2007) maps the rich history of the debates about the cultural status of the novel, in particular the wrangling over whether or not novels make readers better liberal citizens, more tolerant, understanding, and proactive. Do novels succeed in creating empathy between readers and fictional characters, as has been commonly assumed? If so, does that affect encourage stronger empathy for and understanding of real people? Does that result in readers taking practical action? My argument traces an important alternate, but equally pressing, challenge for modern liberal nations. Liberal epics foreground a concerted effort to educate or discipline in the converse direction, namely, not to be sadistic, not to take pleasure in the sufferings, defeats, and deaths of others at the hands of a powerful oppressor. Liberal epics implicitly admit to a deep human pleasure in dominating others—a delight at the surface of Homer—and address the need to control that pleasure as novels do not.

Ian Duncan's *Scott's Shadow* (2008) focuses on a figure and period in which the declining epic and the rising novel came into the closest contact. Scott's progression from heroic poems to historical novels exhibits an attention to the Popeian-Gibbonian poetic dictional rendering of violence, the distinction between heroic and political economic agency, and the declining historical status of war that together strongly support my broader argument. Duncan extends and deepens claims from his earlier study of Scott's status as the first novelist to become a national author. His work emerges from a critical tradition that casts Scott as the crucial figure for elevating the cultural prestige of the popular novel form. Scott enabled it to supplant the epic—in large part because he incorporated epic historical matter into his narratives: "The novel, according to another commentator, has assumed the role of epic to represent 'the different modes of national existence . . . in modern times'" (Duncan 21). Scott's novelization of epic, however, entails anti-heroic consequences best seen in the so-called passive hero, and Duncan's argument extends these implications by associating Scott's strategies for elevating the fictional novel with David Hume's influential views on faith and agency: "Hume's *Treatise of Human Nature* provided a theoretical basis for that 'fundamental practice of modern ideology—acquiescence without belief, without credulousness,' that would find its technical realization in the Waverley novels" (xii). According to Duncan, Scott rendered the novel epic by incorporating heroic historical action, but Hume's liberal skepticism guarded those fictions against epic's ethos of faith and fatefulness: "Hume bequeathed to Scott . . . a historiographic ethos of aesthetic detachment that allows the free play of sympathy and so predicts the liberal horizon of our reading" (137). Hume did not, however, sanction the reader sympathizing with Scott's heroes as triumphant conquerors and killers: such free play did not extend backward to that original sublime pleasure. And though Hume's "deconstruction of causality remains a purely logical operation" for Scott's fiction, one which "does not threaten the ethical foundations of belief and agency" (134), the result is still a world seemingly ruled by a mysterious, intellectualized agency lacking the vividness preserved by liberal epics. In contrast to Duncan's specific claims regarding the Scott novel and Humean skepticism toward agency, truth, faith, and history, my study's liberal epics, even Hume's, exhibit a strong desire to believe in historical great men whose violent heroics are seen changing history. In contrast to the paradigm of the novel as a modern middle-class form succeeding or failing in Adam Smith's marketplace run by the invisible hand, liberal epics are cast as texts that impose themselves upon the public seen not as consumers but as citizen-subjects. Carlyle's reactionary epic histories, which expressly celebrate heroic agency as a matter of faith and do so in explicit literary opposition to Scott's popular novels and in philosophical opposition to Hume's theories, dramatize this rivalry of epic and novel. But epics with good liberal pedigrees also expose their societies' need to retain, for moments of crisis, a committed belief in epic agency and its bloody hand, its scenes of domination, and its ideology of nationalist war.

One novel will allow me further to elucidate these broad claims and, thence, what short list of nineteenth-century novels and novelists will figure in my study. *Middlemarch* (1872) is certainly one of the greatest English

novels and, for some, among the most significant epic experiments of
the nineteenth century. Nevertheless, *Middlemarch* also dramatizes what
heroic narratives that preserve warfare offer that even the most ambitious
narratives without it do not. Often categorized with *Aurora Leigh* (1856) as
a domestic or home epic, *Middlemarch* easily transcends that poem by the
common epic test of canonicity and cultural status, not to mention length
and ambition. Eliot's studious deployment of scientific imagery and discourse grants her focused narrative a universal significance; her linking
of the central Victorian theme of reform to such heroic figures as St. The-
resa and Don Quixote dynamically elevates her subject matter and its
mode; finally, her more than Carlylean development of work or "business"
(Carlyle had famously proclaimed that "tools and the man" would replace
"arms and the man" as the central epic theme of modern society) similarly
aggrandizes her novel both in terms of its subject and its desire to surpass
Victorian England's most outspoken theorist of the heroic. Much more
could be said on this novel's epic strategies, but my simple purpose here
is to draw attention to how this self-consciously epic novel concludes on a
strong note of failure that fairly symbolizes the shortcomings of all novelistic agency and empathy. Here is the concluding paragraph in full:

> [Dorothea's] finely-touched spirit had still its fine issues, though they
> were not widely visible. Her full nature, like the river of which Cyrus
> broke the strength, spent itself in channels which had no great name
> on the earth. But the effect of her being on those around her was incal-
> culably diffusive: for the growing good of the world is partly dependent
> on unhistoric acts; and that things are not so ill with you and me as they
> might have been, is half owing to the number who lived faithfully a hid-
> den life, and rest in unvisited tombs. (838)

The dense literary and historical allusiveness of Eliot's concluding flourish
signals its ambition. Like the novel's "Prelude," its "Finale" foregrounds
Middlemarch's cultural pretensions, first, through its explicit analogy to
high art; second, through its rich offering up, then winding down, of the
novel's central themes; and, finally, through references to major figures of
history and literature and variations upon famous lines such as the final
gesture toward 1 Peter, Cowper's *The Task,* and Gray's "Elegy." These allu-
sions paradoxically function to deny Dorothea any epic or heroic status.
On the positive side, she is cast in the light of a humble Christ-like martyr
working quietly for the good of others. But she is left with "no great name";
her acts remain "unhistoric," her life "hidden" and her tomb "unvisited."
There is to be sure a counterplot based upon the invisible hand of liberal political economy. We are meant to realize that her life has perhaps

been far more helpful, her diffusive streams more nourishing, than the great unbroken rivers or all the brutal conquerors whose tombs are visited or acts remembered because of their success in breaking the strength of others. But the sad overtone of failure overwhelms this quiet alternative, which is raised only so it can be contemplated and dismissed.

Furthermore, the prototypical epic scene of kill-or-be-killed combat lurks beneath Eliot's melancholy envoi—thereby reinforcing its theme of novelistic helplessness. For *Middlemarch*'s elaborate river simile echoes the lengthy simile at the conclusion of Matthew Arnold's "Sohrab and Rustum" (1853). There the imagery of a great river broken and wandering again marks a defeat and the consequent emptiness of a lifetime's efforts, but now that defeat occurs explicitly in a heroic agon, and the pointlessness extends to both the dying son and the father who slew him unaware:

> Then sands begin
> To hem his watery march, and dam his streams,
> And split his currents; that for many a league
> The shorn and parcell'd Oxus strains along
> Through beds of sand, and matted rushy isles—
> Oxus, forgetting the bright speed he had
> In his high mountain-cradle in Pamere,
> A foil'd circuitous wanderer. (881–87)

As in this civilized version of epic, the mood of Eliot's summary is filled with pity for the defeat facing all of us in the modern world. Arnold's liberal modernization leaves little room for admiration of or terror for the conquering warrior, but Dorothea's parallel experience is not an ironic undoing of or contrast to such tragically epic agency. It is rather a logical extrapolation to the conclusion that liberal notions of agency necessarily lead us to see any fully modern "hero" as a failure. By emphasizing Dorothea's selflessness, Eliot corrects (and thereby casts further doubt upon) the paradoxically selfish logic of the Smithian invisible hand. Dorothea's climactic triumph occurred in a single combat between her outward-flowing empathic imagination and Rosamond's enclosed selfishness. The novel's narrator, however, doubts Dorothea's triumph, and in the finale her selfless sacrifices are posed against the selfish victories of Homeric heroes and found forgettable, dubiously effective, and disappointing. *Middlemarch*'s transformation thus concludes with an admission about the continuing appeal of liberal epic narratives that retain terror, though sanitized, and violent triumph, though legalized. Such narratives sought to inspire belief in a great individual's ability to act effectively on the world stage, while hers remains mired in doubt about the effectiveness of even the best-intentioned acts arising from even the most selfless sympathy.

One more major critical study of the novel, Catherine Gallagher's *Nobody's Story* (1996), will complete this discussion of liberal epic's relation to this rival and increasingly dominant genre. *Middlemarch,* though one of the greatest Victorian novels and, certainly, along with Richardson's *Clarissa* (1748) and Joyce's *Ulysses* (1922), the most successful novelization-modernization-transformation of epic, concludes with a contrast between an epic somebody and its own novelistic nobody. Gallagher anatomizes an earlier era, but her argument echoes Eliot's conclusion by demonstrating how "nobody was the pivot point around which a massive reorientation of textual referentiality took place, and the location of the pivot was the mid-eighteenth-century novel" (xvi). Her list of key concepts summons the world of the invisible hand and clarifies how her argument contrasts with mine with its focus on a very visible and bloody one: "The terms 'woman,' 'author,' 'marketplace,' and 'fiction,' sharing connotations of nothingness and disembodiment, reciprocally defined each other in the literature analyzed here" (xviii). Again, I accept Gallagher's thesis, but I qualify it by insisting that too little attention has been paid to the persistence of an alternative tradition of major narratives. Liberal epic emerged during this same period; it cautiously adapted rather than rejecting or radically transforming classical epic; and, above all, its ideology pivoted on the violent stories of great men as told by great men—in short, Somebody's Story. These texts, moreover, succeeded almost in spite of the marketplace. They theorized their achievement in opposition to what they saw as the too easy appeal of the novel. Pope and Gibbon became wealthy men on the proceeds from *The Iliad* and *The Decline and Fall,* respectively. Scott made more money from his *Napoleon* (1827) than from any of his novels, and Carlyle's *Frederick the Great* (1858–65) was the text that made him at last financially secure. These are extreme cases of expensive multivolume editions that were acquired because they celebrate major cultural events and military leaders and were written by renowned men of letters (Scott's identity became known shortly before he decided to embark on this his longest work), but the texts at the center of this study floated up to their cultural heights because they were regarded as important books that one was obliged to acquire and display: the logic of somebody, not nobody, described their success.

Thus the novels and novelists included in this study will be those who speak most directly to and share the most common ground with its liberal epics. Since my working definition of epic is a narrative that seriously takes up the content of war, that sees war as ruled by the logic of

heroic agency, that confronts the reality of killing at war's heart, and that
is written in a high style as part of a "great tradition," the selected novels
will, similarly, include significant representations of warfare, heroism,
and violence in a high style and with lofty cultural ambitions. There are
surprisingly few such texts and even fewer novelists who regularly turn
to such matter. Trollope's *La Vendée* (1850), Kingsley's *Hereward the Wake*
(1865), and Meredith's *Beauchamp's Career* (1876) represent important,
but exceptional, cases by major novelists, but Walter Scott and William
Makepeace Thackeray are the only nineteenth-century writers to regularly
produce novels meeting these criteria, and analyses of their careers and
their oeuvre will deepen my study's claims. For all their hard work, however, even Scott and Thackeray did not produce a single novel with the
epic historical resonance of Tolstoy's *War and Peace* (1862) or the terrifying pleasures of heroic violence found in Flaubert's *Salammbo* (1862).

To consider other novelists who took up heroic warfare on a regular
basis is to realize just how marginal such matter was to the Victorian
novel in general. Charles Lever's popular war novels of the 1830s and
1840s were inspired by the more respected efforts of Napier's great history, while Rider Haggard's bloody imperialist romances of the 1880s
and 1890s owed much to contemporary heroic warfare in Africa, more
to Homer's *Odyssey* and *Iliad,* and themselves did much to shape some of
the greatest examples of twentieth-century fictional warfare (the climactic
battle of *King Solomon's Mines* (1885) is the key source for the battle of
the five armies in *The Hobbit* (1937), which is, in turn, the model for the
numerous battles in Tolkien's epic trilogy), but Lever and Haggard were
never taken very seriously (even by themselves) as culturally ambitious
novelists. Heroic warfare in their narratives sinks to the level of adventure: these narratives aimed for and earned an easy popularity, while,
more often than not, the texts in my study succeeded more as required
texts, exemplars of a culturally esteemed genre that were often read or
acquired because readers felt obligated, not because they could not be put
down.[3] Scott's novels themselves encode a descent from the heroism of
his heroic ballads into the mundane, uninspiring peace of the novelistic
world, and upon the collapse of his novel-based financial success in 1825,
he turned to the prestige of an epic history to restore his reputation and
income. Thackeray's novels internalize even stronger contempt for the
limitations of his chosen genre. His sequence of novels in the 1840s and
1850s dramatically embody his disappointment with his authorial self
by staging a metafictional ascent to an epic war novel that concludes in
The Virginians (1859) with his failure to realize that ambition, a failure
that confirmed both the triumph of the novel genre and the whimpering

deflation of his novelist career. Finally, Thomas Hardy, the third novelist to receive detailed analysis in this study, succeeded where Thackeray
failed by more successfully modeling his career after the epic paradigm of
Vergil. He carefully rose from the self-consciously lesser form of the pastoral novel to an historical epic-drama of Napoleon. That world-historical
material had long hedged around the lesser matter of his novels, casting
its shadow upon their ephemerality. What's more, while Hardy's novels
famously articulate a worldview marked by pessimism and tragic helpless, this internal theme extends to Hardy's conviction of his narratives'
inability to act powerfully in the world. In *The Dynasts,* he found not only
the text that he felt would secure his preeminent literary position, but one
that allowed him briefly to become a progressive liberal and imagine his
epic-drama prophesying and participating in shaping a better world.

INTRODUCTION

The gruesome atrocity of Homeric battles and deaths is the source of all the astonishing power of the Iliad.

—Vico, *New Science* (1725)

My subject is the entwining of two terms or notions, *liberal* and *epic,* one associated with progress, humanity, and self-determination and the other with tradition, war, and violent domination. Adorno and Horkheimer, in their *Dialectic of Enlightenment* (1944), comment cryptically on this paradoxical relation between liberalism and domination: "enlightenment is universally opposed to domination"; "it [enlightenment] was domination itself" (42). The core impulse of Michel Foucault's philosophical studies is best seen as a meditation on this dilemma of liberal self-determination really being a form of social control. In *"Society Must Be Defended"* (1997), his most self-conscious reflection on the rise of liberal historiography, Foucault founds his argument upon a massive educational text assembled for Louis XIV's heir. Foucault cautions that "we are therefore not talking about *Télémaque"* (127), that is, the far more famous prose epic penned by Fénelon to educate the same prince. The fortunes of *Télémaque* in English will be the focus of this introductory survey of my argument; and, suffice it to say, for all its enlightened liberalism, *Télémaque* no less than the text chosen by Foucault "was intended to constitute the knowledge of the king, or the knowledge that would allow him to rule" (127)—violently if necessary. Another far-ranging and various philosopher of modernity, William James, has explored this paradox in terms that precisely anticipate my study's emphases. On the one hand, he angrily observed, in *The Moral Equivalent of War* (1906), that liberal civilization had failed to create a drama with the moral and aesthetic appeal of Homer's violence, whose pleasures he sees essentially in terms of the illiberal domination by the better individual over another, ultimately climaxing in the undemocratic thrill of the "last man standing." On the other, his thinking has gone farther than any other in equating liberalism with humanism, pluralism, and tolerance. His lecture series *A Pluralistic Universe* (1909) presents a compendium of beliefs and arguments implicitly opposed to epic domination, but still fails to propose any aesthetic means for effectively dramatizing those ideological convictions.

Finally, John Rawls's theory of justice as fairness brings the equation of liberalism with pluralism to its contemporary apotheosis, while his behind-the-veil scenario of democratic choice seems the long-sought equivalent of war narrative. It inverts the agon of the Achillean choice for lasting personal fame and early death over equable happiness and long life, and implicitly rejects that preference's result in a series of graphic combats to the death. (Rawls's world-choosing game seems to preclude even an Achilles from opting for an Achillean world of epic contestation, since the hero, in his preliminary position of choosing a world without knowing his position in it, would realize that the likely result would not be victory and fame for himself, but ignominy and death as one of the many victims of some other individual lucky enough to occupy the singular "Achilles" position.) Rawls echoes James in lamenting the continuing appeal of Homer's violent agency and excellence to supposedly democratic societies—"[the new city] contains no alternative idea of the highest good to set against that expressed by the Homeric gods and heroes" (xxiv). Nonetheless, his own liberal storyline falls squarely into the category of a failed effort to offer a successful aesthetic alternative to Homer's: the imaginary worlds of contemporary online play, for example, are dominated by Achillean formulations and Homeric aesthetics, not Rawlsian realms of fair choosing. This study proposes to specify, expand, and explain the theoretical ironies of Adorno, Horkheimer, and Foucault, James's perturbed diagnosis of liberal failure, and Rawls's embodiment of that condition.[1]

The eighteenth-century liberal reformer Cesare Beccaria declared that "every act of authority of one man over another, for which there is not absolute necessity, is tyrannical." Such a sentiment further underscores the unlikelihood of any cultural alliance between liberalism, founded upon the humane ideal of individual self-determination, and epic, centered upon the sublime drama of one person violently besting another. John Locke's political theories were central to most eighteenth-century liberalisms. Less appreciated is how these theories matched Locke's denunciations of the violent heroism of traditional epic poetry and history. His combination of liberal political theory and a humanizing aesthetics, which I will take up below, nonetheless deeply informed one of the Enlightenment's strongest renewals of epic narrative. Voltaire, long the most acclaimed epic poet, tragedian, and historian of the eighteenth century and a definitive influence upon the "school of Voltaire"—Hume, Robertson, and Gibbon—succeeded through the unlikely marriage of a traditionally violent and authoritarian epic heroism with liberal Lockean politics.[2] In a similarly volatile mixture of progressive politics with epic renewal, a second leading Italian liberal of the eighteenth century, the philosopher of humanist modernity Giambattista Vico, claimed, on the one hand, that "poets are the teachers of the masses, and the aim of poetry is to tame their savagery" (356) and, on the other, that Homeric epic had an opposing purpose: "No mind rendered humane and compassionate by philosophy could have created the truculent and ferocious style which Homer uses in describing the great variety of bloody battles, and the great variety of extravagantly cruel kinds of slaughter, which constitute the particular sublimity of the *Iliad*" (357). Vico, who awaited the nineteenth-century historian Jules Michelet to be "discovered" and to emerge as an intellectual muse for Michelet's Romantic epic histories, exerted no direct influence over Alexander Pope comparable to Locke's upon Voltaire.[3] Nonetheless, Pope labored over his translations of Homer's epics (1715–26) during the same years that Vico worked upon his *New Science* (1725). In their accompanying essays and notes, but, above all, in their sanitizing poetic diction, Pope's learned modernizations of Homer exhibit the same dynamic of admiration and repulsion, of traditional respect and enlightened dismay, found in Vico's historicist philosophizing over the bard. Certainly, David Hume combined a similarly vexed marriage of admiration and repulsion toward Homer's war epic.

Thus Pope, when translating Homer, echoes Vico's dismay over the enormous variety of ways to kill enshrined in the *Iliad:* it makes his strange decision to spend years in the prime of his life carefully translating it all the stranger.[4] But he did, and it made him a rich man—and firmly established, according to Coleridge, the reign of poetic diction, along with making Homer-translation a poet's surest route to financial security: "'No author,' says Leslie Stephen, 'had ever made anything approaching the sum which Pope received, and very few authors, even in the present age of gold, would despise such payment. . . .' The returns to [William Cullen] Bryant from his Homer in about the same period of time after publication were about $20,000 as against the returns to Pope of say $45,000" (Bigelow 170). Its unprecedented success led to many original epic poems and to the spectacular growth of epic history—including Scott's heroic poems, his historical novels, and his multivolume *Napoleon* (1828), whose success surprised even his son-in-law and biographer: "The Napoleon (first and second editions) produced for them a sum which it even now startles me to mention—18,000 pounds" (Lockhart 2:573). It inspired Macaulay, author of Victorian England's biggest seller, to devote himself to an epic military biography of another brand of military hero, but a military hero nonetheless. Through all of these examples, this study will document how and why a past-oriented epic found within a future-looking liberalism an apologetic strategy that allowed a revivified heroic tradition to persist in glorifying war and violence in the cause of liberty. It will trace just how Pope's *Iliad,* which mirrored Vico's concerns and influenced David Hume's, proved, along with Gibbon's *Decline and Fall of the Roman Empire,* the key enabling development for the larger phenomenon or genre I call liberal epic.[5]

The workings of this paradoxical phenomenon will be told through the deep stylistic, generic, cultural, and thematic connections between post-Miltonic epic poetry and epic history, after *Paradise Lost* (1667) and *The History of Britain* (1670), in the eighteenth and nineteenth centuries.[6] *Paradise Lost* has long been regarded as the last great English epic. Its critique of classical heroism embraces both long-standing Christian and newfound liberal perspectives. Milton's poem marked and contributed to a cultural shift that made it increasingly difficult for poets to offer up war epic seriously: "Not sedulous by nature to indite / Wars, hitherto the only argument / Heroic deemed" (9.27–29). But his *History of Britain,* published in the same year as his epic's second and definitive edition, presented itself as a compendium of potential epic themes drawn from British history, its kings, and wars: "I have therfore determin'd to bestow the telling over ev'n of these reputed Tales; be it for nothing else but in favour of our English Poets, and Rhetoricians, who by thir Art will know how to use them judiciously" (3). This history's judicious strategies for finding and proffering some heroes and some struggles fit for epic point to a long list of subsequent epic poems and histories that rose to cultural, critical, popular, even best-selling success. In addition, Milton's epic history abounds with strategies for rendering violence in a muted and disapproving manner, strategies that were to be extended and perfected by ambitious poets and historians alike.

A similar ironic interplay of repulsion and attraction to war epic characterizes the writings of Milton's contemporary Thomas Hobbes. His reactionary authoritarianism stood at the opposite end of the political spectrum from Milton's incipient liberalism.[7] Furthermore, Hobbes's historical model found chaotic violence in the original state of nature, whose kill-or-be-killed ethos echoes Homer's. Hobbes thus argued that the best chance for peace lay in advanced authoritarian states. Milton reversed this valuation, locating peace in the original garden and aggressive war in Hobbes's ambitious leviathans. Despite such differences, a key purpose of

Hobbes's writings—one they shared with Milton's—rested in their contribution to an emerging culture opposed to the glorification of war and
military heroism. Their political and historical paradigms oppose one
another, except that both are designed to undermine the high status of
war heroism. In his 1628 translation of Thucydides, a narrative project
that anticipated the concerns of his theoretical *Leviathan* (1651), Hobbes
sought "the few and better sort of readers" (xxiii), who do not, like the
masses, read "history with an affection much like that of the people in
Rome: who came to the spectacle of the gladiators with . . . delight to
behold their blood." Hobbes's readers do not "love to read of great armies,
bloody battles, and many thousands slain at once" (xxiii). Both texts—one
through narrative, the other through theory—sought to describe, assess,
and delegitimize the traditional practice of glorifying the world of heroic
violence.

Late in his life, however, Hobbes turned to the popularity of spectacle
and bloodshed and devoted considerable efforts to translating Homer's
Iliad (1677). To be sure, he did so in a manner that downplayed the celebration of the "state of nature" so prominently on display in that fero-
ciously gladiatorial narrative, but his constraints as a translator left him
firmly in the position of positively portraying a world of sublime violence
his *Thucydides* and *Leviathan* eschewed. Hobbes's embarrassed introduction to his translation fittingly ends with lame answers to some serious
questions—"Why then did I write it? Because I had nothing to do. Why
publish it? Because I thought it might take off my Adversaries from showing their folly upon my more serious Writings" ("To the Reader"). Such
flippancy seems all the odder since Hobbes begins his apologetic introduction by asserting that the primary virtue of an epic poet, Homer above
all, is "discretion," a virtue usually reserved for the judicious Vergil, not
the primitive Homer. Though Hobbes showed little discretion in either
his initial decision to translate Homer or his reckless introduction, he
demonstrated eminent caution in his actual translation. It is characterized by rapidity, concision, and thus by the suppression of the gladiatorial
detail for which Homer was renowned—or abused. Its chief result, the
muting of violence, earns Hobbes's translation some claim to discretion.
This pattern of global self-contradiction corrected by tactical circumspec-
tion will prove the hallmark of all the epic narratives in this study. Hobbes
and Milton variously exemplified this key feature in the early development
of liberal European society—on the one hand, to discredit the seriousness
and the pleasures of war epic, and on the other, to craft strategies for
finding exceptions to such discrediting and to deploy tactics for civilizing
those exceptions.

My study will proceed from the primitive theory and practice of Milton and Hobbes to the more securely liberal, Lockean epics from the three leading liberal nation-states, France, America, and, primarily, Britain, from the War of the Spanish Succession of 1701–14 to the Great War to end all wars of 1914–18. The former is the earliest major war marked by sustained efforts to observe the emerging rules of war, or *ius in bello,* first advanced by Hugo Grotius early in the seventeenth century in response to the horrors of the Thirty Years' War; the latter was a war that seemed to explode the platitudes about European success in civilizing warfare, the achievements of the various legal theorists, international conferences, and Geneva Conventions, all the two centuries' long efforts of liberalism to bind even the Hobbesian leviathans in their armed conflicts. Both developments have been claimed as markers of the end of serious war epic, but both proved only obstacles to be overcome by the devices of liberal epic, whether by Fénelon in 1699 or Churchill in 1938.

At the core of my argument, moreover, lies a precise claim, the consequences of which run through the center of each of the following chapters linking poets and historians, Augustans and Romantics, Victorians and Modernists: the seventeenth- and eighteenth-century founders of the modern, liberal law of war—Hugo Grotius (1583–1645), Samuel Pufendorf (1632–94), and Emmerich de Vattel (1714–67)—first directly influenced and later were themselves affected by the epic poetic diction crafted by the translators and modernizers of Homer, by Dacier, Fénelon, Voltaire, Dryden, and Pope, whose success in sanitizing Homeric violence for modern readers resulted in its adoption as the key, enabling device for heroic narratives of liberating warfare.[8] In Grotius's *De Jure Belli ac Pacis* (1646) and Pufendorf's *De Jure Naturae et Gentium* (1672), the counterintuitive practice of illustrating a modern theory of humanized, rule-bound warfare with choice examples drawn from Homer and Vergil, Livy and Tacitus, ancient poets and historians of unrestrained warfare, directly shaped how Dryden and Fénelon translated and updated Homer and Vergil.[9] They made their epics closely conform to these new rules of civilized, restrained war. The lawyers creatively discovered their modern theories in ancient practices by subtly misconstruing the originals, and this dubious but richly productive practice formed the basis for how poets delicately updated and mistranslated *The Iliad* and *The Aeneid* to produce wars and epics that in turn did their best to conform to civilized, modern rules and tastes. Later, Vattel's decision to write his treatise on *The Law of Nations* (1758) in French, not the Latin of Grotius and Pufendorf, was in part made possible because he could readily adapt his rhetoric, which combined outraged denunciations of the horrors of war with a novel legal defense of wars of liberation, from the liberal epic poems and histories of Fénelon and Voltaire. *Télémaque* (1699) and *La Henriade* (1723) rendered heroic combat in a refined French style that had grown out of the work of Grotius and Pufendorf. These widely acclaimed narratives had already largely succeeded in combining a celebration of wars of national liberty with a softening of violence. Thus Vattel's justification for his novel practice—"I have quoted the chief part of my examples from modern history" (xvii)—makes eminent good sense because his examples already conformed to legally restrained modern warfare and to the sanitized modern style for recounting it.[10]

Grotius and Pufendorf's stylistic and legalistic modernizing through misconstruing ancient epics mirrors the basic logic behind their effort to liberalize and humanize war itself. This logic readily mapped onto the modernizing, civilizing translations of Fénelon and Dryden, which together paved the way for the translational strategies, humanizing commentary, and elegant diction that reached its apotheosis in Voltaire's *La Henriade* (1723) and Pope's *Iliad* (1715–20), the two most important epics of eighteenth-century France and England.[11] Here is one vivid example of how such epics, even as they swathed their wars with liberal justifications and legalistic defenses, simultaneously softened and evaded the ultimate act of heroic killing. This climactic combat in *La Henriade* involves a standard neoclassical reworking of the final confrontations between Aeneas-Turnus and Achilles-Hector. It is a brilliant example of self-consciously not quite looking at what even humane war heroes finally must do:

> On se plaît à les voir s'observer et se craindre,
> Avancer, s'arreter, se mesurer, s'atteindre:
> Le fer étincelant, avec art détourné,
> Par des feints mouvements trompe l'oeil étonné.
> Telle on voit du soleil la lumière éclatante
> Briser ses traits de feu dans l'onde transparente,
> Et, se rompant encor par des chemins divers,
> De la cristal mouvant repasser dans les airs.
> Le spectateur surpris, et ne pouvant le croire,
> Voyant à tout moment leur chûte et leur victoire. (148)

Voltaire confesses that some pleasure ("on se plaît") attends watching mortal combat, but links it to sympathetic fear, not the sadistic pleasure Vico sees in Homer. In describing the combat, Voltaire avoids Homeric precision in favor of whirlwind verbal action whose own feinting parallels the deceptive moves of the heroes' weapons. He acknowledges that this is all a "trompe-l'oeil." The eye is astonished, unable to focus, and then Voltaire moves further off into a simile on the dazzling effect of light on broken water—a fine example of liberal epic's skill in avoiding graphic detail through a quick move into the emphatically poetical (this same simile figures prominently in Pope's theory for translating Homer's violence). When the kill finally comes, it is deliberately presented as a bland anticlimax, after the fireworks of the poetic foreplay—"Enfin d'un coup mortel, il lui perce le flanc"—and other than an obligatory gesture toward "les flots de son sang," that is all Voltaire allows.[12] Voltaire went on to a series of increasingly liberal experiments in verse and prose on subjects from Mohammed to Joan of Arc, Charles XII of Sweden to Louis XIV, most of which were eagerly read on both sides of the channel. They all circle around both the larger paradoxes of liberal warfare and the core problem of humane killing. These dilemmas appear best, because most dramatically, in Pope's landmark translation. His edition's enactment of elegant civilization in tandem with its honoring of primitive violence makes it the most interesting artistic analog to the modern law of war. Its divided logic points to a series of oxymora that range logically from a bizarre literary tour de force to a deeply conflicted cultural pretension—Pope's *Iliad*, liberal epic, humane warfare—lying at the heart of this study.

I will document Popeian poetic diction in epic poems well beyond the terminal point usually assigned to it by literary history. Equally important is the influence of this poetic mode upon a range of major epic historians. The popular twentieth-century narrative historian Cecily Wedgwood, who along with Churchill occupies my concluding chapter, rightly insists upon Gibbon's stylistic indebtedness to Pope: "More important was his discovery of Homer in Pope's translation which, he says, 'accustomed my ear to the sound of poetic harmony.' In his mature style the influence of Pope's fluent precision in the use of words can still be traced" (*Edward Gibbon* 6). Coleridge anticipated her insights, though in a negative vein that denied the precision Wedgwood admired. He pointed to Pope's *Iliad* and Gibbon's *Decline and Fall* as the two premier neoclassical exemplars of the suppression of vivid detail in favor of false elegance: "his [Pope's] Homer, which I do not stand alone in regarding as the main source of our pseudo-poetic diction" (*Biographia* 177), and "Gibbon's style is detestable . . . When I read a chapter of Gibbon I seem to be looking through a luminous haze or fog . . . nothing is real, vivid, or true; all is scenical and by candlelight" (*Table Talk* 1:418–19). Samuel Johnson's biographies of Dryden and Pope dramatize the latter's further refinements upon the former's style, but even for Dryden, the hallmark of his poetic innovation is, according to Johnson, its taming of English verse, its elimination of the "tendency to relapse to its former savageness" (347), an effect Johnson locates in Dryden's giving English poetry "just rules and examples of translation" (348). Note the collocation of justice, rules, and translation all in relation to a modernized account of ancient epic warfare. For Johnson, early Dryden long before the translations of Homeric, Chaucerian, and Vergilian epic, had not achieved this level of civilized restraint. He complains of the ugly technicalities of warfare in Dryden's heroic *Annus Mirabilis* (1667): "Dryden was of the opinion that a sea-fight ought to be described in the nautical language. . . . I suppose there is not one term which the reader does not wish away" (358–59).

Dryden's and Pope's translations had a profound effect upon Gibbon, who recounted ancient battles primarily through translating heroic poets and epic historians. He regularly suppressed the technical specifics of weaponry and killing and the graphic details of anatomy found in his sources. He did so in the manner he learned from these poets, through the use of intellectualizing Latinate vocabulary and nonspecific noun-adjective pairings. In translating the historian Procopius's account of the Persian siege of Amida, Gibbon turns a crude hash involving city prostitutes obscenely taunting the besiegers into the following soufflé: "The women on the ramparts . . . revealed their most secret charms to the eyes of the assailants" (2:608). Here "secret charms" is specific, but elegantly-hazily riddling poetic diction for the straightforward and graphic "kunnos" of the Greek. Furthermore, "revealed," perhaps even "women," is almost as corrective. Readers can, with a bit of effort, discern the precise meanings, but the pleasure shifts to a self-congratulatory exercise in appreciating the writer's coy skills and the reader's own decoding abilities, rather than the simple, but shocking, effect of the Homer-like original. Here Gibbon is reworking the graphic anatomical details of taunting and sexuality for his civilized readers, but the setting remains eminently epic and the translational practice on display applies to how elsewhere he renders the details of heroic violence.[13]

Both Wedgwood and Churchill openly proclaimed Gibbon their principal stylistic model. Their post–World War I practices for rendering warfare and combat largely conformed to what Pope and Gibbon together established after Milton. To a remarkable degree, they eschewed the horrific realism that literary history has assumed won out as the proper anti-heroic style after World War I. Between them and Gibbon, moreover, resides a whole series of Pope-Gibbon epic imitators in poetry and history. These epic poets and historians similarly adhere to the sanitizing artificialities of their neoclassical masters as against an earlier phase of supposedly triumphant realism after Wordsworth, Byron, and Scott. The leading late Romantic historian William Francis Napier, rival of Southey and peer

of Byron, adheres to and adapts the delicacies established by Pope and
Gibbon. Likewise Alexander Kinglake, famously Byronic in his early travel
memoir *Eothen* (1844), becomes explicitly Popeian in his epic historical *Invasion of the Crimea* (1863–87). Perhaps the clearest case is Edward
Creasy's best-selling *Fifteen Decisive Battles of the World* (1851). As a young
Victorian, Churchill first encountered Gibbon via Creasy's popularizing
mini-epics. His history inaugurated an entire subgenre of military histories (Keegan, *Churchill* 57). Creasy's narrative foregrounds a humanizing
and legalistic recounting of war: he at once wallows in its excitement and
longs for the day when it will end. In the meantime he traces a series
of battles in which war's horrors are progressively tamed as freedom advances, and he does so in a style that already exemplifies that final civilized discipline: his is both a stylistic and a thematic end of history.

The major effort of Creasy's later years was a popularizing history of
the law of war, *The First Platform of International Law* (1876), in which
he updates the ancient stoic and early modern natural law restraints on
war's horrors with the latest Victorian utilitarianism. The two texts are
clear parallels in the realms of the narrative practice and the historical
theory of legalized warfare. He sets Grotius, Pufendorf, Vattel, and many
less well-known theorists in context, though Montesquieu emerges as the
most succinct authority, one whom Creasy quotes repeatedly: "Our primary authority may be found in the maxim which Montesquieu considers to be the natural foundation of International Law. That maxim has
already been cited, and partly discussed. . . . 'Nations ought to do each
other as little harm in war as possible, without prejudice to their own true
interests'" (364). Such a minimalist rule (and nicely epic adaptation of the
golden one) extends to any actual representation of historical warfare. In
the end, whether in theory or practice, Creasy insists upon the sad inevi-
tability of some wars, but then allows for the stirring heroism of resisting
aggression. His repeatedly makes those wars as just and humane as possible in practice, whether that involves the actual conduct or the narration
of war. His theory elevates philosophical figures such as Montesquieu and
Grotius, while his history frequently recalls exemplary poetical and historiographical civilizers of war, above all Voltaire and Edward Gibbon: "If I
seem to have given fewer of the details of the battle itself than its importance would warrant, my excuse must be, that Gibbon has enriched our
language with a description of it, too long for quotation and too splendid
for rivalry" (158). Here Gibbon's inimitable brilliance in sanitizing heroic
battle narrative becomes an excuse for further suppression.

Thus the rarefied style of poetic diction had longer life, because it had
deeper and more compelling reasons than has been supposed by literary

and cultural historians. Poetic dictional violence, the original motive for poetic diction, survived and flourished, despite the powerful critique of its inherent falseness that began almost immediately with Richard Bentley's dismissal of the inauthentic prettiness of Pope's *Iliad*, reappeared in Coleridge's and Arnold's famous attacks upon it, and then continued in the modernist critique of the stilted chivalry of Victorian war poetry detailed by Fussell in his study of World War I poetry. Simply put, poetic diction effectively saved war epic from the mortal blow that literary history has so often claimed Milton dealt to it, and just like epic itself, the reports of poetic diction's demise have been greatly exaggerated. Surprising eruptions of supposedly long dead poetic diction appear in the most unlikely places: for example, in the graphic climaxes of ostensibly primitivistic epics by William Morris and Algernon Charles Swinburne.

Chapter 6 will trace the ironies surrounding the Pre-Raphaelite Morris's surprising recourse to neoclassical poetic diction at moments of climactic violence. In *Tristram of Lyonesse* (1882), Swinburne likewise beats a surprising retreat to Pope's poetic diction in order to sanitize and contain one of his epic's rare descents into combat:

> Save that the sheer stroke shrilled aside, and passed
> Frustrate: but answering Tristram smote anew,
> And thrust the brute beast as with lightning through
> Clean with one cleaving stroke of perfect might:
> And violently the vast bulk leapt upright,
> And plunged over the bridge, and fell: and all
> The cliffs reverberate from his monstrous fall
> Rang: and the land by Tristram's grace was free.
> ("The Last Pilgrimage" 163–70)

The triple sanitization wrought by the lightning metaphor's cauterizing bloodlessness, the mortal blow's status as "clean" and "perfect," and then the quick disappearance of the body, now a poetic dictional "vast bulk," all point back to Pope's strategies for translating Homer, though Swinburne goes even further in blaming the dead body for acting "violently" and then granting "grace" to his liberating hero-killer. Though the illogic of allowing a "thrust" to cleave falls short of Homeric, much less Popeian, precision, the brilliant enjambment of "frustrate" perfectly captures the kind of verbal play and Latinate intellectualizing that adorns every page of Pope's hardly graphic but exquisitely shimmering *Iliad*. Swinburne's conservative gestures, moreover, appear in a heady poem whose use of the heroic couplet is, in all other ways, deliberately opposed to Pope's refined style and diction. Swinburne poured his theme of the overwhelming power of love into neat heroic couplets so as then to undo from within the balanced logic of Pope's rational construction of an ordered Newtonian or civilized post-Homeric world. So, too, his poem otherwise deploys an ecstatic, Romantic vocabulary whose soaring Blakean and Shelleyan resonances scorn the elegant Popeian restraint that resurfaces with "frustrate" in this moment of spotless heroic violence. There, at the heart of poetic diction's purposes, its original function reasserts itself.

DRYDEN, POETIC DICTION, AND *IUS IN BELLO*

Our Poet, who all the while had Augustus in his Eye, had no desire he should seem to succeed by right of Inheritance, deriv'd from Julius Caesar; such a Title being but one degree remov'd from Conquest. For what was introduc'd by force, by force may be remov'd. 'Twas better for the People that they should give, than he should take.

—Dryden, preface to *Virgil's Aeneid*

Pope and Gibbon stand at the center of my claims about liberal epic, poetic diction, and the law of war because they perfected trends that began in the seventeenth century and served as the preeminent influences upon practices by later poets and historians alike. Pope, however, identified Dryden and Fénelon as his masters, and Gibbon owed much to Dryden in addition to Pope and Voltaire. The bulk of this introduction will turn to the reception history of Fénelon's *Télémaque* in England as a means of presenting an overview of my larger historical argument regarding the evolution of liberal epic from the eighteenth through the early twentieth centuries. Before I turn to that task, however, it will be useful to pause over Dryden's contribution. For in that poet—who suffered and profited from the liberal revolution of 1688, who imported to England both the French rules for poetry and the new spirit of humane rules for the conduct of war—we possess the simplest and clearest case study of a phenomenon that my subsequent chapters will detail.

Grotius and Pufendorf, the two primary figures in the early development of the modern *ius in bello,* as opposed to the medieval *ius ad bellum,* regularly cite passages and quote text from classical poetry, history, and oratory to illustrate their arguments: "The uncertainty of the outcome of a war leads us to temper its license, for fear the examples we have set may by the hand of fortune be turned against us. See . . . Vergil, *Aeneid,* Bk.X.533: 'By the death of Pallas, Turnus had first removed all friendly intercourse of war'" (Pufendorf 1299).[14] My specific purpose here is to consider such methods in relation to the analogous efforts by neoclassical epic poets to clothe modern humane wars of liberation in the bloody,

ancient garb of Homer and Vergil. This counterintuitive feature of Grotius and Pufendorf's legal writings seems to prefigure the vexed logic of
liberal epic: in each there is a marriage of opposites, humane benevolence
and violent courage, liberal autonomy and epic domination. Pufendorf,
for example, cites Grotius in characterizing "unjust" wars in terms of a
quest for epic glory, a desire "to gather fame from the oppression of their
fellows," which, in case the reader misses his point, is then restated as "a
craving to lord it over others" (1295). Such thinking sums up the liberal
critique of traditional heroic warfare found in both his work and Grotius's.
Their endorsement of individual autonomy and national independence is
the baseline definition of *liberal* deployed in this study. It remains the key
to understanding their legal objections to war and its inevitable logic of
domination.

The impact of their writing upon the subsequent practice of epic appears vividly in Pufendorf's objection to Turnus's abandonment of the
commercia belli (translated here as "friendly intercourse," but best understood as the ancient practice of exchanging prisoners for ransom), which
appears in his chapter "On the Laws of War." Pufendorf is propounding
a new law for the treatment of prisoners and illustrates his theory with
an example from Vergil he twists to fit this category. Vergil refers to a
custom, but one that hardly obligated the participants. Its violation might
point to the enraged hero's carelessness about financial gain, but it did
not constitute a crime. In Dryden's subsequent translation of this line
from the *Aeneid,* the original phrase is colored by Pufendorf's previous
use and classification of it as a law, and it thus becomes a straightforward
example of breaking well-established codes: "Thy Turnus broke / All the
Rules of War" (10.739–40); not only has a financial transaction, ransom,
become a rule, but the addition of "all" references the lurking presence
of an entire legal framework. This is but one of many instances in which
Dryden projects back onto an ancient epic the thinking and even the vocabulary associated with the seventeenth-century project to humanize,
restrain, and codify the practice of war.[15]

In Dryden's case, these cultural and legal developments were reinforced by French neoclassicism's simultaneous efforts to rationalize the
rules of tragedy and epic. Like Fénelon's *Telemachus* of 1699, Dryden's adaptations and translations of epic poetry in the 1690s vividly exhibit the
parallel developments of civilized rule-making in warfare and decorous
rule-making in poetry. Dryden, however, is a more revealing mirror of that
process, because, unlike Fénelon, he was responding to and reflecting
these developments, and not directly involved in making them happen,
as we will see with Fénelon. In addition, Dryden touted his patriotic resis-

tance to these civilizing influences from the overly refined and unmanly French—both in their practice of poetry and in their combat. Thus, his clear trend toward ever-fuller submission to the rule of law in poetry and war seems all the more striking as evidence of an emerging genre of liberal epic.[16] Finally, Dryden, bound by his need to translate, better shows the essentially compromising logic of neoclassical liberal epic. Fénelon was adapting Homer and Vergil. He also granted himself the freedom of prose. Indeed, given Dryden's stated resistance to this largely French project, the fact that he was translating could well have served as an excuse not to liberalize, after the manner of Grotius, Pufendorf, and the French rule-makers, the depiction of warfare in Homer and Vergil. That he did so despite his loud objections and ready-made excuses is telling evidence of the power of the ongoing liberal transformation of epic.

Dryden confessed to taking liberties in translating Chaucer—"I have not ty'd myself to a Literal Translation" (533)—and there is a clear pattern in his version of *The Knight's Tale,* which Dryden labels an "epic" not a "romance," of calling attention to the horror of war by adding editorial denunciations of its barbarity. Such freedom did not extend to his avowedly faithful translations of Homer and Vergil. Even so, a pattern of subtle interpolations pushes these "literal" versions in a liberal direction. His *Iliad* responds to contemporary fears of Louis XIV's domineering intolerance at home, his universal ambitions abroad, and his haughty treatment of his fellow European kings. In several small touches, Dryden aggrandizes Homer's Agamemnon into a similarly haughty king lording it over his fellows. The following passages highlight Dryden's small additions, ones that are not, for example, picked up by the more literal Pope, who otherwise showed a happy willingness to borrow from Dryden's version: "But he the Tyrant, whom none dares resist . . ." (1.139); "'O first in Pow'r, but passing all in Pride'" (1.183); "'O, Impudent, regardful of thy own, / Whose Thoughts are center'd on thy self alone, / Advanc'd to Sovereign Sway, for better Ends / Than thus like abject Slaves to treat they Friends'" (1.225–28); "The King, whose Brows with shining Gold were bound: / Who saw his Throne with scepter'd Slaves incompass'd round" (1.257–58). These lines are additions to Homer's depiction of Agamemnon's arrogance and are best understood as expropriations of contemporary criticisms of Louis XIV. In that regard, they achieve a liberal goal, but in negative terms. They play up a post-1688 sensitivity to illiberal tyranny. Dryden's theoretical claims regarding Vergil's humane and republican values, however, set up a context for seeing his *Aeneid* in positive terms as a liberal epic. As the epigraph attests, Dryden responded to the fall of his patron James II by holding that Vergil's epic refused to endorse Augustus's legitimacy in terms of inheritance or divine right and that it boldly asserted his need for popular approval. Similarly, in his *Aeneid,* there is a subtle, but clear pattern of coloring his translation so as to make Aeneas and his heroic warfare just—and not in terms of traditional Catholic just war theory, but the emerging liberal notion of justice in the humane conduct and the liberating justifications for war.

Out of nearly twenty occasions in which Dryden uses some variation of the word "just" or "unjust," only once does the original have an exact equivalent in the Latin: "Whom just Revenge against Mezentius arms" (8.658) from "Quos iustus in hostem / Fert dolor" (8.500–501). More often, Dryden's use of "just" or "unjust" is an interpolation or interpretive coloring of what he wants his reader to see as the injustice of Turnus's or the justice of Aeneas's cause. Sometimes there is warrant for such additions, but nonetheless he pushes stronger for the notion of justice than Vergil does. Thus in book 11, Aeneas pleads with the Latin leaders with whom he desires peace, "nor wage I wars unjust." In the Latin this is "nec bellum cum gente gero," which translates literally to "nor do I carry on war with your people" and stands in opposition to "rex" later in the line. One could follow Dryden in interpreting such a distinction as the difference between a just and unjust war, but Aeneas in the original is making a canny rhetorical plea to the enemy king's people to see their interests as different from their monarch's.[17]

It is not simply this postclassical just/unjust war model that Dryden repeatedly adds into the poem. His *Aeneid* commences its account of Aeneas's invasion of Italy as follows: "The Pious Chief, *who sought by peaceful Ways, / to found his Empire,* and his Town to raise" (7.203–4, my italics). The portion in italics has no correspondent in the original. Here Dryden takes one of his largest liberties with the text in order to defend Aeneas from the charge of being an unjust foreign conqueror of Italy, a view increasingly common from the mid-seventeenth century onward with the rise of liberalism.[18] Indeed, a crucial liberal innovation during this period was the legal repudiation of conquest enshrined by Grotius's Treaty of Westphalia in 1648. Conversely, in appealing to the Arcadians for an alliance against Turnus's Rutulians, Dryden's Aeneas points to the fear of Turnus gaining "Universal Sway" (8.194), again an interpolation with no direct sanction in Vergil, but a timely bit of rhetoric in 1697 when such charges were frequently made against Louis XIV. Aeneas is exposing Turnus's ambitions, but it is absurd to imagine that a Roman epic, especially one dedicated to Augustus Caesar and taking as its theme the foundation of Empire, would base a serious criticism upon an assumption that "universal sway" was a bad thing. Dryden's Aeneas implicitly invokes the modern European balance of power, a concept, like the modern European law of war, opposed to the historical fact of the Roman *imperium*, to bolster his call for allies in his just war.

Within the severe limitations of a translation that tries to follow the original closely, these shadings, interpolations, and blatant additions to the text exhibit the post-Miltonic effort to celebrate war only when it is seen as justified, primarily by being a war of defense or national liberation and not a war of conquest. When wars did come, the legal effort centered on restraining their violence within a civilized code. Finally, when confronted by that violence, these translations deploy poetic diction to avoid the graphic and technical realities of combat. They never allow visceral descriptions of just how a specific weapon enters a specific part of a human body to kill with artistic skill worthy of a reader's appreciation and approval. Dryden maneuvers as best he can within these constraints by insisting that Aeneas's intentions are peaceful and his war is just, that Turnus's aggressions are unjust and that he is the real illiberal conqueror, the seeker after universal empire, and that in the battles he thrust upon Italy, Turnus is the violator of the humane "rules of war" (10.740).

THE EVOLUTION OF LIBERAL EPIC: THE ENGLISH RECEPTION OF FÉNELON

> *For the custom of tormenting and killing of Beasts will, by degrees, harden their Minds even towards Men. . . . All the Entertainment and talk of History is of nothing almost but Fighting and Killing: And the Honour and Renown, that is bestowed on Conquerors (who for the most part are but the great Butchers of Mankind) farther mislead growing Youth, who by this means come to think Slaughter the laudable Business of Mankind, and the most Heroick of Vertues.*
>
> —John Locke, *Some Thoughts concerning Education*

Epic long throve not so much, as Bakhtin and others would have it, because it was once a living poetic tradition or because historical memory trumped empirical attentiveness, but because its military content rested on a set of widely accepted presumptions: that the test of war and combat was morally invigorating; that the graphic violence of killing was the terrifying essence of the aesthetic sublime; that wars were the most important of historical events; and that individual heroes possessed the agency to determine their outcomes. All these enabling assumptions were cast into doubt by the progress of liberal ideology. Hayden White's monumental *Metahistory* (1973) dismisses the category of epic for eighteenth-century historical narrative largely on these grounds. For him epics, in this age of irony (irony, in political economy, plays out in terms of the theory of beneficial self-interest and the invisible hand), could only be accepted as very rare exceptions or freakish tours de force. Liberal epic, however, flourished precisely in terms of the logic of the exception, the special case that eludes the ironic, ethical, and materialist dismissal of traditional heroism. What's more, there were many of these exceptions. Indeed, they are legion. These multiplying exceptions point to a new rule of epic persistence, not decline, forming a living tradition of "exceptional" epic narrations. White's study articulates, from the perspective of historiography, the old theory of epic senescence. Like Bakhtin's, his theory rests on the neglect of a monumental tradition.

Thus Fénelon's *Télémaque* (1699) became the most popular French book of the eighteenth century, was translated into English over six times—once by Tobias Smollett, who modeled more than one novel after it—and exerted a profound influence upon Pope. It proved a potent model for success as a modern heroic war narrative founded upon a pattern of critiquing most wars and most heroes: its reception in England demonstrates both the evolution of liberal epic and an important constant—persistent popularity. Locke, who lamented the ill effects of youthful reading of Homer and Livy, proposed Grotius and Pufendorf as the best civilizing reading for young men in contrast to the truculent fare from the past: "It may be seasonable to set him upon *Grotius de Jure Belli & Pacis,* or which perhaps is the better of the two, *Puffendorf de Jure naturali & Gentium* [sic]; wherein he will be instructed in the natural Rights of Men, and the Original and Foundations of Society, and the Duties resulting from thence" (239).

In *Emile* (1762), which honored Locke's views on education, Rousseau lobbied hard for *Robinson Crusoe* (1719) to be adopted as a better alternative: an enjoyable yet instructive book for young readers. This choice owes much to Defoe's allegory of individual self-determination and economic enterprise, but also stems from his strong liberal denunciations of heroic killing. Crusoe considers ambushing the cannibals, but retreats from such lethal aggression on the liberal grounds that they had not threatened him directly, that he had no claim to self-defense: "What authority or call I had, to pretend to be judge and executioner. . . . It was not my business to meddle with them, unless they first attack'd me" (135–36). Crusoe carries his argument to a humane extreme, holding not only that he must wait until it is clearly a matter of self-defense, but that it was his "business if possible" (136) to ensure that situation would not arise: it was his humane duty to hide from them behind an elaborate planting of twenty thousand sapling trees. Rousseau admitted that Fénelon's *Télémaque*, with its more ambivalent relation to this problem and its avoidance of any such foresting cowardice, remained the most popular book for young French boys—and girls. Rousseau's classicizing rival Voltaire followed the lead of Fénelon and fashioned a long and successful literary career writing epic poems and heroic histories and historical dramas that did not eliminate epic violence, but sanitized and liberalized it. Even Defoe followed *Robinson Crusoe* (1719) with *Memoirs of a Cavalier* (1720), a novel of aristocratic filiopiety, ambivalent militarism, and numerous battle pieces imbued with the critical, but heroic, spirit of *Télémaque*. Its protagonist is a critic of war, but also a brave, often eager soldier with little of Crusoe's latent cowardice. *Memoirs of a Cavalier,* which Scott edited and adapted in his own war novels, demonstrates the challenges to Locke's and Rousseau's hopes for the triumph of nonviolent entertainment—and how a subtle, attractive middle way was established by Fénelon's prose epic.[19]

David Hume fixated upon Fenelon's popular redoing of Homer as the best example of the evolution of morals from the ancient to the modern world: "The ethics of Homer are, in this particular, very different from those of Fénelon, his elegant imitator" (*Enquiries* 333), and he achieved his greatest literary success, not as an essayist or philosopher mulling over such rich paradoxes, but as an epic historian practically negotiating them as he found ways to produce his own sanitized accounts of glorious battle and refined heroism. (Thomas Carlyle, for one, considered Hume's narrative of the English Civil War and the career of Cromwell to be a major English epic.) In his *History of England* (1754–62), he registered his ambivalent faith in heroes, and again—as is fitting for this determined skeptic—the logic of the exception proved the rule, even against his own theories. The best example is Hume's account of the reign of King Alfred.[20] It concludes with a strange wish for negative testimony against his protagonist's perfection: "Fortune alone, by throwing him into that barbarous age, deprived him of historians worthy to transmit his fame to posterity; and we wish to see him delineated in more lively colours, and with more particular strokes, that we may at least perceive some of those small specks and blemishes, from which, as a man, it is impossible he could be entirely exempted" (1:75).This scenario, in which a great king sadly lacks Humean historians to perpetuate his fame by recording his shortcomings, matches an earlier paradox in Hume's narrative of this king whose "great virtues, and shining talents . . . saved his country" (1:63); Alfred stands not just as a war hero, but as an early, indeed much too early for Hume's historicist theories, example of an enlightened monarch: an eighth- not eighteenth-century king who toiled over internal improvements, even on such progressive matters as public education. Alfred seemingly grew up reading Fénelon, not Homer. Of course, he read neither, but his Anglo-Saxon favorites were closer to the latter's barbarity. Alfred's boyhood reading consisted of primitive heroic poems of the sort Hume otherwise found morally objectionable to elevated moral tastes: "His genius was first rouzed by the recital of Saxon poems, in which the queen took delight; and this species of erudition, which is sometimes able to make a considerable progress even among barbarians, expanded those noble and elevated sentiments, which he had received from nature" (1: 64). Hume's embarrassment here is palpable. His historical theories did not allow for civilizing and benevolent poetry to be produced by savage cultures. Like Gibbon, Hume doubted the authenticity of Ossian because the heroes seemed too humane and their violence too restrained. Gibbon scoffed at the illogic of barbarity in the civilized Romans and humanity in the primitive Britons in those stories: "the generous clemency of Fingal" and "the bravery, the tenderness, the elegant genius of Ossian" (1:152) uses praise to insinuate fraud.[21] Hume's Alfred would not have been reading Ossian or any modern imitation of primitive epic, but heroic poetry in the raw, filled with brutal violence and replete with sympathetic identification with the actions of killers. Hume therefore struggles. He carefully cites this poetry's appeal to a presumably refined woman, the queen, Alfred's caring mother. In addition, Hume advances a suitably vague possibility of poetry (recast as "erudition") "sometimes" achieving "progress even among barbarians." In the end, Hume retreats to a theory that Alfred's inherent "genius" was naturally "noble and elevated" in order to explain or mystify an outcome his historical models frankly do not allow. This projection of liberal epic, liberal education, and a liberal hero back into the eighth century telescopes the dilemmas confronting Hume's own liberal epic history in the eighteenth. His heroic history of Alfred is trapped by its own enlightened ironies: at once forced to be less critical in treating a hero than it would like and more uncritical in its assumptions about primitive epic than is its wont. Such illogic and paradox, such thwarted skepticism and self-imposed credulity (and from Hume!), anticipate many similar crises in the tradition of liberal epic—and such unexceptional exceptionality has proven to be the norm in the history of liberal epic.

NEOCLASSICAL FÉNELON: VOLTAIRE AND SMOLLETT

*Those monstrous heroes, though almost deified by the foolish admiration of the
vulgar, are in effect the most cruel enemies of the human race, and ought to be
treated as such.*

—Emmerich de Vattel, *The Law of Nations*

Vattel here reworks Fénelon's standard rhetoric on the horrors of war and
the dangers of false hero-worship: "No, no: far from being demi-gods,
they are not even men; and, instead of being admired, as they expected, by
future ages, they ought to be execrated" (208). That popular French epic,
here translated by Smollett, served as the legal theorist's main touchstone
for his humane outrage regarding his core theme. Similar outbursts regularly punctuate *Telemachus,* and these denunciations were the primary
vector for Fénelon's influence upon Voltaire, Rousseau, and Hume. But
novelists, too, particularly Smollett in *Roderick Random* (1748), whose
larger plot and focused critique of war were modeled after *Telemachus,* and
William Godwin, whose *Caleb Williams* (1794) represents that philosopher's novelization of his Fénelon-based theories, exemplify the centrality
of this epic for eighteenth-century anti-heroic narratives. *Telemachus* was
also the intellectual origin for the economic system known as physiocracy, which Fénelon deployed in opposition to Louis XIV and Colbert's aggressive mercantilist policies and their focus upon promoting preferred
industries and urban development, on the state support of foreign trade,
and on military expansionism to support economic goals. Physiocracy favored a largely agricultural policy as the foundation of peaceful internal
improvement. *Telemachus*'s pages are filled with moral and intellectual denunciations of war, pragmatic criticisms of its enormous economic costs,
and lessons to the young prince about the value of favoring agricultural
policy and internal improvement in conditions of peace. In the eighteenth
century, physiocrats such as Melon, D'Argenson, Goudar, then Quesnay
and Turgot, and thence Adam Smith, argued powerfully against nationalist war policies in terms largely derived from Fénelon (Howard, *War* 24).

Fénelon composed *Telemachus* for the young Duke of Burgundy, the
oldest son and heir of the Dauphin, in the neoclassical spirit of flavoring
the medicine with sugar, though Voltaire thought there was still too much
unadulterated medicine.[22] Louis XIV was so displeased by his grandson's
indoctrination in theories critical of his actions that Fénelon was banished
from court. Fénelon compounded more concentrated dosages, however,
particularly in the *Examen de conscience sur les devoirs de la royauté* (1734)

and its appendix or *Supplement*, which propounds, without adventures, essentially the same arguments against aggressive warfare, for peace and internal improvement, and, on those occasions when war comes anyway, for laws of war based upon the principle of humanity: "These enemies are still men, still our brothers, that is, if you are a true human being yourself" (*Oeuvres* 994, my translation).[23] Fénelon surveys Europe and its ongoing wars and advocates an ideal opposed to Louis XIV's aggressive policies and to the historical vision of Bossuet, Fénelon's chief rival, of a universal monarchy bestriding Europe and presided over by the French Catholic king. Instead Fénelon appeals to the theory of a balance of power, but pushes it beyond that of his contemporaries to an ideal Europe formed around equal, securely independent, self-determining states that coexist as part of a universal republic: "The fourth system is one in which the power of each state is nearly equal to that of the others, whereby it will achieve equilibrium and thus a kind of public safety. To be in this state and not to desire to abandon it through ambition is the wisest and happiest condition" (1008, my translation). Fénelon expands on his vision of this Europe (he even deploys the term "republic") by insisting that a just king must aim for not merely the reality of equality, but the abiding desire for such. This European system rests upon the essentially liberal ideal of the inviolability of self-determination and then further proposes an anti-heroic spirit of equality as the key to maintaining itself. Later in the century, Adam Smith and Edward Gibbon would both restate this republican alternative to the Roman model of universal monarchy, though Gibbon, in particular, did so with less focus on the French ideal of equality and more upon regulated competition as the system's dynamo.

Still, in Fénelon hero-princes retain the power to transform nations and history for good or ill, and occasions present themselves when such a hero-prince can earn his just fame through fighting battles deemed necessary. There are numerous combats, many battles, and even several full-blown wars in *Telemachus*—most unjust or foolish, but some presented as necessary, and thus as opportunities to win glory. Its most extended scene of heroic combat reworks both the climactic Achilles-Hector and Aeneas-Turnus mortal combats. It establishes two key liberal epic motifs: first, it excuses its hero of all of Achilles's or Aeneas's vengeful cruelty and injustice by making Telemachus's foe Adrastus, the analogue for Hector or Turnus, wholly unreliable in his promises to surrender; second, it softens the graphic detail of killing and thus the dangerous thrill of epic terror. As I will show, these strategies guided Pope's rendering of Homer. Smollett's translation, sanitized as it is, actually increases the anatomic specificity by rendering the original's "he plunged his sword" ("il enfonce son glaive" [455]) with the addition of a bodily object for the plunging sword—"into his bosom" (253). Earlier in the same battle, Fénelon registers his most graphic killing (here literally translated with no additions by Smollett): "In the mean time, [Telemachus] with a javelin pierced the throat of Periander, whose voice was choked by the blood that gushed from the large gaping wound" (247). That killing is Fénelon's most detailed in twenty books, but he quickly corrects it with a scene of Telemachus's pity and, unlike Achilles, his pious return of the body to Periander's domestics. After his victory over Adrastus, Fénelon further burnishes his hero's liberal credentials (and reverses Aeneas's illiberal conquest of Italy) by having him reject any rulership over the Daunians and their lands. Though forced by his enemy's treachery into the inhumane act of denying him his autonomy—and his life—Telemachus adheres to Fénelon's principles of international justice by refusing to extend this necessary act of domination borne of self-defense to Adrastus's people.

Fénelon, as a royal tutor, played the most stellar pedagogical role of the modern era: he criticized Louis XIV's aggressive wars; he taught his heir to act differently; he sought to induce sympathetic horror at the prospect of war's results; he set forth a theory of national progress achieved through peaceful development not military expansion; and he did all this by civilizing Homer—or should I say, but he did all this by compromising with Homer? For Fénelon's own integrity, assuming one accepts that high praise, did not guarantee that his formula for adapting epic, his implicit compromises and casuistry, could not easily lend themselves to more questionable compromises—even abuse. Timothy Dwight's *Conquest of Canaan,* though dedicated to Washington as a humane liberator, and though marked by the usual liberal evasions of graphic violence, tactics borrowed from Fénelon by way of Pope, deploys the newly conventional liberal apologetics for violent killing to justify the extermination of the Canaanites—and thus native Americans. A more subtle example of Fénelon's influence on later neoclassical writers, one that embraces two more committed liberals than Dwight, involves Voltaire and Smollett on the epic heroism of the Swedish warrior-king Charles XII. This pairing demonstrates the key feature of neoclassical liberal epic: its penchant for endless debate, subtle distinctions, and ethical quibbling—in short, for casuistry.

Voltaire certainly knew, admired, and imitated *Telemachus.* His own epic, *La Henriade,* makes this plain, without the need of any explicit comments, though those exist in Voltaire's appended survey of great epic poets.[24] This epic presents a humane, war-hating hero who proves fully capable of fighting when necessary; its violence is sanitized; and its ideology focuses upon religious toleration in the greater cause of physiocratic internal development. Nonetheless, Voltaire went on to write his enormously popular heroic history of the military adventurer Charles XII. The productivity of this text is remarkable: Byron openly acknowledges it as the source for his popular comic-heroic poem *Mazeppa* (1819); Shelley adopted the central idea for *The Revolt of Islam* (1817) from Voltaire's account of an almost bloodless revolution in the Ottoman Empire (making his revolution actually bloodless is the clearest sign of Shelley's Romantic distinction from the neoclassical Voltaire); and Voltaire even seems to be the source for Gibbon's ubiquitous Odin suggestion: "It is chiefly from Sweden . . . that those swarms of Goths issued forth, who like a deluge overran Europe, and wrested it from the Romans" (*Charles XII* 12). Here, in a text well-known to Gibbon and in a translation preceding his history, we have the same metaphorical word "swarms," the same verb "issue," and the same ambivalent, typically neoclassical wavering, as Voltaire continues, between admiration and revulsion, liberating and savage energies.

Voltaire's history was popular reading for budding epic historians and poets; in the next century, both William Prescott and Macaulay reread and remarked upon it as a prime model for popular history writing: "Voltaire's Charles the Twelfth [is] perused with delight by the most frivolous and indolent" (Macaulay, *Essays* 1:303). Still Voltaire himself hardly viewed it as a straightforward epic history: "The Swedish king is presented as a hero and nothing else, a conqueror whose conquests have no meaning" (Pocock 2:76). It follows *Telemachus*'s lead as a powerful critique of the false allure of military glory. Charles's single-minded military ambitions mark him as dangerous and lead to failure for him and ruin for his country. He is an extended case study of the kind of counterproductive Homeric heroism repeatedly denounced by Fénelon, and an object lesson, as in Johnson's satire on the vanity of such human wishes, where Charles substitutes for Juvenal's Hannibal as the prototype of disastrous military ambition. In both Voltaire's opening and closing gestures, Charles is judged harshly. Even so, Voltaire's narrative cannot hold back in sometimes admitting its attraction to its hero's excellence. Voltaire's exercises in apologetics, his occasional compulsion to find something humanly redeeming in his hero, prompts his translator Smollett to intervene with his own further round of corrective footnotes to Voltaire's effort to find some tenderness in Charles: "If we many judge from the whole tenor of his life and character, he had in fact no tenderness in his nature" (46). In a fuller outburst, Smollett again denies this figure any redeeming virtues, with the emphasis expanding from the lack of a feminizing "tenderness" to a broader lack of "liberality" and "humanity": "We cannot perceive the least tincture of liberality or greatness of soul in Charles. . . . We find in Charles an insensibility to danger, a contempt of wealth, a clownishness of manners, a brutality of disposition, an implacable thirst for revenge and dominion; without taste, sentiment, or humanity" (172). Ironically enough, though Smollett novelized *Telemachus* in the foul *Roderick Random* (1748) with its brutal and heartless protagonist, he here objects to Voltaire's too sympathetic recuperation of Charles.[25]

Smollett takes just the opposite tactic with another debatable hero from Voltaire. Peter the Great has only a supporting role in this heroic biography, but figures as a much greater king: Charles's rival on the battlefield, but superior as an internal improver. Ample praise flows despite Peter's cruelty, and Voltaire settles for a paradoxical summary judgment upon his reign: "He civilized his subjects and yet himself remained a barbarian" (42). In a fuller version of this balanced judgment at the conclusion of a later history devoted to Peter, however, Smollett, as J. G. A. Pocock has noted, finds Voltaire's praise inadequate and chooses to augment his assessment with several laudatory additions of the word "noble" into his translation of Voltaire (Pocock 2:82). Together Voltaire and Smollett, in their self-conscious indebtedness to Fénelon, in their wavering efforts to apologize for imperfect epic heroes, in their insistence that heroism must have a measure of humane liberality, in their petty disputes over giving too much or too little praise or blame, finely illustrate the basic paradigm and logic of neoclassical epic—one founded upon ambivalence, apologetics, and ceaseless casuistry. Finally, they share a greater tolerance for heroic power when used for economic development than Fénelon allowed. For ultimately, both accept and admire the mercantilist policies and concomitant wars pursued by Peter the Great—in part because they succeeded. Though they variously read, translated, admired, and imitated *Telemachus,* and though they happily engaged in Fénelon's own effort to humanize and liberalize epic warfare, both retreated from Fénelon's stricter standards for using power. In all these ways, Voltaire and Smollett apart, and even more together, demonstrate the active casuistry that allowed neoclassical liberal epic to flourish by ceaselessly amending its stated principles and spinning troublesome facts.

ROMANTIC FÉNELON

It is in the contemplation of these circumstances, that Fénelon has remarked, that "kings are the most unfortunate and the most misled of all human beings." . . . More forcible and impressive description is scarcely anywhere to be found, than that of the evils inseparable from monarchical government, contained in this and the following book of Fénelon's work.

—Godwin, *Enquiry concerning Political Justice*

Romantic epic righteously rejects compromise and casuistry by charging forward to the simple certainties of ideal humanism, or backward into the sureties of Old Testament bloodthirstiness. Godwin's reading of *Telemachus* is a touchstone of this development. It strives to free that text of the charge of casuistry and compromise, pushing toward a perfected benevolence of nonviolence. Godwin interprets Fénelon's standards so strictly that *Telemachus* becomes not the education of a humane hero-prince, not an explanation of the kind of wars a liberal epic could justly celebrate, but a scathing demonstration of the impossibility of such a noble creature, such a humane war, or such a poem. In the event, none of Godwin's Romantic followers wrote one. For Godwin, no royal education can succeed, since the logic of princely power inevitably subverts liberal principles: "Nothing can appear more adventurous, than the reposing, unless in cases of absolute necessity, the decision of any affair of importance to the public, in the breast of one man. . . . Where powers, beyond the capacity of human nature, are intrusted, vices, the disgrace of human nature, will be engendered" (2:80–81). This anticipation of Acton's "power corrupts" apothegm highlights a deeper indictment of all heroes who would claim the right to lead or represent an entire nation or people. Godwin's *Telemachus* effectively represents the uncompromising logic of Romantic epic, particularly on the question of any celebration of a hero's domination and killing of another human being. He thus begins by acknowledging Gibbon—"It is an old observation, that the history of mankind is little else than the record of crimes" (1:6)—and then proceeds: "But . . . man is of all other things the most formidable enemy to man. Among the various schemes that [man] has formed to destroy and plague his kind, war is the most terrible. Satiated with petty mischief and the retail of insulated crimes, he rises in this instance to a project that lays nations waste, and thins the population of the world" (1:7). War, epic only in scope, is thus little more than the greatest of all crimes, the horrifying consequence of our insatiable desire for more of a bad thing. For a poet or historian to glorify war seems little better than aiding and abetting. As with his interpretation of *Telemachus,* so his humane ethics allow only a logical impossibility: "The utmost benevolence ought to be practiced towards our enemies" (2:162–63). Godwin's is the most "worked-out statement of rational anarchist belief ever attempted . . . [, one] carried through to its logical conclusions, however surprising and absurd these might be" (Joll 31).

It is worth pausing to admire the absurdist brilliance of Godwin's logic, particularly here where such rigidity meets the compromised suppleness of neoclassical war heroism and its poetic and legal refinements.[26] Hume saw in Fénelon the leading modern exemplar of epic and the clearest evidence that for modern civilization, benevolence was the highest value. Godwin puts the two together and discovers that taking an epic of benevolence seriously can lead to only one conclusion: enemies must be treated with kindness. Such a paradox does not winnow things down to a few or maybe only one admirable war (and thus one perfect neoclassical war epic), but rather requires the progressive disappearance of war altogether: "Why should not war, as a step toward its complete abolition, be brought to such perfection, as that the purposes of the enemy might be baffled, without firing a musket, or drawing a sword?" (2:162). Godwin rides the logic of liberal epic, warfare, heroism, and killing to its only possible destination, "perfection": epic must abandon the matter of war or epic's wars must involve no killing, only baffling. The fruit of such thinking appears throughout the actual practice of Romantic epic, but perhaps most clearly in Shelley's tragedy *The Cenci* (1819). Already Shelley has moved from epic to tragedy: his *Prometheus Unbound* (1820), completed after but begun before *The Cenci,* simplifies the messiness of *The Revolt of Islam,* while Prometheus's suffering achieves an agency denied to Laon's martyrdom. But then, just to emphasize the point, Shelley balances Beatrice Cenci against his Prometheus. He forces her to act, but the violent revenge of the horribly oppressed Beatrice is still judged a crime, and her defense casuistry: "the restless and anatomizing casuistry, with which men seek the justification of Beatrice, yet feel that she has done what needs justification" (240). Shelley likens her to Milton's Satan, whose heroism stands squarely upon casuistical feet: "The character of Satan engenders in the mind a pernicious casuistry" (133). Both of them fall short of the guiltless Prometheus, who is characterized simply, strictly, and cleanly as possessing the "highest perfection" and the "purest and truest motives" (133), which purity is made easier by this hero's not being in an epic.

Nonetheless, Godwin, for all his radical and utilitarian embrace of self-interest, the invisible hand, and thus the impossibility of the selfless hero-ruler, cannot quite abandon the epic ideology of the hero. His recovery of heroism avoids neoclassical compromise by resorting to a deeper Romantic paradox. Curiously, it is Fénelon himself who emerges as the one great hero for Godwin, a hero for destroying the idea of heroism, prose-poet of the epic to end all epics: the perfect Promethean poet-hero of the Romantics. Indeed, like Prometheus, he was exiled from heaven, that is to say, Versailles, for his service to humanity. Godwin's exploration of this irony spins down into a veritable mise en abyme of logical illogic as he imagines the need for others to be prepared to sacrifice themselves to save this one last hero. Now the hero no longer kills, but demands the self-sacrifice of others for himself, and of himself for his perfectly nonviolent book. Nearly a century later, Lord Acton evinced a similar opinion of Fénelon, though his praise is shielded from self-contradiction through its indirection:

> Fénelon, the cherished model of politicians, ecclesiastics, men of letters, the witness against one century and precursor of another, the advocate of the poor against oppression, of liberty in an age of arbitrary power, of tolerance in an age of persecution, of the human virtues among men accustomed to sacrifice them to authority, the man of whom one enemy says that his cleverness was enough to strike terror, and another, that genius poured in torrents from his eyes. (Acton 308)

A terrifying hero of humane benevolence! The same logic leads Godwin, who elsewhere belittles abstractions regarding collective or national glory in contrast to the reality of individual happiness and self-interest, to cast such dogmatically selfish thinking aside and imagine a melodramatic scene in which Fénelon's valet—a loaded choice given La Rochefoucauld's cynical maxim—is expected to sacrifice himself for this hero: "A man is worth more than a beast; because, being possessed of higher faculties, he is capable of a more refined and genuine happiness. In the same manner the illustrious archbishop of Cambray was of more worth than his valet, and there are few of us that would hesitate to pronounce, if his place were in flames, and the life of only one of them could be preserved, which of the two ought to be preferred" (Godwin 1:126–27). In this variation on the traditional epic primal scene of kill-or-be-killed, Godwin weaves an agon in which his anti-heroical hero does not himself kill, but his selfless greatness requires the immolation of the unheroic human nonentity; "higher faculties" do not kill, but do call for the death of others: "It is a fascinating problem in casuistry" (Brailsford 94).

The logic of survival is different from that found in the *Iliad* or even in *Telemachus,* but the result is the same—the smoke clears to show the greater man left standing and the lesser man dead. Godwin further ratchets up the drama of this example by supposing that the moment of crisis came just as Fénelon "conceived the project of his immortal Telemachus," which has "cured" so many of "error, vice, and consequent unhappiness" (1:127), and further imagines the valet as either himself or "my brother, my father or my benefactor" (1:128).[27] Clearly, too, the reader is asked to include him or herself in this challenge to die—for *Telemachus,* for Fénelon, and perhaps, by the same logic, for Godwin, another heroic critic of heroism. The utilitarian calculation in favor of greatest happiness holds here, but the dilemma of a strict philosopher of self-interest advocating such a heroic act of selflessness cannot be made to disappear. Furthermore, the paradox is redoubled with the inclusion of the second "benefactor," presumably the category Fénelon belongs to as well, but here Godwin points to a lesser and, therefore, relatively expendable philanthropist. By a strange twist, the core of epic has survived, insofar as the greater hero triumphs in a fatal contest. Alternatively, since the reader is the one being challenged, the willingness to accede to the sacrifice of a direct benefactor to save the indirect, anti-heroic Fénelon dramatizes that what is really being offered up here is selfishness itself, though such a resignation makes little sense within Godwin's rigid system. Or not—for lurking at the core of this passage lies the deepest, strangest implication of all, namely, that, given the choice, Fénelon should sacrifice himself for his book, since that is the true heroic agent, and since this overdetermined scene's various elements include both the author and the text in a variation upon the ethical chestnut about a burning museum, an old lady, and a Rembrandt. The logic of Godwin's Fénelon subsequently played out most richly in the poetry of Godwin's son-in-law Shelley, where heroic self-sacrifices are made to result ironically in heroic triumph and where the poet-hero ultimately sacrifices himself for his books so they can set the world alight in a bloodless revolution that will confirm their creator's heroic agency. Godwin's scenario of Fénelon, *Telemachus,* and the fire was reworked repeatedly by Shelley as his core myth, though nowhere more succinctly than in his "Ode to the West Wind."

Finally, even with regard to actual killing and death on the battlefield—the chronic challenge for liberal epic—the vexed logic of Godwin's Fénelon reveals much about the dangerous purity of Romantic epic. Lord Acton pointed to how some saw in Fénelon's power the terror of the traditional hero flashing from his eyes. In Godwin's most extended passage on the horrors of war, he adapts the rhetoric of Voltaire, Rousseau, Vattel, and, behind them, Fénelon, but there now enters the lurking Romantic admiration for the apocalyptic destroyer:

[War] is that state of things, where a man stands prepared to deal slaughter and death to his fellow men. Let us imagine to ourselves a human being, surveying, as soon as his appetite for carnage is satiated, the scene of devastation he has produced. Let us view him surrounded with the dying and the dead, his arms bathed to the very elbow in their blood. Let us investigate along with him the features of the field, attempt to divide the wounded from the slain, observe their distorted countenances, their mutilated limbs, their convulsed and palpitating flesh. . . . Whence came all this misery? What manner of creature shall we now adjudge the warrior to be? What had these men done to him? Alas! he knew them not; they had never offended; he smote them to the death. . . . Is not this man a murderer? (2:174–75)

Godwin's declamation means to contribute to a rejection of heroism. Nonetheless, this passage exhibits the fundamental strategy of liberal epic: it emphasizes horror and pity; it lightly induces in the reader an identification with the killer ("imagine to ourselves a human being surveying" and "investigate along with him," where the "to" and the "along" flirtatiously hold full identification at elbow's length); such near sympathy, however, is invoked to achieve a stronger revulsion and turn to a better sympathy with the victims. For all the self-satisfied honesty, Godwin does not dare to recreate the very different, more compelling, more pleasurable effect of Homer and his terror, precisely the effect most troubling to liberal epic poets and to theorists of the sublime like Burke. The sympathetic identification with the hero in the midst of combat terror and in the moment of triumphant killing lurks within this denunciation, but is not so much faced and refuted as warily refused.

Even his evasion does not avoid a brush with the pleasurable guilt of the Byronic hero. The final accusation—"Is not this man a murderer?"—has a slight ring of self-accusation, of the sort that the Byronic hero so often suffers from when surrounded by the devastation he has wrought. As with Byronic guilt, this passage's rhetorical intensity creates an equal and opposite sense of the dangerously effective heroic agency of the "warrior-murderer." Here he appears single-handedly to have caused all this devastation. Part of Romanticism's reaction against neoclassical artificiality arose out of its scientific empiricism, a practice that necessarily disavowed Pope's poetic diction, which was fashioned as a means of suppressing Homer's near-medical graphic realism. Byron provides many instances of his empirical observation of death and killing. *The Siege of Corinth* (1816) includes a gruesome scene of dogs tearing at the bodies of fallen soldiers that self-consciously outdoes the opening of *The Iliad*. In a footnote Byron assures us he has personally witnessed such events: "The spectacle I have seen, such as described, beneath the wall of the Seraglio at Constantinople" (*Selected Poems* 373). Likewise a footnote to *The Giaour* (1813) claims firsthand experience:

> I trust that few of my readers have ever had an opportunity of witnessing what is here attempted in description, but those who have will probably retain a painful remembrance of that singular beauty which pervades, with few exceptions, the features of the dead, a few hours, and but for a few hours, after "the spirit is not there." It is to be remarked in cases of violent death by gun-shot wounds, the expression of it is always that of languor, whatever the natural energy of the sufferer's character: but in death from a stab the countenance preserves its traits of feeling or ferocity, and the mind its bias, to the last. (*Selected Poems* 170)

Again, the possibility that Byron was guilty of killing some of those whose deaths he observed seems part of the reader's sympathetic pleasure here. By ranging between the effects of gunshots and stabbings with such grand qualifiers as "always" and "whatever," Byron elevates himself to a virtually Homeric status of experiential knowledge of combat and its anatomical and now even spiritual effects. He combines sentimental comments on the beauty and calm of some deaths with lurid attention to others of a more "ferocious" quality. Finally, all such scenes are bound with pain, not so much of the dying man or woman, but of the viewer whose intense interest is thus subtly rendered as masochistic—or sadistic. Where neoclassicism practices evasion and excusing, Romanticism delves into details and flirts coyly, not with dubious innocence and lame self-justifications, but with guilty sins and painful or pleasurable regret.

Shelley, though a bit less empirical, describes visits to charnel houses and often masks the pleasure of contemplating his terrifying poetic power to destroy with the pathos of martyrdom, self-destruction, and guilt. In addition to following Godwin's strict logic and thereby denying themselves the ability to compromise and celebrate heroes like Odin or Wolfe, Napoleon or Wellington, these poets resembled Godwin in thereby arriving at another kind of hero, the poet-hero, who, though superficially free of the violent murderousness of the warrior-hero, and thus in no need to be handled with neoclassicism's kid gloves, actually seems to attract by his power to demand the death and destruction of all those around him, and ultimately even himself, for the sake of his salvational, anti-heroic epic art. In any case, these godlike heroes will too have blood—their own or someone else's. The avoidance of neoclassicism's casuistries thus does not result in the expected innocence, but in an even deeper sense of guilt, particularly because it is so very enjoyable. Shelley and Byron represent the radical continuation of Godwin's critique of neoclassical epic, while Southey and Wordsworth react by turning to conservative politics and religion. Nonetheless, as I will argue, the strict logic of the Godwinian reading of Fénelon works itself out in Southey too. There the turn away from the sprightly dance of neoclassical benevolence in wartime takes the form of a heady plunge into self-righteous vengefulness of the bloodiest, most vindictive variety, especially when the victims are the French, the ultimate exemplars of enlightened, civilized, and casuistical pretense. The convoluted ethical apologetics and military legalisms of neoclassical liberal epic become impossible for the Romantic poets focused on a rhetoric founded upon empirical facts, firsthand experience, and stylistic plainness.[28] Though Southey traded mockery, recrimination, and invective back and forth with Shelley and Byron, in pursuing a liberal ideal of epic, all of these poets were in fact following out the logic of Godwin's reading of Fénelon: the younger group escaped the delicate balancing act of neoclassical epic by embracing a rhetoric of purity and a psychology of guilty pleasure, while Southey retreated to a self-righteous and self-pleasuring hatred of the French and fierce delight in contemplating their violent deaths, which revealed his own vindictive and guilt-ridden bloodiness. In either case, self-questioning casuistry had ripened into liberal epic marked by schizophrenic, self-assertive certitude.

VICTORIAN FÉNELON

If I had the pen of a Napier, or a Bell's Life, I should like to describe this combat properly. It was the last charge of the Guard (that is, it would have been, only Waterloo had not taken place)—it was Ney's column breasting the hill at La Haye Sainte, bristling with ten thousand bayonets, and crowned with twenty eagles—it was the shout of the beef-eating British, as leaping down the hill they rushed to hug the enemy in the savage arms of battle—in other words, Cuff coming up full of pluck, but quite reeling and groggy, the Fig-merchant put in his left as usual on his adversary's nose, and sent him down for the last time.

—Thackeray, *Vanity Fair*

The Victorians manage an even stranger feat: war epic becomes largely a province of childhood and a pleasure reserved for children—or for adults relaxing into a juvenile mood. Creasy's *Fifteen Decisive Battles of the World*, as a reading experience and as an argument, was clearly aimed at the fifteen-year-old in all of us. Carlyle's contemptuous reference to Tennyson's *Idylls* as "lollipops" emphasizes his insight that, however beautiful or well-wrought or thematically rich, their essential appeal was a nostalgia not just for the past, but for the simple faith and narrative adventures of childhood. Tennyson in his anxiety over his obsolete epic anticipated such objections when he referred to his Arthurian epic as a "sugar-plum" ("The Epic," line 43). Carlyle would know. The progress from the mature challenge of *The French Revolution*'s (1837) rich medley of disparate voices and incongruous events to *The History of Frederick the Great*'s (1858–65) forced march through a series of great battle pieces marks a largely identical regress into nostalgia for recognizable stories and simple lessons. Indeed, the monstrous length (more than 3,000 pages in my seven-volume edition; the hero is born around page 300) of Carlyle's final epic history is best read as his strenuous effort to make it seem that this history was very serious, was in fact for adults—though what adult would ever have time to read it, unless he or she enjoyed summers off and a sabbatical now and then, I would not know. Even the Victorians, sometimes thought to have had ample leisure time for reading long novels, do not seem to have gone beyond buying and displaying Carlyle's multivolume magnum opus.

So, too, Thackeray reserves war heroism for childhood and realistic social comedy for adults. When his narrative reaches Waterloo, many years after the schoolyard fight quoted above, Thackeray does not describe such epic events as "the last charge of the Guard." Instead he spends his time, in a chapter titled "In Which Jos Takes Flight, and the War Is Brought to a Close" on prototypically novelistic events and emotions involving snobbery, money, cowardice, silly clothes, and awkward horseback riding. To be sure, Thackeray prefaces this chapter with one of his illustrations—a figure of the goddess Bellona with streaming hair and sword in hand. In contrast to the early chapter, the juxtaposition of the illustration and the contents, of epic convention and novelistic reality, creates a thoroughly mock-epic effect. For there will be no killing and dying here—or, to be precise, when George's offstage death is recorded at the chapter's close, it is a realistic, harsh, and bitterly ironic reflection on all the previous comedy: "Darkness came down on the field and city: and Amelia was praying for George, who was lying on his face, dead, with a bullet through his heart" (406). In the earlier chapter from which the epigraph is drawn, entitled simply "Dobbin of Ours," there is also an evocation of epic followed by no death. It seems misguided, however, to apply Rawson's logic and regard the action as mock-epic.[29] The chapter title itself has a heroic ring to it, unlike the ironic juxtaposition of phrases in the Waterloo chapter mentioned above. There is fine humor in "Dobbin of Ours": *Vanity Fair* follows Fielding's classicizing definition of the novel as a "comic epic in prose," but comic epic is not necessarily mock-epic. The chapter's rendering of Dobbin's schoolboy suffering is only partially mock-epic, if at all, in its celebration of his great triumph. Though Thackeray surrounds these small events with references to much greater ones, such matters are not small to the participants, nor is it reasonable to suppose that Thackeray implies children should learn to put bullying into perspective, as, say, Pope's Belinda is told to do. Finally, Thackeray's small epic of the school-yard led directly to the larger epic of *Tom Brown's Schooldays* (1857) and thence, without too big of a jump, to the vast, unfolding saga of the Harry Potter fantasy series—neither of which is parodic or mocking. Indeed, each has become the epic source of its own mock-epic shadows, above all in the *Flashman* novels.[30]

Thus when, as a result of defending young George, Dobbin turns his life at the school around, becomes "Dobbin of Ours," and later, to the delight of his mother, wins *Telemachus* as a "prize-book" at the "public midsummer examination" (56), it seems plausible to read more into this particular award. For Dobbin's victory is the essence of liberal epic: he selflessly defends the oppressed against a tyrant. The "war" is fully justified even by Fénelon's rigid standards. Dobbin was not looking for a fight, but reading quietly by himself. Young George was the weak and unoffending victim of Cuff's naked aggression:

> "Take that you little devil!" cried Mr. Cuff, and down came the wicket again on the child's hand.—Don't be horrified, ladies, every boy at a public school has done it. Your children will so do and be done by, in all probability. Down came the wicket again; and Dobbin started up.
>
> I can't tell what his motive was. Torture in a public school is as much licensed as the knout in Russia. . . . Perhaps Dobbin's foolish soul revolted against that exercise of tyranny; or perhaps he had a hankering feeling of revenge in his mind, and longed to measure himself against that splendid bully and tyrant, who had all the glory, pride, pomp, circumstance, banners flying, drums beating, guards saluting, in the place. (52)

Thackeray, as a good Victorian, first justifies his use of epic by putting these events into an appropriately primitive venue, then clinches this episode's liberal credentials by comparing Cuff's surprise at Dobbin's intervention to that of George III at the revolt of the American colonies. In any case, although the battle itself, a twelve-round boxing match, does not result in death or any life-threatening injuries, it involves real wounds— knockdowns, black eyes, cut lips, and flowing blood—that transcend mock-epic's conventional send-up of the seriousness of epic wounding: "His face being quite pale, his eyes shining open, and a great cut on his under-lip bleeding profusely, gave this young fellow a fierce and ghastly air, which perhaps struck terror into many spectators" (54). With its qualifying "perhaps," this passage signals a careful approximation to the absolute terror of looking upon epic death (there is no adult supervision of this brawl). With such violence at its center, Thackeray's references to Waterloo, to the last charge of the Guard, and to Ney seem far from simply belittling.

Fénelon's *Telemachus,* an adventure with a clear pedagogical purpose and written in elegant but eminently readable French, was a fine choice for an elevating prize. Its place in Thackeray's chapter, while suggesting a larger liberal epic symbolism, functions smoothly as part of a realistic portrait of a typical English public school around the year 1800: the boys' equivalent of *Johnson's Dictionary* for Miss Pinkerton's girls. Nonetheless, a more dispiriting implication accompanies this usage. Fénelon composed his prose epic as part of the neoclassical project to civilize and soften the graphic terror of Homer and traditional epic for an era that was attempting to limit the emotional and intellectual appeal of war and violent combat. Though written for a child, *Telemachus* mirrors an effort that extended to other increasingly literate groups such as women and the upper working or artisanal classes. It also extended its disciplinary program back to the traditional, unruly ruling elite—for that child was the heir to the throne of France. The good Victorian liberals, perhaps thanks to their confidence in having transcended the emotional appeal of war and having exposed its political-economic irrationality, reversed the neoclassical project. Now instead of beginning with children as part of the larger effort to suppress the natural allure of war and war epic, they preserved that violent matter and rescued that oldest of genres by consigning what they discounted as its primitive, obsolete pleasures to children. Both Tennyson's *Idylls* and Carlyle's *On Heroes and Hero-Worship* quickly became standard school reading—embraced for their relative accessibility, their high moral tone, and the easy (and unthreatening) pleasures of their heroic battling. Their fundamental argument and core themes are the same: to rescue modern faith in heroes by self-consciously appealing to primitive, childish beliefs. William Morris, in so many ways the child of Tennyson and Carlyle, followed their lead, with a good admixture of Scott and Ruskin, and produced a series of epic poems, romance epic collections, and, finally, fantasy epics in prose—all of them essentially juvenile in their appeal.

In these ways, Fénelon has become for the Victorians a subtle antithesis of what he himself sought: for epic violence was allowed to become a childish pleasure, something deadly serious for Rousseau and Locke, but now seen as an innocent amusement for a securely civilized society. The all-important process of beginning, at the level of a child's education, the task of leading society away from heroic violence had ended with children being allowed to indulge in violent entertainment by a society confidently at peace—at least with its own claims to peaceableness. The tale of Homer's fate is similar, but starker. For all their differences, the young J. S. Mill and the young John Ruskin found their greatest reading pleasures in Pope's *Iliad*. Among the Victorians, that poem and that translation became largely the provenance of children, particularly boys. Mill himself recognized, however, that his love of Pope could hardly be taken as normal "or natural to boyhood" (*Autobiography* 8). As the century wore on, the publishing industry expanded the appeal of Homer by providing ever more accessible versions, and near its end they hit upon the obvious solution of prose. The first was forged by a team including Andrew Lang, famous for his series of color-coded fairy-tale collections, but in 1897 the novelist and satirist Samuel Butler produced his own prose *Iliad*. Its preface makes clear that the target audience was boys, and that his goal was to render it fit for them with clear, simple English. Such a translation would necessarily abandon the civilizing project elaborated by Pope's *Iliad* with its refined diction and corrective commentary. Lest parents worry, as Locke or Fénelon or Rousseau or Blake or Pope or Hobbes worried, about the ill effects of Homeric savagery on tender minds, Butler concludes with a startling claim in the form of a bland assurance:

> All I claim is to have done my best towards making the less sanguinary parts of the Iliad interesting to English readers. The more sanguinary parts cannot be made interesting; indeed I doubt whether they can ever have been so, or even been intended to be so, to a highly cultivated audience. They had to be written and they were written; but it is clear that Homer often wrote them with impatience, and that actual warfare was as distasteful to him as it was foreign to his experience. Happily there is much less fighting in the Iliad than people generally think. (vi)

Such sentiments from an author who specialized in mocking Victorian moral pretensions were published at a time when the Rider Haggard–derived "bloody imperialist romance" dominated the marketplace for young men and boys, and when older men and boys were gobbling up newspaper accounts of imperial victories—Churchill had just proudly participated in the bloodiest of all at Omdurman, which he would soon celebrate in his popular history *The River War* (1898). Butler's claims cynically give the lie to the late Victorian liberal empire and its complete self-confidence in its humane benevolence. (In five years of labor on his

Iliad, Pope never ceased complaining about all the graphic violence; Butler's claim is manifestly absurd, though not to the Victorian objects of
his satire.) No doubt, just as Homer's violence "had to be written," the
Empire had to crush its primitive enemies. Perhaps, too, there was "much
less fighting in the [empire] than people generally" thought. All that was
needed was one additional assumption, namely, that even Victorian children, not to mention Homer's ancient listeners, were already a "highly
cultivated audience," uninterested in bloody adventures. Mill implied a
"natural" taste in boys for unadulterated Homeric fare, while Butler asserted that it was really "distasteful" even to Homer himself. The first was
noting that Pope's humanizing correctives had come to be an impediment
to lesser boys' readiness to find pleasure in straightforward violence. Butler allowed himself to remove these floodgates, because, with a wink and
a sneer, there was, he said, nothing there to be held back and no one, in
England, hungered for it anyway.[31] It is a long road from Fénelon's daring struggles to humanize the young Duke of Burgundy amid the palatial
lion's den of his conquering grandfather to this cozy, familial, Victorian
self-confidence that no such education was needed, a complacency Butler
could safely mock to his enormous profit. Perhaps this might be taken
as a wondrous sign of the moral progress of the West. In any case it was
the realm of Churchill's own education, and, as we shall see, he ironically capitalized upon the civilized confidence of his fellow Victorians in
his bloody, popular, epic celebrations of Britain's unparalleled achievement as the most liberal, most imperial, and most glorious end of history
imaginable—with himself as its heroic-heir and historian-beneficiary.

THE CRITICAL LANDSCAPE

The dominant mode of twentieth-century criticism of Homeric violence
has lost contact with the insights of Fénelon and Hume and unironically
embraced the satire of Butler. The last century largely ignored the anxiety that readers might respond sympathetically to Achilles's displays of
terrifying domination in favor of reading Homer as a critic of violence
and warfare, in short, as a tragedian, a mourner of human suffering. Our
prevailing modern theories of tragedy, however, are almost as maudlin
as such theories of epic. A. D. Nuttall in *Why Does Tragedy Give Pleasure?*
(1996) dissects the critical tradition, largely derived from Aristotle but recently reinvigorated by, for example, Martha Nussbaum, for suppressing
the obvious possibility that audiences enjoy watching others fail, fall, suffer, and die. Aristotle's theory makes a belabored elevation of tragedy over
epic, and one suspects that Aristotle's hierarchy was partially motivated

by epic's even more intense focus upon the pleasures of watching one hero kill another. Unlike the offstage violence of most tragedy or tragic violence's obvious realistic limitations when staged, epic is much better equipped to proffer realistic accounts of the drama of violent combat and its graphic killing. Homer, as James and Vico observed, is renowned for his detailed anatomical denouements, for offering the richest repasts to connoisseurs of killing.

In 1940 Simone Weil's seminal essay *The Iliad, or the Poem of Force* brilliantly summed up and extended this dominant attitude of modern Homer scholarship. She works hard to suppress the possibility, even the consideration, of readerly pleasure in the scenes of graphic violence. Instead the reader is being taught to deplore and reject the depersonalizing reality of force, the excesses of Achilles, and thus of warrior violence generally. Again, a dubious reading of tragedy has been expanded to become an even more dubious reading of epic. Weil's strategy is simply to deny the status of poetry to Homer's graphic violence, claiming that it is pure realism: "Whatever is not war, whatever war destroys or threatens, the Iliad wraps in poetry; the realities of war never. No reticence veils the step from life to death" (31). She deeply appreciates Homer's achievement in rendering the violent details of killing, but constructs a false opposition whereby all that content is set in opposition to poetry, art, civilization, and morality—which she equates with reticence, a verbal analogue to refinement and restraint. Such a position deserves repudiation as morally appealing but practically absurd: Homer labors as assiduously making his energizing violence poetic and beautiful as he does making his calming similes poetic and beautiful. For Homer, as Hume and Vico realized, the techniques of violent domination are the essence of his culture's ethical system. It is only to be expected that a detailed representation of heroic violence would be the central concern of Homer's high art. One of the most searching contemporary critics of war and violence, Elaine Scarry, has largely followed Weil and the tradition she epitomizes. Her influential *The Body in Pain* (1985) is a passionate and subtle work of ethical persuasion. Nonetheless, it relies upon a similar assumption that violence represents mere destructiveness in contrast to civilization as construction. She ignores the possibility that art and civilization are beholden to the pleasures and techniques of graphic violence, especially when it results from the trained abilities of a heroic agent whose expertise is being displayed to a discerning audience. Rather than being merely dehumanizing, is it not likely that Homer's scenes of violent killing are meant to celebrate the acquired skills of the supremely human hero-killer? When Scarry turns to Homeric violence, she stresses how the graphic representation of the destruction of a hero's body functions as a powerful allegory for war's destruction of culture: her analysis falls under the heading of "To Die" and stresses the "unmaking of civilization as it resides in each of those bodies" (122). In so focusing her analysis, Scarry suppresses the rival possibility that what is really being represented is "To Kill," the learning and power in the body of the victorious hero, an allegory of a culture's acquired ability to dominate its rivals and for its leaders to secure their desires through their mastery of their culture's highest skill, one matched by the verbal skills of their poets to celebrate such hero-killer-agents. They only acknowledge the victim's powers and gruesome death as a further embellishment of the winning culture hero's glory.

The positions of Scarry and Weil fairly sum up the prevailing modern critical view of Homer.[32] Still, such noble intentions do not substitute for the clear facts about Homer's own valuations, about Homer's art of violence, and about his influence. At the very least, they clash with the understanding of Homer's barbaric love of the kill that predominated at the time of Pope's culminating effort to civilize Homer for his increasingly liberal culture through translation and commentary. This late nineteenth- and twentieth-century view of Homer and Homeric violence also informs a range of contemporary critical responses to war literature in general. John Keegan, in his influential modern study of the literature of war, particularly the subgenre of the battle piece, shares Scarry's fundamental assumption that the muted or evasive descriptions of killing that characterize battles in military histories arise from the inherent difficulty historians face when contemplating and describing violence against the human body: "The act of misdescribing torture or war . . . is in either case partially made possible by the inherent difficulty of accurately describing any event whose central content is bodily pain or injury" (Scarry 13). "What went on at Agincourt appalls and horrifies the modern imagination which, vicariously accustomed though it is to the idea of violence, rarely encounters it in actuality and is outraged when it does" (Keegan 115). Keegan does not consider the possibility that historians' realistic failure is actually an artistic triumph. Beginning with Hume and Vico or Pope and Fénelon, however, my study calls Keegan's assumption into question. The archaeological evidence of the battle piece suggests this opposite paradigm: Western literature began with an easy, accepting, eager embrace of detailed descriptions of killing; modern, liberal epic poetry and history were premised on the effort to suppress that delight and to discipline its readers into thinking that their natural response ought to be one of disgust, of being appalled and horrified. What Keegan sees as hidebound or "inflexible" in the battle piece is in fact a remarkable achievement of one of the most subtly wrought poetic efforts of a self-consciously humane society, a labor of love by the likes of Alexander Pope and Edward Gibbon—two supreme artists of our modern "story of civilization." Keegan's undoing of that great if artificial tradition has indirectly, and sometimes directly, contributed to the current deluge of proudly and frankly graphic American military histories and novels, meticulously violent films and video games, to the first-person shooter, to *Halo* and *Doom*.

ONE

THE ETHICAL-AESTHETIC CHALLENGE TO EPIC

POPE, GIBBON, AND SCOTT

This chapter will move from the seventeenth-century origins of the liberal critique of war, through the rise of liberal epic and its enabling device, poetic diction, on to its triumph in the works of the leading poet of the eighteenth century, then to its greatest, most popular, and most influential historian. It will conclude with the poet, historian, and novelist central in establishing the preeminence of the novel early in the nineteenth century. In his *Iliad* preface, Pope acknowledges the influence of Fénelon's French modernization and Bossu's French rules, but gives his highest praise to Dryden for rendering portions of Homer and all Vergil: "the most noble and spirited translation I know in any language" (20). This chapter will in turn demonstrate Gibbon's indebtedness to Pope's practices for his translation and modernization of classical warfare. Scott's most famous novel, *Ivanhoe* (1819), repeatedly signals its dependence upon both Pope and Dryden—in the form of epigraphs from their Homer, Vergil, and Chaucer along with battles in his main text directly modeled after theirs—for its own efforts to adapt medieval heroic warfare to the tastes of his contemporary audiences. *Old Mortality* (1816), his starkest war novel, expressly thematizes the transition from an aristocratic culture of martial heroism to a middle-class world of democratic and capitalist peacefulness. His epic history of Napoleon is similarly shaped by the sanitized warfare and refined heroics of Gibbon. All three of these figures, though Gibbon most of all, have remained important, though largely unacknowledged, influences upon modern war epics—whether in the form of poetry, history, or the novel. In sum, this chapter will transition into the nineteenth century, where the phenomenon of liberal epic reached its climax, and it will establish that this tradition is a highly self-conscious one that spread from poetry to history to the novel. Lastly, it will frame this analysis of a stylistic and narrative evolution with a demonstration of how, parallel to it, the aesthetic and ethical discourse of the sublime went through a similar liberalization that theorized, justified, and exploited what the poets and historians were doing.

THE HOMER PROBLEM: THE LIBERAL SUBLIME FROM
HUME AND BURKE TO RUSKIN

The close connection between the good and the beautiful has been always felt. . . .
We all feel that there is a strict propriety in the term moral beauty. . . . Poems
like the Iliad or the Psalms, springing in the most dissimilar quarters, have com-
manded the admiration of men, through all the changes of some 3,000 years. The
charm of music, the harmony of the female countenance, the majesty of the starry
sky. . . . And in the same way types of heroism, and of virtue, descending from the
remotest ages, command the admiration of mankind.

—W. E. H. Lecky, *History of European Morals*

Numerous cultural, philosophical, artistic, and literary developments, some trivial and some momentous, measure the growing intensity of early modern liberal distress over the glorification of war and heroic violence. It was, first, this ethical discomfort and, later, intellectual doubts that drove traditional epic into its post-Miltonic crisis.[1] David Friedrich Strauss's groundbreaking survey of the evolution of biblical scholarship, for example, shows how Enlightenment critics grew increasingly restive over the illiberal, indeed newly illegal, actions of God's chosen people in the book of Joshua. Their exhibit A was the Bible's closest approach to a classical epic: "According to Chubb, the Jewish religion cannot be a revelation from God, because it debases the moral character of the Deity by attributing to him arbitrary conduct, partiality for a particular people, and above all, the cruel command to exterminate the Canaanitish nations" (Strauss 45). Strauss notes how the ironic rhetoric of various Deists and humanists used the ethical paradoxes provoked by the book of Joshua, particularly due to Grotius's and Pufendorf's influential legal writings, to disturb their readers and advance their agendas. Lord Bolingbroke, who affected a potent combination of liberal humanism and religious skepticism, compared Attila to Joshua: "Attila extended his conquests farther than Joshua; but it may be doubted whether he shed more blood. . . . Attila gave quarter often, Joshua never. . . . It was criminal among the Israelites . . . to show mercy to those they had robbed" (4:210). It is in what I call the Homer problem, however, that the most telling ironies and best evidence abound, for the effort to align ethics and aesthetics also peaked in the eighteenth century, above all in the writings of David Hume. This synthetic project inevitably led to moments of profound dissociation between the good and the beautiful, to sharp conflicts between the so-called moral taste and the aesthetic taste. For Hume, this potential tension found its most delicious irony in the case of Homer—the artistic acme and moral nadir of Western culture.[2]

Lecky, a leading nineteenth-century historian who aspired to greatness in the tradition of Gibbon, produced several studies of the evolution of Western law and morality and capped his career with a multivolume history of the eighteenth century whose theme was the progress of enlightened humanism. His overview of the problem of the good and the beautiful owes much to Hume. At this point in his introductory survey, Lecky has reached the eighteenth century and the thinking of Hutcheson, Shaftesbury, and Kames, along with Hume. That this last is Lecky's likely source becomes clearest in the Victorian's neoclassicizing appeal to Homer's long-standing position of aesthetic preeminence: as Hume also asserted, his three thousand years of permanent canonicity secured his claim to greatness. Such an argument made more sense in Hume before the historicizing Romantic revolution than after, but Lecky repeats it anyway. Indeed he goes beyond Hume. Though ostensibly engaged in a history of morals, Lecky affirms an ahistorical thesis ("always been felt") that strictly aligns moral and aesthetic beauty. His narrative becomes a testimonial to this universal rule of our nature. He forgets Hume's ironic purpose, one present in the *Enquiry concerning the Principles of Morals* (1751) but central to the essay "On the Standard of Taste" (*Essays* 1757). This essay plays upon the parallels between moral taste and aesthetic taste, and repeatedly points to Homer as a constant standard of artistic merit, but also as a disturbing compendium of dated, barbaric ethical codes. Between the age-old respect for Homer's artistic greatness and the modern withdrawal from his moral ugliness lurks an impossible dilemma—one that causes problems for Hume's local ethical philosophizings but energizes his broader commitment to skeptical empiricism, to disruptive facts over comprehensive theories.[3] He enjoys finding exceptions even to his own rules. Homer is a monkey wrench in the workings of Hume's effort to align the two tastes, but a godsend to Hume's project to undermine all such philosophical certainties. This dilemma is ratcheted up by Hume's repeated appeals to Fénelon, whose adherence to Homeric standards of poetic artistry opposes his ongoing effort to reform Homeric standards of virtue.[4]

For Hume, the earlier poet becomes the basis for his claim that classical morality was centered upon the notion of courage, while Fénelon's revision of Homer offers the strongest evidence that benevolence was the essence of modern liberal virtue. More pointedly, Hume implies that for Homer, the hero himself is the key standard. His individual success, excellence, and glory outweigh all other considerations, while Fénelon limits his heroes by subjecting them to principles that elevate the rights of others: "When [Homer] draws particular pictures of manners, and represents heroism in Achilles and prudence in Ulysses, he intermixes a much greater degree of ferocity in the former, and cunning and fraud in the latter, than Fénelon would admit of . . . [Ulysses's] more scrupulous son, in the French epic writer, exposes himself to the most imminent perils, rather than depart from the most exact line of truth and veracity" (228). "Courage" becomes the dominant virtue of a system based upon outstanding individuals; "benevolence," the prime virtue of a system organized around mutual respect. Hume deploys this contrast to dramatize that, while across the ages writers might use the same names for ethical excellence—"justice, humanity, magnanimity, prudence, veracity" (228)—in the meanings there lie enormous differences. In contrast, Lecky, the historian, oddly struggles to minimize these historical differences. He subordinates the "great diversities of detail" to a theoretical "far larger amount of substantial unity" (1:78)—reversing Hume's empirical point. Lecky is narrating a history of moral thinking, but when he arrives at the Humean position, he is suddenly less of a historian and more of an advocate—and what he is advocating is a timeless rationale for epic. He wants an easy alignment of ethics and aesthetics, of the teachings and the beauties of Homer. He draws on Hume, but subverts Hume's skeptical project in order to preserve the modern relevance of Homeric virtue, its courage and violence, and thus the epic hero and epic itself: "War is, no doubt, a fearful evil, but it is the seed-plot of magnanimous virtues, which in a pacific age must wither and decay" (1:147–48).

Hume was rightly noting that for Homer, killing in battle was ethically and aesthetically unproblematic.[5] For Fénelon it was this conjunction that his Homeric narrative sought to deny and decouple. Edmund Burke added the "Introduction on Taste" to the second edition of his *Philosophical Inquiry into the Origin of Our Ideas of the Sublime and the Beautiful* (1759) as a direct response to Hume's provocative essay on taste. His first sentence references Hume's historicist quandary, then rejects it ("the standard of both reason and taste is the same in all human creatures" [Burke 11]), and his theory of the sublime becomes his way out of Hume's dilemma. Like Lecky, he thereby defends the ethics of epic. Burke's introduction and Hume's essay ultimately derive from Pope's Fénelon-inspired correction of Homer's *Iliad,* and its terrifying pleasures: Burke's first quoted example comes from it; Hume's juxtaposition of Homer and Fénelon merely labels the schizophrenic halves that together comprise Pope's *Iliad.* What critics of Burke's treatise have not noted is that Burke's response to Hume and Burke's overall theory of the sublime both work to smooth over this

Homer problem.[6] Burke disputes Hume's insistence that an inherent taste, not universal reason, is the only way to explain our aesthetic (and moral) judgments; an underlying purpose is that it allows him to theorize the sublime as something different from the beautiful, but equally ethical and rational in its own terms.

Burke generates two kinds of beautiful, each with its own logic rendering it ethical—indeed, liberally ethical. He also defines two kinds of pleasure: one a joyful pleasure, drawn from the beautiful, and the other a painful pleasure, which Burke labels "delight," imposed by the sublime. "As I make use of the word Delight to express the sensation which accompanies the removal of pain or danger; so when I speak of positive pleasure, I shall for the most part call it simply Pleasure" (34). Burke's specification of his terms here is misleading, since he elsewhere claims that sublime delight is also a positive experience, more than simply the cessation of pain. This distinction accomplishes a subtle moral purpose: it aligns the sublime with masochism, when, as Locke, Vico, Hume, and Pope feared, the real challenge of the Homeric sublime was its sadism. Burke links the sublime with fear—for another and for oneself. The reader fears for the characters in danger in a tragedy or an epic, and thus comes to experience, through empathy, fear for him- or herself. Finally, the reader comes to enjoy sublime terror because of its intense frisson followed by relief, by escape from that fear. But Hume and Vico's point was that Homer's reader experienced the truculent pleasures of causing fear or empathizing with the dominator, the terrorizer, the killer, not the terrorized victim. Thus the Burkean sublime rescues Homeric terror for liberal culture by obscuring its illiberal thrill of domination—and rendering it an eminently liberal fear for another's well-being and thus for oneself, a frightful lesson in the need for all to enjoy individual autonomy, not to adore the power of a heroic few to violate it at will.[7]

Burke's fundamental maneuver was enabled by Pope's *Iliad*, which strives to downplay the terror of domination and increase the relief of pity. His first example of the sublime presents Homer in the original and then Pope's version as a trustworthy rendering. This simile describes the surprise of Achilles and his followers at Priam's appearance in his tent:

> ὡς δ' ὅτ' ἄν ἄνδρ' ἄτη πυκινὴ λάβῃ, ὅς τ' ἐνὶ πάτρῃ
> φῶτα κατακτείνας ἄλλων ἐξίκετο δῆμον
> ἀνδρὸς ἐς ἀφνειοῦ, θάμβος δ' ἔχει εἰσορόωντας,
> ὡς Ἀχιλεὺς θάμβησεν ἰδὼν Πρίαμον θεοειδέα.

> As when a wretch, who conscious of his crime,
> Pursued for murder from his native clime,

> Just gains some frontier, breathless, pale, amaz'd;
> All gaze, all wonder! (Burke 32)

Burke's follow-up analysis of this passage refashions what in Homer is an ambivalent scene of anxiety for Priam in danger coupled with admiration for the fearsomeness of Achilles firmly toward the former, toward fearful sympathy for someone at risk: "This striking appearance of the man whom Homer supposes to have just escaped an imminent danger, the sort of mixt passion of terror and surprize, with which he affects the spectators, paints very strongly the manner in which we find ourselves affected upon occasions any way similar" (32). Pope's translation augments this sense of fear, relief, and escape so important to Burke. Its language of consciousness of crime, of pursuit, of the man's "breathless, pale, amaz'd" appearance has little warrant in the Greek. There the amazement applies only to the onlookers: "Ἀχιλεὺς θάμβησεν" (24.483; line 484 then reapplies this verb to Achilles's followers). Pope doubles it, giving "amaz'd" to the man fleeing and "wonder" to those seeing him, thus exhibiting his translation's basic strategy to increase the mood of pity and empathy between spectator and endangered characters whenever possible. The Greek presents a simple scene of a murderer arriving as an exile in a new land, and being looked upon with amazement. Are the onlookers fearful of him or relieved for him—or merely surprised? Moreover, Homer's simile shades into both Priam and Achilles: it hints at the danger Priam has put himself into, and the murderous power of Achilles's hands. Burke's emphasis remains fixed upon Priam and thus upon the viewers' fear for the exile, but even Pope admits, though he intensified the passage's effect of making one fear for someone in danger, that the larger passage and the simile itself also emphasize admiration for Achilles's terrifying abilities: "The poet recalls to mind all the noble actions performed by Achilles in the whole Ilias; and at the same time strikes us with his utmost compassion for this unhappy king" (24.1142). Pope here fudges with the adjective "noble," which he otherwise seems to question. Homer leans toward the terror of Achilles, toward an expectation of the reader's knowledge of his ready anger and dangerous powers. In Homer even the undeniable effects of pity are ultimately there to magnify his terrifying heroes. The final mourning for Hector is proof positive of Achilles's power to reduce an entire city to tearful despair, and to force a father to go begging on his knees to his son's killer. Pope gestures cautiously toward this savage dimension but eagerly busies himself to create readerly sympathy with Priam in danger. Burke shifts almost entirely to this sympathetic fear, and then designates this new effect "the sublime."

As further confirmation that this pattern is a distinct feature of Pope's translation, which Burke could then exploit, consider this outburst: "That wretch, that monster, who delights in war: / Whose lust is murder, and whose horrid joy, / To tear his country, and his kind destroy!" (9.90–92). Pope frequently boasts that he, unlike previous translators, resisted the urge to add new ideas and images to the original. In this case, however, he greatly exceeds his normal inflation rate by rendering one line of Greek into three lines of English, and that original line condemns something quite different: "ὃς πολέμου ἔραται ἐπιδημίου ὀκρυόεντος" (9.64). In his notes, Pope admits taking "liberty" in this rendering of an "original [that] comprizes a great deal in a very few words" (455), but his follow-up analysis focuses entirely on his translation of the line just before it. In fact, the unit of meaning involves two lines in Homer and six in Pope: Pope's note attends to the first of Homer's two and the first three of his six, where he more or less literally translates a series of dense adjectives. He never acknowledges his more serious breach and more expansive reinvention of Homer's second line. Modern commentators read it as a quotation of proverbial language, by the voluble and wise old Nestor, "outlawing . . . someone who introduces civil war into a community" (Willcock 272). It translates literally into "who is in love with horrible war at home" (my translation). The scenario recalls key elements of the passage quoted by Burke in referring to a murderer within a community, but now Pope has wrenched it into something not subtly, but fundamentally, different. Knowing the original, one can look back and realize that Pope's "tear his country" could be invoking civil strife, and "his kind" means his fellow countrymen, but the larger effect of Pope's three-line expansion absent such knowledge is clearly to condemn war in general, to curse any killing of a human being by another, and thus to deplore the essence of the Homeric sublime itself. It renders all admiration for skill on the battlefield, all excellence in killing and dominating an enemy, into a "lust." The core narrative material of *The Iliad*, the reliable pleasure it provided a Greek audience, has been made a sin.[8] Indeed, in transforming an intra-community rule into a code applying to all humankind, into a boundless inter-community bond, Pope has foisted upon an unwitting Nestor the essential first step of international law—and his poetic diction is the wand whereby Homer's simplest, most elemental thrill has been transmogrified into an off-putting "horrid joy."

Derived from such translational strategies (indeed falsifications), Burke's sublime passed on to another great liberal, Immanuel Kant, who further defanged the bite of the sadistic Homeric beautiful-sublime by marginalizing even masochistic Burkean terror; intensified the sublime's intellectual or logical dimension, which Hume had rejected and Burke partially reinstated; and matched this aesthetic project with Fénelon-inspired strategies for pushing Europe away from war and toward a new order of universal peace founded upon national autonomy and federative peace-keeping.[9] Kant was nothing if not a determined liberal, one dedicated to correcting Hume's corrosive skepticism, whether in epistemology, history, ethics, or aesthetics. The prime case of subsequent English thinking on the sublime, however, appears in John Ruskin's voluminous writings. His early heroic poem "The Battle of Montenotte" (1842) is filled with the Burkean sublime of fear-inspiring mountains and skies but has few fearsome details of battle, and no opportunity for the reader to identify with heroic infliction of terror. Indeed, the poem's premise reverses any Homeric identification with the killer. It asks, what if Napoleon had been defeated in his first great battle, and none of his glory had arisen to plague the world? About the same time, Ruskin began his five-volume *Modern Painters* (1843–60). This treatise follows Burke's (and Locke's) theories closely, and, not surprisingly, it mirrors Ruskin's poem in stressing the sublime of mountains, skies, the ocean, clouds—the natural phenomena of terrific awe. Nonetheless, like "The Battle of Montenotte," Ruskin's particular subject in *Modern Painters,* the art of J. M. W. Turner, includes both the grandeur of nature and the violence of epic, empire, and war. Many of Turner's historical paintings are drawn from Gibbon's *Decline and Fall* and its Vergilian source. Thus, the striking feature of *Modern Painters* is how determinedly it evades this inevitable subject. Chapter after chapter, and volume after volume, Ruskin inches up to the central place of heroic violence in the theory of the sublime—but then puts it off, looks away. Written at the height of the Victorian era, *Modern Painters,* which was widely influential upon poetry and history, is the final and most revealing example of the Homer Problem, here morphed into the Turner Problem.[10]

By his own admission, Ruskin grew up loving, reading, and rereading Homer—in Pope's translation—and coming to venerate the power of heroes. He offers this fact as evidence for his long-standing political opposition to democratic liberalism. Ruskin thus rejects the liberal paradigm that takes pride in the historical progress away from a culture of war and its heroic ideals. He asserts the opposite—"as peace is established or extended in Europe, the arts decline" (18:463). Ruskin oftentimes shows himself determined to challenge liberal ideals by Homerically associating ethics and aesthetics, sometimes even stressing the congruity of the virtues of martial heroism and its aesthetic beauty: "There is no great art possible to a nation but that which is based on battle" (18:460). This quotation comes from a deliberately provocative lecture intended to impugn the increasingly powerful liberal thesis that true virtue resides with the peaceful, antiwar values of capitalism. In that lecture, titled "War," from *The Crown of Wild Olive* (1866), Ruskin articulates the most insightful characterization of the Homeric primal scene: "But, remember, so far as this may be true, the game of war is only that in which the *full personal power of the human creature* is brought out in management of its weapons. And this for three reasons—First, the great justification of this game is that it truly, when well played, determines *who is the best man*, who is the highest bred, the most self-denying, the most fearless, the coolest of nerve, the swiftest of eye and hand" (18:470). Curiously, Ruskin omits the signature Achillean quality of swiftness of foot, which enabled him to chase down his victims. He also backs away from Achilles's most famous characteristic: "The conduct of the Spartans in battle denotes a high and noble disposition, which rejected all the extremes of brutal rage" (18:473). This tweaking of Homer's ideal figure underscores that, even at such a high heroic moment, Ruskin hedges with his rhetoric of war as a "game," his qualification of "well played," which seems to suggest the existence of rules or laws of war, and his emphasis upon heroic self-denial and fear-lessness as opposed to Homeric self-assertion, rage, terror, and speedy brutality. Despite all his trained insight and all his ideological opposition, Ruskin's writings on war and the sublime become a lesson in how far modern writers, even ones who claim not to be liberals and to love war as the highest of arts, will go in order to sanitize and liberalize combat and not to look at the graphic details of killing. Thus, according to Ruskin, even the Greeks designed their war gear to hide what they were doing: "the dark-red of the purple mantles, which were meant both to adorn the combatant, and to conceal the blood of the wounded" (18:473). Certainly, Ruskin did his best not to look—and, in the great tradition of liberal epic, to teach his readers not to want to either.

POETIC DICTION AND NEOCLASSICAL KILLING: POPE AND GIBBON AND SCOTT

Let him with glorious Slaughter smear'd, affright
And please us too, with terrible Delight.
—Blackmore, *Advice to the Poets*

Gibbon's *Memoirs* tell how as a young reader he first learned to appreciate beautiful writing by reading Pope: "The verses of Pope accustomed my ear to the sound of poetic harmony: in the death of Hector . . . I tasted the new emotions of terror and pity" (36–37). Gibbon's uncompleted final revisions of *The Decline and Fall of the Roman Empire* record how these early lessons in rhythm, euphemism, and humane restraint persisted throughout his life: "Late generations and far distant climates may impute their calamities to the immortal author of the Iliad. The spirit of Alexander was inflamed by the praises of Achilles: and succeeding Heroes have been ambitious to tread in the footsteps of Alexander" (Bury, *Decline and Fall* 1:xxxvi). Here, Gibbon in the 1790s expands his 1776 critique of the conquering ethos of the emperor Trajan. He elaborates the movement of the prose and clarifies that this judgment arises from Pope's Achilles and Voltaire's Charles XII, whom Voltaire roundly condemned for thus imitating the Achillean Alexander. Readers at the time detected Gibbon and Pope's shared project—only to reject it as merely a more polished, more insidious form of the original barbarity. Blake explicitly denounced Homer and the classics, but implicitly targeted Pope's Homer and, above all, Gibbon: "The Classics, it is the Classics! & not Goths nor Monks, that Desolate Europe with Wars" ("On Homer's Poetry" 428)—Gibbon being the notorious indicter of Goths and Monks as the twin destroyers of ancient civilization.[11] Joel Barlow, a contemporary of Blake's and America's first epic poet, states in more measured terms this same complaint: "I think every person who will give himself the trouble to form an opinion on the manner in which actions, called heroic, have been recorded must find it faulty; and must lament, as one of the misfortunes of society, that writers of these two classes almost universally, from Homer down to Gibbon, have led astray the moral sense of man" (849). Barlow binds epic poetry and history, Homer and Gibbon (with Pope implied). He goes on to fashion a determinedly anti-heroic formula that makes harm to humanity directly proportional to the greatness of Homeric fame—whether hero's or poet's.

Pope's translation of Homer and Gibbon's of Ammianus Marcellinus are my principal examples for more closely specifying how poetic diction was conceived and deployed to defang heroic violence—and how Pope's practices were handed on to and extended by Gibbon. The foundation for Pope's *Iliad*, both its text and its notes, was Madame Dacier's pioneering late seventeenth-century French prose translation and learned commentary.[12] Dacier acted as the primary vector by which the special sensitivities of women readers and French high culture entered into Pope's own version, a marked feature of his *Iliad* that was noted at the time by critics such as Johnson and Bentley and has recently been given renewed attention.[13] Dacier's concern for her women readers leads naturally to strenuous efforts to address this core problem of graphic violence. For on this precise point, Dacier's dedication to translate as literally as possible (not a strong point of earlier French or English versions, and thus a prime selling point for Pope with his accomplished French but dubious Greek) clashed with her humane and polite objections to Homer's graphic energies. This tension was increased by Pope's also acknowledging the influence of Fénelon's child-directed and antiwar-inflected adaptation of Homer. Gibbon, too, was a favorite with the sort of young boys who grew up on Pope's *Iliad* and Scott's poems and novels—thus the need for Bowdler in the 1820s to do to him what he'd already done for Shakespeare. Bowdler attended to the sexuality in the playwright and the irreligion in the historian, for he had little need to strain out any graphic violence. Gibbon had already recast his lurid sources so as not to offend sensitive modern readers. He boasted of his brisk sales in a simile that underscored his successful rivalry with contemporary novels and his text's evident ability to appeal to both sexes: "My book was on every table, and almost every toilette" (*Memoirs* 160). His biographer Patricia Craddock chronicles his accommodations in the themes and the tone of his later volumes to the presumed sensitivities of women readers (84–85). As with Pope, Gibbon apologizes for what graphic violence he includes and downplays the possibility of taking any pleasure in it, but his main tactic focuses upon translating his graphic originals into a softer form.

The clearest evidence of Pope's direct influence upon Gibbon's practices appears in a related case of barbaric and graphic bluntness versus refined delicacy: food preparation. Gibbon advances many theories regarding violence—why some take pleasure in it and others do not; why the ancients and barbarians celebrate it and the civilized moderns bemoan it. One cautiously proposes that "if it be true, that the sentiment of compassion is imperceptibly weakened by the sight and practice of domestic cruelty, we may observe, that the horrid objects which are disguised by the arts of European refinement, are exhibited in their naked and most disgusting simplicity in the tent of a Tartarian shepherd." Here Gibbon implicitly corrects Rousseau's ready assumption of English barbarism. In a footnote, he responds to Rousseau's claim that "la barbarie Angloise" arises from the English being such prodigious meat eaters: "Les grands mangeurs de viande sont en general cruels et feroces" (1:1026). The Greek versus Modern contrast is reworked as English versus French. For Gibbon, at pains to defend the English from the accusations of their French superiors in polite civilization, such cruelty comes only from seeing the butchering of the living animals, not from merely encountering them on the dinner table "disguised . . . by refinement." This comment on the presentation of animal meat suggests how his narrative will offer its modern readers the butchering of human bodies in war. It typifies the refining process of such liberal epic poets and historians as Pope, Voltaire, and Gibbon in contrast to the more radical (one is tempted to say vegan and cite Peter Singer) positions of Rousseau, Blake, and Barlow. Gibbon characterizes these Tartars as "unfeeling murderers" of their familiar pets, before speculating that such voracious meat eaters nonetheless possess a distinct military advantage over their civilized bread-eating enemies when it comes to supplying an army.

Later Gibbon returns to this same logic in a comment on a medieval Russian: "Swatoslaus, the son of Igor, the son of Oleg, the son of Ruric . . . usually slept on the ground, his head reclining on a saddle; his diet was coarse and frugal, and, like the heroes of Homer, his meat (it was often horse-flesh) was broiled or roasted on the coals" (3:463). This vignette has a geographical setting and "military and savage" logic that recalls not just Homer's heroes, but Voltaire's throwback conqueror Charles XII, who deliberately eschewed Western European comforts for the pleasures of fighting and sleeping on Ukrainian ground. But it is the appended footnote (note 68) that clinches things: "This resemblance may be clearly seen in the ninth book of the Iliad (205–21), in the minute detail of the cookery of Achilles. By such a picture, a modern epic poet would disgrace his work and disgust his reader; but the Greek verses are harmonious, a dead language can seldom appear low or familiar; and at the distance of two thousand seven hundred years, we are amused with the primitive manners of antiquity" (2:463). Gibbon's comment comes from Pope's note on the relevant lines from Achilles's cooking scene, lines exhibiting all the techniques of poetic diction in replacing simple, graphic terms with nice word combinations. Furthermore, Pope's commentary is itself a quotation-translation from Dacier:

> Madam Dacier's general note on this passage deserves to be transcribed. "Homer, says she, is in the right not to avoid these descriptions, because nothing can properly be called vulgar which is drawn from the manner and usages of persons of the first dignity; and also because in his tongue even the terms of cookery are so noble, and of so agreeable a sound, and he likewise knows how to place them so well, as to extract a perfect harmony from them: so that he may be said to be as excellent a Poet when he describes these small matters, as when he treats of the greatest subjects. 'Tis not so either with our manners, or our language. Cookery is left to servants, and all its terms so low and disagreeable, even in the sound, that nothing can be made of them, that has not some taint of their meanness. This great disadvantage made me at first think

of abridging this preparation of the repast; but when I had so well considered it, I was resolv'd to preserve and give Homer as he is, without retrenching any thing from the simplicity of the heroick manners. I do not write to enter the lists against Homer, I will dispute nothing with him; my design is only to give an idea of him, and to make him understood: the reader will therefore forgive me if this description has none of its original graces." (461–62)

To draw this chain link to a close, Pope-Dacier's meditation upon the difference between ancient and modern attitudes toward food preparation is echoed by Pope's later complaint as a modern against Homer's ancient delight in pure violence. Dacier had contemplated "abridging this preparation of the repast," and that is exactly what Pope eventually did to the worst of Homer's concentrated violence: "This is the only book of the Iliad which is a continued description of a battle. . . . [The] spirit which animates the original, is what I am sensible evaporates so much in my hands; that, tho' I can't think my author tedious, I should have made him so, if I had not translated this book with all possible conciseness" (832). Gibbon follows Pope, who manifestly copies Dacier on the question of the offensiveness of Homer's graphic accounts of cookery for modern readers. Gibbon aligns his trouble over that matter with his struggles over epic's graphic violence. He deploys that connection to theorize on the reasons behind civilized horror and compassion and barbaric pleasure at the sight of a skilled killer's handiwork. All three moderns evince a determination to lessen such graphic material and its precise vocabulary, though Dacier's defensiveness leads her to deny the act of abridgment she perpetrates, while Pope's subtlety allows him to apologize through Dacier and thus commit less of a falsehood when he, too, proceeds to do for grilling fresh meat what he then directly confesses when it comes to unrelieved human slaughter. For when Pope says "conciseness," he means abridgment. Gibbon, with more freedom in relation to his sources than these two translators, more easily indulges in their strategies of evasive refinement, civilized truncation, and apologetic commentary.

Scott prefaced *Ivanhoe* with a statement about his translational strategies both at the literal level for lessening the offense of uncivilized vulgarity and violence and at the metaphorical level for tweaking his medieval history and customs to reflect the manners and culture of his era: "It is necessary, for exciting interest of any kind, that the subject assumed should be, as it were, translated into the manners as well as the language of the age we live in. No fascination has even been attached to oriental literature equal to that produced by Mr Galland's first translation of the Arabian Tales" (9). Much as Fénelon's elegant updating of Homer shaped a generation of English translations and adaptations of Greek epics, so here Scott singles out another smooth French rendering of primitive "splendour" and "wildness." Scott speculated correctly that his story told in this way would lead "multitudes" to "devour it with avidity": the consumption metaphor is apt. The first chapter of his narrative is headed by an epigraph from Pope's Homer referencing Odysseus's swineherd: the reader is being assured that Scott's version of an eleventh-century swineherd has the same relation to the raw reality of such a creature as Pope's Eumaeus has to Homer's. When we meet Scott's Gurth, we find him discussing (in modern English) the difference between polite upper-class French words for food in contrast to the rougher Saxon terms for the live animals, to wit, "pork" versus "swine," and so on: Dacier to Pope to Gibbon to Scott.

POPE'S SANITIZED LIBERALIZATION OF HOMER

Some of [Homer's deaths] are so exceedingly exact, that one may guess from the very position of the combatant, whereabouts the wound will light: Others are so very peculiar and uncommon. . . . Another cause of this variety is the difference of the wounds that are given in the Iliad: They are by no means like the wounds described by most other poets, which are commonly made in the self-same obvious places: The heart and the head serve for all those in general who understand no anatomy, and sometimes for variety they kill men by wounds that are nowhere mortal but in their poems.

—Pope, "An Essay on Homer's Battels"

Despite Milton's success in undermining war epic, literary culture still required an ambitious poet to crown his career with an appropriately classicizing epic poem, but no leading poet—not Dryden, not Pope, not Cowper—did more than translate, however brilliantly, the *Aeneid,* the *Iliad,* or the *Odyssey.* Pope's experience illustrates the paradoxes of this high cultural dilemma: beginning with his youthful pastorals, Pope evinced the intention to follow the standard Vergilian path that progressed from pastoral to epic; yet, despite his brilliance and learning, Pope was consistently thwarted at the level of epic—succeeding in various mock-epics, completing major portions of a philosophical epic, famously translating and hugely profiting from the *Iliad,* and repeatedly planning his own *Brutus,* but never actually composing more than a few scattered lines. In the greatest of the Augustans emerges the central problem: a complete mastery of the style and conventions of classical epic, but an inability to find or dedicate himself to a suitable subject.

A closer scrutiny of Pope's translation of the *Iliad* confirms the essential obstacle. This text, eagerly awaited by Pope's public and lucratively produced by subscription in expensive editions, is much more than a translation. In it Pope includes extensive prefacing materials and three appendices, lengthy notes distilling the millennial tradition of Homeric commentary, and, perhaps most interesting because anomalous, extensive, interpolated essays—one appearing between books 4 and 5 ("An Essay on Homer's Battels") and one between books 18 and 19 ("Observations on the Shield of Achilles"). The preface concentrates on an exposition of Homer's greatness as a poet, stressing his role as the "Inventor of Poetry," insisting repeatedly, with all the weight of his era's anxiety of imitation, on his transcendence of all other poets in originality and invention: "his fable more extensive and copious than any other, his manners more lively and strongly marked, his speeches more affecting and transported, his sentiments more warm and sublime, his images and descriptions more full and animated, his expression more rais'd and daring, and his numbers more rapid and various" (10–11). Pope's assertion that Homer is more original leads to the conclusion that he possesses more of everything. The remainder of the preface seeks to demonstrate these claims in detail, to explain how Pope has gone about the paradoxical task of translating such originality, and, finally, to defend Homer against his detractors, particularly against any claim of Vergil's superiority. Amid all this praise and vindication, Pope does concede the one undeniable problem of Homer's content, the sad fact of the savagery of his heroes and the extreme violence of their actions: "Who can be so prejudiced in their favour as to magnify the felicity of those ages, when a spirit of revenge and cruelty, join'd with the practice of Rapine and Robbery, reign'd thro' the world; when no mercy was shown but for the sake of lucre, when the greatest Princes were put to the sword, and their wives and daughters made slaves and concubines?" (12–13). Pope's adulation halts abruptly before the "more" of Homer's violence and savagery.

His two interpolated essays therefore disturb the otherwise smooth progress of books and notes in an effort to address this outstanding challenge.[14] The "Observations on the Shield of Achilles" provides Pope with a joyful respite, as he turns from rendering the relentless battling of the later books to this explicitly aesthetic episode (it is an ekphrasis), with peace surpassing war as its content and with the highest example of Homer's unsurpassed inventiveness as its mode: "The invention is shown in finding and introducing, in every subject, the greatest, the most significant, and the most suitable objects" (898). Pope's superlatives announce the ease with which he will jaunt through not only the technical beauties of Homer's pure poetry but also the now wholly acceptable content. The "Essay on Homer's Battels" undertakes the more difficult task of confronting this rough fact. The dominant note of Pope's analysis is to detail how the poetic style variously "relieves and softens these descriptions of battels" (216). Rawson's word "sanitization" has arisen as the best term for describing what Pope's translation does to Homer, but here we see Pope projecting it back on to Homer—and then deriving his own strategy from this imposition. Although Pope begins by admitting that the bulk of the *Iliad* is devoted to minute descriptions of intense combat and gory death ("no other [poet] has describ'd half so many deaths" [214]), he then proceeds to demonstrate how Homer's "astonishing variety" works to vary the depressing monotony of this material and to relieve the reader: "As the perpetual horrour of combates, and a succession of images of death, could not but keep the imagination very much on the stretch; Homer has been careful to contrive such reliefs and pauses as might divert the mind to some other scene, without losing sight of his principal object" (215). Pope continues with an elaborate simile that sums up his argument and reveals his desire not to look at the Homeric subject of combat killing, but rather to limit his civilized appreciation to Homer's immense variety and artistic embellishments. He thus defends Homer's use of simile to counter the burden of his graphic realism:

> Those cricks who fancy that the use of comparisons distracts the attention, and draws it from the first image which should most employ it . . . [;] those, I say, may as well imagine we lose the thought of the sun, when we see his reflection in the water, where he appears more distinctly, and is contemplated more at ease, than if we gaz'd directly at his beams. For it is with the eye of the imagination as it is with our corporeal eye, it must sometimes be taken off from the object in order to see it the better. (215)

Pope's final metaphorical remark about the "eye of the imagination" exposes the logical problem of his simile on Homer's similes. For the reader's encounter with Homer's verbal depictions of violence is hardly the same as any actual vision of such horrors. Those descriptions are already distanced reflections in the mirror of language of some unbearable reality—but Pope's discriminating mind's eye cannot long look even at these.

In sum, Homer's poetry renders killing beautiful and precise, a matter of realistic style and skillful content for his reader's heroic sympathy and nice appreciation. Pope prefers to apply such terms and effects only to his similes, to reserve his steady-eyed appreciation only for the reflection of the violence, and to avoid acknowledging the beauty of Homer's primary efforts. Together with his later comments regarding his concision in translating Homer's violence and his implicit omission of the nonpoetic material reality of Homer's battle scenes, this passage on simile outlines the basic poetic and ideological theory behind Pope's rendering of the immediate and technical original into his more distanced and generalizing heroic couplets. Pope's preference for a reflection's reflection, for a poetic verbal analogy of the primary verbal description or plain-style representation of some original violent act, betrays his fundamental objection to epic.

As Burke realized and exploited, Pope's analysis follows a pattern of dividing Homeric death into two distinct components—"terror" (its basic subject, the vivid moment of anatomical killing) and "pity" (its poetic relief, the stylistic and emotional diversions). Pope prefers "pity." His thinking follows Aristotle's theory of tragedy. Homeric terror is far more overwhelming than its tragic descendent, however, far more weighty and vivid than the tragedians' offstage killings, and thus, too, Homeric pity comes as more of a relief than tragic pity, less of a viewer's identification with the common humanity of the victim than an escape and flight into poetry from reality. This radically divided model extends from the basic narrative content to Pope's sense of Homeric characterizations: "The Pathetic of Patroclus's speech is finely contrasted by the Fierté of that of Achilles. While the former is melting with sorrow for his countrymen. . . . Achilles . . . speaks of the total destruction of the Greeks as of too slight a cause for tears" (775). Pope's exquisite Frenchifying of Achilles's distinguishing rage echoes his basic dictional strategy for translating this unpleasant dimension of Homer's poem.

When Pope moves on to the business of translating book 5, the first of the battle books and the first in volume 2 of his deluxe edition, he prefaces his descent into unrelieved violence with an epigraph from Horace expressing a civilized, humanistic dismay at, even disdain for, the task of writing about war: "Who can write, in a dignified way, about Mars wrapped in his adamantine armor? or of Meriones black with the dust of Troy?" Later, in his opening observations on book 17, Pope's dignity reaches the breaking point over violence "without any digression . . . to refresh the reader [and translator]": "Homer seems to have trusted wholly to the force of his own genius, as sufficient to support him, what soever lengths he was carried by it. But that spirit which animates the original, is what I am sensible evaporates so much in my hands; that, tho' I can't think my author tedious, I should have made him seem so, if I had not translated this book with all possible conciseness" (832). The passage dramatizes Pope's growing exasperation: Homer has gone too far, and he cannot follow. Since now it is only the vaunted originality of Homer that saves this narrative from tedium, Pope, in the role of unoriginal translator, can only plead the utmost concision as a remedy.

Here at its most intense, this challenge warps a fundamental feature of Pope's translation: its comparatively greater length. Because of the pithier nature of the inflected Greek, but also because of Pope's decision to translate unrhymed dactylic hexameter lines into rhymed iambic pentameter couplets filled with noun-adjective pairs in place of Homer's plain and/or technical vocabulary, Pope's version is significantly longer, measured either by lines or words, than the original. This fact unravels in the face of the later books' unadulterated violence. It reaches a crisis here where Pope boasts of his version having "but sixty five lines more than the original" (832). Such a small increase over the original number of lines is unprecedented in Pope's *Iliad:* from an original of 761 Greek lines to only 854 in heroic couplets for an increase of 93. This is significantly smaller, both absolutely and as a percentage, than any other in the translation, though one must note Pope's striking overestimation of his concision (he says 65 lines, but it's 93), betraying his nervous desire. In contrast, Pope's books 1 and 24 have 781 and 1016 lines, the Homeric originals 611 and 804, for increases of 170 and 212 lines, respectively. In noting his achievement, Pope also makes the curious claim that "nothing material [was] omitted," when, of course, it is precisely the material reality of dismemberment that Pope evidently does want to omit.

Pope's assertion that Homer poses a violent and unpleasant reality against a refreshing and diverting poetic thus finally results in an explicitly acknowledged program of reducing the former and enlarging the latter in his translation. Moreover, in book 17, even the similes, which Pope generally views as diverting refreshment, take on a brutal tone and ugly violence that render them anything but poetic in Pope's freighted, beautifying, and ideological use of that term. Here is Pope's version of Homer's infamous stretching-the-bull-hide simile to dramatize the fight over Patroclus's body—followed by the original:

> As when a slaughter'd bull's yet reeking Hide,
> Strain'd with full force, and tugg'd from side to side,
> The brawny curriers stretch; and labour o'er
> Th' extended surface, drunk with fat and gore. (17:450–53)

> ὡς δ' ὅτ' ἀνὴρ ταύροιο βοὸς μεγάλοιο βοείην
> λαοῖσιν δώῃ τανύειν μεθύουσαν ἀλοιφῇ·
> δεξάμενοι δ' ἄρα τοί γε διαστάντες τανύουσι

κυκλόσ᾽, ἄφαρ δέ τε ἰκμὰς ἔβη, δύνει δέ τ᾽ ἀλοιφὴ
πολλῶν ἑλκόντων, τάνυται δέ τε πᾶσα διὰ πρό· (17:389–93)

Pope uses this same image of stretching the imagination to characterize
the demands all the violence exacts from the weary reader: here that effect
extends into the relieving simile. Thus his translation, for once, proves
actually shorter than the original—in terms of both words and lines (5
lines and 37 words in Homer; 4 lines and 33 words in Pope). Because he
strenuously compresses where Homer's simile stresses muscular expansion, Pope's sharp departure from his usual practice seems especially
striking. As a vivid contrast, Chapman's *Iliad* (1611) renders this simile
significantly longer than the original:

> And as a huge Oxe hide
> A Currier gives amongst his men to supple and extend
> With oyle, till it be drunke withall; they tug, stretch out, and spend
> Their oyl and licour liberally, and chafe the leather so
> That out they make a vapour breathe, and in their oyl doth go;
> A number of them set to worke, and in an orbe they pull
> That all waies all parts of the hide they may extend at full. (17.335–42)

Chapman reverses his normal pattern. He usually translates the original
into fewer lines (his are very long), but here he generates more (6.5 versus
5) in his exuberant intensification of this simile's violent energies. Above
all, he multiplies the verbs—"to supple and extend," "they tug, stretch
out, and spend"—where both Pope and Homer have only two: "strained"
and "tugged," "τανύουσι" and "ἑλκόντων."[15]

In contrast to Homer and Chapman, Pope's more recent fellow translator Madame Dacier also exhibits a distinct resistance to the realistic
detail of such violence. Dacier's usual practice is to expand her translation in order to emphasize meaning implicit or only suggested in the
original. For the most part, as with Chapman, Pope objects to this practice
of addition and interpolation: "[Chapman] appears to have had a strong
affectation of extracting new meanings out of his author" (19); "[Dacier's]
practice of refining and adding to Homer's thought in the text, and then
applauding the author for it in the notes, is pretty usual in the more florid
modern translators" (291). Given such purism, it is notable that on one
occasion Pope chooses to follow Dacier's practice of adding to Homer so
as to lessen any possible offense to women readers:

> Mr. Dryden has translated all this with the utmost severity upon the
> Ladies, and spirited the whole with satyrical additions of his own. But
> Madam Dacier . . . seems willing to give the whole passage a more

important turn, and incline us to think that Homer design'd to represent the folly and danger of prying into the secrets of providence. 'Tis
thrown into the air in this translation, not only as to make it more noble
and instructive in general, but as it is more respectful to the Ladies in
particular. (71)

Pope's delicate admission of his willingness to fold in more nobility,
instruction, and respect proves even more significant when it comes
to the question of how, on a regular basis, to translate Homer's vividly
anatomical accounts of death. Pope from the more moderate position
of eighteenth-century English culture refuses to follow Dacier into the
seventeenth-century French battle of the ancients and moderns. He does
not, like her, feel obliged to insist on Homer's command of an almost
universal knowledge of science, history, and art. He does, however, sometimes exhibit the effect of this debate, as in his championing of Homer's
command of the art of sculpture or Homer's mastery of the science of
medicine and anatomy: "It appears from so many passages in Homer that
he was perfectly master of this science [chirurgery and anatomy], that it
would be needless to cite any in particular. One may only observe, that if
we thoroughly examine all the wounds he has described, tho' so infinite in
number, and so many ways diversify'd, we shall hardly find one which will
contradict this observation" (214). Pope's metaphor of examination finally
works to cast both himself and his readers as medical school understud-
ies to Homer, the master physician, whose skill is celebrated in a series
of superlatives—"so infinite," "so many," "hardly find one"—though note
no details of any particular example are closely admired. These render
him not only inimitable but impervious to even the most searching criticism, except, of course, for the unfortunate fact that the fiction of medicine hides the reality of murder, that Homer's skill is put to use to kill,
not heal.

Despite the intensity of her advocacy of Homer's greatness in every
regard, for which Pope often mocks her, Dacier's translation nonetheless
often anticipates liberal corrective practice in eschewing Homer's anatomical detail, the very basis of her (and Pope's) extravagant claims. Her version of the climactic killing of Sarpedon by Patroclus withdraws to exactly
the type of generalized vagueness preferred by modern poets: "Patrocle
plus heureux ne lance pas son javelot inutilement; il le place près du
coeur de Sarpédon" (qtd. in Hepp 649). Here is the original: "ἀλλ' ἔβαλ'
ἔνθ' ἄρα τε φρένες ἔρχαται ἀμφ' ἀδινὸν κῆρ" (16.481). Fagles's contemporary translation, one noted for its efforts at brevity and literalism, renders
the same lines as follows: "Patroclus hurled next, / the bronze launched

from his hand—no miss, a mortal hit, / He struck him right where the
midriff packs the pounding heart" (16.567–69). Fagles catches the anatomical and technical precision of Homer in contrast to Dacier's softer
"near the heart," which vagueness she confesses in a note giving a literal
translation like Fagles's: "Frappe Sarpédon à l'endroit ou le diaphragme
se resserre autour du coeur compact." Here is Pope: "Not so Patroclus'
never-erring dart; / Aim'd at his breast, it pierc'd the mortal part / Where
the strong fibres bind the solid heart." Pope's stated ideal of remaining
close to the original and avoiding either interpolation or vagueness results
in a translation closer to Homer's detail than Dacier's vagueness. Even so
Pope's poetic diction grants him a degree of euphemism when it comes
to this killing of the hero he himself most admired for his qualities of
disinterestedness and gallantry. Pope's guiding preference for "refreshing" simile over "wearying" realism finds expression in his translation's
recourse to the standard neoclassical avoidance of technical terms (here
"diaphragm") and favoring of generalized adjective/noun euphemism:
"mortal part," "strong fibers," and "solid heart." Instead of a primer on
surgery, Pope gives his reader the poetic delight of balanced structure and
intellectualized imagination so dear to the civilized Augustans. He flees
the painful Homeric sun for its pastoral antithesis, for the cool shade and
reflective waters of his balanced couplets and diction.

GIBBON'S LIBERALIZATION OF ROMAN WARFARE

*In strict philosophy, a limitation of the rights of war seems to imply nonsense and
contradiction. Grotius himself is lost in an idle distinction between the ius naturae
and the ius gentium, between poison and infection. . . . Yet I can understand the
benefit and validity of an agreement, tacit or express, mutually to abstain from
certain modes of hostility.*

—Gibbon, *Decline and Fall*

Gibbon first critiques and then accepts the humane philosophy behind
what he confesses to be Grotius's "great work De Jure Belli et Pacis" (2:
676). Similarly, he openly praises plain narration, but his practices are
very different: "The same horrid circumstance is likewise told of the sieges
of Jerusalem and Paris. For the latter, compare the tenth book of the *Henriade* and the *Journal de Henri IV,* tom. i. p. 47–83; and observe that a plain
narrative of facts is much more pathetic than the most laboured descriptions of epic poetry" (2:190). Gibbon adheres to the belabored elegance of
Voltaire and Pope, not the prosaic bluntness of Henri IV or Caesar. Here,
for example, his footnote vaguely references, with its poetic dictional

"horrid circumstance" (2:190), what his main text renders with even more elaborate circumlocution. He refuses to translate the graphic anatomical reality—starving mothers eating their dead newborns—from the original Latin: "recipit utero, quem paullo ante effuderat"—"the mother received into her stomach what only a little before she had given birth to" (2:189, my translation). Indeed, *The Decline and Fall,* for all its indebtedness to Pope's *Iliad,* surpasses that compendium of civilized responses to Homeric barbarism in its role as a virtual encyclopedia of Enlightenment thinking on the broader subject: it is a treasure trove of euphemistic rephrasings and cutting-edge theories on the culture of violence. Gibbon follows and broadens Pope with a narrative that repeatedly refers to, translates, condemns, and civilizes epics, poems, histories, wars, heroes, and battles from the ancient world. Like Pope, Gibbon's central challenge is to limit the truculent appeal of his sources. Unlike Pope, his argument is deeply informed by the latest scholarship, not the long tradition of Homeric commentary.[16] Earlier, this chapter looked at one such theory, Gibbon's notions regarding the differences between barbaric and civilized food preparation. As just one more example, Gibbon's political-economic analysis speculates that it was savage warriors' lack of property, their dearth of responsibility over the management of their own landed estates or yeomen farms, much less a modern commercial business, and their resultant "carelessness of futurity" (1:237), that led them to direct their energies into achieving distinction through war and killing. The unpropertied German had the time and the inclination to risk his life—and kill other men—for the one kind of cultural capital his society offered. Such theories lead Gibbon repeatedly to discern a distinction between ancient and modern attitudes to the presentation of violence: "We cannot . . . even conceive the enthusiasm of. arms and glory, which [the bards] kindled in the breast of their audience. Among a polished people, a taste for poetry is rather an amusement of the fancy, than a passion of the soul. . . . [In contrast,] the desire of fame, and the contempt of death were the habitual sentiments of a German mind" (1:247). Here Gibbon admits that, for savages, epic poetry and heroic killing are two aspects of one art: a bond he and Pope will assiduously but, as Blake and Barlow insist, only partially unwind for their civilized readers.

Gibbon's productive Odin suggestion is just one of many occasions in which he indulges in the common neoclassical exercise of trying to find just the right subject for an epic poem. He contemplates a similar potential in the story of the liberation and revenge of the Turks who, led by "a slave and mechanic," use the tools of their bondage (forging hammers) as "instruments of freedom and victory" (2:695): again, such matter hints at its own illiberal and ugly disqualifications. Gibbon exhibits a recurring epic rivalry with Milton, whose radical Christian republicanism challenges Gibbon's secular and aristocratic liberalism. From another perspective, *The Decline and Fall* as an epic history opposes Augustine's *City of God* and Bossuet's Augustinian *Histoire Universelle* (1681): Gibbon blamed Rome's fall on Christianity and harbored no desire for an earthly universal monarchy mirroring that on high. He occupies a liberal epic compromise between Milton's radical individualism and Bossuet's universal monarchism. In contrast, he exhibits a friendly interest in Tasso, owing to his sense of how much they have in common, in terms of both Tasso's careful adaptations of historical accounts of war to his own epic— "It is pleasant enough to observe how Tasso has copied and embellished the minutest details of the siege" (3:604)—and Tasso's long search, so similar to Gibbon's, for the perfect theme: "A splendid scene! Among the six subjects of epic which Tasso revolved in his mind, he hesitated between the conquests of Italy by Belisarius and by Narses" (2:751). This aside dramatizes how Gibbon himself is just then writing his own epic account of Belisarius. Conquests, however, whether carried out by Belisarius or told by Tasso, especially ones motivated by religious fanaticism, are hardly proper matter for liberal epic. Indeed, a helpful way to conceptualize *The Decline and Fall* is as a series of experiments in epic, trial runs: each individually found liberally wanting, all together embodying the civilized victory resplendent in the Enlightened condition of the historian's world—recorded in the endlessly erudite footnotes.[17] One of the best of these smaller epics is Gibbon's history of the attractive but flawed figure of Julian the Apostate, who appeared to oppose Christian fanaticism, sadly turned into a pagan fanatic, and, finally, fell into the dangerous role of an Alexander-style conqueror. Gibbon's account is another "failed" epic, here adapted from Ammianus Marcellinus's heroic account of the emperor he long served.

The biggest stumbling block for all these epics is that even the most progressive war hero in the most progressive cause succeeds through victorious killing. This disclaimer typifies numerous battle prefaces, apologies, and rationalizations scattered throughout Gibbon's narrative:

> The single combats of the heroes of history or fable, amuse our fancy and engage our affections: the skillful evolutions of war may inform the mind, and improve a necessary, though pernicious, science. But in the uniform and odious pictures of a general assault, all is blood, and horror, and confusion; nor shall I strive, at the distance of three centuries

and a thousand miles, to delineate a scene, of which there could be no spectators, and of which the actors themselves were incapable of forming any just or adequate idea. (3:961)

This passage echoes Pope's dismay and precedes the concluding scenes of Gibbon's final battle, the fall of Constantinople to the Turks in 1453. This self-consciously Iliadic episode sharply contrasts with its Homeric paradigm, where the central effort of the narrative is to testify to the specifics of violent conflict and triumph. Here Gibbon's historiographical claim that "the actors themselves were incapable of forming any just or adequate idea" of the scene of carnage subtly implies a further humanizing rationalization that there is no such thing as a "just" idea of such activity. Gibbon's odd term "adequate," while performing its intended exclusionary function, makes little sense. Logically, it fits in with Gibbon's role as a philosophical and humane Enlightenment historian who questions the prejudiced testimony of the eyewitness actors, but practically it is an unusual gesture for him to sniff at such rare firsthand testimony.

Gibbon possesses several contemporary sources, but he takes the unusual step, out of anxiety not to look closely, of dismissing them all. His rhetorical struggles not to show this horror and to justify not showing it are registered in his ambiguous and inadequate qualifications. The last emperor, Hector's literary and historical heir, dies amid confusion that denies to the reader any detailed representation of his killing:

> Amidst these multitudes, the emperor, who accomplished all the duties of a general and a soldier, was long seen, and finally lost. The nobles, who fought round his person, sustained, till their last breath, the honourable names of Palaeologus and Cantacuzene: his mournful exclamation was heard, "Cannot there be found a Christian to cut off my head?" and his last fear was that of falling alive into the hands of the infidels. The prudent despair of Constantine cast away the purple: amidst the tumult he fell by an unknown hand, and his body was buried under a mountain of the slain. After his death resistance and order were no more. (3:962)

Elsewhere in his scholarly history Gibbon scorns those historians who court popularity by cultivating heroic conventions at the expense of military reality: "But these operations are neglected by the Byzantine historians, and, like authors of epic poetry and romance, they ascribe the victory, not to the military conduct, but to the personal valour, of their favorite hero" (2:925). Here, however, Gibbon sins against his own dictum and seeks to combine epic romance with military-historical logic. He insists

that the emperor fought like a frontline "soldier," not merely a command-
ing "general," but he still "accomplished all the duties" of both; he makes
his hero the central actor in this scene, but surrounds him with an appropriately noble supporting cast; he suggests a parallel to Hector's fear of
bodily mutilation; and he epically exaggerates his hero's importance by
asserting, on the one hand, that no one saw him fall and, on the other, that
the Greek resistance collapsed when he did.

Gibbon's usual method, when balancing rival accounts, is to justify
his choice of one or some combination: here each of the sources, Ducas,
Phranza, and Chalcocondyles, presents a graphic account of the battle—
and the main hero's death. Gibbon dismisses all three, claims that it was
not witnessed reliably, and then cites a death from a Dryden play as the
closest, most appropriate parallel:

> We may, without flattery apply these noble lines of Dryden:
>> As to Sebastian, let them search the field;
>> And where they find a mountain of the slain
>> Send one to climb, and looking beneath,
>> There they will find him at his manly length,
>> With his face up to heaven, in that red monument
>> Which his good sword has digged. (3:962)

This passage, from act 1 of *Don Sebastian,* well illustrates the Augustan
preference for grand effects at the expense of graphic detail, even as it
powerfully plays on the tragic and liberal emotion of pity, not the terror
of epic. The fundamental point is simple: in this last battle of his sprawl-
ing history, Gibbon departs from his ironic, even sarcastic, depiction of
Byzantium; he makes a series of rhetorical flourishes at odds with the historical reality of that battle; at its climax he dismisses the graphic accounts
of his hero's death found in his sources and, instead, cites a neoclassical play, which turns such heroic death into a vague scene of blood and
slaughter with a dead hero seemingly unmutilated, lying at peace with his
face recognizable, in a manner typical of the beautiful battlefield death—
and opposed to its terror and horror.

Such instances of Gibbonian sanitization, evasion, and apology are
legion in *The Decline and Fall.* It is the most thoroughgoing combination
of traditional epic warfare and state-of-the-art liberal theory in English
literature, and is thus packed full of corrected or civilized violence. The
importance of Gibbon's *Decline and Fall*—in relation to Pope, to the French
tradition, to the entire eighteenth-century scholarly project of rethinking
the status of war, and, finally, to the subsequent practice of epic history—
is hard to overestimate. I will, therefore, round out this analysis with a

single case study of his typical strategies and subsequent influence: Gibbon's pattern of translating and adapting one of his most important classical sources, the historian Ammianus Marcellinus. Ammianus is generally regarded as the last important Roman secular historian. A military officer with direct experience of war and an ambitious stylist who saw himself as Tacitus's literary heir, Ammianus, in his surviving books, covers the years after the death of Constantine the Great, with particular emphasis upon his hero the emperor Julian. Gibbon's cautiously heroic treatment of Julian relies on Ammianus's enthusiastic celebration, though Gibbon typically backs off from Ammianus's largely uncritical admiration for Julian's brilliance as a war leader. Inspired by Voltaire's *Charles XII*'s caustic narrative of that conqueror's effort to repeat the career of Alexander the Great, Gibbon finds similar justifications for avoiding any uncritical regard for Julian's similar ambitions—a skeptical attitude made easier by the ultimate defeats deep within their enemies' domains suffered by Julian and Charles.

Not only is Ammianus's history generally epic in its focus on war and its celebration of a military hero, but it also declares its literary ambitions by cultivating a high style appropriate for its heroic content (his history breaks off in the midst of one such Vergilian self-admonition: "procudere linguas ad maiores moneo stilos"). Ammianus's richly metaphorical style is decorated with frequent quotations, references to, and echoes of Vergil and Homer. In recounting the death in battle of a young Persian aristocrat—a death that Gibbon adapts and sanitizes and condenses in his history (1:706)—Ammianus compares his death and the fight over his body to Patroclus's fate: "as once upon a time before Troy his companions contended in a fierce struggle over the lifeless corpse of the Thessalian prince" (1:475), thus indicating his ambition to be read next to Homer. Finally, Ammianus offers a particularly interesting case study because of the attention paid to him in Erich Auerbach's *Mimesis* (1952). Auerbach's juxtaposition of the objective surface realism of classical literature versus the realism in depth of the biblical tradition puts Ammianus firmly in Homer's camp for his detailed surface accounts of lurid violence: "A whole gallery of gruesomely grotesque and extremely sensory-graphic portraits can be culled from Ammianus's work" (54). Gibbon's efforts to tame Ammianus for his very different enlightened purposes (and readers) presents him with a challenge comparable to Pope's.

Because he relies so heavily on Ammianus, and in order to defend this dependence, Gibbon insists on Ammianus's direct knowledge and experience of the wars and high politics found in his history—and his objectivity in recounting them. He shows equal vehemence in objecting to Ammianus's rich style and its deliberately disorienting combination of elaborate metaphor and lurid detail to shock and entertain. Gibbon cultivates a cooler, ironically detached mode and an ambivalence toward the super-abundant violence: "We might censure the vices of his style, the disorder and perplexity of his narrative: but we must now take leave of the impartial historian; and reproach is silenced by regret for such an irreparable loss" (1:1063). Gibbon's complaints about Ammianus's poetical style (and it is worth noting that the "perplexity" of his narrative often stems from Ammianus's efforts to recreate the chaos of battle, a feature the rational Gibbon seeks to avoid and so critiques) match his efforts to excise gory details and ugly matter. His account of the Roman disaster at the battle of Adrianople, with which his second volume climaxes, seems little more than a straightforward translation of Ammianus.[18] The Roman historian opens with a ringing epic tonality and metaphorical display— "On every side armour and weapons clashed, and Bellona, raging with more than usual madness for the destruction of the Romans, blew her lamentable war-trumpets" (3:473)—and follows it with numerous exciting flourishes and graphic details: "The battle . . . filled their hearts with terror, as numbers of them were pierced by strokes of whirling spears and arrows" (3:473); "here one might see a barbarian . . . hamstrung, or with right hand severed, or pierced through his side, on the verge of death threateningly casting about his fierce glance" (3:475); "and so the barbarians, their eyes blazing with frenzy, were pursuing our men, in whose veins the blood was chilled with numb horror" (3:477).

None of this frenzy appears in Gibbon. His narrative opens matter-of-factly: "On the ninth of August, a day which has deserved to be marked among the most inauspicious of the Roman Calendar" (1:1063). When he reaches the disaster, Gibbon shows little interest in the minutiae of death and announces his determination to suppress his source's verbal exuberance: "The event of the battle . . . so fatal to Valens and the empire, may be described in a few words" (1:1063–64). The one detail he does grant, Valens's demise, suspiciously resembles his Dryden-derived account of the last emperor's death: "Some troops . . . advanced to [Valens's] relief: they found only a bloody spot, covered with a heap of broken arms, and mangled bodies, without being able to discover their unfortunate prince" (1:1064). Again, Gibbon permits only a bloody absence. Instead of Ammianus's terror and horror, Gibbon substitutes either sanitized observations or nothing at all. His battle of Adrianople, though treated extensively in the build-up and follow-up and said to be enormously important, is, after the practice of Pope, simply made shorter than Ammianus's original. When he does add to his source, his expansions frequently take the form of humane comments on the barbarity, even criminality, of the violence described by Ammianus: "the violation of the laws of humanity and justice" (1:1070) is Gibbon's exemplary interjection into his muted translation of Ammianus's ugly account of a barbarian leader's assassination.

Occasionally, Gibbon closely follows Ammianus in depicting violent death. Two such exceptions nonetheless further demonstrate his fundamental adherence to Popeian practice. Even when he strives to be literal, Gibbon humanizes and sanitizes. The first involves the death in battle of Ammianus's central epic hero, Julian, whose status as a tragically flawed hero in Gibbon's narrative seems to require that the historian not shrink from showing the fate of this admirable man too enamored of the ancient world's ethics of courage. Gibbon's account is an almost literal translation of Ammianus, so I will first quote the original Latin, and then Gibbon:

> Et (incertum unde) subita equestris hasta, cute brachii eius perstricta, costis perfossis, haesit in ima iecoris fibra. Quam dum avellere dextra manu conatur, acuto utrimque ferro digitorum nervos sensit excisos, et provolutus iumento. (2:492)

> And a javelin, after razing the skin of his arm, transpierced the ribs, and fixed in the inferior part of the liver. Julian attempted to draw the deadly weapon from his sides; but his fingers were cut by the sharpness of the steel, and he fell senseless from his horse. (1:943)

The little detail of the fingers sliced by the sharp blade is itself particularly sharp and excruciatingly vivid, but the fatal wound is the main focus here. Ammianus's "costis perfossis haesit in ima iecoris fibra" maps closely onto Gibbon's "transpierced the ribs, and fixed in the inferior part of the liver." But one can point to the subtle distancing of turning "ima . . . fibra," which the meticulously literal Loeb translator renders "lower lobe," into "inferior part," which in English has a Latinate artificiality absent in the Latin itself with its vivid "fibers" for Gibbon's bland "part": "ima fibra" or "lower lobe" is a plain description of a portion of the liver; "inferior part" is classic poetic diction.

This artificiality, however, is most apparent in the verbs: Gibbon's "fixed" has much, but not all, of the vividness of the Latin "haesit," which more closely translates to "stuck." The second verb is more revealing. "Transpierced" seems a close translation (both consist of a preposition + main verb compound) of "perfossis" (from the Latin infinitive "perfodere"—to dig through). But Gibbon's verb, which he uses on several occasions in his history when compelled to show a body being mortally wounded, is a most uncommon construction that distances the graphic terror of those scenes. It seems likely that Gibbon borrowed it from the exquisite word-hoard that is Pope's Homer or Dryden's Vergil. The latter uses it to translate Vergil's account of Laocoon throwing a spear into the side of the wooden horse in book 2: the vivid "utero recusso" ("the womb/belly having been struck loud") becomes the toned-down and technical "the sides transpierced" (2:68). In Pope the change is even starker—or softer. Odysseus tells of killing a stag: "τὸν δ᾽ ἐγὼ ἐκβαίνοντα κατ᾽ ἄκνηστιν μέσα νῶτα/πλῆξα· τὸ δ᾽ ἀντικρὺ δόρυ χάλκεον ἐξεπέρησε" (10.161–62). Graphic modern translators (Fagles and Stanford in his commentary, which closely follows T. E. Lawrence's plain-style prose translation) render the verbal action and anatomical detail thus: "I hit him / square in the backbone, halfway down the spine / and my bronze spear went punching clean through" (10.176–78). These direct and simple verbs and nouns—ἐξεπέρησε, hit, punch through—become elaborate and refined in Pope. He begins with a fancier action, "I launched my spear," and then not only gets yet more artificial, but makes the kill oddly passive, even slightly illogical: "and with a sudden wound / Transpierced his back" (10.188). As Stanford comments, "O. seems to have been unusually proud of this kill" (370). The reader is meant to enter into the hunter's joy. (This kill almost exactly resembles scenes of hero killing hero, but modern commentators rarely allow themselves to observe the text's pleasured representation of those human-on-human events.) Pope's version tempers the boast—and the reader's sympathetic pleasure. Gibbon borrowed the poetic diction and the ethical intention of Pope and Dryden: his "transpierce," while technically accurate, has none of the ugly physicality and immediacy of "perfossis," which translates best as the visceral "having been dug through." Even in this rare instance of literal faithfulness, Gibbon betrays the graphic reality of his grisly source.

My last example is one of the most terrifying in all of Ammianus. After the defeat at Adrianople, the Eastern Empire finds itself virtually without an army and facing the triumphant Goths. The Romans retreat within the walls of Constantinople but, luckily, are reinforced by some wild Saracens. During a siege filled with horrific dangers and thrilling events, this little gem sparkles most brightly: "The Northern Barbarians were astonished and dismayed by the inhuman ferocity of the Barbarians of the South. A Gothic soldier was slain by the dagger of an Arab; and the hairy, naked savage, applying his lips to the wound, expressed a horrible delight, while he sucked the blood of his vanquished enemy" (1:1067). Gibbon seems to indulge himself in showing this act because it carries the ironic, but humane lesson of shocking one group of barbarians with the deeper savagery of another. His civilized readers should derive no direct pleasure from such violence, but only a mixture of horror, self-satisfied humor at the expense of the Goths, and immense humane superiority over the Saracens. Still Gibbon suppresses a few details. Here is Ammianus: "But the oriental troop had the advantage from a strange event, never witnessed before. For one of their number, a man with long hair and naked except for a loin-cloth, uttering hoarse and dismal cries, with drawn dagger rushed into the thick of the Gothic army, and after killing a man applied his lips to his throat and sucked the blood that poured out. The barbarians, terrified by this strange and monstrous sight" (3:501–3). Gibbon judges the event with his corrective term "inhuman," while Ammianus only has somewhat different terms such as "never witnessed before" and "monstrous." In addition, Gibbon's "hairy, naked savage" for Ammianus's longer description, where the specific details of the long hair and the loin-cloth make the nakedness more palpable, seems to intensify the affect of being coyly civilized that is the hallmark of experiencing *The Decline and Fall*. Although there is less horror in Gibbon, he has crafted his translation to focus only on horror and avoid another feature of Ammianus's account, where there is a frisson of terror and excitement around the daring attack of the Saracen who boldly rushes into the enemy ranks. In Gibbon's translation, that exciting action, with which a reader might sympathize, is safely rendered as a passive fact.

This passage has an extra interest because it was adapted by Flaubert for his horrific, gaudy, but meticulously technical and vividly detailed historical novel *Salammbo* (1862). Flaubert inserts this episode into an earlier war between the Carthaginians and their barbarian mercenaries. Flaubert's version, in contrast to Gibbon's, expands the original in order to maximize its graphic assault upon (or appeal to) the reader. Flaubert makes it both more heroic and more poetic, and by rendering the killer un-anonymous increases the possibility, only lurking in Ammianus and wholly lacking in Gibbon, that the reader might cheer him on. For now he is a warrior in the mercenary army, a named character in the novel. The other elements (a siege, a horrible killing, profound shock even to barbarians) remain the same:

> Zarxas ran up, knocked him down and plunged a dagger into his throat; pulling it out, he flung himself upon the wound—and with his mouth glued to it, with grunts of joy and spasms which shook him from head to foot, he pumped out the blood with all his might; then he quietly sat down on the corpse, lifted up his face and threw back his head to breathe more freely, like a deer which has drunk from a stream, and in a shrill voice intoned a Balearic song, a vague tune full

of extended, broken, alternating modulations, like answering echoes in the mountains. . . . The dreadful death appalled the Barbarians, especially the Greeks. (162)

Flaubert's obvious effort to aestheticize this killing appears first in his idyllic epic simile that is not meant, as it would be in Pope, to contrast with the killing by giving relief, but to complement its gruesome luster, to make the drinking of blood seem beautiful. He then reinforces the aesthetics of this murder by constructing a parallel between it and Zarxas's haunting song. These additions reverse Gibbon's ironic and distancing changes to Ammianus's original. Flaubert also intensifies the pleasure of this act, for both killer and reader, by sexualizing it. In these ways, his adaptation reemphasizes that Gibbon works to ensure that his readers can only look upon such events with horror, and that Gibbon has the intent to deny to his humane audience any pleasure in it other than that of feeling morally superior. Flaubert notoriously sought to ridicule the humane values of the liberal middle classes and their self-confident civilization. *Salammbo* insistently dramatizes, in an insulting and confrontational manner, that the pleasures of epic are violent and graphic, but they are, like it or not, pleasures. He implies that readers enjoy looking upon one person destroying, dominating, even violating another, and that such representations are central aesthetic monuments in Western civilization: such indeed is the logic of the novel's notoriously sadomasochistic central love story.[19]

SCOTT'S ROMANTIC POEMS, GIBBONIAN HISTORIES, AND POPEIAN NOVELS

I had Walter Scott's novels, and the Iliad *(Pope's translation) for constant reading when I was a child, on weekdays. . . . From Walter Scott's novels I might easily, as I grew older, have fallen to other people's novels; and Pope might, perhaps, have led me to take Johnson's English, or Gibbon's, as types of language. (13–14)*

—John Ruskin, *Praeterita*

John Burrow's assertion that "Gibbon fascinated scholars in the later twentieth century as he did not, in Britain at least, in the nineteenth" (332) is contradicted by both the testimony and the practices of a wide range of nineteenth- and early twentieth-century historians—James Mill, Thomas Carlyle, W. E. H. Lecky, J. R. Green, G. M. Trevelyan, Winston Churchill, C. V. Wedgwood, and H. G. Wells, along with novelists like Dickens, Trollope, Hardy, Wells (again), and Gissing. One nineteenth-century devotee stands out as himself a figure of preeminent influence. Walter Scott, the point man in English literary history for dethroning epic poetry by the novel, nonetheless outdid his unprecedented novelistic money-making with his Gibbonian epic history of Napoleon—a task he undertook in response to the financial and cultural implosion of his novelistic career, thus establishing a pattern of turning from the discredited novel to the still-venerated epic, which major Victorian novelists such as Thackeray and Hardy later followed. Pope was another model: Scott's popular heroic poems, which in theory appeal to the very different tradition of the vernacular ballad, become poetic dictional when they take up warfare. Ruskin, a master of the theory of the anti-Homeric Burkean sublime, who grew up reading and rereading Pope's *Iliad*, declared that *Marmion* closes "with the truest and grandest battle-piece that, so far as I know, exists in the whole compass of literature" (511)—because it was so thoroughly Popeian and Gibbonian. As to Scott's novels, Henry Adams, himself one of Gibbon's most determined disciples, advanced a curious theory pertinent to my claims. According to Adams, Scott was in fact a follower. His novelistic innovations arose from the more daring experiments by Washington Irving in his *Knickerbocker History of New York* (1809): "Irving preceded Walter Scott. . . . The influence of Diedrich Knickerbocker on Scott was more evident than *Waverley* on Irving" (2:1326).

High among Irving's numerous objects of parody and pastiche stands Gibbon, whose literary glory rendered him the principal target-model for the titular historian Diedrich Knickerbocker. Its opening chapters sketch a life of the historian shaped by Gibbon's *Memoirs;* its penultimate chapter is a comic-philosophical reflection upon decline and fall—"there is [no theme] that occasions such heart rending grief to your historian of sensibility, as the decline and fall of your renowned and mighty empires!" (718)—where Irving takes a further step in making classical epic subject to the presumed tenderheartedness of modern readers and to the humanizing refinements of neoclassicism known as sensibility. Irving's and Scott's careers represent a major qualification to the Romantic critique of neoclassical epic and its poetic diction—and all the literary histories premised upon it—as well as an important continuation of the work of Pope and Gibbon.

Scott's status and oeuvre also provide revealing evidence of crucial differences between the epic and the novelistic, because here the same writer produced major examples of both. Yet it was not just Scott's *Life of Napoleon* but also his novels that demonstrate their continuity with the heroic narrative style of Pope and Gibbon. *Ivanhoe,* his most popular novel and a

showcase of heroism, war, violence, and liberal nation formation is explicitly presented as a sanitized translation of the words and feelings of its
twelfth-century characters. *Old Mortality,* his closest novelistic approach
to an epic content, is described by Lockhart as the first of his novels to be
based on reworkings of the language and events from pre-liberal, ante-
Lockean Britain: "*Old Mortality,* on the other hand, is remarkable as the
novelist's first attempt to repeople the past by the power of imagination
working on materials furnished by books" (28). Lockhart's use of italics
seems to signal that this novel was the first to attempt the kind of historical matter heretofore reserved for his heroic poems. The novel is organized
around a before-and-after contrast centered on 1688. The opposition boils
down to the difference between an era dominated by heroic violence and
heroic agency and one defined by middle-class peacefulness.

What is most interesting about Scott's neoclassicizing strategies for
re-presenting examples of premodern heroic violence to his liberal readers is how within the larger continuity of his practice and style across
poems, histories, and historical novels, there is a subtle but important
break between the poems and histories, which remain largely true to the
neoclassical emphases, and the novels, which work toward rendering violence more plainly. Thus they tend toward the harsher, more unforgiv-
ing attitude of the Romantics regarding heroic violence and the readers
who enjoy it in polished form. Scott produced battle pieces in all three
genres, but his *Napoleon* presents the clearest case of Scott working in a
fully epic mode. His heroic poems expressly disclaim epic seriousness or
grandeur. Similarly his novels, especially his best ones from early in his
career, were published anonymously by an acclaimed poet stooping to a
déclassé form. *Napoleon,* however, was openly published by one of the
world's most famous and respected writers, and it ambitiously sought to
tell the story of modern history's greatest event, the French Revolution
and the Napoleonic Wars, through the life of its greatest actor-agent. Here
are the thoughts of Goethe, in his role as international man-of-letters, on
this much anticipated literary event: "The richest, the easiest, the most
celebrated narrator of the century, undertakes to write the history of his
own time" (Lockhart 2:575). Scott did not dedicate himself seriously to
this long-contemplated work until after the bankruptcy of his publisher
and the revelation of his identity as the author of the Waverley novels: like
Hardy, he turned to Napoleon after disaster struck his novelistic career.
He counted on the kind of intense interest shown by Goethe, and Scott's
reputation in conjunction with the magnitude of his theme had more to
do with the sales and profit of this history than any widespread desire to

read it: "None of our great Reviews grappled with the book at all; nor am I so presumptuous as to undertake what they shrank from" (2:574); even his biographer passed on reading it.

Such a dismissal, however, ignores the allure of the famous battles. Agonistic warfare in a high style is the defining characteristic of epic. And Scott's elevated battle pieces are the heart of his *Napoleon*. There Lockhart implies his own pleasurable reading, and there he locates the real interest and achievement of the text. These war narratives follow Gibbon's elegant example. They certainly do not emphasize, as did contemporaries like Byron and Napier, the horror of war. They do not harp upon its inescapable criminality. There is little effort to incorporate eyewitness accounts by experienced participants. There is no challenge to the readers, who, indeed, are expected to take civilized pleasure in refined and sanitized, but still vaguely Homeric, contests to win or lose, kill or be killed. The agon pits France against England, Napoleon against Wellington. Scott introduces Wellington with a Homeric simile trumpeting the literary heritage behind the rising contest: "Britain, long excluded from the continent, had assumed, with regard to it, the attitude of the Grecian hero, who, with his lance pointed towards his enemy, surveys his armour of proof from head to foot, in hopes of discovering some rent or flaw, through which to deal a wound" (13:107). Such poeticisms appear throughout, and, as here, they consistently recast the Homeric material in a cool, distanced manner: "The broken army resembled a covey of heathfowl, which the sportsman marks down and destroys in detail and at his leisure" (12:179). Never had an epic hunting simile so suavely indicated leisurely discretion. When it comes to the actual killing, not the similes, Scott is equally circumspect. He follows Gibbonian and Popeian practice in rarely looking to individuals in battle. When he does, he favors death (and pity) over killing (and terror). These persons are almost always aristocratic and young, thereby further underlining regret for lost hopes. Above all, he obeys the central neoclassical dictum to suppress details that might evoke a reader's sadistic appreciation: "Prince Louis showed the utmost gallantry in leading his men when they advanced, and in rallying them when they fled. He was killed fighting hand to hand with a French subaltern, who required him to surrender, and, receiving a sabre-wound for reply, plunged his sword into the prince's body. Several of his staff fell around him" (12:170).

To be sure, readers are expected to admire the skill of one general in fashioning and executing a superior plan, but when it comes to actual persons, the style retreats to the purest neoclassicism: balanced phrasing, noble vocabulary, and a haziness regarding death's details. All that Coleridge despised about the pernicious influence of Pope and Gibbon is on full display in Scott's *Napoleon*. Though his concern is to highlight Louis's heroism, he pauses to defend the humanity of the Frenchman who was forced to kill in self-defense. This is typical of Scott's hard work throughout to keep the action within these gated boundaries.

His history's climax at Waterloo confirms such practices. The violence of this notoriously bloody battle is acknowledged but rendered in sentences that verge on being Popeian couplets: "It was made with the most desperate fury, and received with the most stubborn resolution" (16:10). Such balance extends to Scott's consistent effort to build up the Homeric logic of this final duel of two great adversaries, but also to his humane desire to lessen any barbaric thrill or rage for either his British or his French readers:

> Another figment, greedily credited at Paris, bore, that the four battalions of Old Guard, the last who maintained the semblance of order, answered a summons to surrender, by the magnanimous reply, "The Guard can die, but cannot yield." And one edition of the story adds, that thereupon the battalions made a half wheel inwards, and discharged their muskets into each other's bosoms, to save themselves from dying by the hands of the English. Neither the original reply, nor the pretended self-sacrifice of the Guard, have the slightest foundation. Cambrone, in whose mouth the speech was placed, gave up his sword, and remained prisoner; and the military conduct of the French Guard is better eulogized by the undisputed truth, that they fought to extremity, with the most unyielding constancy, than by imputing to them an act of regimental suicide upon the lost field of battle. Every attribute of brave men they have a just right to claim. It is no compliment to ascribe to them that of madmen. Whether the words were used by Cambrone or no, the Guard well deserved to have them inscribed on their monument. (16:19–20)

The logic of "just right," both in a narrow and an expansive sense, rules over Scott's anecdote, this battle, and his Napoleonic Wars generally. Alessandro Barbero, in the most reliable contemporary reconstruction of this battle and this episode, also corrects the legend, but the alterations do not consistently point to refinement, balance, and humane good sense. The French general Cambrone survived, but probably yelled out, "Merde," at the moment of surrender, not the valiant sentiment Scott disallows in reality and then generously grants to their monument. In contrast to Scott's bland account of him giving up his sword and remaining prisoner, which epitomizes Scott's refashioning of the entire event in light of proper and legal behavior, it seems that after surrendering, Cambrone dishonorably attempted an impromptu escape: he was caught again and not treated in so gentlemanly a fashion.[20]

Finally, to anticipate both Romantic and Modernist critiques of this sort of neoclassical tidiness, it is worth looking ahead to *The Dynasts,* a subject of chapter 6, where Hardy narrates this same event, but exactly reverses Scott's sanitizing logic to foreground horror, criminality, and ugliness:

> At last [the Old Guard] are surrounded by the English Guards and other foot, who keep firing on them and smiting them to smaller and smaller numbers. General Cambronne is inside the square.
>
> Colonel Hugh Halkett (shouting)
> Surrender! And preserve those heroes' lives!
>
> Cambronne (with exasperation)
> Mer-r-r-rde! . . . . You've to deal with desperates, man, today: Life is a byword here!
>
> Hollow laughter, as from people in hell, comes approvingly from the remains of the Old Guard. The English proceed with their massacre, the devoted band thins and thins, and a ball strikes Cambronne, who falls, and is trampled over. (516–17)

Hardy typographically exaggerates the authentic and vivid response suppressed by Scott, but retains the dubious slaughter. He also intensifies the horror by suggesting the complicity of the English in the Frenchmen's deaths: "their massacre" carries a double-edged effect exposing the excesses of both sides. The gallant, rule-bound, even commonsensical contest in Scott has evolved, in Hardy, into a crude hash of suffering, criminality, and inhumanity—one not even redeemed by the thrill of a fair fight.

The Dynasts as a whole covers roughly the same events as Scott's *Napoleon,* and both seek an epic status largely by including most of the major battles of the Napoleonic Wars. War narrative became, for each bitterly disappointed novelist, the surest way to recuperate, even aggrandize, his authorial status. *The Dynasts,* moreover, is filled with similarly criminal, brutal, and ugly effects, while a reader would be hard put to find anything but wan valor and stylized combat in *Napoleon.* Much the same is true of Scott's heroic poems, but I will momentarily put aside consideration of their epic status and military content, and turn to the richer, heteroglossic contrast posed by Scott's novels. These regularly include warfare from *Waverley* (1814) onward, but *Old Mortality* and *Ivanhoe* are the two most important for their seriousness and elaboration. They meticulously approximate a Homeric level of detailed, graphic attention to the facts of violent combat that goes beyond anything found in the epic history or the heroic poems. Nonetheless, the novels more energetically thematize the criminality of warfare, the end of heroic militarism, and the decline of epic. The generic logic of Scott's oeuvre exhibits an inverse relation between plain Homeric violence and epic pretension: the more his novels dispense with neoclassical sanitization and polish and increase the graphic realism of their violence, the more they recede from and reject epic; the more his *Napoleon* aspires to the status of epic history by Gibbon or Livy, the more it results in a narrative centered on battle, but battle softened, legalized, and made elegantly neoclassical.

Old Mortality tells of the Covenanters' rebellion against James II's Scottish regime, shortly before the Glorious Revolution of 1688. It includes lengthy versions of two historical battles and one fictional siege. All three include combat violence more graphic and harrowing than anything in *Napoleon*, but the following passage comes the closest of any moment in Scott to Homeric anatomical detail and admiration for lethality. Balfour describes to the protagonist Henry Morton the notches in his sword:

> The fragment of steel that parted from this first gap, rested on the skull of the perjured traitor, who first introduced Episcopacy into Scotland;—this second notch was made in the rib-bone of an impious villain, the boldest and the best soldier that upheld the prelatic cause at Drumclog;—this third was broken on the steel head-piece of the captain who defended the Chapel of Holyrood when the people rose at the Revolution. I cleft him to the teeth through steel and bone. It has done great deeds. (466)

The second example comprises all of *Ivanhoe*'s chapter 29, where Rebecca is put in the position of describing to the wounded hero the attack on the castle where they are imprisoned. The chapter juxtaposes her anachronistically humane dismay over such matters with Ivanhoe's intense, well-informed appreciation for the skill and bravery of the combatants: the stagy scenario obviously genders the novelistic as female and the epic as male. It culminates with an excited question-and-answer narration involving a melee, a single combat, waxing anxiety over who is winning, a sudden turn in favor of one knight, and a concluding struggle over the fallen body of the loser. It is Scott's nearest imitation of the most common narrative unit in *The Iliad*. Both of these examples, however, are contextualized and characterized so as to undermine the epic values that they enact.

At this point in *Old Mortality*, Balfour, who once figured as a seductive friend to Henry, drawing him into a heroic war of liberation, is revealed as not just a dangerous religious enthusiast, but an epileptic madman struggling only half successfully with his inner demons. He appears as an admitted murderer, thief, and blackmailer hiding in a cave that not so subtly transforms him into a monster to himself and others (the chapter begins with an epigraph from *The Faerie Queene*'s allegory of despair). Scott's heavy-handed deployment of the Burkean sublime dramatizes the terrors of the dark cave, its mysterious sounding depths, and the thing lurking within—all of which play off of the fear of nature's vast powers and its symbolization of the mind's equally dark energies. There is little remaining resonance with the Homeric sublime: the reader is not allowed to identify at all with Balfour as a hero who can cause fear, only with Balfour as something to be afraid of, something to be afraid of becoming, or a madman to pity. From this encounter, the novel (now in its post-1688, end of history mode) moves toward its domestic climax (the war climaxed long ago). Here Balfour's final actions anticipate our culture's fascination with killers in the form not of war heroes, but of serial murderers. Balfour vindictively leads an assault on a quiet suburban home. He dies showing no purpose beyond killing whomever (here appropriately a nameless stranger) he can lay his hands on: "They were twice seen to rise, the Dutchman striving to swim, and Burley clinging to him in a manner that showed his desire that both should perish" (476). Allegorically, he is not even a Byronic criminal-hero, but only criminal-madman striving to drag others down with him into the depths of his insanity. Scott's novel systematically evokes, develops, recasts, and then undoes a Homeric hero and his powerful "bloody hands." The potency and terror of this figure sheds all its glory, its embodiment of historical agency (Balfour can kill, but cannot effect any real change), and its monopolization of a sympathetic readerly admiration. This shift is intimately tied up with the narrative's flirting with an epic identification and then rejecting it in order to embrace its status as a novel of a peaceful, settled, middle-class society—one emphatically without Burley, in which even his once heroic protégé Henry has declined from his former military self into a lover, then husband.

Ivanhoe, because it is a more artificial novel than *Old Mortality*, better exemplifies this pattern of graphic intensification marking generic decline. It so obviously emerges from a neoclassical paradigm that it is able to clearly thematize how it also has moved beyond that project and come closer to a Romantic critique. For in *Ivanhoe*, the narrator pauses to insist that even its cleaned up heroic violence is barbaric, criminal, and ugly. Where neoclassical epic subtly restrains sadism and prides itself on its civilized appreciation only for legal violence, Romanticism openly attacks readers for such interests and such self-satisfaction. It will not allow even its putative modern readers to escape its denunciations:

> But the earnest desire to look on blood and death, is not peculiar to those dark ages; though in the gladiatorial exercise of single combat and general tourney, they were habituated to the bloody spectacle of brave men falling by each other's hands. Even in our days, when morals are better understood, an execution, a bruising match, a riot, or a meeting of radical reformers, collects, at considerable hazard to themselves, immense crowds of spectators, otherwise little interested, except to see how matters are to be conducted, or whether the heroes of the day are, in the heroic language of insurgent tailors, flints or dunghills. (479)

Scott rejects Dryden, Pope, and Gibbon's project to allow readers to take pleasure in such fare if gently seasoned. Ivanhoe states the essentials of the Homeric sublime and heroic ideology: "The love of battle is the food upon which we live—the dust of the mêlée is the breath of our nostrils! We live not—we wish not to live—longer than while we are victorious and renowned"; but he is answered by Rebecca's humane riposte: "Alas . . . what is it, valiant knight, save an offering of sacrifice to a demon of vain glory, and a passing through the fire to Moloch?—What remains to you as the prize of all the blood you have spilled?" (315–16). The novel favors the woman's judgment over the man's zeal. Scott's strategy allows the reader to enjoy both the thrilling combat and the sympathetic dismay—Rebecca experiences both too. But more than just providing both, the logic of their combination permits Scott to dramatize how his narrative, in becoming more honest, graphic, epic, and Homeric than the sanitized epics that inspired it, has thereby moved past their compromised position of enjoying etiolated heroic violence, to a more fully humane, liberal, feminized, middle-class, and peacefully novelistic worldview.

That world remains only a prospect for Rebecca, however, and within *Ivanhoe*, within this most Homeric and most novelistic of its chapters, there is yet another paradoxical twist as Rebecca wishes for a time and a place of liberal epic heroism that her people have lost:

> "I am, indeed," said Rebecca, "sprung from a race whose courage was distinguished in the defence of their own land, but who warred not, even while yet a nation, save at the command of the Deity, or in defending their country from oppression. The sound of the trumpet wakes Judah no longer, and her despised children are now but the unresisting victims of hostile and military oppression. Well hast thou spoken, Sir

Knight,—until the God of Jacob shall raise up for his chosen people a second Gideon, or a new Maccabeus, it ill beseemeth the Jewish damsel to speak of battle or of war." (316–17)

Here Scott's most impassioned critic of epic heroism is seen longing for it most intensely. In thus returning to the heroic, Rebecca simultaneously reverts to legalistic neoclassical sanitization: the passage champions only defensive and liberating warfare; it discreetly cloaks Joshua's bloodthirsty conquest under the rubric of a command from God. This double conundrum in *Ivanhoe* also surfaces in *Old Mortality* when, in the concluding state of blessed peace, the authorial figure finds himself unheroically burdened by the demand for an endless supply of conventional happy endings from an imperious band of middle-class female novel readers figured in the person of Miss Martha Buskbody: "Goose Gibbie, Sir?" she demands of the novelist at the tail end of a long inquiry about the fortunes of all the characters down to this obscurest of the obscure. In both *Ivanhoe* and *Old Mortality,* the narrative pushes itself into Homeric epic as a powerful device for finally exorcising the last vestiges of neoclassical falsification. It then ironically becomes more fully novelistic and more completely liberal—only to be bitterly disappointed at the inane result.

Rebecca and Peter Pattieson embody a final counterplot that suggests why Scott would later return to neoclassical epic with his *Napoleon* and why Victorian England would continue to elevate and reward epic histories by Carlyle and Macaulay, despite the novel's apparent dominance. Ultimately, Scott still desired to be more than a novelist. His *Napoleon* represents a daring and arduous quest after the crown of genres. At the same time, part of its appeal is that it enacts an older and still compelling model for historical agency that the liberal novel had too successfully banished. The evidence of Scott's novels and his epic history points emphatically to how the latter, as a text and a narrative, embodied a heroic model of agency, while the former evoked a problematic and frankly disappointing paradigm. As a culturally valorized writer of epic history, Scott could impose himself, his texts, and their often tragic endings on readers. Likewise, the violent heroes of epic continued to symbolize a top-down model of agency that novel heroes, particularly the passive heroes of Scott, not only did not embody, but were expressly designed to undo.[21]

Critics beginning with Alexander Welsh have explored the significance of the Scott passive hero in relation to this problem, but here it is worth observing how other characters, not just the passive hero, but characters like Rebecca or Peter Pattieson, act to extend the logic connecting the novelistic liberal with powerlessness. Both characters participate in the critique of epic values and violence. As a result of this critique, both come to acknowledge their own and their liberal culture's inability to imagine agency convincingly apart from the violence they have cast out. It is because of their powerlessness that Rebecca longs for the war heroes and Peter for war stories they have both banished. These novels demonstrate how much of epic's continuing appeal resides in liberal culture's evident dissatisfaction with its nonheroic and nonviolent model of impersonal agency. Rebecca's humanism is part and parcel of her and her nation's powerlessness; Peter Pattieson finishes his novelistic account of the historical transcendence of heroic violence only to find himself subject to the whim of a novel-renting seamstress. *Napoleon,* however, retains its vision of the still center of a turning world: "[The army] was placed under the command of Sir Arthur Wellesley . . . [,] one of those gifted individuals upon whom the fate of the world seems to turn like a gate upon its hinges, or as a vessel is managed by its rudder" (13:108). On the following page, Scott asserts that "the characters of both [Napoleon and Wellington] serve to show that the greatest actions are performed, and the greatest objects attained" (13:109). Together Wellington and Napoleon, as war heroes at the center of an expansive war narrative, allow Scott's epic history to combine heroic individuals and violent action into a convincing demonstration of historical agency. In conjunction with his novels, *The Life of Napoleon* demonstrates the double-bind of liberal epic—at once repulsed by the facts of heroic violence, vivid in the novels and softened in the history, and drawn to its agential symbolism, vivid in the history and vanishing in the novels.

This paradigm and my argument have passed over the heroic poems. Ruskin, however, ranked the battle piece of *Marmion* ahead of all others. He was not alone in his enthusiasm. They were among the most widely read and widely influential poems of the century: "[Macaulay] was so fired with reading Scott's Lay and Marmion, the former of which he got entirely and the latter almost entirely by heart, merely from his delight in reading them, that he determined on writing himself a poem in six cantos which he called 'The Battle of Cheviot'" (G. O. Trevelyan 1:20)—and Macaulay's hugely popular *Lays of Ancient Rome* (1842) owes much to their example. On the other hand, Macaulay earned his highest cultural laurels by taking up epic through elaborately wrought battle pieces in his *History of England,* not in his explicitly lightweight poetry. Scott himself denies (and note the linking of history and epic) in his poems' prefaces any fully fledged epic status: "Any HISTORICAL NARRATIVE, far more an attempt at Epic composition, exceeded his plan of a Romantic tale" (preface to *Marmion*). The dearth of warfare and heroic violence, even in *Marmion,* mutes any epic resonance. These poems emphasize "customs," "manners," and "scenes highly susceptible of poetical ornament." His ballad form stands opposed to the poetic dictional tactics that allow the *Napoleon* to include so much historical warfare: the poems' popular, ornamental, and naturalistic style requires the exclusion of such matter.

In place of the novels' bluntly criminal violence and the epic history's sanitized heroics, the lesser narrative poems have only glancing dismissals. *The Lay of the Last Minstrel*'s protagonist censors his account for his refined post-1688 audience. He comments upon his need not to offend their sensibilities and nostalgically wishes for the kind of interested Homeric audience that would appreciate a detailed description of skillful killing: "But, were each dame a listening knight, / I well could tell how warriors fight! / For I have seen war's lightning flashing / Seen the claymore with bayonet clashing" (5.21).

Scott dramatizes his knowledge of the Homeric sublime and the neoclassical tactics for remaking it. Earlier in the *Lay*, Scott literalizes the sublime logic of Homeric epic when his poem explicitly wraps poetic knowledge into the same package with lethal skill. He equates the mastery of the rules of poetry and the rules of combat in a fight between two leading bards: "And tuneful hands were stained with blood." But these moments only refer to such matter and such issues: the text never goes into detailed accounts, even via poetic diction, which Scott associates with a higher form of poetry than he is attempting here. The climax of Ruskin's favorite battle piece is similarly emptied of Homeric matter—not sanitized but scrubbed clean. The action stays on the margin with onlookers, who do not often look, and we see very little of the little they do. The narrator happily joins them:

> He saw the wreck his rashness wrought;
> Reckless of life, he desperate fought,
> And fell on Flodden plain:
> And well in death his trusty brand,
> Firm clenched within his manly hand,
> Beseemed the monarch slain.
> But oh! how changed since yon blithe night!—
> Gladly I turn me from the sight
> Unto my tale again. (6.35.1079–87)

There is no Homeric terror here, only sympathy and sadness that moves yet further off into a memory of happier times and fixates on the "trusty brand," but as an ornament of romance, not a realistic weapon. Scott con-

cludes by signaling that his romantic tale takes precedence over this slight
epic interruption.

RUSKIN'S SCOTTISH SUBLIME

The first two of his great poems, The Lay of the Last Minstrel *and* Marmion, *are
the re-animation of Border legends, closing with the truest and grandest battle-piece
that, so far as I know, exists in the whole compass of literature;—the absolutely
fairest in justice to both contending nations, the absolutely most beautiful in its
conceptions of both. And that the palm in that conception remains with the Scotch,
through the sorrow of their defeat, is no more than accurate justice to the national
character. . . . What moor or mountain is there over which the purple cloud of
Scott's imagination has not wrapt its light, in those two great poems?*

—Ruskin, *Praeterita*

Ruskin's characterization of *Marmion* dramatizes his heroic dilemma: replete with the language of fairness, justice, sympathy for the loser, and the
aesthetics of the beautiful, not the sublime, it concludes with eager praise
of Scott's evocation of nature. He acknowledges *Marmion*'s connection
to the eighteenth-century project to make warfare legal, but suppresses
the real challenge posed to that project by heroic violence. The appeal of
fear, even in Burke's masochistic much less Homer's sadistic mode, fades
before the softening glow of sympathetic sorrow.

Ruskin's own "Battle of Montenotte," written at the age of twenty-three
in 1842, displays Ruskin's indebtedness not only to Scott but also to his
successor in the popular heroic poem: Byron. Ruskin exhibits a measure
of Byronic hero worship for Napoleon's satanic military genius ("above
his head a crimson star / Burning continually" [stanza 6]), but his battle
piece pushes beyond sympathy for the defeated to liberal dismay over the
conqueror's triumph. By juxtaposing "battle" and "mountain," the title
sums up the poem's structural and thematic division, but Ruskin always
favors the latter and its Burkean resonances. He opposes the conqueror's
metaphorical "red career" to the reality of the "purple rainbow's resting
light," preferring peace and pity to war and terror. When it finally must
show some combat at the height of the battle, its turns to vivid metaphors
showing the persistent life of the group over any close, realistic attention
to individual death:

> In death's faint shade and fiery shock,
> They stand, one ridge of living rock,
> Which steel may rend, and wave may wear,

> And bolt may crush, and blast may tear,
> But none can strike from its abiding. (stanza 3)

Here within the living metaphor, we can again discern Ruskin's abiding preference for nature's Burkean over war's Homeric sublime.

Ruskin knew Homer, Pope, and Burke, and realized that the roots of the sublime lay not in the overwhelming power of mountains and oceans, but in the terror-delight of killing. When it comes to this sublimity of the trained body, however, and the terror of combat, Ruskin has little to say and is always poised to flee into highly wrought rhetoric of moral outrage against the vulgar or the grotesque: the entirety of chapter 7 of part 9 of *Modern Painters,* tellingly entitled "Of Vulgarity," presents a case study in his various tactics for avoiding most representations of violence inflicted by one body on another. Nonetheless, *Modern Painters* is too large and too ambitious and too knowledgeable. Its core interest in Turner hardly allows it to evade all encounters with the important genre of history painting. Indeed Ruskin is often openly contemptuous of the modern liberal revaluations that would banish war and heroism from great art: "He was eminently warlike. He is now gradually becoming more and more ashamed of the arts and aims of battle. So that the desire of dominion, which was once frankly confessed or boasted of as a heroic passion, is now sternly reprobated or cunningly disclaimed" (3:198). Ruskin has a knack for putting his finger on the center of a problem: his characterization of the epic primal scene is the clearest; here, though expressed sarcastically, is the best brief summation of the cultural and ideological crisis of modern epic.

Though fully equipped to appreciate a vivid representation of heroic killing or heroic death as sublime art, Ruskin consistently eludes that challenge. As the pressure mounts to confront such matters in his fifth and final volume (he has put it off till here), he shies away into ethical allegorizings: "The ruling purpose of Greek poetry is the assertion of victory, by heroism, over fate, sin, and death" (5:271). He allows himself to condemn bad, vulgar, naturalist and mannerist paintings of violence—above all, by the much despised Salvator Rosa.[22] He works himself up into humane rage over great painters showing dogs hunting and killing: "By the more powerful men, Rubens, Snyders, Rembrandt, [the dog] is painted only in savage chase, or butchered agony. I know of no pictures more shameful to humanity than the boar and lion hunts of Rubens and Snyders, signs of disgrace all the deeper, because the powers desecrated are so great" (5:337). Such condemnation soon extends to the pitiless death of a dog in Homer: "My pleasure in the entire Odyssey is diminished because Ulysses gives not a word of kindness or of regret to Argus" (5:339). When it comes to great paintings of heroic violence, the matter is repeatedly approached, then deferred, until, at the end of the fifth volume, it cannot be put off any more. When that task arrives, Ruskin openly balks at analyzing how Turner paints such matter. In the main text he writes that "I need not trace the dark clue farther, the reader may follow it through all his work and life, this thread of Atropos" (5:436–37), and then refers the reader to a note. Our inveterate guide, who otherwise seems perfectly willing to expatiate more than generously on the smallest facets of Turner's art, suddenly leaves us on our own with his most dangerous theme. Ruskin's main text continues by stressing "the intensity with which [Turner's] imagination dwelt always on the three great cities of Carthage, Rome, and Venice"— that is, Ruskin jumps over any specific deaths of heroic individuals to linger upon the grander version of this drama in the rise and fall of imperial cities. He is more than ready to contemplate such sublime landscapes and cityscapes, and to appreciate epic decline and death in a building, as his *Stones of Venice* abundantly demonstrates. In the footnote Ruskin confesses, "I have not followed out, as I ought to have done, had the task been less painful, my assertion that Turner had to paint not only the labour and the sorrow of men, but their death. There is no form of violent death that he has not painted" (5:437). Ruskin's "had to paint" seems to transfer his intolerable burden onto Turner, but, though Turner looked at violent death and showed it on his canvases, Ruskin will not talk about what he saw there, even if that death occurred "where the liberties of the cantons were won by the battle charge of Morgarten" (5:439). This line concludes the long footnote that began with Ruskin's apologetic refusal. The battle referred to, like that in his early poem, took place in the mountains, a sublime landscape that tempted Ruskin to discuss its effects on "military character," but was deferred on this first occasion, then deferred again forever: the title of the concluding chapter, which follows immediately upon this embarrassed note, is "Peace." Ruskin flees with Pope into pastoral.

|||||||||||||||||||||||||||||||||||||||||||||||||||||||||||||||||||||||||||||||||||||||||||||||||||||||||||||||||||||||||||||||||||||||||||||||||||||

TWO

ROMANTIC LIBERAL EPIC

SOUTHEY, BYRON, AND NAPIER

> . . . he cannot bear
> The wound that girds him, weltering there:
> And "Water!" he cries, with moonward stare.
> [I will not read it!" with a start
> Burning cries some honest heart:
> "I will not read it! Why endure
> "Pangs which horror cannot cure?
> "Why—Oh why?"]
>
> —Leigh Hunt, *Captain Sword and Captain Pen*

The Romantics attacked the poetic dictional strategies of eighteenth-century epic as deeply falsifying, which they were partly designed to be, and so extended the Enlightenment project to humanize warfare so as to preclude killing. Godwin read Fénelon as proof that there can be no real liberal war or war hero—only a bloodless benevolence in the former and, as the latter, the writer himself, a direct precursor to the Romantic poet hero. Thus Hunt's "Captain Pen" replaces "Captain Sword" and remains the last man standing, but his agonistic victory demands no bloodshed. Godwin firmly designated the neoclassical effort to generate war epics by finding exceptions to its own humane rules as vicious casuistry: "It is scarcely necessary to add that all false casuistry respecting the application of this exception would be particularly odious" (1:517). This chapter will further trace this basic Romantic critique in Southey's denunciations of French casuistry and Byron's mockery of heroic cant. In William Napier, however, and his multivolume *War in the Peninsula* (1828–40), we will turn to an author who shared Byron's liberal aristocratic background, joined him in literary squabbles with the reactionary Southey, but broke with both Byron and Southey by resurrecting military epic in a form that was aware of itself as coming from a neoclassical tradition, fully attuned to the Romantic revolution, but agile to overcome all challenges and produce a popular and influential heroic account of war. The modern world has come to see that conflict not through Napier's but Goya's eyes. His *El Dos de Maio* and *El Tres de Maio* make it a smorgasbord of inhumanity, criminality, and horror—and the French as its hypocritical perpetrators. Such a contrast underscores the forgotten fact of Napier's long and influential reign as the principal historian of that war, the leading nineteenth-century writer of war epic, and a fiercely eloquent defender of the liberal values of the French Revolution; and it was his strategy of attending to battle's "Janus" face, not Keegan's singular one, that allowed his success in this poetical tradition.[1]

Godwin's extrapolation of the ethical critique had aesthetic implications, but it is Hunt in *Captain Sword and Captain Pen*—an anti-epic in six short books that, with its extensive appended notes, reads more like a treatise on the horrific sublime—who best exemplifies the furthest logical extension of the neoclassical aesthetic critique. Homer stirred readerly interest in, even sympathy for, the lethal skill of his heroes and the beauty of his poetic renderings of their artistry. Pope struggled to limit that barbaric pleasure and promote more readerly pity for his victims. Burke reformulated the sublime in light of Pope's efforts into the humane thrill of feeling, not causing, terror. Hunt aggressively advanced this process past merely emphasizing pity and fear to forcing readers to experience war's horrific ugliness, pain, and suffering. His poem's significance lies in its deliberate challenge to readers, especially women readers or readers figured by female standards, for being too coy, for their wish to be spared the full horrific truth: "I will not read it!" becomes the frequent cry of his offended reader. He complained that readers were implicitly demanding and being allowed to indulge in the matter of war without paying the full price. In short, while neoclassicism had struggled to suppress Homeric terror and replace it with pity, Hunt challenged his readers to face its full horror and thus experience dread of such power that they would no longer be able to stomach any muted rendering of such matter: again, the logic of this theory seemed to require the end of such epic and, in his poem, a poet-hero who writes against war defeats a soldier-hero renowned for it.

Hunt in 1835 summed up these Romantic emphases that Godwin in 1793 anticipated. Their advocacy, synthesis, and influence marked the high tide of the ethical-aesthetic critique. Meanwhile Jeremy Bentham had been adding to the stirrings of a more economic attack upon the status of war: "War is mischief upon the largest scale. . . . In ancient times, there was one system of inducements, under the feudal system another, and in modern times another" (544). By the 1850s all of war's "inducements" would be recast in economic terms—and all would be negative. The aesthetic-ethical critique consequently diminished till Keynes in turn raised doubts about the validity of the economic and intellectual case against war early in the twentieth century. The Romantics occupy a period of transition toward the Victorian era's confidence in the intellectual critique. They were not yet certain, like J. S. Mill or Henry Buckle, that modern economic realities simply precluded war. Malthus's stress on the inevitable supremacy of scarcity left the logic of violent confrontation firmly in place. And David Ricardo saw no easy way to construct an economic system that would eliminate war. He even turned the tables on *Télémaque*'s pacific physiocracy. Fénelon's argument with Louis XIV's militarist mercantilism maintained that an agricultural policy led to peace, to a focus on internal improvements. In contrast to this convention of eighteenth-century thought, Ricardo argued in 1817 that it could just as easily be the landed interest that most benefited and manufactures that most suffered from war. For, in England's case at least, war promoted investment in agriculture that, in times of peace, would flow more naturally to manufactures: "When war interrupts the importation of corn, its consequent high price attracts capital to the land" (Ricardo 318).

Thus the Romantics needed to retain and strengthen the ethical-aesthetic critique, if they were to continue to marginalize war. This critique's intensity largely succeeded, at least until Napier, in making the serious practice of war epic practically impossible. I have already glanced at some aspects of how Shelley's experience with epic encapsulates the Romantic double-bind stated by his father-in-law, but not at his actual epic. *The Revolt of Islam* (1817) adheres to Godwin's strictures: its hero leads a "bloodless dethronement of oppressors" (Shelley 32). It also anticipates Hunt's strictures with its horrifically violent counter-revolution that forces the sensitive reader to experience shock, intense pity, and disgust. His preface touts the most up-to-date code words: the poem possesses a "liberal and comprehensive morality," and its narrative tells of the "progress of individual mind aspiring after excellence, and devoted to the love of mankind" (32). It is at once bloodless, progressive, individualistic, socially benevolent, and triumphant. In good Romantic fashion, it both insists on Shelley's lived, not bookish, experience of war ("I have seen the theatre and more visible ravages of war" [34]) and yet requires that one divorce the goals of liberal idealism from the means of agonizing violence. One climactic moment dramatizes the unreal quality of heroic combat in this most unwarlike of war epics:

> A band of brothers gathering round me, made,
>   Although unarmed, a steadfast front, and still
> Retreating, with stern looks beneath the shade

> Of gathered eyebrows, did the victors fill
>> With doubt even in success; deliberate will
> Inspired our growing troop, not overthrown
>> It gained the shelter of a grassy hill,
> And ever still our comrades were hewn down,
> And their defenceless limbs beneath our footsteps strown. (6.9)

Though "unarmed" and "defenceless," this "band of brothers" is nonetheless heroically military in being "steadfast" and "stern" enough to sow doubt in their advancing killer-conquerors. The absurdity of Shelley's literalization of "unarmed" runs deep as his concluding attention to the "defenceless" dead limbs compulsively reiterates the crucial fact that he had affirmed about them while living. In this poem, even dead arms cannot be thought capable of doing harm. The Vergilian pun is repudiated: arms are not *arma*. The silliness of such a perfected epic is unintentional, but undeniable, and still not good enough. Shelley's rapid move from this ideologically purified graphic violence to tragedy—and tragedy of the most ethereal sort, self-consciously purged of all agonistic struggle—testifies to his radical rejection of even the wannest Homeric sublimities.

Scott, Southey, and Byron (in one exceptional episode) do seemingly break with this "reductio ad absurdum" logic of such heroic and benevolent, Achillean and Godwinian war epic. They all manage reasonably mimetic narrations of combat violence in an epic mode. The previous chapter concluded with Scott's exceptionality among the Romantics in extending the neoclassical tradition of heroic poetry and history deep into the novel. That leaves only Southey and Byron as legitimately Romantic epicists. Each, unlike Scott, performed epic by attacking the casuistry and cant at the core of the neoclassical project. Each, unlike Scott, took up heroic warfare in an explicitly plain style:

> "Reader, I have kept my word at least so far
>> As the first canto promised. You have now
> Had sketches of love, tempest, travel, war,
>> All very accurate, you must allow,
> And epic if plain truth should prove no bar."
> (*Don Juan* 8.138)

But Byron's exceptional achievement nonetheless remains rooted in a very specific set of neoclassical tactics perfected by Pope's *Iliad*. That book, as it was for so many of the writers in this study from Gibbon to Ruskin and J. S. Mill, was Byron's childhood favorite, and an enduring influence on his mature style. In 1810 Byron toured the archaeological site of Troy and there anticipated his later championing of Pope against the Lakers: "I have read it on the spot; there is a burst, and a brightness, and a glow about the night in the Troad, which makes the 'Planets vivid' and the 'pole glowing.' . . . I know of no more appropriate expression of such a heaven . . . than that of a 'flood of glory' " (Prothero 2:241). Byron recited the very passage and phrases singled out by Coleridge as particularly lame in his attack on Pope's translation's poetic diction. Byron's aggressive defense here had deeper implications later: "[Byron engaged in an] 'intellectual war' . . . against the Lake School under the twin banner of the traduced genius of Pope and the betrayal of enlightened political ideas" (McGann, *Byron and Romanticism* 175). His advocacy of Pope matched his defense of liberalism in an era of political reaction. Although Byron's indebtedness to Pope is usually explored in terms of their mutual admiration for Horace's conversational plain style (Ridenour 7–17; McGann 69–74), Byron's single most famous statement on this point—his much discussed Horatian epigraph to *Don Juan*, "difficile est proprie communia dicere"— echoes Pope's own Horatian epigraph for the task of translating Homer's violence: "Quis Martem tunica tecum adamantina digne scripserit?" Ultimately, Byron held that Pope got Homer exactly right, but that view entailed a defense of Pope's efforts to suppress the violence and aggrandize similes and poetic reliefs such as his notorious expansion of the Troad's moon and stars and glowing pole. For all their Romantic rhetoric of honesty, *Don Juan*'s war books surreptitiously follow Pope's humanizing, modernizing, and evasive strategies: if much of the poem struggles "to speak properly about everyday things," books 7 and 8 strive "to write in a dignified way about war." Southey is equally compromised.[2]

Neither poet's strategy provided a way forward for liberal epic, however, and there is no subsequent Southeyan or Byronic tradition of war epic comparable to the long and distinguished tradition of heroic war narrative that springs from Napier. Thus that historian figures as the key exception and pivot point of my larger argument, much as history now begins to shoulder aside poetry as the dominant form for military epic. In Southey's case we can see this larger development playing out within his own career. The difference between his *History of the Peninsular War* (1823–32) and his poem *Roderick, the Last of the Goths* (1814) is exemplary. Though the latter, in telling the story of the Islamic invasion and conquest of Spain, centers upon a fundamentally military event, there is no warfare until the final section, "Roderick in Battle," and there such material is handled in the form of a swift overview that looks forward suggestively to Tennyson's equally impressionistic and rapid practice of making all warfare a matter of criminality and blindness—not agonistic drama and heroic self-assertion. Furthermore, though its plot is self-evidently a historical allegory for the French invasion of Spain and thus directly comparable to Southey's subsequent history, Southey subtitles the former "A Tragic Poem," and like *The Idylls of the King,* its version of epic is distinctly somber and tragic, while the latter does epic in a triumphantly aggressive mode filled with combat and dedicated to the logic of personal and national glory. Still, it was written with a reactionary fervor that helped make it an also-ran to Napier's more liberal, balanced, successful, and violent version. In his capable hands, warfare became Romantically honest, plain, and empirical. He knew more of war and wrote about its horrors more vividly than any of the poets. His war narrations attained a level of agonistic intensity, rhetorical splendor, and world-historical import that made his history an inspiration to novelists (Lever, Thackeray, Meredith), historians and historian-statesmen (Macaulay, Roosevelt, Churchill, Trevelyan) and poets (Hardy, Meredith).[3] His achievement was acknowledged as English literature's answer to Thucydides, much as Gibbon had become its Tacitus, and Scott, so says Lockhart, its Livy. As a result of his success and his distinguished liberal heritage, he emerged as the Whig rival to the Tory's "Captain Sword" Wellington. Napier's success in the context of the Romantic crisis over epic warfare points to how history now self-consciously supplanted poetry as the most fertile ground for war epic. Napier himself bested the reigning poet laureate as the preferred historian of the English in the Napoleonic Wars; Southey saw his epic history as a more serious, more sustained example of epic than his increasingly violence-free epic poems; and in the next generation Carlyle and Macaulay would openly scorn poetry (and the epic efforts of a new poet laureate), while they ascended to the heights of popularity and canonicity as prose historians of battle.[4]

FRANCOPHILIC SOUTHEY TO FRANCOPHOBIC SOUTHEY

> *WAR's varied horrors, and the train of ills*
> *That follow on Ambition's blood-stain'd path*
> *And fill the world with woe; of France preserv'd*
> *By maiden hand, what time her chiefs subdued,*
> *Or slept in death, or lingered life in chains,*
> *I sing: nor wilt thou FREEDOM scorn the song.*
>
> —Southey, *Joan of Arc*

One hundred years after Dryden's translations established neoclassical epic's strategies, Southey's *Joan of Arc* (1796) fulfilled this process,

even as his subsequent career as a prolific heroic poet and epic historian signaled the major countertrends of Romanticism. The epigraph,
which presents that epic's opening lines, both follows and Romantically
intensifies the neoclassical pattern of denouncing war and war heroes
in general, while finding that rare exception "Freedom" will accept as an
epic theme. Later editions dropped this proem, as they similarly removed
the bulk of the original's more obvious formal conventions, such as its
allegorical machinery and *Aeneid* 6–like visionary dream, in favor of a
tighter focus upon the more challenging problem of its violent content.
It is remarkable, however, that even the late and rabidly Francophobic
Southey left this poem's celebration of French nationalism intact. To be
sure, his last edition nearly doubles the notes, largely by adding diatribes
such as the following: "[These English atrocities] seem nothing when
compared to the atrocities which the French exercised upon each other"
(235)—followed by a lurid quotation. Other than such marginal ventings
and a further scrubbing of the original's lingering Spenserian diction,
however, Southey let stand a very early narrative that seemed to offend
against the fierce opinions of the elderly poet laureate.[5]

More even than its politics, the poem's first scandal was the adoles-
cence of its pretentious poet: Southey composed it during his nineteenth
and twentieth years. It nonetheless proved a popular and critical success,
easily outperforming his productions as poet laureate from 1813 to 1843.
Joan of Arc jauntily drove Dryden's translational paradigm to its logical
extreme. It is perhaps the only antinationalist epic poem, as Southey himself observed: "It has been established as a necessary rule of the epic,
that it should be national. To this rule I have acted in direct opposition
and chosen for the subject of my poem the defeat of the English. If there
be any readers who can wish success to an unjust cause because their
country was engaged in it, I desire not their approbation" (17–18). He
makes this point even broader and less parochial by impugning how the
"national vanity of a Greek or Roman" buttressed the "renown of Achilles
or Aeneas," and by contrasting his effort "to engage the unprejudiced" in
a heroine with "more of human feelings than is generally to found in the
character of a warrior" (15).[6] One must be careful to read such universalizing gestures properly: Southey's political ideology (Speck is insightful
and precise regarding Southey's moderately liberal "Girondism" during
this period[7]) lies in his poem's championing of the principle of national
self-determination. Later in his career it would be the French with their
universalizing rhetoric of humanity who would most threaten the nation-
state, but here the English perform that heavy role.[8]

Thus his epic is happily based on French sources, in celebration of

French popular nationalism, with English villains fighting cruelly in an unjust war. It is written in open opposition to the history plays of England's greatest national hero-author, Shakespeare, and his Henry V; in defiance of Hume's skeptical debunking of the Joan legend; and in protest against England's wary response toward newly republican France. Years later, the conservative and nationalist Southey belittled this early hit, seeing its politics as an example of youthful ignorance and its success a function of the liberal press; his later writings, such as his *Life of Nelson* (1813), express a steady, chauvinistic defense of English heroism and war making, as well as an unrelenting view of the French as cruel and rapacious, scheming and perfidious—not just in their contemporary revolutionary transformation, but for all time: "The French, who have never acted a generous part in the history of the world" (63) sums up the attitude of that narrative.[9]

Joan of Arc centers upon her war making, not her martyrdom—above all, on the siege of Orleans where she first earned her lasting fame; and like his heroine, Southey acted very boldly, even heroically, in risking such a venture.[10] The older Southey hardly does justice to the daring of his younger self's *Joan of Arc,* both politically and poetically. Its transnational championing of independence for France against English adventurism prefigures the liberal internationalism that grew in force throughout the nineteenth century and culminated in the English and French support for Garibaldi and Italian nationalism. Its revisionist assessment of Henry V and Richard the Lionhearted anticipates the aggressive liberal project of identifying and vilifying former war heroes as war criminals. One might expect such judgment upon Henry V—and, in typical eighteenth-century fashion, Southey obliges with a lengthy disquisition taking up most of book 2 on the intricate legal and ethical questions surrounding that king's actions. It differs from neoclassical practice, however, in ultimately condemning its subject, not excusing it. But why did it reach back to Richard, who, for the crime of disobeying the medieval church's efforts to ban a particular kind of weapon, is condemned: "An English king, the lionhearted Richard, their decree / First broke, and rightly was he doomed to fall / By that forbidden weapon" (165)? Southey's critique extends to Nuremburg-like charges against the followers of such kings, who "in obedience to our chiefs / Durst disobey our God" (185). The elder Southey explained his poem's success in terms of the biased Whig press, but in doing so he ignored his poem's challenge to the more powerful and entrenched political and social, not to say generic, interests this poem knowingly provoked, forces that would drive England into war against the French Republic.[11]

Joan of Arc goes beyond fulfilling the logic of neoclassical liberalism to anticipate his coming abandonment of that mode altogether. Southey demonstrates his proto-Romantic credentials in dismissing the "fop-finery" of Pope's *Iliad,* and, like Cowper, the leading epic translator of Homer in his day, turns to blank verse. In contrast to Cowper's Miltonic pastiche, Southey praises—"the singular excellence of Milton render[s] it impossible to deduce any rules of epic poetry" (17)—in such a way as to negate both Milton's specific blank verse practices and the more general influence of his argument against war epic. He displays a Romantic resistance to all rule-bound poetry that extends to Pope's and Dryden's French-based rules for obscuring the realistic details of combat. He calls attention to his efforts to render killing with a fresh eye: "Where in battle I have particularized the death of an individual, it is not, I hope, like the common lists of killed and wounded" (17). Largely freed from Pope's poetic diction and Milton's ethical strictures, Southey comes closer to Homeric renderings of the anatomical details of killing and death than any neo-classical poet—and closer than in any of his later epic poems. Moreover, as his judgment on Richard's war crime suggests and insofar as the siege of Orleans was marked by numerous technological innovations, including a very early use of cannon, Southey's poem incorporates this matter, its terminology, and its effects. His account bristles with obscure terms, which offend against poetic diction by their very technicality: "trebuchet," "barbican," "mangonel," "arbalist," "petraries," "beugles," "metafund", and so on. His surrounding narrative depicts the way these defensive and offensive elements actually work, particularly their effect on the human body:

> . . . and that murderous sling
> The metafund, from whence the ponderous stone
> Made but one wound of him in its way
> It met; no pious hand might then compose
> The crushed and mangled corpse to be conveyed
> To where his fathers slept. (164)

("Mangled" proves one of his favorite words: "mangled lungs" appears no less than three times in this Homerically anatomical poem.) The final comment pulls us back to the Homeric concern for the proper treatment of the body and the heroic ethos of lineage, but Southey refreshes this stale convention with his attention to just how this particular weapon cruelly obliterates such pieties. Occasionally, Southey retreats into awkwardly nontechnical poetic diction, but even these exceptions suggest an effort to confront war realistically:

The bowstring twanged, swift on its way the dart
Whizzed, and it struck, there where the helmet's clasps
Defend the neck,—a weak protection now:
For through the tube which draws the breath of life
Pierced the keen shaft; blood down the unwonted way
Gushed to the lungs. (166)

Southey drops the term "trachea," but he is accurate about the wound and its effects. His close attention to the flying weapon, to the failure of armor, indeed to the specific failure of its "clasps," and to the details of anatomy brings him closer to Homer than any post-Homeric poet period.

Southey's choice of his epic subject, by asking his English readers to sympathize with the French cause and its French fighters, furthers the liberal and humanizing goals of the poem, its effort to stress "human feelings" (15) that remain patriotic in the liberal sense that insists upon the virtue of everyone's particular patriotism. But his project struggles mightily when this ideal goal reaches its logical crisis point, when its humane heroine must be shown killing Englishmen. Just there his heretofore confident poem pauses, even stumbles. Joan leads armies of men armed for killing, and she herself kills. *Joan of Arc* must justify such actions. Joan repeatedly becomes caught up in casuistry—openly mulling over the justice of her cause, then over this key problem of exactly why and under what conditions it is legitimate to take another's life. The basic justification follows a liberal formula: "They shall perish who oppress" (45). But Southey's humane Joan never resorts to its blanket application. She takes seriously her impulse to limit the extent of the killing, even when it comes to the English oppressors. Joan sends a herald to the English camp to apprise them of their offenses and give them the chance to withdraw. The English refusal results in claims of justification by both the herald and then Joan for the coming French attack. Such formalities of war can easily serve as excuses for subsequent inhumanity. In a later extended sequence during the battle, Southey implicitly contrasts Joan and Henry V, a war criminal primarily due to his order to kill French prisoners at a crisis point at Agincourt; Joan insists on properly treating captured English soldiers, though the dire circumstances of the battle render this care both difficult and dangerous for the French, though her fellow leaders strongly advise otherwise, and though the English leaders are shown attempting to take advantage of what they consider to be a foolish gesture of womanish humanity (176–77).

Joan becomes a neoclassical epic hero because she fulfills its liberal logic of benevolence acting from within war to correct its logic of escalation, retaliation, and domination. But neither Southey nor the reader can forget or ignore that she remains a hero and patriot because she leads the French to victory. The self-contradictions come to a head at the end of the passage cited above when Joan willingly exchanges "renown, however splendid" for "the thought / That we have saved one victim from the sword" (176). Such a Godwinian sentiment, however, is not quite ready for epic fulfillment in Shelleyan bloodless victory. Southey must and eventually does show Joan personally killing an enemy. He nonetheless approaches this key problem warily. Early in the poem, as Joan journeys to Chinon to offer her services to Charles, she balks at the thought of killing with her own hand: "'I gazed upon it, / And, shuddering as I touched its edge, exclaimed, / 'How horrible it is with the keen sword / To gore the finely fibred human frame! / I could not strike a lamb'" (40). Joan's imagery provides material for a grizzled veteran who articulates the poem's fundamental rationale for killing:

> "Maiden, thou sayest well. I could not strike
> A lamb; but, when the merciless invader
> Spares not gray age, and mocks the infant's shriek
> As it doth writhe upon his cursed lance,
> And forces his foul embrace the wife. . . .
> Almighty God! I should not be a man
> If I did let one weak and pitiful feeling
> Make mine arm impotent to cleave him down." (40)

The human inhibition against killing is cast as a "weak and pitiful feeling" when set against justified rage over invasion, oppression, tyranny, and rape. The nationalist logic of the poem makes the ethical choices easier: why can't the English just go home? Eventually, Joan is armed with a sword of her own and, despite her best efforts to warn the English, is at last confronted with the necessity of using her weapon. When she does finally slay in battle, Southey falls back into the same coyness typical of the neoclassical poems he set out to surpass and that his detailed scenes of killing had thus far escaped. Her scenes become much briefer and vaguer than those of the male heroes. Southey often makes her sword, not the mild Joan, the agent against the raging enemy: "Swift he turned to wreak his wrath; / When, lo! the assailant gasping on the ground, / Cleft by the Maiden's falchion" (149). A miraculous agency signaled by "lo!" distracts the reader's eye from the very action of killing it should have attended to. Here the sword again takes over:

> . . . On high she lifts
> That hallowed sword, which in the tomb for her,
> Age after age, by miracle reserved,
> Had lain, which time itself could not corrode:
> How, then, might shield or breastplate or close mail
> Retund its edge? Beneath that edge her foe
> Fell. (149)

Southey's strategy of diverting the gaze from Joan's agency and the anatomical details of her act is even more obvious here, since the sword has
done it—magically. At the end of the ninth of the poem's ten books, however, Southey finally confronts the task of showing Joan killing in vivid
detail and with no masking of her action. This long delay was originally
even longer, since the poem's first edition did not present this scene at all.
It is the centerpiece of a 200–plus-line narrative interpolation replacing
Joan's book-length dream vision, which Southey dropped from later editions. (Again note how the challenge of epic violence trumps epic machinery. Southey first could not quite bring himself to show Joan actively
killing, but he could indulge in epic machinery. When he corrected this
failure, he did so with notable brevity.)

> . . . With uplifted arm,
> Furious he came: her buckler broke the blow,
> And forth she flashed her sword, and with a stroke
> Swift that no eye could ward it, and of strength
> No mail could blunt, smote on his neck,—his neck
> Unfenced; for he in haste aroused had cast
> An armet on: resistless there she smote,
> And to the earth prone fell the headless trunk
> Of Franquet. Then on Burgundy she fixed
> Her eye severe. "Go, chief! And thank thy God
> That he with lighter judgments visits thee
> Than fell on Sisera, or by Judith's hand
> He wrought upon the Assyrian." (193)

Her agency, "she smote," is finally clear enough, but the poem follows
Fénelon's example by hurrying on to assure us that the forgiving Joan is
no Old Testament Jael/Deborah or Judith (Southey's later epics, in their
illiberal war lust, will embrace such Old Testament deliverers). Far from
coming with the intent to kill the leader of France's enemies, as in the case
of the biblical heroines, Joan has come to warn, and she only kills when
attacked. Southey once again projects the Achillean fury of epic combat

onto the victim—who is notably not English, but Burgundian. Southey never quite faced his ultimate test. Southey's skittishness renders her "stroke" so "swift that no eye could ward it." The pause and repetition over the point of contact ("neck—his neck") cleverly works to avoid having to detail the impact of Joan's sword upon that neck, which, for example, Southey willingly showed in the arrow piercing a trachea. Finally, rather than show that horror, Southey prefers to lay blame on the victim, who, in his fury, forgot to take the proper precautions. Nowhere else in his vivid poem does Southey exhibit such skill at not seeing, and Southey's determined Homeric realism about the fundamental business of war stalls and becomes coy when facing his central figure of liberal heroism performing her one essential task.

SOUTHEY'S NELSON AND WELLINGTON

> The French commandant at St. Elmo, relying upon the strength of the place, and the nature of the force which attacked it, had insulted Captain Foote in the grossest terms; but citoyen Mejan was soon taught better manners. . . . He was informed, that none of his letters, with the insolent printed words at the top, Liberté, Egalité, Guerre aux Tyrans, etc., would be received; but that, if he wrote like a soldier and a gentleman, he should be answered in the same style. The Frenchmen then began to flatter his antagonist upon the bienfaisance and humanité. . . . Monsieur Trowbridge's bienfaisance was, at the time, thinking of mining the fort.
>
> —Southey, Life of Nelson

Leigh Hunt charged that Southey's mature writings celebrated mere conquerors, but while Southey's later epic narratives indulge in retributive bloodlust, their heroes are the enemies of conquerors, indeed conquerors who hypocritically speak the language of liberation. His turn against France thus remains rooted in a deep liberal nationalism, one that the English imperialism offended against in the Hundred Years' War, but the French most threatened in the era of Napoleon. This transformation appears best in his later epic histories with their superabundance of heroic violence in contrast to the etiolated later poems. His heroic biographies of Lord Nelson and the Duke of Wellington perform epic in a high mode, in the "same style," as it were, as a "soldier and a gentleman." Indeed, these two words deliberately point to a blunt, but honest plain style, in relation to which they evoke a pre-liberal, heroic past. Southey had been carefully reading Clarendon, the seventeenth-century aristocratic-Thucydidean historian of the English revolution, and "had his belief in the 'conservative principles' of society fully confirmed" (Storey 169). He returns to the celebration of war heroes, but now with a newly minted bellicose patriotism and reactionary fervor. Whereas Joan sympathized with the English and strove not to kill them, when the English and French roles switch in later Southey, no such humanity remains. Southey and his later heroes delight over the slaughter of the now intensely hated, aggressively republican, linguistically diplomatic, and hypocritically humane French.

The epigraph encapsulates the contest of heroic and liberal rhetoric in Southey's late phase. The fierceness comes from the fact that the French are playing the role of the English in *Joan of Arc*—plus they are smooth-tongued hypocrites. Southey's account depends upon casting the English as reliably true and the French as inveterately false, but its energy pushes beyond such Manichaean categories to suggest something complexly admirable in plain-speaking heroism, even when that quality is engaged in planning the defeat of an enemy during a negotiation. At the same time, there is a simple scorn for the trappings of universal democratic liberalism and its richly humane rhetoric: his contempt for the term "citoyen" is palpable; his ironic delight in deploying "bienfaisance" is both finely comic and ethically grotesque. On the other hand, his willingness to pass over without comment the captain's mock-epic remark about "break[ing] some of their shins," which comes just below and refers to killing the enemy, seems an egregious example of covering over the true effects of war. Clearly, honesty has its privileges—heartily jocular euphemism being one of them.

Therefore, we can safely assume that it was no flaw that Nelson, Southey's hero, so hated the French that it was part of his heroism to declare that emotion on numerous occasions, and that this Achillean rage sanctified the harshest treatment: "I hate a Frenchman: they are equally objects of my detestation, whether royalists or republicans: in some points, I believe the latter are the best" (99); "To serve my king, and to destroy the French, I consider as the great order of all, from which the little ones spring . . . down with the damned French villains!—My blood boils at the name of Frenchmen!" (220–21). Southey wholeheartedly shares these views. Few French individuals are given any praise, and those always with some qualification. Their leader and symbol, Napoleon, is naturally the antithesis of Nelson, and, after granting that he had some military skill and much ruthlessness, the narrative takes every opportunity to accuse him of every possible war crime. All of this heat can be read as so much epic fun in a narrative little interested in shedding objective light on the background or context of these events. Still, Southey has abandoned the neoclassical effort to restrain such bloody-minded sympathy with killer-soldiers in war, and does so precisely against the nation most associated with that sanitizing goal. So much vengeful delight is directed

at the French that it seems more is going on than mere hatred, fear, and
rivalry. Nelson "tempered the exercise of power with courtesy and humanity, whenever duty would permit" (111):

> Nelson, who was as humane, as he was brave, was shocked at this mas-
> sacre—for such he called it—and, with a presence of mind peculiar to
> himself, and never more signally displayed than now, he retired into the
> stern galley, and wrote thus to the Crown Prince: "Vice-Admiral Lord
> Nelson has been commanded to spare Denmark, when she no longer
> resists. The line of defense which covered her shores has struck to the
> British flag; but if the firing is continued on the part of Denmark, he
> must set on fire all the prizes he has taken, without having the power of
> saving the men who have so nobly defended them." (260)

Southey stresses Nelson's plain-spoken honesty in calling a massacre a
massacre, but his further gesture of humanity includes a Henry V–like
threat to kill prisoners amid a crisis in battle (precisely what Joan refused
to do). The complex situation was such that when the Danes inquire
about its implication, Southey allows Nelson's comment—"Lord Nelson's object . . . was humanity" (262)—to pass as a fair clarification of the
deeper logic informing his offer/threat. The narrative then surveys "the
mangled and mutilated Danes bleeding to death" and calls it "a scene, of
all others, most shocking to a brave man's feelings" (265), but this sympathetic comment is set against another: "The fate of these men, after
the gallantry which they had displayed, particularly affected Nelson; for
there was nothing in this action of that indignation against the enemy,
and that impression of retributive justice, which at the Nile had given a
sterner temper to his mind, and a sense of austere delight, in beholding
the vengeance of which he was the appointed minister" (264). "The Nile"
refers to one of Nelson's greatest victories over the French navy, the battle
in which the tragic event that inspired Hemans's "Casabianca" occurred.
Nelson, apparently, viewed even the French boy on the burning deck with
the "sterner temper" of Old Testament vengeance.

I have purposely not surveyed Nelson's various defeats of the French,
where carnage, delight, and sympathetic identification with the hero-
killer readily merge, because this episode (in which the English illegally
launched a preemptive assault on the Danish fleet) better illustrates Southey's awkward efforts to claim some humanity for his hero who regularly
broke the rules of war, not to mention those of liberal epic.[12] Southey's
Nelson has spun 180 degrees from Joan's explicit refusal to be a Deborah and her epic's meticulously documented indictment of Henry V's war
crimes—to become a vivid embodiment of Deborah's vengefulness and

Henry's guilt. Such a revolution suggests that the French symbolize more than just the supreme enemy, more even than a Manichaean opposite, but a poetic and generic negation: the historical exemplars of the hypocritical betrayal of the liberalism Southey began his career celebrating, the national embodiment of the casuistry that even Godwin abhorred, and that even Shelley found simply Satanic—in the deeper sense of ironic diabolism, the thwarting of the Romantic ideal of unified, organic symbolism and true meaning.

One could take such a return to traditional epic rage in *The Life of Nelson* as the expression of the fearful Burkean as much as the terrifying Homeric sublime. It was published in the midst of the Napoleonic Wars when the issue was very much in doubt. Southey's *Life of Wellington* (1816), however, appeared after the Battle of Waterloo and the decisive defeat of the French. It shows no lessening of virulence with the disappearance of the threat, no magnanimity toward the defeated foe. In its much expanded version into a six-volume history of the Peninsular War issued in the late 1820s, Southey's illiberal rage has only grown. The *Life of Wellington* does not have a hero who repeatedly expresses hatred for his enemy and joy in seeing him die, but that lack is more than made up for by the narrator. Every rhetorical opportunity to diminish the French enemy and aggrandize the English is taken. When he expanded this biography into the multivolume history of the Peninsular War, which he considered his greatest epic work, the most worthy "to transmit my name to future ages" (1.1:2), Southey proclaimed a kind of religious patriotism: "The late war in the Peninsula will be memorable above all in modern times. . . . It was a direct contest between the principles of good and evil as the elder Persians, or the Manicheans, imagined in their fables: it was for the life and death of national independence, national spirit, and of all those holy feelings which are comprehended in the love of our native land" (1.1:2). Here Southey aligns nationalism with true religion and even goodness against the religion of French international humanism—seen as evil because it is not just false, but a knowing lie. As ever, a stylistic and rhetorical opposition lurks at the root of the ideological divisions in these epics.[13]

Southey weaves such divisive sentiments into the details of many of the famous battles—Coruna, Talavera, Salamanca, Vitoria. His account of a smallish early battle announces his basic thematic scheme: "The skill of the French was indeed as clearly proved that day as their inferiority to the British soldiers in those moments when everything depends upon native courage" (42). This epic viewpoint becomes a refrain: "The Englishman is the braver animal, the bayonet is the test of that bravery, and the English have never shrunk from it" (42). An ideological yoking of heroism and patriotism is now Southey's ruling principle. In addition, there is Wellington's superiority as a commander—"that brilliant gallantry which, on the proper occasions flashes terror into the eyes of the enemy, and kindles in his own army an enthusiasm which nothing can withstand" (156).[14] Together this native bravery and individual energy render the English victory purely a matter of the epic logic of heroism, not a question of finances and resources, much less the fate of the Grand Army and Napoleon himself far away in the Russian winter.

Along with such conservative and honest scorn for the liberal and rhetorical ambitions of republican France and such heroic disdain for the military pretensions of the typical French soldier or any French general, Southey's account is at pains to dramatize French war atrocities as well as hypocrisy: "As for assassinating friends and enemies indiscriminately the French perhaps accused the allies of it, because they themselves are familiar with such practices" (133). This passage mentions English atrocities, but Southey will have none of it, and, as with bravery, his narrative weighs the humanity of the French against the English and finds the former wanting: "The difference in humanity between the two nations will appear as strongly marked as it is in the treatment which the maniacs Damiens and Hatfield [attempted regicides] experienced for actions precisely similar" (174). Such contrasts between the clever and inhumane French and the brave and kind English persist throughout Southey's narrative. The guerrilla war resulted in many French acts of cruelty and oppression, but other contemporary authorities, including Wellington himself, admitted the gruesome excesses of the Spanish insurgents against both the French and the many Spaniards who supported them, and, more important, the brutalities of English soldiers against both French prisoners and Spanish natives.

Southey's simple dichotomy effectively condones readerly pleasure at the doom falling upon the French monsters. Southey longs for a strict constructionist application of the laws of war that his Joan rejected, one that would allow the killing of French prisoners: "Our troops had humanity enough to grant them their lives. . . . They did not enforce the right which the laws of war allowed them,—laws which, in this instance where they seem most severe, are in reality most merciful; and which we could *therefore* wish to see more frequently exercised" (133–34). Southey's retributive logic italicizes "therefore" so as to emphasize the strict sequence of vengeance: his critique of casuistry has reached the point where he only admires the rules of war when they ask for punishment, never their guiding spirit that resists it. He does not even seem to be speaking about the modern *ius in bello,* but of some harsh *lex talionis* drawn from the horrors of the book of Joshua. Such thinking appears often in Southey's heroic narrative, as in gleeful comments on the ironic justice of the bayonet that the English soldiers wielded so skillfully and gruesomely: "Bayonne itself is a place memorable in military history for the invention of the bayonet, a weapon which in British hands has proved more destructive than any other to the nation by which it was invented" (145). Again, a poetic justice that *Joan of Arc* liberally applied to the English hero-king Richard is now evoked vengefully for the French.

This process culminates in his account of Waterloo, where in the aftermath he is pleased that the Prussians were mainly responsible for the pursuit, since they, in their justified rage and hatred, were blessedly less likely to obey the rules of war regarding prisoners than the English, or, rather, more likely to follow an older, more honest code:

> The British army then halted, formed on the hill, and gave the Prussians three cheers as they passed; a moment which all who were present will remember as having given them the sublimest emotion of their lives. The pursuit could not have been given over to better hands; the enemy had deserved and found no mercy from the Prussians and they found none. . . . Thus insolent, thus brutal, thus inhuman in success, [the French] were equally treacherous and abject in defeat. . . . Some of these villains [prisoners] were deservedly sabred . . . [,] but when they heard . . . the sound of the Prussian trumpet, the blast of which was as dreadful as if it summoned them to the Last Judgment, their panic returned. . . . Eight hundred of their bodies were found lying here, where "they had suffered themselves (it is a German who speaks) to be cut down like cattle." General Duhesme . . . fell in this place. A black hussar of the Duke of Brunswick's corps sacrificed him to his master's memory. "The Duke fell yesterday," said the Brunswicker; and "thou shalt also bite the dust"; and so saying he cut him down. (250–51)

Southey's reference to the sublime here goes back to Vico's sense of the Homeric sublime, not Burke's liberal redefinition: it's all about delighting in causing fear and death, not feeling such emotions oneself. So, too, the concluding death in this passage is modeled after the death of Hector or Turnus, and Southey sympathizes with the vengeful killer and his Homeric locution. It is just this sort of scene of epic vengeance that his early epics had been most at pains to correct, or justify, or suppress, usually by making the suppliant beg forgiveness and then sneakily attack yet again, thus forfeiting his life. Here Southey takes the opposite tactic of suppressing the French general's plea altogether: we can no longer bear to hear French hypocrisy. In a final gesture, Southey inserts a little anecdote that works to deny Christian sympathy to the French and to imply their eternal damnation—"It marks too the character of the different nations, that among the pillage of the dead, French novels are enumerated, (we know of what description!) and German testaments" (256). Perhaps Southey's audience found more to sympathize with in French novel-readers than German Bible-bearers, but such was not Southey's intent.

Southey's summary judgment upon the Battle of Waterloo begins with exactly the sort of gesture Hunt's *Captain Sword and Captain Pen* takes to task: "The state of the field of battle is too dreadful for description. Let us rather relate such facts as are honourable to our nature, and mitigate and relieve those horrors. It has been said in the French papers that the British soldiers exerted themselves to form litters and carry off the wounded from the field. Some of our wounded, who had still the use of their limbs, employed themselves in binding up the wounds of their enemies" (255). But Southey is intent not so much upon hiding the horror of war from tender, modern readers, than upon making sure they experience no liberal affect of humane pity for the French. Hunt's critical point, therefore, is deeper and more specific than might first appear. He sees that this Wordsworthian and Southeyan literature of the Tory reaction, while trotting out the language of humanity as an excuse for not showing the horror of war, actually uses the liberal rhetoric of sympathetic horror as an inhumane device for further justifying the keen pleasure of hating enemies. Casuistry has been horribly reversed. Even Homer had some pity, if only after an intense jolt of terror, but not Southey. What Hunt's critique misses, however, is that Southey's deeper purpose shares one key point with his own: to attack the lies of liberal epic and the very notion of humane warfare which, for him as for Dryden, originated with the French—and for which they must pay.

MISANTHROPIC BYRON: THE CANT OF HEROISM AND HUMANITY

> Three hosts combine to offer sacrifice;
> Three tongues prefer strange orisons on high;
> Three gaudy standards flout the pale blue skies;
> The shouts are France, Spain, Albion, Victory!
> The foe, the victim, and the fond ally
> That fights for all, but ever fights in vain,

Are met—as if at home they could not die—
To feed the crow on Talavera's plain,
And fertilize the field that each pretends to gain.

—Byron, *Childe Harold's Pilgrimage*

Byron strives to see every war in terms of horror, vanity, and cant, an affair of criminals and victims, not exciting contests. All three nation-combatants participate blindly in an enterprise marked by a polished vocabulary of rhetorical glory and a grotesque reality of material death. His ironic stanzas repeatedly inflate themselves into a facsimile of epic's high style before succumbing to the logic of their conversational bluntness and deflating rhymes. They are "a versified aurora borealis, / which flashes over a waste and icy clime" (*Don Juan* 7.2).[15] Southey is consistently bombastic and grandly oratorical, but he shares with Byron a commitment to expose and deflate the pretensions of humane, progressive warfare:

> Marshal Soult will deservedly be recorded with lasting infamy. . . . In a memorable dispatch, which the peasantry of Gallicia intercepted, he had complained of the moral debility (*affaiblissement moral*) of some of his officers, and gave it as his opinion that the generals who were employed in such a war ought to be men whose hearts no circumstances could soften. . . . This *impassibility*, or, in other words, this Satanic indifference to the means which he used, the crimes which he committed, and the misery which he occasioned, Marshal Soult possessed almost as completely as the monster whom he served. (*Wellington* 120–21)

Given that he is equipped to denounce far more than to praise, his heroic narration comes very close to Byron's in its negative energies, and his vision of Soult is eerily close to Byron's Suwarrow, the gloriously callous general who dominates the military action of *Don Juan*. Both writers question the military enthusiasts who delight in praising skill on the battlefield without regard to its inhumanity and criminality. Both writers also question the neoclassical project to sanitize the harsh reality of war with verbal refinement. Thus Southey pauses to gloss the eminently poetic dictional "impassibility" with his own blunt "in other words . . . Satanic indifference" (121). For all their superficial and polemical differences, Southey and Byron shared this deep commitment to set forth war's ugly reality and strip away its civilized, legalized, sanitized façade. It is just that Byron subjects both parties to this process, while Southey reserves his debunking for the French. Cant was a universal problem affecting all epic, but casuistry was the special disease of Frenchified liberal epic.

Byron famously launches his epic poem with a survey of war heroes, all of whom are quickly rejected, before settling on the semi-autobiographical theme of Juan's adventures in love. Despite the vehemence of his proem's apparent dismissal of war heroism, his poem never abandons heroic warfare as the essential matter of epic. The renunciation is echoed and undone by a later boast upon the completion of his Iliadic siege: "Reader, I have kept my word . . . / you have now / Had sketches of love, tempest, travel, war, / All very accurate" (8.138). With this declaration, books 7 and 8 of *Don Juan* confess what is clear from their very existence. Their apparent exception to the Romantic rule of not being able to do war epic is best read as a daring effort to illustrate with more vividness (and accuracy) than a dismissal the same fundamental crisis. Unlike Wordsworth, Byron will perform heroic violence to show precisely why he rejected it; unlike Shelley, his war will be real, not an idealized confection. This episode shows the centripetal pull of epic's core matter (the poem's ironic opening turns out to be still more ironic, a promise here fulfilled), as well as the centrifugal repulsiveness of such themes (the poem keeps delaying this fulfillment; war is the list's first mentioned and last completed).

Beyond embodying this global attraction and repulsion to war, *Don Juan* precisely articulates the crisis points of the Romantic double-bind in taking the project of neoclassical epic to its sublime and ridiculous extreme, but with more knowing comedy and empiricist determination than Shelley. It looks back to the eighteenth-century effort to find and clean up one worthy hero and one good war, but it burdens that task with the demands of Godwin and Shelley for bloodless benevolent heroism and of Hunt for war to be made grotesque and offensive to readers. Byron references Fénelon in a context that confirms his Godwinian reading of *Télémaque* as a cynical debunking of the very possibility of battlefield heroism, not a delineation of one stellar exception:

> They accuse me—me—the present writer of
>   The present poem of—I know not what—
> A tendency to underrate and scoff
>   At human power and virtue and all that. . . .
> I say no more than has been said . . .
>   By Swift, by Machiavel, by Rochefoucault,
> By Fénelon. (7.3–4)

Later he singles out the same Wordsworthian lapse that Hunt indicated as the origin of his polemic: " 'Carnage' (so Wordsworth tells you) 'is God's daughter' " (8.9). Neither Byron nor Hunt tolerates the Wordsworthian, much less its fuller Southeyan twin, swerve into assuming that heaven is on his side, that celebrations of war can be justified by blaming the godless losers, and that readers can be rightly satisfied with graphic accounts of the slaughter of such monsters. Byron's continuation echoes Hunt's fascination with the wounded suffering on the battlefield, particularly their burning thirst: "All common fellows, who might writhe and wince / And shriek for water into a deaf ear" (8.11). Byron pivots from this critique of self-righteous, vengeful inhumanity and from these scenes of unglamorous agony to two more prime emphases of Hunt's poem: the grotesque reality of war and the sad ironies surrounding the literary, political, and financial profit reaped by its eulogizers and heroes. Stanza 12 proffers an extended metaphor of a cannonade as an "emetic" with bombs as "pills" resulting in a "bloody diuretic," while stanza 14 turns ironically to the self-interest of "glorious" accounts of war for soldiers (and poets): "Yet I love glory—glory's a great thing / . . . Thus in verse to wage / Your wars eternally, besides enjoying / Half-pay for life, makes mankind worth destroying." Byron anticipates Hunt when he directs his most vigorous satire at the readers of such softened versions of war. To be sure, canto 8 itself repeatedly indulges in sentimentalized heroic action—"The drying up a single tear has more / Of honest fame than shedding seas of gore" (3). It wraps up its own Iliadic siege with a humanizing variation on the tragic story of Priam and all his sons killed in battle.[16] Byron suppresses the sublime Homeric pleasure of crushing an enemy: *Don Juan*'s concluding reference to Hector (8.41) carries none of *The Iliad*'s deeper point that that hero's funeral is evidence of Achilles's greatness. But Byron undercuts even these gestures and repeatedly reminds his readers that the oceanic horror of war overwhelms its occasional upsurges of pity: in short, Byron mocks the evident limitations of Pope's strategy of pathos. Thus Suwarrow is the true agent here, not Juan. Therefore Byron mocks and attacks his readers for desiring such sentimentality and for only wanting war in a softened form: canto 8 begins with a satirical address to the "too gentle reader" (1); at its climax, the canto returns to this point where we discover that all modern readers suffer from such gentility: "Cockneys of London! Muscadins of Paris! / Just ponder what a pious pastime war is. / Think how the joys of reading a Gazette / Are purchased by all agonies and crimes" (124–25). That Byron managed to write anything at all, given his adherence to the impossible demands articulated for him by Godwin and extracted from him by Hunt, is surprising, and it is instructive to look to just how he managed it. Pope and Voltaire showed him the way, but his purpose was consistently to push their practices to an extreme, thus undoing his models from within. In good neoclassical fashion (and in spite of his earlier Romantic claims to empirical knowledge of war and killing), Byron bases his account on an enlightened French history of a modernizing, internally improving Russia, that is to say, his source was a Voltaire- or Fénelon-inspired history of a benevolent monarchy. His hero Juan's most memorable act in war, the rescue of a young girl amid the storming of a city, is borrowed from that history's hero: "Some of the incidents attributed to Don Juan really occurred, particularly the circumstance of his saving the infant, which was the actual case of the late Duc de Richelieu, then a young volunteer in the Russian service, and afterwards the founder and benefactor of Odessa, where his name and memory can never cease to be regarded with reverence" (261). Byron now recalls the neoclassical, not Godwinian, Fénelon, the one whose *Télémaque* was a blueprint for educating liberal heroes who would pursue such schemes. But Juan never goes on to such a prototypically epic founding of a new city in a progressive Russia. Instead the poem reverts to *The Iliad*, emphasizing not the building but the siege and destruction of Ismail. The driving agent is not the humane Juan or Richelieu, but a comic grotesque, whose success comes from his disdain for human life: "that lover of / Battles to the command, Field Marshall Suvaroff . . . 'You will take Ismail at whatever price'" (7.39–40); "'Let there be light,' said God, and there was light! / 'Let there be blood,' says man, and there's a sea!" (7.39). The narrative juxtaposes Juan's passive, accidental, fictional, and tear-sized heroism to the reality of Suwarrow's well-directed and oceanic destructive powers. This contrast results in the dismissal of Juan's one famous action as inconsequential amid the wider horrors unleashed by Suwarrow:

> If here and there some transient trait of pity
>   Was shown, and some more noble heart broke through
> Its bloody bond and saved perhaps some pretty
>   Child or an aged, helpless man or two,
> What's this in one annihilated city . . . ? (8.124)

Byron belittles the act of pity he grants to Juan, denies him the memorable act of epic foundation, and elevates, even as he deplores, the opposing Iliadic act of annihilation. (Most caustically of all, Byron tests his hero over his humane rescue of the girl, one that explicitly contrasts liberal and Homeric values. Juan is told to choose "between your fame and feelings, pride and pity" [8.101], but is subtly allowed a casuistical way out: someone else is found to guard the girl, while he goes off to battle, someone who swears not to abandon her to join in combat, as Juan does.) Byron thus evokes and undoes the neoclassical hope, whether in poetic or historical form. *Don Juan* invokes the Godwinian reading of Fénelon, turns back to the neoclassical one, and then returns definitively to Godwin's. As

Fénelon's Telemachus or Fénelon's royal pupil proved to be will-o-wisps, false ideals dramatizing their realistic impossibility, so Byron's Juan in this war episode functions as a symbol of empty uplift and self-serving casuistry when set against the ugly fact of Catherine's blunt but deadly tool Suwarrow.

Nonetheless, amid this ironical contrast, Byron seems to cling to some hope that the neoclassical project, if not in the person of his slender lover, then through imposing personages from history, can sometimes bear real fruit:

> Yet in the end, except in freedom's battles,
> Are nothing but a child of Murder's rattles.
> And such they are, and such they will be found,
>   Not so Leonidas and Washington,
> Whose every battlefield is holy ground,
>   Which breathes of nations saved, not worlds undone.
> How sweetly on the ear such echoes sound. (8.4–5)

These two stand as actual instances, however rare in the general course of history, of heroes who championed national freedom and whose means of heroic violence are excused by their glorious end. The poem once again falters, however, when it does not sustain its position with any actual details from "freedom's battles." The liberal ideal of the free nation-state still requires real killing, an unacceptable cost for Romanticism. When it comes to echoes sounding "sweetly on the ear," Byron swerves away, in the book's lengthiest digression, to yet another exemplary hero from history. But this figure's freedom rejects the ideology of the nation-state, and only here can Byron realize his pure ideal: "The General Boon, backwoodsman of Kentucky / Was happiest among mortals anywhere, / For killing nothing but a bear or buck, he / enjoyed the lonely vigorous, harmless days" (8.61). Here, "lonely, vigorous, harmless" succinctly establish that the one authentic hero whose "harmless" actions can be plainly described emphatically did not participate in any sort of nation formation, however enlightened.

This Boon episode covers seven stanzas out of a total of 141 in canto 8. It is the longest and most revealing example of the "digressive intertextuality" that Stabler sees as the distinctive feature of the two siege cantos, and it sums up their evasive neoclassical relation to war.[17] It provides a lengthy break from the horrors of battle that Byron had finally gotten to after so much delay. Such refreshment is obviously its purpose. Indeed, each of its main features—setting, action, family, mood—expands key pastoral motifs from the *Iliad*'s epic similes, where Homer flashes away from the death of some hero to a vision of his family busy with their peaceful chores on the farm. Pope's sanitizing translation inflated these moments, as rest from the wearying terror of killing. Byron's poem takes that practice to a breathtaking extreme. It also deepens the ideological implications of such pastoral escapism by folding in a measure of Rousseau-derived noble savagery: this "child of nature . . . shrank from men even of his nation" (8.63–64). Boon's freedom and innocence are a function of his separation from even the liberty-loving United States of America: "The free-born forest found and kept them free" (8.65). Byron's transition back to his main narrative abruptly dismisses Boon—"so much for Nature"—before sarcastically taking up its violent matter, "back to thy great joys, civilization" (8.68). In effect, Byron insists that civilization of the sort most closely associated with the economic and societal sophistications of the France of Voltaire and Fénelon necessarily entails their kind of falsely humanized warfare. But, as my introduction noted, Rousseau's *Emile,* which advocated a Locke-inspired education, sought to clear itself of even a whiff of the kind of aristocratic heroism advocated by Fénelon. He tried to replace *Télémaque* with Defoe's *Robinson Crusoe.* There is more than a hint of Robinson's flight from European culture, his fashioning of an isolated refuge, and his similarly vigorous and lonely articulation of a wholly unwarlike paradigm (secured, one recalls, by his own forest) in Byron's Boon. In its expansion of Popeian techniques of sanitization, its antinationalist referencing of Rousseau, and its echoing of Defoe's peace-loving capitalist hermit, this digression manages a multilayered refutation of the heroic pretensions and nationalist ideology of even Leonidas and Washington. Byron dismissed, evaded, and then finally rehearsed the liberal epic of free nation-states. His eventual performance, however, flirts with becoming an elaborate exorcism rather than a final summoning.

Still, though *Don Juan,* as the most important Romantic exemplar of war epic, simultaneously represents Romanticism's single most powerful deconstruction of the neoclassical defense of some heroic violence, there is a larger literary-historical context in which even Byron's expert dismantling underscores the persistent strength of heroic warfare's appeal. *Don Juan* begins by praising Pope and ridiculing Wordsworth's "The Thorn," one of the earliest exemplars of polemical rusticity, Byron's epic remains a thoroughgoing proponent of the same combination of empiricism, realism, and everyday bluntness set forth by Wordsworth. The theory and practice of the plain style are also principal features of cantos 7 and 8—and contribute directly to its version of epic and its Romantic deconstruction of liberal epic sanitization: "We only can but talk of escalade, / Bombs, drums, guns, bastions, batteries, bayonets, bullets— / Hard words, which stick in the soft Muses' gullets" (8.78). The critic Michael Murrin has asserted the end of serious war epic as early as the Renaissance, given the practical difficulties of rendering modern warfare poetically, but here we see Byron incorporating modern technical terms, as indeed Southey did in *Joan of Arc*. In a passage such as this, Byron not only insists on using technical language but also makes plain that the difficulty is one posed to poetic diction, not epic itself. Even Byron's numerous swerves into evasive sentimentality function, as I have argued, less as devices for themselves sanitizing war epic, less as actual occasions for readerly relief, and more as mockeries of neoclassical softening. His prefacing critique of Wordsworth's own use of the plain style to paper over with sentimentality the horror of child murder and madness is thus best read as an early signal of the ironic, self-exposing purpose such episodes will serve in his own later rendition of epic violence. In choosing a siege for his epic episode, Byron opted not only for a kind of warfare that most recalls *The Iliad*'s siege of Troy, but for warfare that typically offers more intense horror, criminality, and suffering than set-piece battles between opposing armies. Sieges in epic histories from Thucydides and Livy to Gibbon and Macaulay regularly provide far more vivid horror (largely owing to the presence of civilians, the effects of starvation and disease, and the climactic storming with its usual consequence of dire struggle, mass casualties, and raping and pillaging). Despite maneuvering onto such favorable ground for his polemical purposes and despite much rhetoric and some plain reality on the horrors of war, Byron's fundamentally anti-heroic narration indulges in evasion at several key moments, perhaps most obviously here toward its concluding climax:

> All that the mind would shrink from of excesses,
>   All that the body perpetrates of bad,
> All that we read, hear, dream of man's distresses,
>   All that the devil would do if run stark mad,
> All that defies the worst which pen expresses,
>   All by which hell is peopled, or as sad
> As hell, mere mortals who their power abuse,
> Was here (as heretofore and since) let loose. (8.123)

In sharp contrast, Napier, to whom I am now transitioning, crafted a fundamentally heroic narration that bluntly and vividly presents the detailed reality of war, especially in its numerous sieges. Out of many, the final assault of Badajos seems to most resemble Byron's Ismail. The narrative overflows with the kind of detailed horror that Byron glosses here at his climax. At the same time, Napier's narrative reenergizes the basic agonistic logic of Homeric sublimity, which is absent in Byron's lopsided slaughter. Indeed, Napier dwells on this siege and relates its realistic horrors with special relish because here Wellington's genius in attack met its match in the French commander's "direful skill" (3:370) in defense:

> Now a multitude bounded up the great breach as if driven by a whirlwind, but across the top glittered a range of sword-blades, sharp-pointed, keen-edged on both sides, and firmly fixed in ponderous beams, which were chained together and set deep in the ruins; and for ten feet in front, the ascent was covered with loose planks, studded with sharp iron points, on which the feet of the foremost being set the planks moved, and the unhappy soldiers, falling forward on the spikes, rolled down upon the ranks behind. (3:373)

Napier's lengthy account of Badajos easily matches and outstrips the horrific detail of Byron's Ismail, but its superiority in both realistic detail and heroic drama appears best in its own version of a concluding praeteritio. In Napier's case, the reader is summoned to picture what Byron, now unironically, allowed him to dispel:

> Let any man picture to himself this frightful carnage taking place in a space of less than a hundred square yards; let him consider that the slain died not all suddenly, nor by one manner of death; that some perished by steel, some by shot, some by water, that some were crushed and mangled by heavy weights, some trampled upon, some dashed to atoms by the fiery explosions; that for hours this destruction was endured without shrinking, and that the town was won at last; let any man consider this, and he must admit that a British army bears with it an awful power. And false would it be to say that the French were feeble men; for the garrison fought manfully and with good discipline, behaving worthily. Shame there was none on any side. Yet who shall do justice to the bravery of the soldiers? the noble emulation of the officers? Who shall measure out the glory of Ridge, of Macleod, or . . . (3:377–78)

Byron's list allows for sanitized ignorance. Napier's forces upon the reader imaginative detail beyond even the vivid realism he does provide: indeed, this passage's "let any man picture" represents a later edition's active personalization of the first's passive "let it be considered." Byron finally retreats to the kinds of evasions he otherwise attacks. Napier challenges the reader to see still more than he graphically supplies and still manages to make all that horror subservient to a heroic purpose. Napier erects an epic combat of two worthy opponents, and his narrative obeys the fundamental principle of epic in keeping the exciting agon of "awful power" right in front of his readers' eyes. We have the sublimity of Homeric epic, without the sanitization of Pope, and with a full measure of Romantic empiricism and plainness.[18] In the end, it is hard to tell whether Byron is exaggerating Popeian techniques to expose the mistakenness of their commitment to fashioning one good war epic—or is surreptitiously obeying Pope's core impulse not to look and not to indulge in the heady pleasures of the Homeric primal scene. For in Napier's steady gaze and deep plunge, we see the danger that all that horror might be only a stage upon which the epic scene of ultimate human triumph can occur—with the duly horrified reader nonetheless experiencing the yet deeper pleasures of the Homeric sublime. Napier inches far closer to this thrilling edge than Byron (or Southey) in his intensely heroic narrative of the epic agon of equality and aristocracy, France and England, Wellington and Napoleon, the British line and the French column, but he too balks at a final reunion with Homeric terror.

NAPIER'S COY ROMANTIC AGONY AND JOY

The piteous spectacle . . . completed a picture of war which, like Janus, has a double face.

—Napier, *The History of the War in the Peninsula*

For Napier, war narrative is as Janus-faced as war itself. He outdoes his rivals in both celebrating and bemoaning warfare, in both heroic intensity and humane disgust, and, most ironically, in both the progressive French-inspired rhetoric of war in the service of humanity and equality and the darker French rage over the recalcitrant backwardness of their Spanish enemies and victims. Sir William Francis Napier, to give him his due respect, author of "the finest military history in English" (Gooch 286), was active in the determined, sometimes desperate, political efforts to reform Parliament, even as he was laboring over his magnificent *History of the War in the Peninsula* (1828–40). Because of his military experience and his subsequent political journalism and, of course, his epic history, he was approached in 1831 by a group of reformers asking him to be the commander of a "national guard" to defend the process of democratic reform against the anticipated reaction. Given his history's vehement defense of Napoleon as Europe's champion of the "principle of equality" and the people against the reactionary "principle of privilege" and the aristocracy, Napier's evolving historical composition clearly echoed his increasingly active politics.[19] Indeed, it seems more than plausible that the rapid surge in the sales and recognition of his history's later volumes, after the first's slow start in 1828, had everything to do with the growing political strife that ended in 1832's exhilarating triumph of a peaceful liberal compromise just on the brink of conservative and antidemocratic victory—with the feared further descent into civil violence. So, too, such circumstances intensified the heady republican prose of his history—along with its denunciations of Spain's many failures, its horrific insurgency, selfish aristocracy, benighted church, and wretched people who ignorantly and savagely refused the equality offered by France.

Despite the intensity of his enthusiasms, Napier remains the gallant nobleman in his narration. In a revealing coda to his battle of Salamanca, Napier turns from matters such as the successful retreat of the French and the sudden wounding of Wellington to this anecdote:

> The wife of Colonel Dalbiac, an English Lady of a gentle disposition and possessing a very delicate frame, had braved the dangers and endured the privations of two campaigns, with the patient fortitude which belongs only to her sex; and in this battle, forgetful of everything but that strong affection which had so long supported her, she rode deep amidst the enemy's fire, trembling, yet irresistibly impelled forwards by feelings more imperious than horror, more piercing than the fear of death. (4:64)

(Hardy, whose double-sided representation of the glory and the horror of battle derives from Napier, dramatized this scene in *Dynasts* 3.1.2.) The aristocratic tone of this passage is palpable. Napier's gallant compliment to the lady's gentleness and delicacy combined with her remarkable patience and fortitude, his desire to record how her anxious love overcame her natural fear, and, most of all, his own polite allusiveness toward a horror that he will not quite show (is her husband dead? what does she see?)—all testify to an elaborate rhetoric of chivalry that contrasts with Napier's ideology of equality.

The pattern in this passage exemplifies how Napier's history alternates between a heroic, glorified appreciation for how war brings out the best in men (and women), and an apprehensive withdrawal from the horror and death that are the necessary conditions of that glory. More precisely, the passage demonstrates Napier's liberal confidence that "horror" and the "fear of death," the ugly elements of epic, can be made to dramatize the triumph—"more imperious," "more piercing"—of our higher, chivalric, noble, and humane attributes. Napier's insistence nonetheless remains suspicious—for it generally comes, as here, with an ever-nagging failure to show the terrifying Homeric details that are so happily overcome. Indeed, his rhetoric only goes so far as to touch upon horror and fear—and

consistently avoids the deeper challenge of terror altogether. Thus, to return to Pope's useful terminology, Napier gestures toward the moment of
terror itself, the scene of killing, but he effectively avoids the core problem
of terror by radically dividing it. On one side, the immediate scene of conflict and death, as with Madame Dalbiac, draws forth the most admirable
human attributes; and on the other, not shown here, it reveals men at their
most savage, degraded, and disgusting. In the first, death is actively present but unseen, while the humanized bravery and sympathy are admired;
in the second, the death is palpable, as the savage murderers kill their
victims, and the civilized disgust waxes strong. In sum, although Napier
attends to the Janus double face of war, one key result of this division is
that nowhere do the two merge into an Achilles. There is never any Homeric identification with the terrifying power of a heroic killer, and thus
nowhere are killing and heroism joined into one sublime whole. This
epic history—for all its Romantic vividness and honesty—thus contrives
its own unique system for obeying the fundamental impulse of Pope's
liberalization of Homer by refusing to admire the terrifying skill of the
hero-killer-conqueror. Still, the reference to some compelling emotion,
one "more imperious" and "more piercing than fear," just beyond the
boundary of his portrait, though here it must be love, also points to a repeated hinting at or coding throughout Napier's text of his willingness to
flirt with actual Homeric terror, with the agonistic thrill of triumphantly
killing a foe.

This key division shows up in a larger pattern of self-division throughout Napier's text: chivalric narration versus democratic ideology; admiration for bravery and disgust at death. This rivenness extends to its literary
inheritance. *The History of the War in the Peninsula* negotiates its specific
relation to the epic tradition through its self-conscious descent from the
great military history of Thucydides.[20] Thucydides told the history of a
larger Grecian struggle between the forces of aristocracy and democracy
in terms of a focused account of the contest of Sparta and Athens; Napier
applies the Thucydidean model in his narrative of the European contest
between what he labels "privilege" and "equality" by concentrating on the
war between England and France in Spain. Thucydides based his account
on his role as an active participant and his reliance on the accounts of
firsthand witnesses; Napier derives his authority from exactly the same
materials. But Napier's history and Napier himself reverse the political
dynamic of his Greek model. There the soldier-historian, though an Athe-
nian, favored the aristocratic principle represented by Sparta. Here the
soldier-historian, though an Anglo-Irish aristocrat, sympathizes with the
cause of France and the people:

> The hostility of European aristocracy caused the enthusiasm of repub-
> lican France to take a military direction, and forced that powerful na-
> tion into a course of policy which, however outrageous it might appear,
> was in reality one of necessity. . . . Whether aristocracy or democracy
> should predominate, whether equality or privilege should henceforth
> be the principle of European governments. . . . The French Revolution,
> intrinsically too feeble to sustain the physical and moral force pressing
> it down, was fast sinking, when the wonderful genius of Napoleon, baf-
> fling all reasonable calculation, raised and fixed it on the basis of victory.
> (1:15–16)

Spain is the stage upon which this great question will be decided between
the aristocratic English led by their own genius Wellington and the democratic French inspired by an absent but overseeing Napoleon. This situation, not surprisingly, greatly complicates the question of who the hero
of his narrative will be, and thus further extends this history's divided,
conflicted dynamic—and its avoidance of full Homeric terror.

For in Napier's narrative, both leaders ascend to the role of premier
hero. Neither is the Hector figure; neither will defeat the other. Napier
could not resist the general who emerged triumphant in every one of his
battles, the favorite of a victorious England, and the very type of the aristocratic ideal: "Yet shall his reputation stand upon a sure foundation, a
simple majestic structure, that envy cannot undermine, nor the meretricious ornaments of party panegyric deform. The exploits of his army were
great in themselves, great in their consequences, abounding with signal
examples of heroic courage and devoted zeal. They should neither be
disfigured nor forgotten, being worthy of more fame than the world has
yet accorded them—worthy also of a better historian" (1:v–vi). Such language of monumentality and authorial modesty is prototypically epic.[21]
But Napier's anxiety over Wellington's "meretricious ornaments of party
panegyric" sounds a discordant note and alerts the reader to the problem of Wellington's Tory politics. His history maneuvers on the difficult
ground of wanting to glorify Wellington's deeds, but of despising his political motives. Although Napier's Wellington largely fulfills the requirements of liberal epic, an aristocratic liberator of an oppressed land, the
final overthrower of a tyrannous oppressor, Wellington was not himself
Spanish; Spain was hardly free before its conquest; and the hero did not
fight for the cause of freedom and equality. Napier chooses Wellington,
but immediately makes clear his sense of having deeply compromised.
Napoleon, in contrast, is undoubtedly a foreign conqueror, one whose actions Napier cannot approve: "a deed that . . . was unhallowed either by

justice or benevolence" (1:17).[22] Yet Napoleon overthrew a corrupt and oppressive Bourbon regime and replaced it with an enlightened one. The
subsequent insurrection, of which the English took advantage, was the
work of national and religious bigotry and ignorance: "The Spanish insurrection presented a strange spectacle. Patriotism was seen supporting a
vile system of government; a popular assembly working for the restora-
tion of a despotic monarch; the higher classes seeking a foreign master;
the lower armed in the cause of bigotry and misrule" (1:v).[23] By definition,
Napoleon, as a foreign conqueror, cannot be the liberal hero, but strangely
should be, since what he overthrew was the very antithesis of Napier's
liberal, progressive, and humane ideal. Wellington fits the technical or
formal requirements of liberal epic heroism, while Napoleon is the clear
choice by Napier's ideological standard. Further complicating matters, despite being victorious, Wellington is portrayed as the lesser general and
the lesser man: once again Wellington is the hero on account of a technicality (he won), whereas Napoleon deserves the title of hero in reality (he
should have won).

Wellington, in his role as dubious liberator, triumphs over Napoleon's
lieutenants, not the man himself—"Napoleon, the greatest man of whom
history makes mention" (5:220). Wellington's brilliance cedes to the absent Napoleon's: "The battle of Wellington was the stroke of a battering
ram, down went the wall in ruins; the battle of Napoleon was the swell
and dash of a mighty wave before which the barrier yielded and the roar-
ing flood poured onward, covering all" (5:217). Wellington appears on the
ground leading brilliantly and winning again and again, but Napier repeatedly reminds the reader that Napoleon's brilliance, exercised from
afar and imperfectly heeded by his lieutenants, was greater, and that matters would have gone very differently if Napoleon had been at hand. Regarding one of the many missed opportunities, Napier comments, "On
such an occasion Napoleon would have been swift and deadly" (2:148).
Fortune, an epic goddess who frequently favors the lesser man and the
lesser cause, brings about an appropriately ambiguous result for this divided epic: "Fortune, however, always asserts her supremacy in war. . . . It
was not so ordained, Wellington was victorious, the great conqueror was
overthrown, England stood the most triumphant nation of the world. But
with an enormous debt, a dissatisfied people, gaining peace without tran-
quility, greatness without intrinsic strength, the present time uneasy, the
future dark and threatening. Yet she rejoices in the glory of her arms! And
it is a stirring sound!" (5:219). The divided heroism of this passage extends
to its curious rhythm and finely exemplifies the extended divisions of this
ceaselessly ambivalent text. For there is little irony in the concluding ex-

clamations. Napier is honestly proud, in an epic and aristocratic manner, of the "glory of [English] arms!" He is equally disturbed, as a political advocate of democracy and equality, by England's domestic weakness. His national pride exists side by side with his national shame, but without infecting one another, as if they were held in airtight compartments. Here England, just like its champion Wellington, is the formal or technical winner of epic played by the rules, but, at one and the same time, its actual historical condition, when judged by the standards of liberal progress, indicates a deeper reality of defeat. Napier's curious solution to the problematic demands of liberal epic is to separate the terms—to be sometimes "liberal" but not "epic," and sometimes "epic" but not "liberal." The problem becomes acute (and fascinating), when, as here, he performs this trick within the same paragraph, from one sentence to the next.

The liberal epic quest for the right hero thus satisfies itself, in Napier's history, with two choices, two equal heroes who never meet in Napier's narrative. Likewise his war narrative displays a divided, Janus-faced solution. Napier's history clarifies its epic pretension and prepares for its lengthy series of combats by dramatically setting up the great contest of France and England: "Thus the two leading nations of the world were brought into contact, at a moment when both were disturbed by angry passions, eager for great events, and possessed of surprising power" (1: 18).[24] Here Napier deploys an Achillean psychology of anger and desire for greatness. But by applying them to nations, not individuals, such a strategy, when it comes to the actual depiction of war, allows him to narrate their struggles without the possibility of death: we are allowed to admire the courage of the adversaries, to revel in the drama of their conflict, but never to indulge in the final terrifying pleasures of Homeric destruction. Napier goes on to glorify the English army as "the best equipped and best disciplined soldiers in the universe," while for their opponents, he supplies a daunting lineage: "an army in number nearly equal to the great host that followed the Persian of old against Greece . . . but they were trained in a Roman discipline, and ruled by a Carthaginian genius" (1:18).[25] When these epically inflated opponents meet in battle, Napier's accounts veer strongly toward an unironic vocabulary of "glory," "bravery," "honor," "gallantry," and "chivalry"—for the rivalry of these mighty hosts brings out the best in both: "The battle of Talavera was one of hard honest fighting, and the exceeding gallantry of the troops honored the nations to which they belonged" (2:164). The word "honest" here clarifies Napier's effort to portray the combats between the French and English almost as sporting events, whose law-of-war rules were honorably obeyed by both sides, and where fair fighting tested the fine mettle of true men and great nations.

When Napier does acknowledge the horror of such honorable, rule-bound warfare, it remains largely atmospheric and pictorial, eschewing the vivid individual dismemberment and death of Homer: "The allied host, righting itself as a gallant ship after a sudden gust, again bore onwards in blood and gloom; for though the air, purified by the storm of the night before, was peculiarly clear, one vast cloud of smoke and dust rolled along the basin, and within it was the battle with all its sights and sounds of terror" (4:61). The term "host" and the simile of the "gallant ship" keep the reader's eye focused on the army as a single unit, one that will, unlike the individual soldiers who remain unmarked despite the clarity of the air, assuredly survive the encounter. Rhetorically, the passage is most interesting for the way it begins with the clearly marked poetic simile of the ship in the storm, but then subtly naturalizes that simile by referring to the actual "storm" of the night before, the real "cloud" now looming over the host, and the "basin" in which it operates. Indeed, "basin" performs a double duty that becomes the interpretive crux of the passage and a revealing moment for the workings of Napier's relation to epic violence and combat. On the one hand, "basin" refers to the actual landscape and battle, and here the word contributes to Napier's effort to isolate or frame the conflict safely as a self-contained pictorial scene; on the other hand, "basin" recalls and reinforces the equally isolating and pictorial simile of the ship. Both senses work to the same end—one in the real world, one in the simile. But taken together they so powerfully isolate and pictorialize the epic action as to miniaturize it, making it a mock-epic battle, a toy ship in a small basin, safely vivid and trivially intense. Where Homeric narration directly presents death-in-combat and then looks again poetically with simile, Napier's epic and pictorial rhetoric merge the two in order to intensify, glorify, but also to divide and isolate and ultimately diminish his violent subject matter by rendering it unreal. As with Madame Dalbiac, Napier's narration here manages to look without quite seeing, to discern only the larger honor in a scene it knows is replete with many isolated horrors, and, finally, to flirt with terror, but never consummate that ultimate Homeric lust.[26]

On other occasions, Napier does individualize death and present it with realistic, Homeric vividness. In these cases, however, Napier renders it criminal, offensive, and barbaric:

The principal motive of action with the Spaniards was always personal rancor: hence, those troops who had behaved so ill in action, and the inhabitants, who withheld alike their sympathy and their aid from the English soldiers to whose bravery they owed the existence of their town,

were busily engaged after the battle in beating out the brains of the
wounded French as they lay upon the field; and they were only checked
by the English soldiers, who, in some instances, fired upon the perpetrators of this horrible iniquity. (2:166)

War as a proving ground between mighty opponents remains consistently at the level of the heroic and the metaphoric, but war seen as a
matter of "personal rancor" becomes an object of "horrible iniquity," vivi-
fied by the plain action of "beating out the brains." Napier strictly divides
these two: "personal rancor," like Achilles's toward Hector, does not enter
the epic combats of the British and French, the behavior of these nations
on the field of battle consistently does them "honor," and death remains
a largely unnoticed feature amidst grandiloquent scene-making; on the
other hand, when death becomes personal, it is ugly and shameful. When
death is linked to the political issues associated with the freedom and
degradation of the Spanish people, Napier's history loses its epic distance,
returns to its liberal principles, and becomes sickened by what it sees.

Spain and the Spanish thus embody the messy realities of history in
contrast to the rule-bound honesty and honor of the epic contest: on the
one side a Grotius-bound epic spectacle, on the other an illegal and horrific reality.[27] Napier's history cannot treat Spain as a blank stage upon
which the reader-viewer can safely regard the sanitized terror of epic
combat between its two honorable leviathans. Instead it becomes a reality shocking and horrifying in its distillation of the complications, paradoxes, passions, injustices, and personal violations of history. Despite the
fact that England and France have invaded Spain and taken advantage of
its civil war in order to pursue the most intense and violent episode of
their worldwide war, despite the fact that Spain and the Spanish people
suffer horribly as a result of this foreign war being conducted on their
soil, Napier's epic shields the French and English and consistently blames
the Spanish for their misfortunes. He argues that the Spanish, because of
their repressive illiberalism and aristocratic decadence, are to blame for
the initial French invasion: "No foreign potentate would have attempted to
steal into the fortresses of a great kingdom, if the prying eyes of the press,
had been ready to expose his projects, and a well-disciplined army present
to revenge the insult; but Spain, being destitute of both, was first circum-
vented by the wiles, and then ravaged by the arms of Napoleon" (1:iv–v).
Napier honestly admits Napoleon's craft and aggression, but the explanatory emphasis of this passage weighs heavily upon Spain. Blaming the
victim (and with rape imagery), Napier details the circumstances of a once
notorious French massacre of Spanish civilians. In his account, the Span-

ish assume most of the guilt. He emphasizes Spanish atrocities—"the French soldiers, expecting no violence, were killed in every street . . . and the hospital was attacked"; in sharp contrast to "many authors," he finds it "necessary to remark . . . that it was commenced by the Spanish" and that, though "the affair itself was certainly accidental," it was "not very bloody for the patriots" due to French restraint, but was terrible for the French due to Spanish barbarity: "The whole number of Spaniards slain did not amount to one hundred and twenty persons, while several hundred French fell" (1:31). Even if we accept Napier's numbers (and he gives only one source for hotly disputed facts), there remains the rhetoric of the precise number used to diminish Spanish losses and the vague "several hundred" to aggrandize French sufferings. This tone is typical of his repeated defense of French humanity and criticism of Spanish brutality.[28]

From the English perspective the Spanish are, in the words of Wellington, an "extraordinary and perverse people" (3:16), who inexplicably distrust the nobility of England's efforts on their behalf and contrive maliciously in their own misguided interest. Against Spanish assertions that "the deliverance of the Peninsula was the work of their hands," Napier retorts that "it is unjust to the fame of the British General, and injurious to the glory of British arms" (1:iv). He thus readily resorts to the conventional language of epic heroism to dismiss the historical claims for the efficacy of Spanish partisans and the "disjointed and ineffectual operations of the native armies" (1:iv). Napier details the intricate conflicts between various juntas and competing Spanish governments, in particular between the Regency and the Cortes, and always finds that the Spanish do themselves more harm than good: "Thus the convocation of the National Cortes, far from improving the posture of affairs, dried up the chief sources of revenue, weakened the army in the field, offended many powerful bodies in the state, involved the nation in a colonial war, and struck at the root of the alliance with England" (3:24). Even as they are suffering from foreign invasion, Napier angrily records their willingness to subject their colonies to the harshest treatment: "All parties agreed to push violence, injustice, cruelty, and impolicy to their utmost bounds" (3:23). Spain functions as a third term in this history, one placed between his determined effort to maintain the neat dichotomies of England and France. Upon this term Napier unburdens his liberal disapproval for the moral contradictions, disgusting atrocities, and human imperfections of war in its historical reality.

Thus, at the level of both its individual heroes and its larger theme, Napier's history is deeply conflicted over its evident joy in the unreality of its epic pictures and its obvious despair before its violent realities: heroes at once liberators and oppressors, warfare at once gallant and criminal, a narrative at one excited and embarrassed. Napier's final willingness to cede responsibility and credit the goddess "Fortune" for choosing Wellington over Napoleon hides his own responsibility in showing a textual preference for sanitized epic over historical shame. In contrast, Napier's "Spain" functions both as his recurrent admission of that shame and as his final unwillingness to devote his historical energies to analyzing what he clearly prefers not to confront. One is a fickle but beautiful goddess drawn from the realms of literary convention; the other a human sign of a reality that, in this history, remains inexplicable, undigested, and finally repugnant. Napier's Fortune is both his great explanatory agent for the vexed course of history, and his ready excuse for the pleasures of epic. And sadly for Spain, Fortune favors the brave! Napier's two great nation-combatants may do battle but never really face death, and, as a matter of fact, their leaders did not die in combat. The only real losers in the ultimate sense of that word are the Spanish people, whose sufferings are blamed upon their unheroic and illiberal selves. Despite its author's knowing the face of battle firsthand, as Pope and Gibbon did not, *The History of the War in the Peninsula* conscientiously offers up the pleasures of high rhetoric, high ideals, high drama, and vivid pictures by means of its radically bifurcated and thus civilized combat. It avoids cant and overcomes casuistry by looking intently with its two Janus faces at two sides of war, the heroic and the criminal, but this division cleverly forestalls the Humean-Homeric insight (always lurking just beyond the frame of his vivid word-paintings) that the highest heroism is also the blackest crime and the greatest pleasure.

THREE

EPIC HISTORY, THE NOVEL, AND WAR IN THE 1850S

THACKERAY, MACAULAY, AND CARLYLE

Boz, and men like Boz, are the true humanizers, and therefore the true pacificators, of the world. They sweep away the prejudices of class and caste, and disclose the common ground of humanity which lies beneath the factitious, social, and national systems.

—*Fraser's Magazine*, 1850

Ian Duncan advances a sophisticated case for the precise workings of the novel as mid-Victorian Britain's dominant form, particularly for the logic behind Dickens's inheritance of the mantle of Scott as the country's preeminent national author. Dickens succeeded to this enviable role without resorting to the kind of epic historical matters of war, combat, and violence that figured so prominently in Scott's ascension. The epigraph shows a contemporary articulating the basics of Duncan's thesis as Dickens "sweep[s] away the prejudices of class and caste": his powers echo those of a conquering hero out of an epic, but his novelistic action is peaceful and humanizing. Conversely, the critic Mary Poovey has ferreted out the bad faith in this myth of peaceful national unification carried out by novels and summed up in the career of Charles Dickens. Poovey's reading of David Copperfield as a rising novelist in the publishing market of the 1840s exposes the various limitations wrought by class and gender and papered over by the ideology of the novel and of the popular Dickens figure.[1]

Duncan grants that Dickens faced major rivals in the 1840s and 1850s, and this chapter will explore the three most prominent—Macaulay, Thackeray, and Carlyle. The first two burst upon the scene with spectacular successes in 1848, and each subsequently turned to the matter of heroic warfare to aggrandize his literary position. During these years, Carlyle established himself as the leading man of letters and "writer's writer." But Carlyle, though he advocated, in the name of industrial modernity, moving beyond the traditional epic emphasis upon war, shored up his cultural pretensions by steadily increasing the place of warfare in his writings. He predicted a catchy, new heroic theme of "tools and the man" and "captains of industry" for a factory nation, but he crowned his oeuvre with a massive narrative of the "arms" variety. The years after 1848 saw Carlyle devoted to what proved to be his most successful work, *The History of Frederick the Great* (1858–65). There the attention to battle easily dwarfed that of his earlier narrative histories. Meanwhile, Macaulay reworked his *History of England* (1848–59), whose early volumes chronicled politics, society, judicial tyranny, and the largely peaceful Glorious Revolution, to focus upon William III's heroic contest with Louis XIV. Finally, Thackeray lavished his greatest preparation (of which reading Macaulay was a major part), fullest planning, artistry, and compositional care upon his heroic-historical novel *Henry Esmond* (1852), which he frequently stated was his best work. Of his major novels, *Henry Esmond* was the only one to be written and revised entirely before publication and to be published as a whole, not in parts. Thackeray claimed that his fame would rest mainly upon this novel of an honorable military man amid revolution and European war. Trollope, perhaps his most important admirer, ranked it as the greatest novel in the English language, and he was not alone.

Thackeray's labors over this novel tracked his parallel work on a lucrative series of literary and historical essays, *The English Humorists of the Eighteenth Century* (1853). Swift, Addison, and Steele appear in the essays and as characters in his novel.[2] Fielding, Thackeray's obvious antecedent, is praised enthusiastically. The analysis highlights Thackeray's evolving views on the novel. He remains impressed by the epic and historical dimensions of Fielding's achievement, as his approving citation of Gibbon's prototypically epic encomium suggests: " 'Our immortal Fielding,' Gibbon writes, 'was of the younger branch of the Earls of Denbigh, who drew their origin from the counts of Hapsburgh. The successors of Charles V may disdain their brethren of England, but the romance of "Tom Jones," that exquisite picture of humor and manners, will outlive the palace of the Escurial and the Imperial Eagle of Austria' " (200). Macaulay's reviews influenced these essays even more than his history colored the novel. These works and the subsequent novel align Thackeray closely with Macaulay and Carlyle as a man of letters working in a more serious literary mode than the still often maligned (by Macaulay and Carlyle) popular novel. Again Poovey provides the most incisive analysis of the cultural status of the Carlylean "hero as man of letters" in the 1840s: both the man of letters and the novelist relied on an egalitarian claim that anyone could succeed through hard work and genius in the modern marketplace of letters, but this pious assertion obscured the advantages of education, class, and gender. Even the successful were reduced to the condition of alienated laborers, especially the novelists working in the common form of the novel issued in parts. They wrote to the market. Their monthly allotments were rewritten according to popular demand and reedited by interfering publishers. Their position allowed for hefty remuneration, but at the price of losing both status and control over their work. What Poovey does not note, however, is how epic history resisted this model or, rather, raised the condition of the typical man of letters well above it. Carlyle and Macaulay graduated to successes in this form. It offered considerable monetary success, literary independence, and a high cultural status. Thackeray carefully modeled his own self-elevation after theirs. *Henry Esmond* came the closest of any Victorian novel to being a scholarly epic history. (Thackeray likened his researches for *Esmond* with Carlyle's concurrent work on *Frederick*.) Indeed, Thackeray seriously considered moving on from that work to an actual history of the period, perhaps even a continuation of Macaulay's *History of England*, much as Smollett continued Hume's. Dickens provides a telling contrast here. His historical novels did not seek to rise above his contemporary ones (*A Tale of Two Cities* [1859] is clearly a breather after the strenuous effort of *Little Dorrit* [1857]), and his foray into history was the decidedly modest *Children's History of England* (1869). But his rivals did seek to rise above the authorial double-bind of success and alienation symbolized by the Dickensian novelist—by turning to heroic histories of war.

This chapter will trace Macaulay's, Thackeray's, and Carlyle's sometimes parallel and sometimes divergent career paths as they moved further into such matters in the 1850s. The careers of Macaulay and Thackeray, in particular, mutually influence and implicitly comment on one another. Critics have neglected this fascinating interplay between two of the premier writers of the mid-Victorian period. It reveals the fundamental tension between liberal epic and the novel. No Victorian novelist wrote as much about war, nor with as much mastery of the liberal epic tradition, while no Victorian historian proclaimed so loudly his intention to novelize grand narrative history. Even so Macaulay moved on from his initial success by pushing his novelized history further and further back toward epic militarism and heroic biography. In contrast, Thackeray receded from rivaling Dickens (and Macaulay and Carlyle) because he retreated from the kind of full engagement with epic content that he once envisioned. Andrew Miller has neatly summed up Thackeray's decline in terms that recall Poovey's reading and Trollope's lament: "Dickens can be seen as Lukacs's capitalist and Thackeray as his worker" (146). But this novelistic imprisonment was exacerbated by Thackeray's heroic plan of escape— followed by his epic defeat. Ultimately, Macaulay saw himself as one of the greatest authors in English, indeed European, literature. Thackeray marked his descent into triviality in his declining sales, his strained inter-action with friends and fellow writers, and, more surprisingly, in the often self-mortifying pages of his own novels. One was an epic somebody; the other a novelistic nobody.

Finally, this reversal of fortunes is yet more problematic, because dur-ing these years the intellectual and political economic critique of war reached its peak, both in popular culture and in high theory. Carlyle's *Past and Present* (1843), Mill's *Political Economy* (1848), Buckle's *History of En-gland* (1857–61), and Spencer's *Principles of Psychology* (1855) all vigorously articulated the conviction that war, while not quite gone, had become not just an uglier crime, but an irrational political-economic event. At the Crystal Palace Exhibition of 1851, commercial competition programmati-cally replaced rivalry in war. War itself was no longer regarded as a phe-nomenon ruled by heroic agency, but one subject to the quiet workings of economic reality: population, industrial output, finance. In short, the nobody's invisible hand had supplanted the somebody's bloody one. As Miller documents, however, Thackeray disdained both his novels and the Crystal Palace as symptoms of an increasingly flattened, interchangeable, and empty commodity culture: "The very variety of objects Thackeray ex-hibits behind the windows of his novel . . . only sets off with greater clar-ity the monochromatic, unitary understanding to which he finally reduces them" (51).

THACKERAY'S DUBIOUS AMBITIONS

I hate story-making incidents, surprises, love-making, etc. more and more every day. . . . The last number contains the incidents which should have been filled out into 6. It is a failure that's the fact, and I intended to make a great victory—Farewell Virginians.

—Thackeray, *Letters*

The story of Thackeray's strenuous ascent and lazy decline is an old chest-nut of literary history that Peter Shillingsburg meticulously documents. Janice Carlisle presents the most fine-tuned analysis of its pivot point: "*The Newcomes* is indeed Thackeray's 'last great work'; *The Virginians* (1857–59), an equally 'great falling off'" (142). Carlisle attends to the "de-cline of his powers as a novelist" (142) and highlights his failures in terms of his increasingly self-undermining handling of narrative techniques. It is illuminating, however, to chart Thackeray's decline from a different perspective, in terms of his plans to rise above the novel altogether or to import the seriousness of epic and war into his narratives—and not to update and improve Scott's novels, but to adapt and rival Macaulay's history. In the 1850s Thackeray realized he could earn the money he needed through this more esteemed genre of grand narrative history. Two interrelated purposes will therefore guide my argument on the rhetoric and reality of novelistic versus epic content in Thackeray's writings and career. First, I will follow the correlation between Thackeray's rising ambitions and his decision to fold more extensive representations of warfare into his novels. Thackeray regularly belittled the content and conventions of the typical novel, especially his own, and lamented his inability to move beyond such stuff. At the same time, he scoffed at and resisted Dickens's ascent via his dubious adoption of the simple verities of the most perfect goodness and blackest villainy. His conservative solution was to seek the traditional prestige of epic history and heroic warfare. Thus *Vanity Fair* readily internalizes and accepts the anti-novelistic sentiments expressed by the leading conservative and heroic writer of the day; Thackeray's trivializing preface to *Vanity Fair* nods to Carlyle's contemptuous judgment on that rising form: "Of no given book, not even of a Fashionable Novel, can you predicate with certainty that its vacuity is absolute; that there are not other vacuities which shall partially replenish themselves therefrom, and esteem it a plenum" (*Biography* 2:388). This logic is woven into the title and central themes of Thackeray's novel. Second, I will demonstrate both Thackeray's thorough familiarity with the conventions of liberal epic, its neoclassical stylistics and its methods for justifying some wars, and his equal mastery of the increasingly powerful critique of that same cultural project. Thackeray's dilemma intensifies Scott's: he internalized an even lower opinion of the novel genre, though it had ascended since Scott; and he harbored even stronger ethical and intellectual objections to epic history, though it too had risen with the triumphs of Macaulay and Carlyle.

This crisis appears vividly in his troubled relation to the hero, whether a Dickensian waif or a Carlylean berserker. His Byronic contempt for the war hero is a prominent strand in his historical novels: Frederick, Napoleon, Wellington, and Marlborough all become objects of scorn, their great actions castigated as selfish and criminal. But, as his admirer Anthony Trollope observed, when Thackeray first resolved to challenge Dickens for novelistic preeminence on ground first cleared by him ("Of late novels had grown to be much longer than those of the old well-known measure. Dickens had stretched his to nearly double the length" [26]), he moved from the short and bitter novel with an anti-hero, *Barry Lyndon* (1844), to a vast canvas famously without any hero at all, certainly not one of the Dickens type: "The central character with Dickens had always been made beautiful with unnatural virtue,—for who was ever so unselfish as Pickwick, so manly and modest as Nicholas, or so good a boy as Oliver?—so should [Thackeray's] centre of interest be in every respect abnormally bad" (26). "Bad" refers to Becky Sharp. Her unprincipled social ambition harkens back to Barry's machinations more than to any neutral "without." Becky's Dickensian foil Amelia, however, is rendered annoyingly bland in her goodness (Thackeray privately disdained this creation), while, as Trollope admits, "Captain Dobbin does become the hero, and is deficient" (93). Major Dobbin (he gets a promotion) and Colonel Esmond, the similarly modest but more securely heroic protagonist of his next novel in this upward ascent, remain "deficient" in large part because, though Thackeray turns to military men for heroes, he retains deep objections to what they do—and his strategy of avoidance compounds their shortcomings. So, too, Thackeray shows a keen awareness of the developing intellectual critique of war. He acknowledges the vast scale of its destructiveness and horror, but insists that it is not actually important, that it in the end it never accomplishes much of anything. The arc of his novels articulates a generic double-bind through its attitude toward heroes, whether epic or novelistic, and their wars or trivialities: his novels attack historical war heroes, but belittle novelistic ones; they then turn to aggrandizing their fictional protagonists by making them ever more honorable soldiers, even as they exhibit an ever more precise critique of war, war heroes, and the sneaking liberal epic strategies for redeeming them.

One can readily explain this dilemma in terms of Thackeray's great theme, his repeated cry that all is vanity: he is bored by novels, but sickened by epics. Still, this double-bind offers more interesting (and illustrative) implications than such reinforcement of his vanity theme. It registers a strong dissatisfaction with the novelistic tendency, symbolized by Dickens, to portray its heroes as too good in their humanity and too weak in their agency. Though his war novels always conform to the liberal epic project of correcting the primitive pleasures of domination, Thackeray nonetheless remains more interested than most of his contemporaries in thematizing the human interest in the thrill of watching a hero, a Barry or Becky, sometimes kill or, more often, dominate and rule over others. The shock of Barry's often defeated and abused wife's final effort to return to her master, or Lord Steyne's exclamations of delight at Becky's domineering feats are only the most obvious examples of Thackeray's willingness to flirt with this dangerous delight.

Thackeray follows the conservative and epicizing tradition of Fielding. Novels such as *Barry Lyndon, Henry Esmond,* and *The Virginians* have an eighteenth-century setting and affect an eighteenth-century style through their fictional first-person narrators. Thackeray's stylistic renown peaked with the earnest pastiche of *Henry Esmond*.[3] In his parallel scholarly study, Fielding enjoys near constant praise: "Such a brave and gentle heart, such an intrepid and courageous spirit, I love to recognize in the manly, the English Fielding" (*English Humorists* 207). Tillotson demonstrates that Thackeray shares with Fielding a penchant for adapting "epic imagery" to their novels (a practice handed on to Thackeray's disciple Trollope).[4] These novelists share a conservative project (Thackeray's and Trollope's version of it is openly nostalgic) to defend, even champion, the category of "gentlemen" against various Christian, democratizing, or economic critiques— by Richardson, Smollett, or Dickens. All three also explore the tension between the values of their gentlemanly heroes and the more dangerous epic hero of the classical texts they invoke and often seem to admire. Their novels move closer to the concurrent liberal epic tradition, and this trend is reinforced by their various attempts to realize Fielding's classically normalizing definition of the novel as a "comic epic in prose." Fielding's key term "comic" sometimes means satirical or anti-heroic (*Barry Lyndon*), sometimes mock-epic (large portions of *Vanity Fair*), and, eventually, serious heroic epic rendered novelistically (*Vanity Fair* on occasion, Henry Esmond in general, and *The Virginians* in theory). Readers and scholars have long noted that Thackeray's individual novels constitute one larger narrative. The usual evidence involves the novelist's web of recurring characters and families (the Barrys, Crawleys, and Esmonds), of narrative sequels, and of fictional characters who become narrators or editors and vice versa (Pendennis is first a character and later an editor-narrator of *The Newcomes;* Rachel Esmond is a marginal narrator-editor and then a character subject to another's narration). Such gestures give a unity to Thackeray's novels not common among the Victorians. Thackeray's disciple Trollope is a major exception, though his version takes the simple form of sequels. My assertion of a Thackerayan metanarrative is therefore hardly unique, but it is both more focused and more evanescent: there is a coherent, meaningful progression from novelistic anti-epic to a combination of mocking, childish, and serious epic to a somberly serious and adult epic ("glum" is Thackeray's disparaging characterization) to, finally, a planned tragic epic with high cultural appeals to leading historians such as Carlyle, Macaulay, and Prescott. This progression sheds much light on the most common academic interest in Thackeray, his descent from Dickensian canonicity, especially because Thackeray's collapse becomes a matter of his ethical and intellectual second thoughts that led to the abandonment of his high literary ambition.

The tension between the consistently anti-heroic tone of the individual novels and their larger development toward the heroic tells the basic story. In *Barry Lyndon,* Thackeray reworks Fielding's *Jonathan Wild* (1743). Both novels extrapolate from the traditional tale of the captured pirate challenging Alexander the Great: the latter's greatness becomes a function of the scale of his piratical crimes. Thackeray's version technically differs from Fielding's by having its villain-protagonist tell a first-person memoir: a short novel with a lying, thieving, gambling, wife-abusing, murdering narrator. Barry comically portrays his crimes as evidence of his greatness, but then Thackeray unironically allows him to be a trustworthy ethical critic of the hypocrisies, tyrannies, and aggressive wars of its "Alexander": "This [criminal] destroyed two sentinels to get his liberty; how many hundreds of thousands of his own and the Austrian people did King Frederick kill because he took a fancy to Silesia? . . . I am not going to give any romantic narrative of the Seven Years' War" (100–101). Lyndon's own criminality, as with Alexander's pirate, gives him real insight into Frederick's putative greatness, but a passage like this one does not read as a minor tyrant's comment on a major, but as a pronouncement filled with authentic moral fervor. The novel thus contrives to be anti-epic in every possible way—in its tawdry slightness, its ironic unreliability, its cynicism toward heroic rhetoric, and then in its earnest telling truth to power.

Despite similar contempt, *Vanity Fair* manages to become more epic and more heroic. Becky is "bad" and Dobbin "deficient," but the novel strives for Dickensian scope and cultural dignity and for a degree of affirmation not found in the previous novel. There is nothing to compare to the rank cynicism of *Barry Lyndon,* and its schoolyard episodes rise to the authentically epic in mood and action. Even so, the critique of war itself remains. It also ambitiously extends beyond *Barry Lyndon*'s older ethical and aesthetic denunciations of the selfishness of war heroes and the horror of battle to include more up-to-date intellectual attacks. As with the equation of Barry and Frederick, *Vanity Fair* juxtaposes Becky's career as an adventurer with Napoleon's. But though the novel relishes Becky's agency and her ability to dominate and manipulate, it repeatedly questions the effectiveness of Napoleon's power. Above all, *Vanity Fair* discredits the fundamental epic presumption that wars are the important, decisive matters of history, their heroes its agents, and their results determining for men and nations. Thackeray's treatment of Waterloo in chapter 32 turns away to a mock-epic account of Jos Sedley's cowardice back in Brussels. His summary judgment of the offstage battle refuses any epic decisiveness to all its sound and fury: "Its remembrance rankles [Frenchmen]. . . . There is no end to the so-called glory and shame, and to the alternations of successful and unsuccessful murder, in which two high-spirited nations might engage. Centuries hence, we Frenchmen and Englishmen might be boasting and killing each other still, carrying out bravely the Devil's code of honour" (405). Thackeray's novel sees this, the greatest of all battles—or any coming greater one—as a matter of shame and empty boasting that, in the real world, will only serve to provoke another round. The novel undercuts the cultural claims of epic decisiveness by drawing it into its own world of spinning novelistic vanity and meaninglessness.

Nonetheless Thackeray returned compulsively to epic warfare—and with an intensified effort to treat its heroic violence seriously. His increasingly powerful critique of epic somersaulted into a more vigorous grab after it. The crux of this process comes with *Henry Esmond* and its sequel, *The Virginians*—the same marked as "the great falling off." *Henry Esmond*'s literary ambitions dramatize themselves most clearly in an extensive *Aeneid* parallel: the narrator-hero has, like Aeneas refounding Troy in Italy, built a country house, Castlewood, after the original in England. Such an analogy is just one method by which the novel moves beyond the deficient heroism of Major Dobbin.[5] Esmond has all the high-born heroic qualities Dobbin lacks plus all his virtues and a Vergilian pedigree. As is typical of liberal epic, Esmond finds means not to show his prowess on the battlefield. Unlike Aeneas, for example, we are never troubled by seeing him conquer the natives. Although he steadily rises in rank and numerous officers refer to his valor, he declines to mention his actions therein: "The present narrator . . . does not intend to dwell upon his military exploits" (240). He pauses, however, to record his humanity, tolerance, and brave opposition to war crimes: "The only blood which Mr Esmond drew in this shameful campaign, was the knocking down an English sentinel with a half-pike, who was offering insult to a poor trembling nun" (241).

What his extensive soldiership does is make him an eloquent, firsthand denouncer of the horrors of war. Lyndon's experience and criminality render him an especially potent critic of Frederick's, while Esmond's experience and humanity make him an equally incisive critic of Marlborough, observer of the inhumanity of war and, conversely, strong proponent of its new rules and codes. These criticisms extend to the shortcomings of heroic poetry and history:

"I admire the license of you poets," says Esmond to Mr. Addison. . . . "I admire your art: the murder of the campaign is done to military music, like a battle at the opera, and the virgins shriek in harmony, as our victorious grenadiers march into their villages. Do you know what a scene it was? . . . What a triumph you are celebrating? what scenes of shame and horror were enacted over which the commander's genius presided, as calm as though he didn't belong to our sphere? . . . To my belief the leader cared no more for bleating flocks than he did for infants' cries, and many of our ruffians butchered one or the other with equal alacrity. . . . [The battle was] hideous, bloody, and barbarous . . . [,] ugly and horrible, not beautiful and serene. Oh, sir, had you made the campaign, believe me, you never would have sung it so." (297)

(In an 1843 essay on Addison, Macaulay praised this once famous poem for its "manly and rational rejection of fiction," judging it a critical turning point in literary practice away from Homer's emphasis upon bodily strength and individual prowess and thus from any "nauseous" poetic "narrative . . . made up of hideous wounds" and toward a truer and more civilized view of war as "a science" [*Essays* 3:32, 33]. Macaulay particularly admired Addison's focus upon "the firmness of [a leader's] mind which, in the midst of confusion, uproar, and slaughter, examined and disposed everything with the serene wisdom of a higher intelligence" [34]. Addison's "Campaign," which "ranks high among the poems that appeared between the death of Dryden and the dawn of Pope's genius" [32], marked for Macaulay a major advance in the evolution of liberal epic and poetic diction, and, as I will show in detail below, this poem's techniques directly shape Macaulay's own intellectualized style for narrating battles. Of course, he relies on precisely the tactics that Thackeray's narrator-hero Esmond here savages. In a further complication, Thackeray's understanding of Addison as expressed in his 1851 critical study and this 1852 novel was initially guided by Macaulay's earlier essay. This example is one of the clearest demonstrations of how heroic poetry shaped the writing of self-consciously realistic and progressive military history. It also dramatizes how a novelist, though envious of a contemporary historian's fame and attentive to his opinions, could not follow him down an epic path he saw as inhumane and self-deluded.)[6] Thackeray's novelistic realism carefully prepared for this attack on Addison's heroic poem by first showing Esmond experiencing the same critical feelings on the field of battle: "Why does the Stately Muse of History, that delights in describing the valour of heroes and the grandeur of conquest, leave out these scenes, so brutal, mean, and degrading, that yet form by far the great part of the drama of war?" (277). Similarly, his reflections upon Marlborough's demeanor ("always cold, calm, resolute like fate") in the face of the battle's various horrors such as peasants "slaughtered" or batteries "vomiting flame and death" (277) anticipate his subsequent reaction to Addison's Marlborough by reworking and darkening Addison's famous comparison of Marlborough to an avenging angel of God (a simile Macaulay's essay lengthily defends).

Esmond's outrage over heroic poetry and the "stately muse of History" not showing the horrors of war and his challenge to tender readers ("you, pretty maidens" [277]) who wish to read of war without being shocked are, however, anachronisms that reveal Thackeray's intensifying aversion to epic even as he finds himself attempting to embrace it.[7] The Romantics—Scott, Hunt, and Byron—championed such critiques of bookish neoclassical coyness in the name of their own blunt empirical plainness. Hunt and Byron in their poems and Scott in his novels, though not in his poems or epic history, castigate readers for their desire not to be shown the ugly horror of war. Thackeray is their heir. But his carefully historicized narrator should not have attacked but rather appreciated Addison's then up-to-date humanism in softening his account: the eighteenth-century concern was to defuse any readerly tendency to sympathize with heroic killing, to resist the Homeric thrill of inspiring terror. Disgusted horror at the reality of warfare appears in Fénelon, Voltaire (particularly in *Candide*'s [1759] satirical exposé), Smollett, and Godwin, but as a critical keynote of the higher genres, it is a later development. Indeed, the principal eighteenth-century critique of Addison's poem came from Voltaire, whose heroic poem on Fontenoy celebrated a great French victory over the English thirty years later. In its notes, Voltaire points to the excessive "bile" in Addison's poem, which was a model for his own, but a model to be further refined. In it the French not only win but conspicuously follow the laws of war, as the English do not, and even triumph in politeness when, at the climax, they graciously insist that the English fire first. For the eighteenth century, the battlefield had become the place to display the proud advance of civilized behavior, not the inhumane horrors of mutilation and death. *Fontenoy* was one of Voltaire's most popular works.[8]

But angry disgust, not polite refinement, is the strongest war note in *Henry Esmond,* though Thackeray labored to re-create an accurate early eighteenth-century style and attitude. The implied critique of Addison as knowing war from books, not from lived experience, is also largely a later development: at the time, it was the project to refine linguistically the terror of war as found in premodern accounts. If such anachronisms in *Henry Esmond*'s literary criticism have gone unnoticed, its attack on the English great man Marlborough, is among its most commented-upon features. My conclusion will take up Winston Churchill's very different account of his ancestor—and his arguments with Macaulay and Thackeray. Here there are two key points. First, Thackeray was so influenced by Macaulay's history that he reworked the substance of *The History of*

England's most damaging (and dubious) indictment of Marlborough into a second instance of the same crime. Macaulay uncritically relied on dubious evidence to claim that Marlborough betrayed the details of a British expedition, which resulted in defeat and much loss of life, in order to destroy the reputation of a rival general. Thackeray invented a further case of such betrayal: "[Marlborough] meant to sacrifice the little army, which covered this convoy, and to betray as he had betrayed Tollemache at Brest" (329). Both were pursuing one of the most common of liberal critiques of great generals, namely, that they behaved for their own selfish purposes, not for the greater good of their nation. Thus Esmond also accuses Marlborough of rushing into Malplaquet, the bloodiest battle in these wars. He "won" at the cost of twice the number of casualties as the French: "This dreadful slaughter very likely took place because a great General's credit was shaken at home, and he thought to restore it by a victory" (361). By this time, Macaulay was well out ahead of Thackeray in reshaping his *History of England* into a more positively heroic account of epic war. I will turn to Macaulay's refashioning of his narrative in the second part of this chapter, but here merely observe that *Henry Esmond*'s negative version of epic was both inspired by Macaulay and left behind by him.

In turn, when Thackeray planned and began *The Virginians* in 1856, Macaulay's hugely successful third and fourth volumes had appeared—filled with stirring accounts of battles and sieges in Ireland and the Low Countries. Thackeray fashioned his novel to match Macaulay's William III with its own George Washington, a higher figure in the liberal pantheon. In addition, Thackeray went in the other direction by choosing a darker epic plot: "I shall lay the scene in Virginia, during the Revolution. There will be two brothers, who will be prominent characters; one will take the English side in the war and one the American, and they will both be in love with the same girl" (Ray 382). This scenario modernizes perhaps the starkest classical epic theme, which comes to us in Statius's spectacularly bloody *Thebaid*. Thackeray never lived up to this dire conception: all the planned horror and terror were emptied out, leaving only a domestic novel. The brothers love different women; never join in battle; and live happily ever after. Very late in the novel, he toys with them meeting in a minor skirmish, but even that does not come off, for which both (they never harbored any animosity) are relieved. The narrative is mainly taken up with matters that long precede and have little to do with the Revolution. He delays and evades showing his fictional protagonists at war (to his own disappointment). Washington fails to rival William III's heroics and appears primarily in a domestic drama (the brothers fear he is courting their wealthy widow mother), to the disgust of Thackeray's American admirers. They appreciated the accuracy drawn from the author's travels in the country and his avoidance of the usual British scorn for the young republic, but they resented this novelistic reduction of the national hero. Thackeray's grand ambitions fizzled out in a maze of anecdotal episodes. The war sneaks in as an afterthought, appended to the last number, not occupying the last six as he once hoped, certainly not the whole thing as he originally planned.

What makes this failure all the more interesting is that Thackeray goaded himself by repeatedly evoking his rivalry with leading contemporary narrative historians who celebrated war heroes and faced the tragedy of battle.[9] It had become an expected exercise of any serious military historian to inspect closely the actual locations of the set-piece battles. We will see that Macaulay embarked upon his heightened recasting of his *History of England* by ostentatiously drawing up a long itinerary of such hallowed spots—and then solemnly visiting them, while rereading epic poems. Thackeray toured Blenheim, the setting of Addison's poem and Esmond's disgust, as part of his work on *Henry Esmond*: "[I] returned from a trip to Blenheim which I wanted to see—an hour by rail and 2 hours by a coach further—What I was pleased with was to find that Blenheim was just exactly the place that I had figured to myself except that the village is larger" (*Letters* 218). As the anxiousness of "just exactly" suggests, this "research" was done after the novel's completion. Later in the year, indeed in the month just before the novel's publication, he carefully noted that Carlyle was "away in Germany looking after Frederick the Great" (225). Carlyle was visiting various battlefields before he wrote. This work resulted in meticulous accounts of warfare of which he was later very proud and widely acclaimed. Such implicit self-comparisons dramatize Thackeray's lurking sense of his weakness and laziness in contrast to these historian's serious efforts.

The Virginians begins by explicitly evoking comparison with another leading historian of the day (note the envious honoring of Prescott's secure fame):

> On the library wall of one of the most famous writers of America, there hang two crossed swords, which his relatives wore in the great War of Independence. The one sword was gallantly drawn in the service of the King, the other was the weapon of a brave and honoured Republican soldier. The possessor of the harmless trophy has earned for himself a name alike honoured in his ancestor's country and his own, where genius such as his has always a peaceful welcome. The ensuing history reminds me of yonder swords in the historian's study at Boston. (1:1)

These swords are still on display at the Massachusetts Historical Society. It is often forgotten that American literature made its first strong impression upon Europeans with the Boston Brahmin Historians—Prescott, Bancroft, Motley, Parkman, and Henry Adams together established a remarkable canon. (In 1866 Kingsley similarly began his fierce historical novel *Hereward the Wake* by evoking Motley: American historians were a common benchmark for epic achievement, even in England, as were contemporary French historians.[10]) Thackeray's novel did not, however, rise to this opening self-challenge. Later *The Virginians* returns to a narrative touchstone, confesses its author's inferiority to Carlyle, and then further abases itself by abusing Richardson:

> It is a mercy for both of us that Harry Warrington did not follow the King of the Borussians, as he was minded to do, for then I should have had to describe battles which Carlyle is going to paint: and I don't wish you should make odious comparisons between me and that master. Harry Warrington not only did not join the King, but he pined and chafed at not going. He led a sulky useless life, . . . He dangled about the military coffee-houses. He did not care for reading anything save a newspaper. . . . He even thought novels were stupid; and, as for the ladies crying their eyes out over Richardson, he could not imagine how they could be moved by such nonsense. (2:114)

Much like his "hero" Harry, who encapsulates Thackeray's waxing frustrations, we see the novelist first aspiring to epic, then castigating epic matter as ethically, even intellectually, backward, but then showing even greater contempt for the emptiness of novelistic conventions and trivialities. Macaulay, Prescott, and Carlyle first appear within and around *The Virginians* as certain benchmarks of cultural success, as high standards of literary ambition; then figure what he, like his protagonist, had once been "minded to do," but seemed fearful of entering upon; and, finally, symbolize what he could look back upon as something he failed to live up to in his once ambitious but now empty novel—and career.

One might read this melodrama of meta-disappointment as the grandest example of Thackeray's central theme of vanity: the plain realism and humane ideology of the novel are employed to denigrate the horror and selfishness that constitute heroic greatness, while the prestige of epic is marshaled to scatter the trivial conventions and little happenings propagated by the novel. In good New Critical fashion, Thackeray's formal double-bind fits perfectly with his meaning: all is vanity. In this light, my argument inverts Nicholas Dames's study of Thackeray and the rise of celebrity culture: "Thackeray's fiction [documents] the gradual formation of a new category of public experience called the celebrity, unmoored from the political or aristocratic underpinnings of older forms of public notoriety and increasingly unlike earlier conceptualizations of fame" (24–25). Even Napoleon is reduced to a popular celebrity, not a historical great man, in Dames's reading of Thackeray's stance. This view, however tempting, ignores the evidence that Thackeray envisioned rising to an epic military narrative. This ambition was wedded to his effort to leap over even the importance of "political and aristocratic . . . notoriety" to the more fundamental glory of the war hero. His pathetic failure in this endeavor, rather than his hollow successes with novelistic ephemera, largely accounts for Thackeray's declining reputation versus Macaulay, Carlyle, and Dickens. Literary history has made much of the rivalry with Dickens that began with the spectacular success of *Vanity Fair* and peaked with their concurrent fictional autobiographies: both *Pendennis* and *David Copperfield* appeared serially and concluded in November 1850. But Thackeray's rambling, plotless, and increasingly ineffective novels after *Henry Esmond* and *The Newcomes* tell the story of a one-sided contest. By 1954 a major study could begin by claiming that "most of the critics whose work achieves print dislike or slight [Thackeray's novels]" (Tillotson 5). Such a result was obvious by the time of his death in 1862: he received no honorific Victorian "life and letters" biography such as the hero-worshipping culture produced for Dickens, Macaulay, and Carlyle. Even his committed defender Trollope compares the two and finds Thackeray, like his heroes, sadly wanting in self-confidence: "He seems to me to have been dreaming ever of some high flight, and then to have told himself, with a half-broken heart, that it was beyond his power to soar up into those bright regions. I can fancy as the sheets went from him every day he told himself, in regard to every sheet, that it was a failure. Dickens was quite sure of his sheets" (19–20).[11]

Thackeray's role as Dickens's chief rival was largely to play a straw man. His status now serves to confirm the towering achievement of Dickens, but his contemporary decline in relation to the epic historical successes of Carlyle and Macaulay weighed far more on his mind and authorial self-fashioning. Thackeray's aborted plan to carry on Macaulay's history after his untimely death in 1860 testifies both to his abiding admiration for *The History of England* and to his deepening dissatisfaction with his chosen genre. Macaulay's and Carlyle's waxing successes in the 1850s pointed forward to their canonical enshrinement after their deaths and contrast with Thackeray's sorry tale of decline. Virginia Woolf, a vigorous spokesperson for the Modernist view of the evolving English canon, continued to rate Macaulay and Carlyle with Gibbon, while famously wondering what had happened to poor Thackeray. During the years of Thackeray's retreat,

Macaulay acknowledged only one peer in the preeminent form of narrative history, namely, Thucydides, and confidently recorded his hilarious pleasure at the sight of a bookseller advertising David Hume as a mere introduction to his own great work: "I have at last attained true glory" (G. O. Trevelyan 2:165). That success rivaled the popularity of the novel, even those of Dickens, while it basked in the assurance of its obvious cultural superiority, but it was only able to achieve that success and that assurance by adopting the poetic dictional devices of an Addison, Pope, and Gibbon—the very tricks of sanitization that Thackeray and his Esmond, in their self-doubting humanity, could never quite stomach.

MACAULAY: EPIC HISTORY, NEOCLASSICAL POETICS, AND NOVELISTIC REALISM

October 27—Huzza! Good news! Lucknow is relieved. Delhi ours. The old dotard a prisoner. God be praised. Another letter from Longman. They have already sold 7600 more copies. This is near 6000 pounds, as I reckoned, in my pocket. But it gratified me, I am glad to be able to say with truth, far, very far, less than the Indian news.

—Trevelyan, *Life and Letters of Lord Macaulay*

The epigraph demonstrates the potential for heroic narratives of war to succeed handsomely in the modern literary marketplace. Macaulay provides a particularly interesting case study of this phenomenon, because traditionally his achievement has been explained in terms of his novelization of content. His appeal to the novel, however, was undertaken primarily as a means of reinvigorating the traditional style of epic history, not for jettisoning its inherited content and forging ahead into social history. Bakhtinian formal and stylistic crises had modern solutions, but modern ethical and intellectual objections to heroic violence vexed Macaulay's desire to center his narrative around it. He worked successfully to rescue narrative history from the sterility of what he identified as its inherited neoclassical rules. At the same time, Macaulay reconceptualized his history to include as many battles as possible and was ultimately obliged to preserve, despite his romantic-novelistic program for a realistic plain style, the decorum neoclassicism had devised for the presentation of violence in his battle pieces. He wanted to write a best-selling epic history; he appealed to the modern ease and facile realism of the novel to make that happen; but he retained exactly those neoclassical elements he otherwise scorned in order to preserve the essential but troubling matter of violent combat.[12]

Macaulay worked on his history from the mid-1840s through his death in 1859, and it appeared in installments in 1848 (volumes 1 and 2), 1855 (volumes 3 and 4), and, after his death in 1859, 1861 (volume 5). These dates and volumes are frequently said to center upon 1851, the year of the Great Exhibition, the historical climax of international liberalism's conviction that the Homeric bloody hand had ceded to the Smithian invisible one. The Crystal Palace represented the architectural version of a great commercial epic of peace—as here, for example, in the peroration of one of Victorian England's most popular military histories, Sir Edward Creasy's *Fifteen Decisive Battles of the World* (1851): "We see the banners of every civilized nation waving over the arena of our competition with each other. . . . No battlefield ever witnessed a victory more noble than that which England, under her Sovereign Lady and her Royal Prince, is now teaching the peoples of the earth to achieve over selfish prejudices and international feuds, in the great cause of the general promotion of the industry and welfare of mankind" (418). Creasy was a contemporary of Macaulay. The rhetoric of his popular history and the grand event evoked in its last lines equally inform the progressive boosterism of Macaulay's great work. Both narrate a tale of the epic victory over war itself, but do so in terms of a series of battle narratives: the end of epic is located in the triumphant era of the present-day narrator-historian. Furthermore, within *The History of England*'s progress toward its final peace, there is a paradoxical intensification of heroic warfare. For there is another historical center for Macaulay's volumes, 1854–56, the years of the Crimean War, and 1857, the Indian Rebellion, which underscore its imperial and militarist strain. The first two volumes focused upon the Glorious Revolution of 1688, a pragmatic compromise that foreshadowed the peaceful commercial prosperity of 1851, and happily climaxed in the successful flight of James II rather than, for example, his Homeric death at the hands of Macaulay's hero William.[13] *The History of England*'s later volumes, however, were reconceived more in line with Creasy's aggressively popularizing militarism. It became less a focused history of a successful and relatively bloodless national rebellion against a tyrant, and more an expansive narrative of William's titanic struggle with Louis XIV, a contest for empire and hegemony focused upon battles and heroic agency:

> On the 8th of February, 1849, after the publication of his first two volumes, he writes in his journal: "I have now made up my mind to change my plan about my History. I will first set myself to know the whole subject; to get, by reading and travelling, a full acquaintance with William's reign. I reckon that it will take me eighteen months to do this. . . . I

must see Londonderry, the Boyne, Aghrim, Limerick, Kinsale, Namur again, Landen, Steinkirk." . . . The notes made during his fortnight's tour through the scenes of the Irish war are equal in bulk to a first-class article in the Edinburgh or Quarterly Reviews. (2:142–43)

This list of place names indicates the battles and sieges that will figure prominently in the coming volumes of Macaulay's narrative. Even the bloody conquest of poor little Ireland will be recast as part of the march of democratic freedom and national self-determination. Beyond such ironies, this history came to rely on generating the imperial pleasure of domination—for much of the enjoyment of *The History of England* for its vast Victorian readership lay in its story of how the firm foundations for their world empire, including their resplendent Indian jewel and their muddy Irish embarrassment, were laid by the results of these battles. Thus, too, in the present, Macaulay rejoiced over the sales of his history, rejoiced yet more over England's victories in India, but combined the two into one celebration of prosperous national liberation at home and imperialist conquest abroad.

Sometimes said to have been outsold only by the Bible, Macaulay's *History of England* was and remains one of the most impressive successes in the history of best-sellerdom. Macaulay's ambitions, however, rose above mere sales to matters of his cultural status and his nation's progressive achievements in peace and war. Though Gibbon now looms over him in what remains of the canon as the greatest historian-writer in the English literature, at the time Macaulay was certain of his preeminence.[14] Furthermore, though Dickens was then, as now, heir to Scott's popular throne, at the time Macaulay saw himself as a truer, better successor— and with some reason.[15] Macaulay, like Carlyle, commenced his career as a writer of essays on history and culture in the 1820s when Scott was at his peak—just before his embarrassing bankruptcy and descent into hack self-exploitation. In their early writings, they envied Scott's unprecedented cultural and popular celebrity and recognized that it was earned primarily through the Waverley Novels. Macaulay, again like Carlyle, ultimately rejected the allure of that most easily popular form and sought a higher, more traditional, more secure status by writing epic in the form of epic history—and history centered not on the experience of some Scott passive hero tossed about by larger impersonal forces within a novelistic world, but history determined by the agency of great men, or the one greatest man.

In 1824, years before he began work on *The History of England*, Macaulay wrote a short essay with a long title: "A Prophetic Account of a

Grand National Epic Poem, to Be Entitled 'The Wellingtoniad,' and to Be Published A.D. 2824." Macaulay's jeu d'esprit works a simple variation on a long-standing tradition of mocking neoclassical epic conventions. Though such mockery intensified with the rise of Romantic poetry, it goes at least as far back as Pope's own satirical accounts of literary sterility. Still, neoclassicizing epic poems by serious poets continued to be written.[16] The currency of Macaulay's essay, therefore, testifies to the persistence of war epic, indeed neoclassical war epic, well past 1789. After outlining the biography of the future English-speaking poet (from China) and comically reviewing its conventionalities (Mars is Napoleon's secret father), Macaulay summarizes the twelve books. Book 2's synopsis is the shortest, but most revealing: "Napoleon carries his narrative from the battle of Leipzig to his abdication. But, as we shall have a great quantity of fighting on our hands, I think it best to omit the details" (*Essays* 1:122).

Four years later in another essay, "On History" (1828), Macaulay engages in a serious version of his earlier comic romp. He again advances a critique of neoclassical style, whether poetic or historical. He outlines a history that would achieve "immense popularity" and leave "the new novel [lying] uncut" (*Essays* 1:303). Though he appeals to the example of Scott for lessons in how to use "those fragments of truth which historians have scornfully thrown behind them" (307) to enliven his narration, Macaulay remains intent on plans for histories of great heroes, battles, and empires. His sober argument eventually brushes up against his earlier comic one, when he joins his admiration of Scott to a critique of history's neoclassical snobbery: its "aristocratical contempt" for memoirs, its "code of conventional decencies as absurd as that of the French drama," its sense of the "majesty of history" that cannot be bothered with the "trivial" (303). He thus works to incorporate a Romantic or novelistic plain style, one attentive to lowly realistic detail, in explicit contrast to the neoclassical tradition of decorum and good taste. Still, Macaulay here outlines a plan for bringing the enlivening charms of the trivial to a history of the deeds of great men, of the revolutions of nations, and of the origins of empires.

A curious anomaly in his two essays' larger argument now becomes clear. Though he strives to free epic history from conventional constraints and complains that "interesting circumstances are omitted or softened down" (303) because of the "majesty of history," when it comes to epic violence, Macaulay clings to all the conventional strategies that lie at the root of neoclassical epic's dignified proprieties. Thus, to return to book 2 of the "Wellingtoniad," he claims, "I think it best to omit the details [of fighting]" (122): such omission being the simplest of all liberal epic devices, and a neoclassical sin Macaulay otherwise scorns. Thus, too, his comic essay stages a conventional epic combat, Wellington versus Napoleon, but, of course, Napoleon lives: "The heroes fire their pistols; that of Napoleon misses, but that of Wellington, formed by the hand of Vulcan, and, primed by the Cyclops, wounds the emperor in the thigh" (126). In the last book, Napoleon, apprehended wearing the "belt of the Duke of Brunswick," is about to suffer the fate of Turnus, but "piety and hospitality . . . restrain [George III's] hand" (126). These examples are from a comic essay, not an epic poem or history, but if we turn to a survey of the 2,500 pages of *The History of England,* filled as it is with battles and sieges, there is much outraged commentary on the horrors of war, much self-satisfied commentary on the humane advances in its conduct, and some irate condemnation of the occasional relapse into barbarism. But there is almost nothing graphic: certainly nothing comparable to what regularly appears in Macaulay's sources, whose vivid details he otherwise prides himself on rescuing from conventional oblivion.

One of the best extended examples of Macaulay's success in ostentatiously removing the illiberal thrill of violent killing from his battle-laden epic history appears at the conclusion of the battle of Landen, one of the bloodiest in the seventeenth century and the deadliest in *The History of England.* After dutifully foregrounding humane condemnation of this fact, his narrative retains and exploits the terrifying drama of kill-or-be-killed that invests any epic single combat, minor skirmish, major battle, or war. Though narrated in a heroic manner ("the whole greatness of William's character appeared" [4:325]), Macaulay chooses, at its climax, to redirect the reader's attention to a tellingly different version of the epic agon. He breaks away from combat and killing into a comparison-contrast of the two opposing generals, William and Luxemburg. This juxtaposition, while remaining a kind of combat, emphasizes its liberal purpose to show "the progress of civilization" in terms of how, in the modern world, mental power has superseded bodily strength. Macaulay surveys past examples of heroism, all focused on size and strength and the ability to kill with one's hands, and contrasts them with the sickliness and deformity of his two modern heroes—distinguished by their cool ability to command amid such confusion: "It is probable that among the hundred and twenty thousand soldiers . . . the two feeblest in body were *the hunchbacked dwarf who urged forward the fiery onset of France, and the asthmatic skeleton who covered the slow retreat of England*" (4:327, my emphasis). In exquisitely balanced prose, here coquetting with the heroic couplet, Macaulay fashions a facsimile of epic warfare's essential drama, but in a manner that adheres to the deeper purposes of poetic diction by allowing him to avoid looking at the graphic violence surrounding warriors of the old-fashioned muscular variety. This intellectual redirection is precisely the innovation Macaulay singled out for special praise in Addison's "Campaign." His review essay on Addison outlined ten years in advance exactly the overall conception and detailed rhetoric on display here in his history:

> There are at this day countries where the Lifeguardsman Shaw would be considered a much greater warrior than the Duke of Wellington. Bonaparte loved to describe the astonishment with which the Mamelukes looked on his diminutive figure. Mourad Bey, distinguished above all his fellows by his bodily strength and by the skill with which he managed his horse and his sabre, could not believe that a man who was scarcely five feet high, and rode like a butcher, could be the greatest soldier in Europe. (*Essays* 3:32–33)

The exaggeration—Napoleon was five feet six inches, not "scarcely five feet"—confirms the rhetorical and sanitizing purpose, though "butcher" neatly resists any pure refinement. Macaulay concludes with a further elegance not found in Addison for registering the horror of all the death at Landen, death that he would not show being dealt out by hero to hero. He looks away from the killing itself and concentrates instead upon its pitiful aftereffects. He indulges in Popeian similes and beautiful imagery as a more refined suggestion of horrific reality: "The next summer the soil, fertilised by twenty thousand corpses, broke forth in millions of poppies. The traveller . . . could hardly help fancying that the figurative prediction of the Hebrew prophet was literally accomplished, that the earth was disclosing her blood, and refusing to cover the slain" (4:328). This "Flanders Fields" avant la lettre shifts from terror and killing to pity and death. It sees the conventionally beautiful and vaguely imagines the horrific.

Such apologetics extend to Macaulay's account of the siege of Londonderry where his self-consciously progressive version of war narrative and heroic patriotism must somehow justify the long history of British oppression of the Irish. This siege climaxes the larger account of war in Ireland found in chapter 12 of volume 3, itself the principal fruit of Macaulay's more epic, heroic, and war-centered reconception of *The History of England*. Now he not only bases his style of heroic narration upon neoclassical verse, but the very content of his siege narrative is drawn from a contemporary poem: "My authority . . . is an epic poem entitled the Londeriad" (3:114). Macaulay struggles to justify his use of this obviously biased, frankly sectarian poem as a legitimate source for both the hard facts and the heroic mood of that war. He elevates his narrative by comparing Londonderry to Troy: "The truth is that there are almost as many mythical stories about the siege of Londonderry as about the siege of Troy" (157). This dubious exaggeration reveals Macaulay's ambitions. Eventually, he overcomes his scruples and insists that the legends as well as the facts of Londonderry form a crucial part of the greatness of modern England, a key aspect of England's heroic sense of itself and its progressive civilizing mission. Now, however, that liberal logic and mission are firmly expressed in a narrative of war, of aggressive conquest, not glorious revolution. His illogical reliance upon *The Londeriad* pushes him to downplay that poem's climactic moment of epic violence as a genre-induced falsification, when that moment inevitably claims a spot in Macaulay's historical narrative, but to embrace that same moment as one worthy of epic glory, when it becomes a patriotic symbol in a memorial church. He suppresses the recorded reality of graphic violence, but elevates the legendary heroism of *The Londeriad*'s epic sword. Most tellingly, he allows the victory to serve as a final judgment upon the English and the Irish: "It was a contest . . . between nations; and the victory remained with the nation which, though inferior in number, was superior in civilization, in capacity for self-government, and in stubbornness of resolution" (189). Civilization and heroic self-determination—backed up by superior lethality on the battlefield—are the positive forces celebrated by this self-consciously progressive epic.

In the elaborate peroration to his heroic narrative, Macaulay echoes Creasy's evocation of the Crystal Palace, but whereas there the symbolism evoked an alternative to war epic, here it falls back into that mode in a manner that also shades over into suggesting that Macaulay's *History of England* aspires to be a grand architectural embodiment of England's heroic legends and relics:

> Five generations have since passed away; and still the fall of Londonderry is to the Protestants of Ulster what the trophy of Marathon was to the Athenians. . . . The cathedral is filled with relics and trophies. . . . The white ensigns of the House of Bourbon have long been dust: but their place has been supplied by . . . the fairest hands of Ulster. The anniversary of the day on which the gates were closed, and the anniversary of the day on which the siege was raised, have been down to our own time celebrated by salutes, processions, banquets, and sermons . . . and the sword, said by tradition to be that of Maumont, has, on great occasions, been carried in triumph. (3:190–91)

There is a long-standing analogy between epics and great buildings and great cities, one which Ruskin had recently brought to its literal fulfillment in his architectural epic *The Stones of Venice* (1851–55), and which Macaulay evoked in his early "On History": "At Lincoln Cathedral there is a beautiful painted window, which was made by an apprentice out of the pieces of glass which had been rejected by his master. . . . Sir Walter Scott, in the same manner, has used those fragments of history which historians have scornfully thrown behind them" (1:307). In these concluding comments on the siege of Londonderry and that heroic city's memorializing cathedral, Macaulay's ambition to make a cathedral-like epic history, not just a novel-like window or Crystal Palace–like exhibition hall, is abundantly clear: fictional novelistic color has been redeployed for epic monumentality. Five generations have passed in England since the Glorious Revolution of 1688, but Macaulay has come to believe that the legends of epic loomed larger than the realities of history. Here Maumont's sword reappears, not as a fraud or as an example of *The Londeriad* poet's lack of invention (for, according to Macaulay, the poet conventionally "imagines" his hero Murray slaying the French champion Maumont with the sword), but as a worthy part of an invaluable heroic "tradition." Macaulay's history becomes more war- and hero-focused as it proceeds, and in defiance of its own humane rhetoric; it drifts back into a close literary relation to epic poetry; its relation to novelistic narrative becomes progressively limited to opportunistic efforts to decorate its narrative with trivial, but enlivening details.[17] Red is reserved for beautiful poppies and similes, not for the actualities of anatomical wounding. Wars are won by superiority in liberal "self-government," not by superiority in killing. In the case of the climactic combat, in the account of Maumont's death, Macaulay scrutinizes and rejects the *Londeriad*'s detailed action (personalized there in the hand of the hero Murray and the sword preserved in the epic cathedral) and replaces it with a suitably depersonalized and bland event: "He was struck in the head by a musket ball, and fell a corpse" (3:157).[18]

CARLYLE'S LIBERAL ILLIBERALISM

It was the bloodiest battle of the Seven-Years War; one of the most furious ever fought; such rage possessing the individual elements; rage unusual in modern wars.

—Carlyle, *Frederick the Great*

In contrast to the self-defeating Thackeray's stylistic integrity and historiographical laxity, Macaulay and Carlyle prospered in the 1850s by embracing long-established sanitizing techniques, though both regularly denounced them, and by following up-to-date research requirements, particularly the meticulous battlefield tour, which both proudly proclaimed. The result of such false rhetoric and hard labor was Carlyle's longest history and greatest financial success, a fact surprising even to Carlyle:

December 28th, 1858.—Book was published soon after my return; has been considerably more read than usual with books of mine; much babbled of in newspapers. No better to me than the barking of dogs. . . . Officious people . . . put reviews into my hands . . . but it would have been better not, so sordidly ignorant and impertinent were they, though generally laudatory. . . . However, the fifth thousand is printed, paid for I think—some 2,800L. in all—and will be sold by-and-by with a money profit. . . . One has to believe that there are rational beings in England who read one's poor books and are silent about them. . . . I am fairly richer at this time than I ever was, in the money sense. (Froude 2:228–29)

In addition to these earnings, Carlyle's official biographer asserts a grand claim for this history's central feature: "There are no mistakes. Military students in Germany are set to learn Frederick's battles in Carlyle's account of them—altogether an extraordinary feat on Carlyle's part" (2: 227). Much as with Macaulay, however, Carlyle's turn to military history came in the wake of more innovative writings that struggled to transcend such traditional matter: *Past and Present* (1843) articulated the progressive insight that "tools and the man" would replace "arms and the man" as the modern world's central epic theme; *The French Revolution* (1837) partially anticipated that claim by having precious little to say about its military dimension, though its political focus resists economic explanations; his biography *Oliver Cromwell* (1845–50) is far more interested in Cromwell's speeches than his battles; but his culminating *Frederick the Great* (1858–65) reverses this pattern. It finds little to be impressed by in all of Frederick's writings (especially the scurrilous French poetry), but much to admire in his deeds of war. It attends minutely to all his many battles, then scants his years of state-directed economic reconstruction. A revealing feature of *Frederick the Great*'s battle pieces in this regard is how Carlyle's lengthy descriptions of the landscapes, which he frequently supplements with a quoted description from a "tourist's note"—the tourist being himself incognito—linger over evidence of agricultural improvement and industrial progress from Frederick's day to Carlyle's: "The country is now much drier than in Friedrich's time; the human spade doing its duty everywhere: so that much of the Battle-ground has become unrecognizable, when compared with the old marshy descriptions of it" (6:381). In this "past and present" drama, the spade has productively transformed the field of battle; Carlyle has brilliantly literalized his arms into tools prophecy-adage; but then the epic historian refuses the tourist's insight, marches back to the past, meticulously reconstructs some once-famous,

now forgotten battle, and passes over the dull truths of the spade for the allure of the sword.

When it comes to style, not substance, though the early Carlyle re-echoed Thackeray and Macaulay in critiquing neoclassical sanitization, he eventually (and quietly) adopted those techniques along with their associated Burkean sublimity to soften the horrors of violence as he moved ever further into war narrative. Thus Carlyle lauds Shakespeare's historical plays as a great English "National Epic" (*Heroes* 109), from which he singles out "the battle of Agincourt . . . as one of the most perfect things . . . we anywhere have of Shakespeare's" (110). In contrast to his embrace of Shakespearean energy and truth, Carlyle dismisses the grace and skepticism, the rules and sentiments, of Pope and Gray: "Gray's fragment of Norse Lore, at any rate, will give one no notion of it;—any more than Pope will of Homer. It is no square-built gloomy palace of black ashlar marble, shrouded in awe and horror, as Gray gives it to us: no, rough as the North rocks, as the Iceland deserts, it is" (34). "Rough" (along with "honest") are frequently deployed by Carlyle to set up a masculine contrast to the contrived and feminized falsifications and of the neoclassical style of epic heroism that, as we have seen, was regarded by the English as essentially French, and was especially despised by Carlyle for that reason: the basic logic of *Frederick the Great* arises from the dichotomy of his truly heroic Prussia and Voltaire's, Louis XV's, and, above all, Madame de Pompadour's flimsily civilized France, whose feminized overrefinement of all things, but especially warfare, is repeatedly damned by Carlyle under the allegorical rubric "Dauphiness Bellona"—and sent packing by the rough hands of Frederick's severely drilled men. But, as we have also seen, the honest roughness of Homer or of primitive epic generally was not a matter of granite rocks as opposed to ashlar blocks, vast deserts versus vast cities, and not a matter of nature's true sublime versus man's contrived one, but of epic centered on the pleasure of sympathizing with killing to which Pope and Burke responded by transforming that affect into pity for the dying and into the sublimity of feeling, not causing, fear and awe.

Carlyle's version of epic fully participates in this fundamental effort of liberal epic. Even when he characterizes one particularly violent battle "as the old Nibelungen has it, 'a murder grim and great' going on" (6:135), his response to such matter is invariably some variation upon the excuse he gives here for not following the lead of the Nibelungs: "No human pen can describe the deadly chaos which ensued in that quarter" (6:134). When he evokes the *Iliad* in his account of a particularly grim siege, his deeper un-Homeric purpose shines forth: "It is by no means our intention to describe the Iliad of miseries, the agitations, terrors and disquietudes, the

tribulation and utter harrowing to despair, which poor Frankfurt underwent incessantly from that day forward, for about five weeks to come" (7:60). Over and over again, Carlyle evokes close combat as an unintelligible chaos best seen through metaphors that keep the face of battle at a safe distance. Only afterward do his narratives leave poetry for hard facts by obsessively registering the statistics of the killed or wounded, thereby certifying the superior industrial warfare efficiency of the Prussian soldiers and celebrating how willingly they sacrificed themselves for their hero-captain-king. On one of the rare occasions when he actually shows one brave man sacrificing himself for king and country, he betrays his anxiety by swerving into melodramatic exaggeration. He first narrates the death of Schwerin thus: "Five bits of grape-shot, deadly each of them, at once hit the old man; dead he sinks there on his flag; and will never fight more" (6:135). Later he directly quotes his less emphatic and more realistic source, as if to confess his pathetic fabrication: "But before he could succeed in the attempt, this excellent man, almost in a minute, was hit with five case-shot balls, and fell dead on the ground" (6:144). Carlyle makes "a minute" into an "at once"; he adds, without sanction, the pathetic-patriotic detail of the hero falling "on his flag"; finally and tellingly, he unrealistically insists, again without sanction, that each one of the five shots was deadly—and reinforces this superheroic surmise with a sobbing echo, "deadly . . . dead." One of the even rarer equivalents showing Prussians doing Homeric killing, not Popeian dying, is, no surprise, a matter of killing at a distance, and includes an even greater exaggeration: "[Prussian] cannon batteries enfilade the thick masses of Russians at a frightful rate ('forty-two men of a certain regiment blown away by a single ball')" (6:387).

This example comes from the war's "bloodiest battle" invoked by the epigraph. Carlyle, as usual, there strives to poeticize and distance its bloodiness and "rage unusual," as he insists, "in modern wars." He thus introduces it with a headnote whose poetic imagery will consistently be used to soften, or just avoid, the narrative's potential graphic detail—"Theseus and the Minotaur over again,—that is to say, Friedrich at Handgrip with Fermor and his Russians (25th August, 1758)" (6:383). This classical myth sets up an allegorical (and racial-ideological) battle between advancing civilization and half-human chaos, but it also becomes a poetical device, which "over again" confesses and "that is to say" explains, for regularly avoiding any realistic details of the "handgrip": "Half of the Minotaur is gone to shreds in this manner; but the attack upon it, too, is spent: what is to be done with the other half of the monster, which is again alive; which still stands, and polypus-like has arranged a new life for itself . . . ?"

(6:389). Carlyle's narrative here moves from one metaphor to another, and that remains its strategy throughout, except for the occasional lapse into the graphic realism of one Prussian cannonball killing forty-two Russians.

Late in the history, Carlyle's ever-present determination to look away from his subject matter's violence results in a much grander departure from his hero's endless battling with Austria over Silesia (it now belongs to Poland) to a much vaster contest, the battle between France and England for North America:

> Wolfe silently descends; mind made up; thoughts hushed quiet into one great thought; in the ripple of the perpetual waters, under the grim cliffs and eternal stars. . . . Next morning . . . Wolfe, with his five thousand . . . stands ranked (really somewhat in the Friedrich way, though on a small scale); ready at all points for Montcalm [;] . . . and in a space of seventeen minutes, have blown Montcalm's regulars, and the gallant Montcalm himself . . . into ruin and destruction. . . . Wolfe himself died in it, his beautiful death. . . . There have been far-sounding Epics built together on less basis than lies ready here, in this Capture of Quebec;—which itself, as the Decision that America is to be English not French, is surely an Epoch in World-History! (7:142–47)

Francis Parkman, perhaps America's greatest epic historian, had already noted these possibilities—and had begun the lifework that would climax with this same decisive battle on the Plains of Abraham, though Parkman would extend the liberal project by emphasizing the tragic fate of Montcalm, whom he explicitly makes the Hector of his more pitiful Iliad. Carlyle stresses the falseness surrounding Gray's transformation of Norse legend's epic sublimity into the paraphernalia of Burkean horror and awe, but in escaping from his monstrous mini-epic into a vision of a seemingly smaller, but actually greater, contest, Carlyle betrays both his weariness with Frederick's wars and his penchant for landscape sublimity and "beautiful death" in the form of his hero's noble sacrifice. As he says, moreover, Wolfe's battle plays out "somewhat in a Friedrich way," and this claim reflects that Carlyle's Friedrichan battles are just bigger, longer, and uncut versions of this one, though inevitably fought for vanishingly smaller stakes. Those battles, too, suppress realistic details of killing, cultivate the Ruskinian-Burkean sublime along with the pity and beauty of self-sacrifice, and thereby flee Homeric terror.

If we return to his theoretical championing of epic presented with Homeric or more than Homeric honesty, we find that even there, though Carlyle may begin with a rhetorical emphasis upon the rugged realism of "a veritable Norse rage" registered in how Thor " 'grasps his hammer till the knuckles grow white,' " he nonetheless quickly moves away from such anatomy (never returning to that hammer's actions) to highlight the "beautiful traits of pity too, an honest pity" (*Heroes* 34). The adjective "honest" is Carlyle's usual fig leaf, but, whether honest or contrived, whether his own cliffs and water and stars or Pope's infamous "stars unnumber'd gild[ing] the glowing pole" (8:692), the rule of Burke's Pope-inspired transformation of Homeric sublimity remains confident. Carlyle turns gladly from Thor's bashings to the tearier matter of Balder. His lecture tends with relief to the softer details of Balder's story and anticipates the sentimental sublimity on display in Arnold's "Balder Dead" (1853) or the pitiful poeticisms of "Sohrab and Rustum" (1853). These patterns in his early theorizings play out, as we have seen, in his later practice. Certainly, such turns out to be the case even for Carlyle's "perfect" model: there Carlyle's actual recounting of Shakespeare's Agincourt stresses the endurance of the soldiers ("the worn-out jaded English; the dread hour . . . that deathless valour" [110]) and how they rise to their task. He ignores what Shakespeare says about any actual combat or face of battle, which is not quite as "deathless" as Carlyle's rhetoric allows, much less Shakespeare's ambiguous version of possible war crimes on that battle's notorious backside.

Carlyle's *Frederick the Great* is hardly a liberal epic. It was, after all, Hitler's favorite book. Nonetheless, *Frederick the Great* testifies to liberal epic's growing dominance by conforming to this genre's conventions whenever and however it can, even against its own pronouncements and even as it tasks itself to explode liberalism's political ideology of constitutionalism and popular consent. Carlyle's antithetical variation on this genre thus naturally seems more conflicted than the usual specimen, both more determined to make love to war (in nearly 2,000 pages of unadulterated battling after 1,000 pages of foreplay) and more squeamish about its inevitable chaos and messy realities; more in awe of its own hero, then more anxious about, finally even weary of him. This confusion, moreover, usefully exposes a corresponding and profound illogic in the liberalism this history so strenuously battled. The account of Hitler's predilection for Carlyle's *Frederick* appeared first in Hugh Trevor-Roper's *The Last Days of Hitler* (1947). In Trevor-Roper's narrative, Hitler is at once the dupe of Carlyle's great-man theory and a club with which the twentieth-century historian can beat the Victorian reactionary: "In [Hitler] we see the last, the logical consequences of Carlyle's dream" (232). At the same time it takes aim at Hitler and Carlyle, this history offers its account as telling evidence against the claims of another very different rival, namely, the intentionally anti-heroic, economic, statistical practice of history as a science: "There used to be a school of thought which held that the course of human history was determined largely by political and economic factors rather than the characters and actions of individuals" (xiii). The next chapter will turn to the surprisingly angry reaction of leading liberal theorists, from Acton to Berlin, to this phenomenon of scientific history that began with Henry Buckle in the 1850s. Buckle's history appeared during the same years as *Frederick the Great,* but though Acton was infuriated by the former's obscure radicalism, he was unperturbed by Carlyle's popular anti-liberalism. Acton preferred a world with heroes, of whatever sort, to one without. Trevor-Roper's portrayal of Hitler's career presents a similarly disturbing picture of liberal anxiety at the prospect of history without heroic agents. His narrative is torn between wanting history to be the record of great men, so as to keep the liberal ideal of a human agent, and fearing that the "logical consequence" of this desire is the horror of epic's primal scene or, here, its operatic aggrandizement in the form of a Wagnerian apocalyptic orgy of destruction: "the ancient froth of Nibelung nonsense . . . Hitler's formula of *World Power or Ruin*" (233).

Trevor-Roper's relation to Hitler neatly parallels Carlyle's to Frederick: both historians desire to retain the idea of the great man, but both find themselves compelled toward figures of war and conquest as their only evidence that individuals do have such power. Trevor-Roper theoretically prefers the democratic Churchill and Carlyle the nonmilitary Abbot Samson. But the convincing proof of Churchill's greatness lies in his rivalry with and defeat of the Führer, and only by turning tools back into arms, Abbot back into Kaiser, could Carlyle finally write his modern epic. Only when war was the industry in question and soldiers the workers, could Carlyle fully devote himself to celebrating the power of a captain of industry. His proto-Fénelonian internal improver and proto-Victorian "reformer of a religious order" (*Middlemarch* 3)—much as Eliot's own Dorothea—proved incapable of carrying that literary and cultural burden.[19]

FOUR

UTILITARIANISM AND THE INTELLECTUAL CRITIQUE OF WAR

MILL, CREASY, AND BUCKLE

It must happen, that as the intellectual acquisitions of a people increase, their love of war will diminish; and if their intellectual acquisitions are very small, their love of war will be very great.

—Henry Buckle, *The History of Civilization in England* (1857–61)

This chapter will examine the intellectual critique of epic warfare—the one implied by Buckle, who frequently belittled the moral critique emphasized thus far: "If it can be proved that, during the last thousand years, moralists or theologians have pointed out a single evil caused by war, the existence of which was unknown to their predecessors,—if this can be proved, I will abandon the view for which I am contending" (1:147). Apparently, the work of Grotius and Pufendorf in developing the modern theory of ius in bello did not impress Buckle as a sufficient advance. He never abandoned his utilitarian view that neither Christian morality nor humanist benevolence, but economic self-interest, particularly the middle class's growing understanding that its interests were not served by war, had led to the phenomenon that Buckle did accept—namely, the decline of war, the culture of war, and its epic literature: "With us [the English] intellectual progress is so rapid, and the authority of the middle class so great, that not only have military men no influence in the government of the state, but there seemed at one time even a danger lest we should push this feeling to an extreme; and lest, from our detestation of war, we should neglect those defensive precautions which the enmity of other nations makes it advisable to adopt" (1:153). Buckle's concluding point marks a slight increase in war thinking after its lowest ebb about the time of the Crystal Palace Exhibition in 1851. Crimea led to a reevaluation of the need for the state to focus on more than simply maximizing wealth: the gross incompetence of the war office dramatized the need to plan intelligently for war. Writing in the 1850s, Buckle subtly retreats from the radical position, which we shall see on display in the writings of John Stuart Mill in the late 1840s, that the richest nations had little reason to ready themselves for war, that a vibrant economy was in and of itself the best defense.[1]

My argument will proceed by focusing upon the pattern of an intensifying marginalization of war as the intellectual critique developed from the eighteenth to the nineteenth centuries, from Gibbon and Smith to Macaulay, Mill, and Spencer. At the same time, it will trace a counterplot lurking within this superficially confident Victorian rejection of heroism and warfare. This second pattern betrays a still powerful attraction to the fundamental epic presumptions of the importance of individual agency and of the test of combat. It highlights the flourishing of epic poetry and epic history during the period—in spite of the surface critique, perhaps even because of it. The primarily political-economic mode of the intellectual critique exhibits less interest (usually it is actively disdainful) in the nexus of humane, ethical, and aesthetic objections to the horror and terror of war and of epic. Instead of rhetoric of moral outrage, it adopts a self-consciously cool headed debunking of epic for its reliance on the notion of heroic agency versus the blind workings of the unseen masses, what Adam Smith termed the "invisible hand," or what Herbert Spencer, with his more pronounced anti-epic agenda, called "impersonal agency": "[In militant societies], personal causation is alone recognized, and the conception of impersonal causation is prevented from developing. The primitive man has no idea of cause in the modern sense" (*Sociology* 2:599). The economic historian Emma Rothschild has traced the literary-historical memory within Smith's use of his famous phrase, how it is a knowing response to and reworking of Achilles's and Jupiter's "bloody hand" of classical epic and myth (Rothschild 19). Spencer dropped the poeticisms, but, even as he hid the heroic antecedents, he deliberately intensified the opposition to the logic of epic, making the agency not just ingloriously invisible, but unheroically "impersonal."[2] The high Victorians' intellectual marginalization of heroism and war through an internal argument with or correction of the language of Enlightenment theorists thus often functions as a rhetorical ploy of self-consciously revising the terms, thinking, and vocabulary of earlier critiques so as to suggest war and heroism have become of steadily lesser concern—to the point of vanishing from nineteenth-century analyses altogether. That so much of the intellectual antiwar argument boils down to a question of imagery and diction will guide this chapter's exploration of this repression, then return, of war.

John Stuart Mill provides a helpful preliminary. In his austere political economic writings, he, first, self-consciously propounded an intensified version of the intellectual critique and, second, followed that up with an ironic return to liberal epic with noble heroes, glorious war, and florid rhetoric. A recent critic has pointed out, with evident intent to shock, that "Mill actually wrote the first important fully developed liberal defense of nineteenth-century English imperialism" (Sullivan 599), but such surprise stems from not realizing Mill's position within a liberal epic tradition and that his challenge went deeper than imperial temptation. His contemporary Herbert Spencer, the sociologist and social Darwinian, presents an equally dramatic example. Not only do both make a powerful intellectual case against epic warfare, but they do so by registering the advance of the liberal critique of war in self-conscious comparison to their eighteenth-century predecessors, particularly Adam Smith. Both coyly rework Smith's thinking on the theory of progress in ways that marginalize, even eliminate, war's role in modern civilization. Their writings embody a simple case study of a larger category of evidence that this chapter will trace in Creasy and Buckle, namely, the intentional effort to prove that war and epic are declining by making one's own analysis of that process evidence for it. Such a circular method simultaneously exposes the inadequacies of their argument. Their knowledge of their own contrivances points to the deeper challenge of their abiding attraction to heroic action and decisive war.

Smith's *Wealth of Nations* (1776) theorized a historical model that reduced the role of war and violent heroism. It did so, however, with significant caution, doubt, and irony. Mill and Spencer's effort to demonstrate that war and heroism have been superseded involves a deliberate simplification of Smith's sophisticated analyses, a reworking of Smith's ambiguous paradigm into straightforward, black-and-white contrasts. Spencer reduces Smith's four stages of civilization (hunters, pastoralists, agriculturalists, mercantilists) into two (militarist and industrial), the first based on wealth acquisition through war and the second through industry. Smith's model is meant to reflect accurately the broad outlines of political-economic development, and it acknowledges both a decrease in heroic militarism and an increase in military capability. Spencer's ideological distillation promotes a belief in progress in terms of a simple opposition of war and peace, violent acquisition and peaceful commerce. Smith speculated that citizens of advanced commercial societies remain interested in their nations' military victories, even when these wars cost them dearly in taxes and newspaper subscriptions: "In great empires the people who live in the capital, and in the provinces remote from the scene of action, feel, many of them, scarce any inconveniency from the war; but enjoy, at their ease, the amusement of reading in newspapers the exploits of their own fleets and armies. To them this amusement compensates the small difference between the taxes. . . . They are commonly dissatisfied with the return of peace" (920). Smith shows a level of doubt regarding the power of any political-economic critique of war to dissuade modern citizens from paying for its pleasures. Mill and Spencer ignore and sometimes suppress this point, which William James would later famously reiterate in the context of Pulitzer's popular fomentation of American imperialism.

Mill, like Spencer, places his own political economic analysis of the problem of war and heroism next to Smith's, and then makes his diminishment of epic starker and thus, in contrast to Smith's, itself evidence for the very decline that he claims to observe. Mill consciously assumed the role of Victorian heir to Adam Smith. He was the great systematic exponent and popularizer of political economy in the classic liberal tradition begun by Smith, passed on to David Ricardo, then Mill, and then Alfred Marshall, the teacher of Keynes's father. In his *Principles of Political Economy* (1848), Mill extends Smith's critique of war to the point of ejecting it from Europe. But a few years after completing that analysis and partially in response to revolutionary events in the year of its publication, Mill appeared in the very different guise of advocating a military alliance under the selfless leadership of freedom-loving England that would stand against the oppression of Europe's empires and for the legitimate aspirations of its repressed nations. Mill's stirring call to arms reintroduces war back into the heart of Europe and does so in terms of a heroic liberal politics desirous of purposeful action that contradicts his self-interested liberal economics and its invisible agency. In short, his self-divided writings on the topics of war and heroism combine, on the one hand, an intellectual condescension to their very existence in modern, capitalist Europe with, on the other, a heady emotional and moralistic clarion call to England, otherwise the still center of Mill's peaceful, economic, selfish worldview, to take up the role of selfless hero in championing wars of liberation—but only in nationalistic Europe, not colonized Africa or Asia.

Smith's analysis of war in *The Wealth of Nations* empties heroism out of modern battle. It allows for the decisive role of individual heroic agency in primitive warfare, of the supreme warrior artist or craftsman there, but theorizes that, in advanced states, warfare has become a matter of drill, of training men to move and act en masse, of the industrialization of the battlefield: "Before the invention of fire-arms, that army was superior in which the soldiers had, each individually, the greatest skill and dexterity in the use of their arms. Strength and agility of body were of the highest consequence, and commonly determined the fate of battles. . . . Since the invention of fire-arms . . . [,] all the dexterity and skill . . . can be well enough acquired by practicing in great bodies" (699). Though Smith explains in political-economic terms the decline of individual heroism, he deploys a metaphor of leveling, "puts the awkward on a level with the skillful" (699), which tellingly echoes one used by Pope to the same effect in his *Iliad:* "The arms we make use of put all men on a level" (220). Both writers see guns as weapons that undermine individual excellence: they reverse our modern sense of the level playing field to eliminate the epic primal scene from modern warfare. Their analyses dehumanize in the sense of deheroicizing warfare: the rule of division of labor makes it a matter of mechanical drill and mass organization rather than human will, courage, and skill. Despite this declinist theory, book 5, part 1, chapter 1 of Smith's work, "Of the Expenses of Defence," surveys the subject of war itself as one of some lingering importance—and growing expense. Smith pauses carefully to recount the history of warfare in his four stages of civilization. He looks to specific historical examples such as Rome and Carthage, and renders judgment upon the comparative advantages and disadvantages of militias versus standing armies. Ultimately, for Smith, the progress of civilization has rendered the primal scene of traditional epic increasingly distasteful and inhuman, but in conjunction with advances in the division of labor, the capitalization of industry, and the development of technology, historical progress has made war so elaborate, so logistically demanding, in short, so expensive, that the conduct of war has become increasingly subject to the logic of national wealth: "In modern war the great expence of fire-arms gives an evident advantage to the nation which can best afford that expence" (708).

In the mid-nineteenth century, however, Mill pushed Smith's thinking to an antiwar extreme. Smith cautiously observed the need for even the wealthiest nation to be prepared for war—to the point of advocating for standing armies (a logical position given his conviction that all depended on the smooth operation of an expensive, elaborate machine), as against the long-standing English preference for militias. In *Principles of Political Economy,* Mill not only drops any Smith-like discussion of the government's need to plan, tax, and spend upon national defense, but on the very rare occasions when he even glances at that subject, he also asserts that national defense has been reduced to purely a matter of national wealth. Here is one of the rare instances, and really the clearest for all its faintness, in which a careful reader can discern its ghostly presence. Once again, Mill intentionally simplifies Smith's nuanced position: "In the meantime, those who do not accept the present very early stage of human improvement as its ultimate type, may be excused for being comparatively indifferent to the kind of economical progress which excites the congratulations of ordinary politicians; the mere increase of production and accumulation. For the safety of national independence it is essential that a country should not fall behind its neighbours in these things" (2:337). Mill's progressive condescension toward his era's "very early stage of human improvement" hardly obscures the key fact the he nonetheless considers it beyond that theorized by Smith for his own. There is no discussion of a need to plan ahead for war or, for example, any consideration of the advantages of a militia versus a standing army for safeguarding national independence. That liberal ideal now depends only on "not falling behind" in "production and accumulation."

What's more, Mill's evocation of his era's earliness, though meant to recall Hobbes's vicious state of nature with its war of every man against every man, has optimistically civilized that stark scenario into mere metaphor: "I confess I am not charmed with the ideal of life held out by those who think that the normal state of human beings is that of struggling to get on; that the trampling, crushing, elbowing, and treading on each other's heels, which form the existing type of social life, are the most desirable lot of human kind, or anything but the disagreeable symptoms of one of the phases of industrial progress" (2:336). Whether in reference to Hobbes or Smith, Mill's apparent self-critique marks a self-confident progress away from an era of real warfare to one of metaphorical contests that he also anticipates leaving behind. The Homeric primal scene is only poetry now, but, even in that form, it remains an unpleasant survival to be exorcised by liberal humanity. Mill shares with his more conservative contemporaries Tennyson, Carlyle, and Ruskin the perception that modern society has substituted a concealed, internalized form of war for an earlier era's open battlings, but he does not, like them, suggest a preference for honesty.[3] Mill rejects any desire to overcome the daily struggle of capitalism by a return to a regimented, military ordering of society. His rhetoric emotes, not nostalgia for the real thing, but annoyance over its imperfect transcendence.

Such self-dismissive superiority reigns throughout his text. Mill's scanty references to war include little more than a few offhand references to soldiers, and these comments consistently demote such to a subspecies of policemen in the fight against "force and fraud" (2:390). Otherwise, there is a total banishment of war itself to the frontiers of the empire where, in accordance with Mill's progressive logic, native savagery, not imperial encroachment, is blamed for its persistence: "Wars, and the destruction they cause, are now usually confined, in almost every country, to those distant and outlying possessions at which it comes into contact with savages" (2:274). By insisting that wars take place "in almost every country" on their "outlying possessions," Mill's assertion, with its dizzying, almost illogical, combination of "confined," "in," "at," and "out," in-sinuates the desire that war become a realistic impossibility. This passage also helps paper over the problems with his claim that increasing wealth precludes war: here wealth remains peaceful by simply assuming the re-gions of savage attack are, in fact, "possessions" of the Europeans, not of the greedy natives provoking the wars.

Mill's dearest opinions on wealth, progress, and the liberal marginal-ization of war are well summed up in the following passage, where these same views are put forth in deeply conflicted rhetoric that at once fur-thers Mill's explicit liberal thesis and calls into question its determined optimism:

> Another change, which has always hitherto characterized, and will as-suredly continue to characterize, the progress of civilized society, is a continual increase of the security of person and property. The people of every country in Europe, the most backward as well the most advanced, are, in each generation, better protected against the violence and rapac-ity of one another, both by a more efficient judicature and police for the suppression of private crime, and by the decay and destruction of those mischievous privileges which enabled certain classes of the community to prey with impunity upon the rest. (2:273)

In Smith's paradigm, the progress of civilization is marked by the dimi-nution of the glory and increase in the expense of war: war's emotional appeal grows ever weaker even as its expense and need for state planning increase. Mill evokes Smith's calculus and then, characteristically, passes over its distinctive feature of decline and increase for the simpler and clearer model of increasing safety. Moreover, here war has gone beyond even a state of decline, and is merely a ghost lingering within the domi-nant term of waxing "security." That term, when coupled with "the people of every country in Europe," at first seems to be moving toward a system of international security, one that would necessarily treat the problem of war and its evolving international laws, but Mill does not allow that possi-bility to become explicit. Whereas Smith's analysis in *The Wealth of Nations* was fascinated by the problem of war between "backward" and "advanced" states—a contest that favored the former in the ancient world but, so he and Gibbon argued, advantaged the latter in the present—Mill's passage raises those contrasts only to shy away from such international warfare and pivots to the more important matters of intra-national security. Mill flirts with his readers, holding out the possibility of a discussion of war in the context of the modern European system, only to snatch it away as yet another means of insisting on war's obsolescence. That historical process has at last reached the point where a liberal theorist such as Mill can celebrate the end (or at least the "decay and destruction of . . . privileges"—and here too lies a verbal hint of an era of wars of revolution not quite passed away, but nothing more will Mill say) of upper-class oppression of the lower classes in even the most backward European states.

As a corollary to this belittling of even the consideration of war, Mill asserts that oppression by one's own government (and its police) is a far worse threat than any oppression by foreign conquest (and its soldiers): "By security I mean the completeness of the protection which society affords to its members. This consists of protection *by* the government, and protection *against* the government. The latter is more important. . . . The only insecurity which is altogether paralyzing to the active energies of the producers, is that arising from the government. . . . Against all other depredators there is hope of defending oneself" (1:152–54). Mill does not openly name wars of conquest, only suggesting their existence as the lesser of two "depredators." This passage further clarifies Mill's slippery usage of the term "security." It can sometimes refer to military security provided by the government against foreign attack. On the other hand, since Mill's diminishment of war goes so far as to find conquest less terrible than internal insecurity in the form of government oppression or over-security, security more often carries the ironic happy meaning of a lack of governmental power, that is, security from government and, no doubt, from its taxation to pay for its protection. Thus, even internal security is figured rhetorically so as to valorize the diminishment of state power: we become more secure as its security apparatus declines. Mill performs an entirely verbal exorcism of war from the discourse of political economy. Whatever his analysis is, it is not a sustained or realistic treatment of the then still sizeable military budgets and military-political ambitions of the major European states.

In contrast, in his political essay "A Few Words on Non-intervention" (1859), Mill does explicitly raise the fact of European warfare, now not as a specter but as a noble opportunity. His rhetoric and imagery change accordingly. He calls upon England to assume its rightful leadership in carrying wars of liberation throughout the continent: "The prize is too glorious not to be snatched sooner or later by some free country; and the time may not be distant when England, if she does not take this heroic part because of its heroism, will be compelled to take it from consideration for her safety" (263). Though it has a literally diminutive title that highlights inaction, these suspiciously overmodest features contrast with the grandeur of its heroic rhetoric and ambitious goals.[4] Scholarly interest in this essay usually attends to the famously liberal Mill's defense of colonial imperialism, on the benefits savages will reap from civilized rule.[5] That aspect of the essay, however, is fully in accordance with Mill's earlier political economy. What is unexpected is the essay's long-delayed acknowledgment of the events of 1848, and its break with his economic theory in now admitting the reality of war in civilized Europe and in advocating military intervention to free proto-liberal nation-states longing to escape imperial oppression. Its tone is remarkable: the essay rings with language of heroism, liberty, and selfless idealism. It begins with an eloquent assertion of England's selfless devotion to peace and freedom and fair play. It concludes with an ominous warning that seems to confess a deeper, selfish reason for its earlier call to arms: "[England] will be compelled to take it from consideration for her safety" (263). Now "safety" does refer to warfare and armed vigilance. Nonetheless his use of "it" suggests Mill's doubts regarding heroic warfare. That word refers back to the phrase "heroic part," which itself points to taking up the leadership of the battle for freedom against tyranny in Europe. The odd shrinking to a mere "it" in the final phrase reveals much, but seems to occur mainly because the final sentence makes clear how very selfish and unheroic that part really is—the role of a fearful agent responding to threats, not an honorable liberator championing ideals. Such self-contradictions underscore, once again largely through structural and rhetorical devices, a fundamental strategy observed in his political-economic treatise. Without ever saying so directly, Mill implies that war is a minor matter in the nineteenth century. For Mill on liberal war speaks softly in a minor essay with a shrinking negative title, while Mill on peace and economics pronounces boldly in a massive political-economic treatise claiming descent from the great founding hero of his science—a "few words" of epic versus the "principles" of its intellectual rival.

Still the heady, overdetermined, almost riddling epic rhetoric of the quoted passage—"too glorious not to be," "heroic . . . because of its heroism"—seems out of keeping with Mill's usual tone, mainly because it is. This departure from his coolly logical prose both highlights and hides Mill's violation of his intellectual commitment to the notion of self-interest—and how that ugly or invisible principle has permanently undermined the place of war and the role of heroes in the modern world. Indeed the essay begins by sadly noting the general European suspicion of English selfishness, particularly when the English claim to be acting selflessly, and nowhere, least of all here, can Mill refute that charge. The irony spins out of control, as our theorist of self-interest complains of European charges of selfishness where Mill only sees selflessness—until the final, sneaking admission. The essay's argument is thoroughly self-interested: it advises that England will gain politically and financially by the advance of democracy and free markets; it warns against the waste and cost of wars of liberation, unless in support of homegrown revolutions; it thus comes down strongly in favor of supporting revolutions that would succeed without English support, except for oppressive outside aid, as in the Czar's intervention to help the Austrian empire retain Hungary. Given such "lofty" principles, it is striking that Mill chooses to frame the essay in terms of a defense of English idealism and English shock at being doubted. Ultimately, the excited heroic tones of the internationalist weirdly echo the studied anti-heroic silences of the economist. Both are designed to hide an inconvenient truth for the intellectual opponent of war, a truth that we will see Keynes thoroughly exposing: war did still serve both the self-interest and the self-regard of liberal middle-class nations—and not just easy colonial wars, but strenuous local ones. The intellectual and moral ground for both the complacent certainty that there could be no great European war ever again and the eagerness with which such a heroic fulfillment was solicited was already there in Mill's paradoxically congruent writings on war or peace.

MILITARY HISTORY VERSUS SCIENTIFIC HISTORY: THE ODD CONGRUENCE OF CREASY AND BUCKLE

Those of us who read Buckle's first volume when it appeared in 1857, and almost immediately afterwards, in 1859, read the "Origin of the Species," and felt the violent impulse which Darwin gave to the study of natural laws, never doubted that historians would follow until they had exhausted every possible hypothesis to create a Science of History.

—Henry Adams, *Letters*

Edward Creasy's *Fifteen Decisive Battles of the World* (1851) appeared in the interval between Mill's cool economic treatise and his heated heroic essay. It shared with Mill the optimistic response to Europe's long post-Waterloo era of peace, but anticipated his later willingness to imagine wars of liberation. Both nonetheless held the strong conviction that the future of national competition would lie almost entirely within the realm of commerce and industry, not on the field of battle. Creasy accepts Mill's political economic banishment of war and concludes with these unwarlike reflections:

> In closing our observations on this last of the Decisive Battles of the World, it is pleasing to contrast the year which it signalised with the year that is now passing [1851] over our heads. We have not (and may

we long be without) the stern excitement of martial strife, and we see no captive standards of our European neighbours brought in triumph to our shrines. But we behold an infinitely prouder spectacle. We see the banners of every civilised nation waving over the arena [the Crystal Palace] of our competition with each other, in the arts that minister to our race's support and happiness, and not to its suffering and destruction. (418)

This heady peroration (the parenthetical prayer for peace is particularly touching), whose tone fairly represents the entire history, concludes with a condemnation of war that recalls Creasy's anxious opening:

It is an honourable characteristic of the Spirit of this Age, that projects of violence and warfare are regarded among civilised states with gradually increasing aversion. . . . For a writer, therefore, of the present day to choose battles for his favourite topic, merely because they were battles; merely because so many myriads of troops were arrayed in them, and so many hundreds or thousands of human beings stabbed, hewed, or shot each other to death during them, would argue strange weakness or depravity of mind. (ix)

Both at the beginning and the ending of his narrative, Creasy evinces a strong antipathy between the values of modern liberal civilization and traditional epic ideology. His anthology of mini-epic histories ultimately figures itself as the epic to end all epics that concludes with the battle to end all battles, whether that be Waterloo or its finer commercial successor, the Crystal Palace. Moreover, in so doing, Creasy clearly echoes the core rhetoric of the exhibition. The official "History of the Great Exhibition," for example, which prefaces a catalog of the exhibits, lingers over the happy evidence of Anglo-French cooperation and approvingly quotes Shakespeare on the advantages of peace as a better kind of conquest in which "neither party loses" (xi).

Creasy's book was a best-seller in his more overtly humanizing and disciplinary age, especially with young readers. His history ran to more than five editions in less than five years, and it rivaled the best-selling novels of Dickens and Thackeray—with only Macaulay's epic *History of England* outselling it: "Its subject, style, and treatment brought it close to fulfilling Macaulay's contemporary dream of writing a serious book that would replace current popular novels on England's nightstands" (Showalter 206). Creasy's success helped nudge Macaulay toward a more heroic refashioning of his *History of England*. Creasy gained wealth along with a knighthood—and later the chair of history at Oxford. His narrative inspired a whole subgenre of popular "great battles" histories (still going strong) that literally belies his text's declaration of the end of warfare.[6] One even sought to capitalize upon Creasy's success in the form of a sequel, but Thomas Knox's *Decisive Battles since Waterloo: The Most Important Military Events from 1815 to 1887* (1887) both flatters Creasy with imitation and explodes his humane premise by continuing what Creasy declared over and then assuming sequels to itself.

Creasy's liberalism is more serious than just these pro forma gestures at the opening and closing of his history. I will pass over the ample evidence of his sanitization of graphic violence in which Gibbon is often cited as his model, because the purpose of this chapter is to focus on persistence in the face of, not ethical and aesthetic objections, but intellectual doubts about the importance of war and the agency of individual heroes. Creasy's enabling decision to focus his narrative upon only fifteen battles underscores his awkward position. Creasy adamantly dismisses most battles, including all the bloodbaths of the Asian world. He thereby affirms his liberal humanism by rejecting the ugly idea that the numbers of killed signals historical importance, and underscores his Whig liberalism, an ideology that, according to its own thinking, is only concerned to praise battles that led the way to the progressive civilization of contemporary Europe and, above all, parliamentary England. In short, his "fifteen," while implicitly a convenient and market-oriented limit to his task, is explicitly a humane intellectual rule for excluding nearly all history's battles from the status of "decisive": the whole world only yields these few cases of truly epic warfare. The concluding prayer for a world of peace and commercial competition also suggests the likelihood that fifteen is an upper limit, a proleptic example of the liberal logic of a battle to end all battles and a battle to make the world safe for democracy applied to Waterloo, the last in his list: "It is an ultimately sober description of war as a means of progress, not in a Social-Darwinist, determinist sense, but as a manifestation of specific human decisions and specific human actions" (Showalter 206).

Showalter is mistaken in calling these colorful narratives "sober," and too confident in dismissing the specter of determinism. For in addition to Creasy's explicit concern over his decision to persist in narrating history in terms of war, there is a deeper scholarly and ideological anxiety over his effort to champion heroic agency that Creasy suppresses in dramatic fashion. His preface confesses that his original idea for the book came from reading a note in a history of *The Middle Ages* (1818) by Henry Hallam, father of Tennyson's Arthur: "[Hallam] says of [Poitiers], that 'it may justly be reckoned among those few battles of which a contrary event would have essentially varied the drama of the world in all its subsequent scenes: with Marathon, Arbela, the Metaurus, Chalons, and Liepsic.' It was the perusal of this note of Hallam's that first led me to the consideration of my present subject" (Creasy x). Creasy goes on to justify his particular battle selections, while also admitting "no two historical inquirers would entirely agree in their lists of the Decisive Battles of the World" (x). What he passes over in silence, though, is that Hallam is discussing what he refers to as the battle of Poitiers, because it "was fought much nearer to Poitiers than Tours" (1:8), while Creasy prefers the rival designation "battle of Tours." Hallam raises serious questions about this battle because of the inability, despite good written sources for its location and the reputedly huge numbers of slain, of numerous modern French antiquarians to find any archaeological evidence for it. Hallam therefore asserts that it might not have happened—"it is now, however, believed . . . that the Saracens retired without a decisive action" (1:8).

Hallam's denial of the key term and notion central to Creasy's entire epic project—"decisive"—in the very passage that inspired Creasy is disturbing enough by itself, but Hallam's note continues with a further specification of that doubt, one that Creasy fails to quote in acknowledging his so-called inspiration: "The victory of Charles Martel has immortalized his name. . . . Yet do we not judge a little too much by the event, and follow, as usual, in the wake of fortune? Has not more frequent experience condemned those who set the fate of empires upon a single cast, and risk a general battle with invaders, whose greater peril is in delay?" (8). Patriotically, Creasy ends with Waterloo, but this comment suggests that Hallam might very well have been thinking of how Napoleon was really destroyed by the Russian winter, by the cagey refusal of the Russians to give him a decisive battle. Thus Hallam's continuation begins with a grand gesture toward Martel's immortal glory, but then follows with two antithetical points: first, a caution against ascribing undue importance even to what seems the most critical battles, from which Creasy's entire thesis suffers in knowing silence; second, Hallam also questions the heroic leadership or agency thought to lie behind war's spectacular events. Hallam's discretion-is-the-better-part-of-valor point about the danger posed by Charles Martel's accepting, even forcing, a major battle, and his suggestion that the reality of geography and the weight of population were much better guarantees of final victory to those invaded than the risk of open battle, not only cast doubt on epic's working assumptions but also expose the false ideology of heroism. For Hallam, this cultural ideal, which in all likelihood influenced Charles Martel's decision to seek immortality in battle, was the real danger. Or rather, since Hallam disputes there ever was a decisive action, it appears that Charles Martel himself might well have avoided decisive battle, rejected the Achillean allure of glory, and relied on deeper forces for his victory. Only the false emphases of subsequent historical accounts, written in the conventional heroic mode of Creasyan decisiveness, manufactured the necessary epic event—and the properly violent immortality. In sum, Creasy's account of his inspiration contains (and buries) a profound intellectual critique of his entire project.

Creasy points us to, then suppresses, Hallam's explicit doubts. On the larger point, Creasy defends his intellectual focus on battles and his heroic theory of historical cause and effect. Again, he does so in revealingly reticent fashion, never admitting the real problem. Indeed he falsifies the debate by claiming the logic of probability for himself, while his rhetoric betrays that he knew it belonged to his opponents:

> But when I speak of Causes and Effects, I speak of the obvious and important agency of one fact upon another, and not of remote and fancifully infinitesimal influences. I am aware that, on the other hand, the reproach of Fatalism is justly incurred by those, who, like the writers of a certain school in a neighboring country, recognise in history nothing more than a series of necessary phenomena, which follow inevitably one upon the other. But when, in this work, I speak of probabilities, I speak of human probabilities only. (xii)

Henry Buckle is usually regarded as the inventor of scientific history.[7] Buckle proclaims his reliance upon a statistical model of historical causation derived from the work of the French statistician Quetelet and, more generally, an adherence to the sociological models developed by Comte.[8] It is just such systems that Creasy here alludes to in his vague and scornful fashion, but those historiographical models deal precisely in "human probabilities," in the weight and momentum of vast groupings of men and women, that is, in a more scientific version of the invisible hand. In contrast, though he begins by appealing to hard facts, Creasy concludes by indicating that he only means human heroes: "obvious" and "important" "human probabilities." He turns back to the heroic hand, to what might be fairly regarded as "human improbabilities," the rare heroes and the fifteen decisive events in all of history over which their miraculous powers presided. To add to this problem, in Hallam's contrast of the dangerous historiographical reliance upon the "event" and "fortune" as against the realism of "frequent experience," there lurks (again in the very note that inspired Creasy) the basic logic of sociological history, of the probable and the usual, as against the flash of heroic action that renders history vulnerable to the fortune of big events like battle.

The anxiety revealed by Creasy's resort to such suppression and rhetorical trickery also appears in his flinging of the old charge of "Fatalism" and his concluding appeal to "the wisdom and power of the Supreme Lawgiver, the design of the Designer," which for Creasy "we recognise emphatically" in the action of heroes in history, in decisive battles. For the Whig Creasy to find himself appealing to the rear-guard position of a Carlyle, that is, to a defense of heroic history that relies on turning it into a hero-worshipping article of faith equivalent to believing in God in this dark age of skepticism, is for him to reveal how weak and self-doubting his rendition of heroic history is. The logic of his preface's invocation of Carlyle reappears in the body of his history when he turns to an explicit defense of his heroic model. He avoids the deeper intellectual challenge to the thesis of heroic agency so obliquely and nervously raised by the preface, and, instead, defends heroism through a sleight of hand: he maneuvers onto the ground of championing his heroes, not against the political-economic critique of the limitations of seeing history in terms of individual agency, but against the eighteenth-century tradition of skeptically questioning the morality of great men:

> It might be easily shown that the defensive tendency which distinguishes the present and recent best historians of Germany, France, and England, has been equally manifested in the spirit in which they have treated the heroes of thought and the heroes of action, who lived during what we term the Middle Ages, and whom it was so long the fashion to sneer at or neglect. (59)

> If any person can be found in the present age who could join in the scoffs of Voltaire against the Maid of Orleans . . . let him read the life of the wisest and the best. . . . Let him not dare to deride or vilify Joan of Arc. (228–29)

Ethical questions regarding the morality of warfare are the core problem for epic in the modern, liberal world, but those challenges are not the only ones, and not the ones raised by Hallam. Creasy's use of the vocabulary of moral skepticism, not intellectual critique, allows him to flee to the nostalgic Carlylean rhetoric of belief to defend heroic agency and to evade the real issues. Like Mill, whether in his treatise or his essay, Creasy is alternately heroic or anti-heroic, traditionally epic or economically modern, as it suits his purposes. He succeeds, but only by knowingly looking away from the challenges to whatever he wants to be or write to maximum effect at the moment.

Henry Buckle's scientific, sociological, and statistical *History of Civili-*

zation in England (vol. 1 [1857], vol. 2 [1861]) represents an inverse situation: a text openly dedicated, not to preserving some select remnant of epic against skeptical criticism, but to dramatically ending history's emphasis on wars and heroes. This anti-epic project suffers from one major flaw: it keeps falling back into the heroic mode of the decisive victory. As we saw in one of Buckle's intellectual heroes, William Godwin, the most radical Romantic critic of all forms of heroism, is still able to cast Fénelon as a hero by right of his deconstruction of heroism. The same paradox of the heroism of destroying heroism plagues Buckle's argument, though for Buckle, Smith and Voltaire assume Fénelon's role. Creasy represents a profoundly self-doubting persistence of epic, one that terminates in its end; Buckle a proudly heroic effort to defeat epic, one that concludes in triumph and transcendence. The first typically succeeds through silencing or falsifying his fundamental critics; the second typically through both belittling epic and, oddly, exaggerating the agonistic struggle of heroic and scientific modes. Here is Buckle on the historical ephemerality of heroes—good and bad:

> The actions of bad men produce only temporary evil, the actions of good men only temporary good; and eventually the good and the evil together subside, are neutralized by subsequent generations, absorbed by the incessant movement of future ages. But the discoveries of great men never leave us; they are immortal, they contain those eternal truths which survive the shock of empires, outlive the struggles of creeds, and witness the decay of successive religions. (1:178–79)

This passage obeys Buckle's ongoing project of discounting ethical factors and aggrandizing intellectual ones: here the category of "great men" excludes ethical agents of the "good" or "bad" sort, but is allowed to hold firm for intellectual heroes—scientists, inventors, economists, scientific historians, and the like. Buckle's developing narrative does not, however, boldly leave these figures in the limbo of moral neutrality: all are made good. The following is the strongest such claim and the most paradoxical: "Well may it be said of Adam Smith, and said too without fear of contradiction, that this solitary Scotchman has, by the publication of one single work, contributed more towards the happiness of man, than has been effected by the united abilities of all the statesmen and legislators of whom history has preserved an authentic account" (1:169). Adam Smith, the formulator of the invisible hand metaphor, figures as Buckle's greatest hero of all time!—and not a hero of conscience or symbolism, but of agency; one whose actions expressly outweigh those of multitudes. His rhetoric has a deeply epic resonance and logic. Its "solitary" and "single" besting the "united abilities of all" seems clear enough, though one notes Buckle's sense of thus contradicting his own Smithian thesis in his anxious addition of "and said too without fear of contradiction." For, of course, Smith hardly worked alone, and in his fuller narration Buckle admits that if the culture had not been prepared for Smith's ideas, they would have been ignored.

This elevation is particularly interesting because of its context: Buckle is presenting the three reasons for the modern world's progress away from a culture of war, away from any epic veneration of war's glory and historical importance, away from warmongering mercantilism to the pacific emphases of Fénelon-Smith-Mill. According to Buckle, these are, first, the invention of gunpowder; second, of steam engines; and third and most important, the science of political economy that teaches people their real interest lies in commerce rooted in peace, not wealth seized in war. Smith's status as a great man lies less in his writings on economics per se and far more in his deconstruction of the epic ideology of war and its great heroes, that is, in his anticipation of Buckle's own heroic project. Adam Smith is the heroic progenitor of William Buckle. It is in European history writing more than in history itself, in the trend of historical narratives away from war as a great subject toward matters of society, the masses, and economics, that Buckle finds the best evidence for his claims. His *History of English Civilization* mirrors Mill's argumentative strategies in his *Principles of Political Economy:* the internal process of rhetorically and intellectually marginalizing the discussion of war becomes the major self-verifying argument against the traditional status of that great epic theme. Each makes its strongest case against epic warfare in largely literary and rhetorical terms. Buckle's version of this generic and rhetorical trick, however, is by comparison far more self-aggrandizing: Mill empties war out; Buckle reintroduces a new kind of hero and new kind of combat, but heroes and combats they remain, and their greatest action is to have begun then what Buckle is finishing now.

Buckle's larger argument embraces many English and French historians—but his two principal exemplars (again the great man thesis returns in the form of heroic historians who made this happen) are Voltaire, whom he judges "the greatest historian Europe has yet produced" (2:255), a writer whose greatness owed much to the ironic fact that he "was always at war" (2:248) with military historians; and, as an implicit heroic agent in the present day, there looms Buckle himself. That Buckle and his scientific history could serve such a role follows logically from his larger use of the progress of history writing away from war to prove the progress of history itself along the same route. Buckle had the tact never to make such a claim openly. Nonetheless, that implication remains strongly present throughout, and his fiercest critics, Tolstoy, Acton, and Berlin, were quick to use it against him. There's an obvious mise en abyme generated by a historian trying "to incorporate within an inquiry into the progress of the history of Man, another inquiry into the progress of History itself" (1:237). The effort to demonstrate the cultural decline of the appeal of war by finding in history writing a movement away from epic and toward sociological history leads, not surprisingly, to a situation in which Buckle's history itself tends to play up its own antiwar credentials, even as, conversely, it exaggerates the degree to which traditional history was obsessed by war and its heroic killers. His pacific vision of history's destination is, like Creasy's, ironically drawn to an especially agonistic vision of the journey thither: his history of history sports its own unique variation upon which fifteen battles were decisive, now not Persia versus Greece, for example, but Voltaire versus Bossuet, or Diamond versus Hanson, since Buckle was a fool to imagine military history was done with in the 1850s—any more than decisive battling was over at Waterloo.[9] His historiography is ruled by the logic of intellectual combat, struggle, and triumph—all played out between a series of famous men. Thus, to begin with Homer, at a time when many liberal critics, from Matthew Arnold to William Gladstone, were struggling to extend Pope's liberal epic project and reclaim Homer for modern liberal civilization by sanitizing the violence of his poetry, Buckle ignored all such efforts to moderate and humanize Homer and showed an opposite eagerness to insist on Homer's simple love of violence as clear evidence of his culture's barbarity: "The same turn of mind is shown in the frequency and evident delight with which Homer relates battles—a peculiarity noticed . . . where an attempt is made to turn it into an argument to prove that the Homeric poems were all by the same author; though the more legitimate inference would be that the poems were all composed in a barbarous age" (1:149). Such an observation lumps the concentrated violence of the *Iliad* with the very different emphases of the *Odyssey*'s romance adventure story.[10] Buckle's unwillingness to distinguish between the two narratives underscores his motivation to find an intensified and generalized Homeric love of violent battles and to see this fact as evidence of barbarity. Buckle fashions improbably stark facts and figures where, in Hallam's words, there were really only "human probabilities."

The leading nineteenth-century Germanic theory of Homer saw the *Iliad* (and the *Odyssey*), not as a composition of a single author, but as the editorial construction by a later age of smaller ballads, the preserved remnants of an earlier barbaric culture. In his chapter entitled "Origin of History, and State of Historical Literature during the Middle Ages," Buckle argues that history writing began with that essentially barbaric and warlike form: "At a very early period in the progress of a people, and long before they are acquainted with the use of letters, they feel the want of some resource, which in peace my amuse their leisure, and in war may stimulate their courage. This is supplied to them by the invention of ballads, which form the groundwork of all historical knowledge" (1:239). Buckle is at pains to insist that these ballads and the matter they relate are true: "All such productions [ballads] have one feature in common. They are not only founded on truth, but, making allowance for the colourings of poetry, they are strictly true" (1:241). By truth, the utilitarian Buckle means hard historical fact: at times his utilitarianism really does render him a caricature out of Dickens's *Hard Times* (1855). Buckle's theory grounds history writing in a ballad form that, first, he makes as warlike and barbaric as possible, and, second, insists is far more historically reliable than eighteenth-century historiography ever allowed and which nineteenth-century historiography, pushed along by the theory of Vico and the practice of Niebuhr and Michelet, found useful for some purposes, but hardly regarded as "strictly true," even when allowing "for the colouring of poetry." Buckle spins his evidence to barbarize and militarize the origin point of history—and then contrasts it with the age of civilized, self-interested opposition to war in which Buckle's history optimistically theorizes he and his readers safely reside.

This basic pattern of agonistic contrast stands at the core of Buckle's history of history's advance beyond war. It figures most prominently in his most extended case study, that of the "greatest" historian, Voltaire, whose lifework as a historian conveniently serves as a microcosm of Buckle's larger thesis. According to Buckle, Voltaire's career spans the gamut from the heroic celebration of a conquering war hero in the very popular *History of Charles XII* (1728) to a massive experiment in social history, *Morals, Manners, and Character of Nations* (1756): Voltaire's career internalizes Buckle's thesis, though, of course, only because Buckle is the one who is describing the course of that career. He begins by contrasting Voltaire with Bossuet, the leading historian of the preceding era of Louis XIV: "The best way . . . will be to compare the works of Voltaire with those of Bossuet; because these great authors were probably the most able, and were certainly the most influential, Frenchmen during the periods they respectively represented" (2:237). Fénelon, a contemporary and rival of Bossuet, informed Voltaire's vexed attitude toward heroic war and toward matters of political economy. Buckle has nothing to say on such matters—Fénelon spoils the "extraordinary" contrast. He does sketch

Louis XIV's persecution of Fénelon, and does indulge in the heroic claim, one too tempting for a pedagogue like Buckle, that Fénelon reformed his wayward pupil-heir and, through such educational success, "would have rendered . . . immense service . . . to the whole of France . . . , if his pupil had come to the throne" (2:224). Again, Buckle does not escape the hero thesis, but merely transposes it from warriors to scholars—and kings, too, if they be students first.

Buckle casts Bossuet as a simple celebrator of war: "It was this, again, that, in those magnificent orations which are among the greatest wonders of modern art, caused him to exhaust the language of eulogy, not upon intellectual eminence, but upon mere conquerors, those pests and destroyers of men, who pass their lives in discovering new ways of slaying their enemies, and devising new means of aggravating the miseries of the world" (2:236). The reader must accept my assurances that Bossuet did not, in any simple sense, perform such a role, though analyzing Buckle does alert the critic to Buckle's own temptation to spin evidence to strengthen an argument. Many of Bossuet's funeral orations were for noblewomen, not military heroes, and all were subjected to Christian judgment, especially the heroic sin of pride. This same pattern of exaggerating contrast in order to claim dramatic progress marks his reading of Voltaire. Buckle remains bent on narrating what is supposed to be a history of probabilistic trends as a series of dramatic set-tos.

> The first historical work of Voltaire was a life of Charles XII, in 1728. At this time his knowledge was still scanty, and he was still influenced by the servile traditions of the preceding generation. It is not, therefore, wonderful, that he should express the greatest respect for Charles, who, among the admirers of military fame, will always preserve a certain reputation; though his only merits are, that he ravaged many countries and killed many men. . . . Indeed, the admiration of Voltaire for Charles is unbounded. (2:238–39)

Buckle promotes his intellectual mode: Voltaire's early error is a result of his ignorance, not his moral values. But Voltaire's *History of Charles XII* yields, as chapter 1 detailed, not Buckle's interpretation of that text, but the reading that Buckle himself offers as a correction. Buckle's willingness to attack Voltaire with Voltaire's own argument demonstrates the inveterate blindness created again and again by his pursuit of the before-and-after.[11]

Buckle's argument extends its exaggerated contrast by making much of the fact that Voltaire, following the publication of his history of Charles, spent several years studying "some of the noblest subjects . . . to mathematics, to physics, to jurisprudence, to the discoveries of Newton, and to the speculations of Locke" (2:240). As always, intellectual explanations trump moral ones. After this intellectual refreshment, Voltaire's next history, *The Age of Louis XIV* (1751), whose title alone, for Buckle, marks a shift from the hero to the age, from the king to the society, turned sharply away from epic history—"while he is contented with giving a summary of military achievements, on which Bossuet hung with delight, he enters at great length into those really important matters which, before his time, had found no place in the history of France" (2:241). Again, while many critics have noted the significant increase of attention to social and cultural history in Voltaire's *Age of Louis XIV*, it still devotes nearly half of its narrative to Louis's wars—hardly a mere "summary." And though, in good liberal epic fashion adapted directly from Fénelon, Voltaire criticizes Louis XIV for his unjust aggressions and negligent cruelties in war, much of the account is unabashedly heroical: "All these actions, following so rapidly upon one another, conducted with so much art, managed with such patience, and executed with so much promptitude, were equally admired by France and her enemies. But Turenne's reputation received a considerable addition" (1:177). This passage is one of many such from a chapter entitled "The Glorious Campaign and Death of Marshall Turenne," which, to be sure, also comments legalistically on its hero's excesses. As with most neoclassical liberal epic, this history is a mixed bag of epic rhetoric and humane demurs. But much of Voltaire's harshest criticism for Louis's ambitions stems from his failure. Indeed Voltaire's critique is significantly less critical and less progressive than Fénelon's earlier one—made at the height of Louis's successes.

Buckle winds down his argument by appending an analysis of Montesquieu's historiography. According to Buckle, Montesquieu took the logical next step of freeing history entirely from biography—"the complete rejection of those personal anecdotes, and those trivial details respecting individuals, which belong to biography, but with which, as Montesquieu saw, history has no concern" (2:256–57). Logically, Buckle's phrasing should be "trivial details *of* individuals," that is to say, for the new history, individuals qua individuals are by definition trivial, even unhistorical, unavailable for statistical and scientific explanation. But for Buckle, as for many an epic historian, only the vast majority of individuals are trivial, and some are a very big deal indeed. And here, in sum, is the largest irony of Buckle's history, for it is quite obviously an epic. Its strange effort, evident in the title, to figure the triumph of civilization in terms of the national story of England in part reveals the logic of patriotic epic penetrating into scientific history, but it primarily resides in Buckle's undeniable emphasis upon glorifying great men, upon explaining history in terms of their contests with one another. That such a project can be best achieved through repeatedly telling history in terms of the dramatic struggles of good and bad men, or of great men against the masses, inevitably pushes Buckle not just back toward heroes, but toward heroes in an epic narrative of progress and final triumph. If that triumph, ultimately, is over war and its culture of violence, over figures representing physical domination and oppression, then Buckle does embody an advance to celebrate—the same that Creasy boasted of in his history. Moreover, it remains the advance typical of most ethics-based liberal epics, just the sort of liberal progress his scientific history began by scorning in favor of an intellectual, self-interested improvement. What Buckle seeks is a world of intellectual contests that is ethically superior to one of physical domination, a fine new version of epic battles among intellectuals at the head of generational contests, but not the ruthlessly anti-heroic world ruled by democratic masses and statistical trends he first ambitiously projected.[12]

Buckle had little of Creasy or Macaulay's popular success, though anecdotal evidence suggests an underground popularity at odds with the scorn poured upon his history by the reviewing and academic world.[13] Its intellectual daring earned it considerable scholarly attention, as Creasy's popularizing did not. Buckle's radical historiography, with its superficial effort to eliminate the residue of heroism and elevate such explanations as the carboniferous content of food for the rise and fall of civilizations, surprisingly earned the most ire from self-consciously liberal historians. In a fascinating late Victorian compendium of the various, mostly negative, responses to Buckle, entitled *Buckle and His Critics* (1895), some critics, like Herbert Spencer, responded harshly, but seem motivated primarily by the desire to discredit a rival in the task of first applying Comte and the new science of sociology; others, like Carlyle's protégé J. A. Froude, articulated the views of a romantic, heroic, and conservative historian (his own beautifully written *History of England* [1856–70], second only to Macaulay's in popularity, found its great hero in Henry VIII and his supposedly anticapitalist central planning). He saw Buckle as so misguided that he could be treated with kindly condescension. None matched the vitriol of Lord Acton. He took the trouble of composing two back-to-back review essays in consecutive volumes of *The Rambler* in 1858: "Mr. Buckle's Thesis and Method" and "Mr. Buckle's Philosophy of History."[14] It is fitting that given Acton's low opinion of Buckle's effort to exclude individual agency—"having thus made the individual soul of no account in his investigations on the history of human progress . . . [,] only one manner of looking at mankind remains . . . [;] they must be considered as bodies in mass" (6–7)—his critique, first, observes that Buckle hardly follows through on "reduc[ing] history to such dry chaff . . . [but] makes persons his centers, and reduces it to what it always must be, an intricate and interlacing tissue of biographies" (18) and, second, turns upon Buckle's own implicit self-heroicization with dry sarcasm: "Taking a survey of literature from the pinnacle of his self-esteem, Mr. Buckle repeatedly affirms that history has generally been written by very incapable men; that before his time there was no science of history. . . . [He] thus cleared the way for his own appearance on the neglected field of history and philosophy" (23). His basic critique becomes an ad hominem attack on this hero-villain of historiography and history, a severe and mocking assessment of Buckle's poor credentials as a scholar and, so Acton argues, often duplicitous exponent of grossly illogical arguments.

His reviews turn Buckle, an autodidact who read voluminously to support his novel theories, into a kind of Edward Casaubon before the fact, though one who managed to complete and publish his *Key to All Mythologies*. Acton's mockery of Buckle's vulnerable combination of bumptious theory and island isolation from cutting-edge European thought suggests the distinct possibility that Eliot could have been thinking of these review essays in fashioning her Casaubon. Acton faults Buckle for his fallacious understanding of the relations of parts to the whole, asserting that Buckle ignores the truism that "in nature totals are made up of parts similar to the whole . . . [and] every chip of wood has the same construction as the block" (17). This critique closely resembles the faulty underlying assumptions of Eliot's isolated researcher-failures—Casaubon on the structure of myths and Lydgate regarding tissues in the body, though here it is Acton who holds the view of Eliot's misguided researchers, not Buckle. Acton often stands on stronger ground when charging that Buckle's scholarship is hopelessly outdated and too removed from the work of internationally connected scholars. Buckle repeatedly goes "to the wrong place for information" or "ignor[es] the obvious authorities" (30). Buckle's principal sources are positively old-fashioned: "For the history of philosophy we have continual references to Tenneman, who was greatly esteemed at the time of Kant's supremacy" (31). His foundational reliance on the French statistician Quetelet is also impugned: "[Quetelet's] way of applying the theory of probabilities to statistics is rejected even by the French writers" (15). Acton's charge oversimplifies the contemporary debate over Quetelet across the channel—one that even now has hardly concluded with the neat certainty of his declaration.[15] Buckle's understanding is firmly dismissed as follows: "Nowhere do the ignorance and incapacity of the author more visibly appear. . . . Mr. Buckle is totally ignorant of the writings and discoveries of these men. . . . [His] dissertation . . . is of no value whatever at the present day" (33). Acton's concluding summary focuses upon this core issue of individual greatness: "We may rejoice that the true character of an infidel philosophy has been brought to light by the monstrous and absurd results to which it has led this writer, who has succeeded in extending his principles to the history of philosophy only at the sacrifice of every quality which makes a history great" (40). Like Creasy, the liberal retreats to Carlyle's linking of religious faith and historical greatness—and to the easy charge of "infidel" so often flung at the unimpeachable Gibbon. It seems hard not to hear in this "infidel" and the last two words an epic resonance, as well as deep anger over Buckle's effort to transcend that traditional form. Acton's final comment is troubling, precisely insofar as it should be obvious to any reader, and certainly was to Acton, that Buckle did retain heroes and a historical admiration for greatness, so long as it was the greatness of a Descartes or a Newton, a Smith or a Voltaire—or a Darwin if he, like Adams, had known. If it is scandalous that Buckle falls back so readily into hero worship, when the hero is a scientist, then is it not more scandalous that the arch-liberal Acton, the Shelleyan prophet of the corrupting power of power, is so bitterly determined to keep military heroes at the very center of history?

This same pattern of strongly denouncing scientific history as a threat to historical greatness when it really ends up only threatening the very different notion of epic glory in war reappears, nearly a century later, in another leading liberal philosopher of both freedom and history, Isaiah Berlin. Berlin knowingly succeeded to Acton's efforts. He self-consciously follows him in championing the "value of Freedom as Acton had conceived of it—as an end in itself" (*Proper Study* 169). Like Acton, he also seeks to expose, with an excess of anger, the fallacies of Buckle. In his essay "The Concept of Scientific History" (1978), Berlin broadens his critique of scientific history to all such endeavors to turn history into a kind of natural science, but acknowledges Buckle as the central figure in this mistaken larger project (*Proper Study* 20). Again the central riddle is that Berlin's desire for war heroes leads him to reject Buckle's efforts to make the likes of Adam Smith and Voltaire our society's new and better paragons, and to return to classic figures of high politics and war such as Churchill. Whatever ironies and self-contradictions lie within Buckle's practice of history, he did firmly reject war and war heroes in any literal sense of those words. Likewise Creasy, for all his doubts and evasions, did at least theorize an end to war and war history. Why did Acton and Berlin break with Creasy's hope and excoriate Buckle's achievements? Why did the leading twentieth-century theorist of liberty require history and historiography to focus on heroes of war, not heroes of science or human-ity? What motivated such hardening of liberal theory? These questions will have to wait till my conclusion, where I will return to Isaiah Berlin following a more detailed study of the war histories, literary reputation, and cultural status of Winston Churchill. For now, it is best to underline this key point: not just Churchill, but also Isaiah Berlin and Lord Acton, wanted, needed, argued for war, for the history of war, for narratives cen-tered upon violent killing, for the moral and intellectual value of seeing heroes destroy their enemies. Liberalism did not just compromise with violence out of necessity or accept its usefulness in a spirit of hypocriti-cal bad faith, but turned to it as a solution for a crisis within—and woe to whoever denied it them.

||||||||||||||||||||||||||||||||||||||||||||||||||||||||||||||||||||||||||||||||||||||||||||||||||||||||||||||||||||||||||||||||||||||||||

FIVE

POPEIAN STRATEGIES IN PRIMITIVE AND MODERN WAR EPIC

MORRIS, KINGLAKE, AND HIGH VICTORIAN LIBERAL EPIC

Forget six counties overhung with smoke,
Forget the snorting steam and piston stroke,
Forget the spreading of the hideous town;
Think rather of the pack-horse on the down,
And dream of London, small, and white, and clean,
The clear Thames bordered by its gardens green;
Think . . .

—Morris, *The Earthly Paradise*

Morris's longing for the clean and smokeless London of 1400 makes a vivid contrast with Macaulay's heated admiration for the clean and industrial Belfast of 1850: "Belfast has become one of the greatest and most flourishing seats of industry in the British isles. . . . Belfast is the only large Irish town in which the traveler is not disgusted by the loathsome aspect and odour of long lines of human dens far inferior in comfort and cleanliness . . . [,] huge factories, towering many stories above the chimneys of the houses and resounding with the roar of machinery" (3:487). The progressive historian sees mud and sewage in the past, the nostalgic poet smog and filth in the present: both readily ignore what offends the other and find in their favorite a healthy purity.[1] This chapter will explore the form Victorian epic poetry took in the hands of William Morris, but, as here, one thing Morris's epics of ancient German victory over Roman imperialism share with Macaulay's modern epic history of the glorious progress of English capitalism is a representation of heroic killing that remains, despite his self-consciously primitive theme, remarkably sanitary. In the most comprehensive reading of Morris's epic poetics, Herbert Tucker emphasizes how *Sigurd the Volsung,* widely regarded then and now as his finest epic poem and one of the monuments of Victorian epic, "takes the measure of liberal sympathy politics" and possesses an "integrity foreign to the modern mind" (388). This Hegelian analysis of the integrity of Morris's primitivism passes over Morris's strict modernity regarding

epic's essential matter: his obedience to liberal notions of warfare, treatment of prisoners, and the representations of graphic violence. The deep
logic of liberal epic and international law, indeed now the first Geneva
Conventions, guides his archaic narrative as surely as it does those of the
ultra-modern Macaulay.

Chapter 4 explored Herbert Spencer's streamlined version of the
eighteenth-century political-economic model of the four stages of society.
Spencer, moreover, exhibited a determination to suppress any lingering
veneration for war, heroism, and the excitement of combat, when, unlike
his fellow sociological historian William Buckle, who was confident that
modern economic self-interest alone would secure such a goal, Spencer
joined the tradition of ethical critiques of war narratives. He campaigned
against allowing children to read heroic literature or engage in aggressive
sports—or even competitive games: "Nor let us omit to note that while
sanction may rightly be claimed for fiction of a humanizing tendency,
there should be nothing but condemnation for brutalizing fiction—for
the culture of blood-thirst to which so many stories are devoted. . . . Chess,
for example, which pits together two intelligences in such a way . . . [that
it produces] a feeling of shame and humiliation in the defeated" (1:529–
30). In condemning any contest that demonstrates the superiority of one
individual over another, Spencer articulated the most radical version of
the liberal ideal of self-determination, equality, and non-domination. The
dangerous consequences of such youthful sports and reading appeared in
how, even in the Parliament of the world's most advanced industrial state,
the lure of militant values in the form of wars of conquest and domination persisted due to the legislators' youthful epic reading. Indeed, when
Spencer began working on his magnum opus, *Synthetic Philosophy* (1862–
98), the conservative leader and prime minister Lord Derby published a
translation of *The Iliad* (1865), and the liberal prime minister Gladstone
published his massive three-volume *Studies on Homer* (1858–89). The
conservative broke no new ground in returning to the kind of graphic
detail versions after Pope's eschewed, but the great liberal prime minister
proved more original. Instead of merely suppressing Homer's offensiveness, Gladstone recuperated Homer as positive source of liberal ideals by
discovering in his warrior assemblies the cultural origins of Parliament
and constitutional democracy.[2]

Morris's epics do not give that honor to Homer, but follow the more
traditional Whig theory of tracing modern English parliamentary government back to an original Saxon Witenagemot, the "one man, one vote"
meetings of the tribe or clan.[3] The Witenagemot was imagined as a heroic
democracy, a kind of town meeting of warrior-citizens, of men bearing

arms and signaling assent by clashing their swords upon their shields: "'Children of Slains-father, doth the folk go to war?' There was no voice but shouted 'yea,' and the white swords sprang aloft" (*House of the Wolfings* 62). This scene, entitled "The Folk-mote of the Markmen," reflects how the Victorians imagined the great-grandfather of their Parliament worked. It resembles, but for its unanimity, the Homeric assemblages to which Gladstone looked, and also reflects the neo-Roman doctrine of a state founded on the armed liberty of a democratic citizenry, rather than the Lockean notion of a commercial representative republic. For Morris this primitive democracy has not been fulfilled but betrayed by modern representative government, a thoroughly corrupt and unheroic development. In his Northern Cycle, the Romans of the empire prefigure the modern British position of representative republican corruption, of a commercialized and class-riven society, while their heroic German enemies embody not just the origins of England, but the early heroic history of the Romans themselves: *The House of the Wolfings* lingers suggestively over the fact that both the simple Germans and the sophisticated Romans symbolize their polity by a wolf. In this way, Morris's heroic primitives also embody the neo-Roman notion of liberty excavated by Quentin Skinner and Pocock, and behind them, Machiavelli and Livy. They comprise a virtuous little Livian city-state, a self-governing collection of heroic citizens, whose valor inevitably will grant them a future of greater wealth and power, but also an ironic progress toward class division, corruption, loss of liberty, and thence decline and fall.[4] Three key points emerge: first, Morris's retreat to the past is superficially motivated not by liberal modernity's opposition to the values of heroic warfare, but by its corrupt incapability of heroic warfare; second, though the past offers that heroic opportunity, it is ultimately a tragic one that faces inevitable decline; third, although Morris's community possesses the martial characteristics of a pre-liberal democracy, its wars are nonetheless subjected to the liberal rules developed by the corrupt, commercial, Lockean-republican model. Morris's Germans, unlike the historical ones or Livy's early Romans or indeed the heroic, war-loving primitives of standard liberal and radical economic theory (Gibbon's and Spencer's), eschew wars of conquest and aggression, embrace an ethics of benevolence toward their enemies, and even seem to abide by the newly minted Geneva conventions of 1864.[5]

Morris, whose aesthetic and political theories often derive from Ruskin, thus follows him in theoretically embracing an older heroic and graphic aesthetic, but abandoning it regarding violent domination. His ancient German heroes follow the modern rules of war and, in their own accounts of battle, avoid and suppress the graphic details.[6] When they sing their heroic songs of their feats of battle, they exhibit a distinctly un-Homeric lack of interest in their particular skills and powers. Morris might have first become interested in his "Northern Cycle" without the help of Carlyle's popular lecture on Odin, and, certainly, there is little reason to believe that Gibbon's famous suggestion for a Mithradates-Odin epic on the vengeance of Germanic freedom upon Roman tyranny finally found its poet in William Morris. Still, Morris's two finest epics tell key parts of this larger story of German freedom contesting with Roman dominion.[7] They do so by suppressing exactly the mood and tone of savagery that clearly worried Gibbon—and drove off Wordsworth. For much as Morris could dream of a clean Chaucerian London without noticing any mud or sewage, his epic sees only the heroic virtue in its primitive champions, and not the ugly effects, or rather the terrifying pleasures, of their grim deeds.

Morris's epic cleanliness is all the more interesting, because as early as his first collection of poems, *The Defence of Guenevere* (1858), Morris pushed beyond not just neoclassical decorum, but also Tennysonian attentiveness, to register a much franker version of sexuality and violence, as they appeared in his medieval sources, than Tennyson's influential medievalism allowed.[8]

> The long bright blade without a flaw
> Glide out from Godmar's sheath, his hand
> In Robert's hair; she saw him bend
> Back Robert's head; she saw him send
> The thin steel down; the blow told well,
> Right backward the knight Robert fell,
> And moan'd as dogs do, being half dead,
> Unwitting, as I deem: so then
> Godmar turn'd grinning to his men,
> Who ran, some five or six, and beat
> His head to pieces at their feet.
> ("Haystack in the Flood" 141–51)

This scenario of the male hero and lover killed in front of his sexual partner by a bitterly jealous rival resembles the bedroom murder of Sigurd in the presence of his wife—and by one of her brothers—in *Sigurd the Volsung:*

> Then Guttorm laughed in his war-rage, and his sword leapt up on
>   high,
> As he sprang to the bed from the threshold and cried a wordless cry,

And with all the might of the Niblungs through Sigurd's body thrust,
And turned and fled from the chamber, and fell amidst the dust,
Within the door and without it, the slayer slain by the slain;
For the cast of the sword of Sigurd had smitten his body atwain
While yet his cry of onset through the echoing chamber went. (259)

The murder in the short, lyric narrative appears in sharp detail. The combination of ugly brutality (the mashing of the head) and beautiful specificity (the close attention to the "bright blade") has an obvious visual logic absent from the deliberately confusing action of the epic poem. In the lyric, Morris still avoids attending precisely to the final effect of the blade on the victim's neck. But in *Sigurd the Volsung,* it is the heroic elements themselves—the out-of-place war cry in a scene of stealthy murder, the huge leap across the room, the overmuscled blow clean through the body, the fatal casting of the sword by the fatally wounded hero, the melodrama of a body unrealistically cut in half with one piece in and one outside the room, and, finally, the retributive logic of "slayer slain by the slain," which works as a bit of neoclassicizing verbal display and justice—that combine to thwart any Homer-like graphic reality. Indeed, Morris exaggerates the fantastic primitivism of his source material to efface, not enhance, the anatomical details of the killing.

Both of these killings are murders, acts of horror and criminality, not the primal scene of epic. When one surveys Morris's versions of such combats in what purports to be an archaizing exercise in primitive epic, an even clearer pattern of suppressing and humanizing heroic violence appears. Morris reverses his earlier Pre-Raphaelite progress beyond Tennysonian specificity and reverts to neoclassical strategies: he looks away; he plays up metaphors and similes; his translation/adaptation lessens the realism of his original by suppressing simple words and supplying elaborate periphrases; and he interjects modern liberal rules of war where no such concern was displayed in his sources. Tennyson could claim to be representing violence under the rule of chivalry, but Morris's primitive Germans possessed no such courtesies—and all despite Morris's intent to challenge his sheltered Victorian readers with the primitive energies of his Germanic sources.

It is in *Sigurd the Volsung* that Morris's primitivist authenticity receives its fullest poetic development. His earlier medievalist energies had been redirected toward Northern mythologies: Germanic, Norse, and Icelandic.[9] Carlyle's self-consciously masculine preference for what he termed the "sincerity" of Scandinavian mythology underwrites Morris's determination to render his primitive materials authentically: "Superior sincerity (far superior) consoles us for the entire want of old Grecian grace" (*Heroes* 30). In first working on what he called a "monstrous" story, Morris showed great enthusiasm for the incestuous relation of Sigurd's father, Sigmund, with his sister Signy—the sort of material Tennyson wouldn't have touched. Tennyson represses Arthur's incestuous relation with his half sister, even though it is something the sources see as a crime, while Morris's retelling both expands the Sigurd-Signy relation and makes them and their tale of revenge even more heroic and only faintly criminal. On this sexual matter, Morris happily shocks his proper readers with the implication of a primitive and heroic code that can dispense with civilization's strictest taboos. Morris's finest nineteenth-century critic, J. W. Mackail, who because of its detailed attention to sexuality and violence found this poem "unsurpassed in the world of epic grandeur and tragic tension" and "the most Homeric poem written since Homer," responded to this "strange and savagely magnificent epic" by calling it inhuman, even prehuman: "The strangely inhuman life and death of the son of that awful brother and sister, are tragic indeed, but with such tragedy as belongs to the dim and monstrous reign of the older gods"; "the story relapses into something of its earlier horror and savagery. . . . For want of that Greek intelligence, the story is not fully humanized" (1:341–43). Instead of "Greek intelligence," Morris found full compensation in the graceless sincerity of the German epic that he aggressively recreated for his Victorian readers with the addition of some rough sincerity of his own.

A close scrutiny of his warfare tells a very different story. In the two texts examined here—*Sigurd the Volsung,* his most famous Germanic epic; and *The House of the Wolfings,* the most epic of his later prose romances; both rooted in fundamental Germanic myth-histories—joyful warfare and the potential for readerly pleasures in scenes of heroic combat are carefully circumscribed.[10] Though Longmans, Green, and Company advertised the latter as a "story, which has a strong Homeric vein that immediately commands and holds the attention" and which "takes us back to those far off times when the Goths were contending with the Romans," the actual narrative pays no Homeric attention to the precise mechanics of killing and, more to the point, actively eliminates the disturbing and inhumane details Roman historians supply.[11] The historical/legendary battle at the core of *The House of the Wolfings* is based upon the battle of Teutoburg Forest.[12] Whereas Tacitus and modern archaeologists are emphatic in claiming that most of the Roman survivors were cruelly sacrificed by the Germans to their gods (the most frightening episode among many by Tacitus, the supreme artist of history as crime, horror, and terror, occurs when years after the battle, a Roman army stumbles upon the remnants of the grotesque ritual), Morris's narrative has his heroic Germans spare the captured enemy: "and to the rest [of the Romans] they had given peace till the Folk-mote should give Doom concerning them; for pity of these valiant men had grown in the hearts of the valiant men who had vanquished them, now that they feared them no more" (194). Morris's logic of manly and heroic pity is showcased, as is his liberal political thematic: for the Folk-mote is the democratic governing mechanism of his Goths, and this heroic democracy will not lash out illiberally at those now fully in its power.

Later Morris represents the Goths finding and treating the wounded Romans on the battlefield (198), feeding the Roman prisoners (his word is "feasted"), and taking care to bury the Roman dead honorably: "But a little way from the mound of their own dead, toward the south they laid the Romans, a great company, with their Captain in the midst" (207). Here, once again, a logic of liberal epic heroism and the modern law of war replaces the historical record of atrocity and triumphal vengeance. *Sigurd the Volsung* exhibits a similar pattern of altering his source material away from clear war crimes or appalling atrocities. Thus at the climax of the revenge story of Sigmund and Signy against her husband, the Goth-king who slaughtered their family, his palace is surrounded and set on fire. In Morris's epic, Sigmund calls out to the women and children within to come out to safety. They do, and he spares them. In the original, which Morris himself translated, the offer is only extended to his sister and co-conspirator Signy, who with tragic and harsh noblity refuses. Similarly, in the original's concluding revenge story of Gudrun against her two brothers, who murdered her first husband, as well as against her second husband, Atli, she kills her children by Atli. Morris's epic adaptation passes over this Medean flourish.

These changes are relatively small, but there are no comparable alterations in the other direction—no folding in of horrors or crimes absent in the originals. This small pattern accords with another trend in which Morris's epic adaptation suppresses particularly graphic episodes of killing or death from his own translation (with Eiríkr Magnússon) of the *Volsunga Saga* (compare, for example, Sigmund's killing of a wolf with his own teeth: vague and confusing in the poem, detailed and visceral in the translation). Such strategies of confusion, not detailed attention, inform the battles and combats in *Sigurd the Volsung* and *The House of the Wolfings*. Sometimes, after a long buildup, Morris rushes through: "short is the tale to tell, / For with the third stroke stricken to field King Gudrod fell" (50–51). Sometimes, Morris retreats into a combination of grand claims of heroic triumphs, which he then records only in metaphors. The poem's central hero proves his worth in a series of victories in a section entitled "Of Sigurd's warfaring in the company of the Niblungs, and of his great fame and glory." But in this core chapter, where the essence of heroic narrative is foregrounded and summated, all these military triumphs boil down to a series of harvest similes:

> But the slaves of the Kings are gathered, and their host the battle
>   abides,
> And forth in the front of the Niblungs the golden Sigurd rides;
> And Gunnar smites on his right hand, and Hogni smites on the left,
> And glad is the heart of Guttorm, and the Southland host is cleft
> As the grey bill reapeth the willows in the autumn of the year,
> When the fish lie still in the eddies, and the rain-flood draweth anear.
>   (178)

The logic of liberal epic holds here: the people's heroes fight against the slave armies of Kings; Sigurd's heroic preeminence is loudly asserted, but no mention is made of his superior lethality; only the other three are shown vaguely killing. Pope's basic tactic of limiting the moment of killing or terror and maximizing the follow-up similes and pity rules: the violence of war is kept to a minimum, while the poetic decoration surrounding it luxuriates.

Finally, the most famous battle in all the various versions of this story also figures prominently in Morris's, and gets treated at greater length and detail in his poem than in his earlier translation. Still, the siege of the Niblungs culminates in a battle that focuses on horror not terror, on scattered body parts more than on heroic kills, upon a list of disembodied heads, throats, and hands that registers violence without context or understanding, with no intellectual pleasure in the display of skill, just an abundance of horrific gore:

> There he smote and beheld not the smitten, and by nought were his
>   edges stopped;
> He smote and the dead were thrust from him; a hand with its shield
>   he lopped;
> There met him Atli's marshal, and his arm at the shoulder he shred;
> Three swords were upreared against him of the best of the kin of the
>   dead;
> And he struck off a head to the rightward, and his sword through a
>   throat he thrust,
> But the third stroke fell on his helm-crest, and he stooped to the ruddy
>   dust . . .

And the war-cries ran together, and no man his brother knew . . .
And clear stood the glorious Hogni in an island of the fight,
And there ran a river of death 'twixt the Niblung and his foes
And therefrom the terror of men and the wrath of the Gods arose.
    (317–18)

Even the hero does not pay attention to what he is doing: "he smote and beheld not the smitten." This is the most graphic battle in Morris's poem, but it is much more Tennysonian than Homeric—or Germanic. Like Tennyson, Morris indulges in heavy anaphora, which both makes the reading easier (it's merely a list) and eliminates the logistical difficulties of this scene of slaughter in favor of the spectacle of a pile of lines and body parts. The line "and the war-cries ran together, and no man his brother knew" articulates a distinctly Tennysonian view that all warfare, even that which seems justified, is inevitably a result of deep moral confusion, not heroic vision and divinely guided power. In one case, Arthur's knights triumph but "slimed themselves / Nor heard the King for their own cries" ("The Last Tournament" 470–71); in another, "ev'n on Arthur fell / Confusion, since he saw not whom he fought. / For friend and foe were shadows in the mist" ("The Passing of Arthur" 98–100). Such is the central point of Tennyson's only extended battle sequences: the defeat of the Red Knight's forces in "The Last Tournament" (419–86) and the "last, dim, weird battle of the west" against Modred in "The Passing of Arthur" (80–135). The atmosphere of moral and visual confusion reverses the moral and visual clarity of killing on display in Homer.[13]

Morris's lyrics boldly moved beyond Tennyson; his epics revert to the morality of the poet laureate. Morris's two concluding lines, however, seem deliberately to gesture away from his Tennysonian model toward the detailed Homeric terror of Achilles at the height of his rage amid the slaughter in the river Xanthus. But Homer's epic extravagance maintains a high degree of graphic realism, that of a river choked by all the bodies slain by Achilles, while in Morris "the river of death" cannot escape the charge of being mere exaggeration or entirely metaphorical or perhaps just confusing. Is it blood? Is it a string of dead bodies? Is it men running between to their deaths? Is it the strokes of his sword? The terror of Homer resides in how his epic spectacles are graphically real—and amenable to readerly visualization and appreciative understanding. Morris's epics never permit that experience or pleasure, even though in a poem like "Haystack in the Flood," he showed that he could achieve an eminently realistic, graphic, and visual horror, when the circumstances precluded delight in observing the sporting defeat of an active foe.

The half-and-half combination of prose and verse that Morris uses for *The House of the Wolfings* creates an opportunity for a level of graphic realism absent from *Sigurd the Volsung*. In some ways, the former does achieve a much greater aura of realism. Notoriously, a German academic queried Morris about what new scholarly and archaeological work informed his convincing evocation of early Germanic forest life. Though Morris peevishly asserted that it was simply fiction (his word was "lies"), there is a sustained, detailed, anthropological effort to specify and explain the ways of his heroic people that excuses the scholar's mistake.[14] This sort of realistic backgrounding extends to the accounts of war planning, maneuvering, and battle as well, and these, consequently, occupy a much larger portion of his narrative than in *Sigurd the Volsung*, or indeed any of his other narratives. Nonetheless, the accounts of the thick of battle, the killing and dying, have no Homeric realism, despite the claims of Morris's publisher and his official biographer.[15] The first major battle is narrated by a messenger from the front to a group of women, children, and old men left behind. Although the narration is individualized as the direct report of the character Egil, although this eyewitness account enjoys the freedoms of prose, and although Egil was an eager participant who by definition should rejoice in the honor of his own and his comrades' heroic killing, still the battle has all the qualities of a neoclassical battle. The excitement consists of balanced syntax and verbal echoings, not in any realistic evocation of actual fighting and wounding:

> Then was the battle grim; they could not thrust us back, nor did we break their array with our first storm; man hewed at man as if there were no foes in the world but they two: sword met sword, and sax met sax; it was thrusting and hewing with point and edge, and no long-shafted weapons were of any avail; there we fought hand to hand and no man knew by eyesight how the battle went two yards from where he fought, and each one put all his heart in the stroke he was then striking, and thought of nothing else. (99)

After a quick overview of how close-fought the larger battle was, the speaker focuses upon the single combats, but then he takes a further step and reduces it all to weapons without bodies. The "sword met sword, and sax met sax" could have been penned by Pope, and, though in the claim that "we fought hand to hand and no man knew by eyesight how the battle went two yards from where we fought" there is a gesture toward one dimension of heroic ideology and, perhaps, battlefield reality, still there is also an easy, unheroic excuse for not recording any vivid details.

Several smallish battles ensue, but they all build to the final epic siege in which Thiodolf meets the Roman Captain in hand-to-hand combat: in short, the heroic climax. Named "Thiodolf's Storm," after the hero who leads it, it centers upon his actions, namely, breaching the walls and killing the enemy. But Morris's narrative, which thematizes itself as a narration based upon heroic legends of the Goths ("the tale tells," etc.), does a strange thing: "The best part of the Romans faced the onset of Thiodolf, which seemed to them the main onset . . . [,] and at the East gate was the place first won, so that Valtyr and his folk were the first to clear a space within the gate, and to tell the tale shortly (for can this that and the other sword-stroke be told of in such a medley) they drew the death-ring around the Romans that were before them, and slew them all to the last man" (190). First, Morris turns to a frequent abbreviating device—"and to tell the tale shortly"—an expected convention in neoclassical liberal epic, certainly, but a dubious gesture for a professedly primitive tale-teller. Furthermore, although in the first battle Morris's character-narrator advanced a realistic excuse for not seeing and recounting the gory details, now we're asked to believe that Morris's general narrator, who consistently relies on "what the tale tells," possesses no heroic sources that recorded the names and deeds of its heroes in the height of battle. Indeed the rhetoric exhibits a not-so-subtle contempt for the central interest of primitive epic—"this that and the other sword-stroke" could, once again, have been lifted out of a neoclassical handbook on how to deploy verbal sleight of hand to suppress graphic realism. Morris's excuse oddly echoes Gibbon's at the climax of the Turkish thrust into Constantinople and the heroic fighting death of the last Byzantine emperor: each advances rationalizing excuses for dismissing the reliability of reports upon graphic details. But Gibbon was an admittedly enlightened historian, one trying to tell of war while sparing his civilized readers its supposedly unpleasant details. But for Morris, a writer dedicating himself to giving his reader a rough and sincere version of old Northern legend who constructs a narrative frame of a direct retelling of a primitive people's most heroic legends, the embarrassment is palpable. Did he accidentally hit upon Gibbon's solution, or did he borrow it from some Gibbonian narrative? Creasy's Teutoborg Forest narrative, for example, the most famous Victorian account of the battle, is a self-consciously Gibbonian exercise in softening a horrific classical source, here Tacitus. In any case, Morris does not acknowledge any such sources, preferring to leave the implication that the sanitized content and the elegant rhetoric rested in some primitive chest, some Ossian he expects us to accept as no enlightened fraud, though it exhibits all the humane characteristics that alerted Hume and Gibbon.

All these trends meet in the combat of Thiodolf and the Roman Captain, where Morris obeys epic convention by staging the final hero versus hero meeting, but then refines it:

> But on the threshold, the fire and flames of the kindled hall behind him, stood the Roman Captain clad in gold-adorned armour and a surcoat of sea-born purple; the man was cool and calm and proud, and a mocking smile was on his face, and he bore his bright blade unbloodied in his hand. Thiodolf stayed a moment of time, and their eyes met. It had gone hard with the War-duke. . . . He looked into the scornful eyes of the Roman lord for a little minute and then laughed aloud, and therewithal, leaping on him with one spring, turned sideways, and dealt him a great buffet on his ear with his unarmed left hand, just as the Roman thrust at him with the sword, so that the Captain staggered forward on to the next man following, which was Wolfkettle the eager warrior, who thrust him through with his sword and shoved him aside as they all strode into the hall together. Howbeit no sword fell from the Roman Captain as he fell, for Thiodolf's side bore it into the Hall of the Wolfings. (192)

Despite forcing his often realistic-seeming narrative to build to this improbable "leader versus leader" climax, Morris severely limits the primal scene he has so carefully contrived. Robert Graves makes much in *Claudius the God* (1935) of the Roman fascination with such commander-meets-commander combats and their extreme rarity in all the long history of Roman warfare: "What immortal glory I would have won" (319), exclaims the thwarted hero. Here Morris indulges his readers in such an event and pauses over the atmospherics of their meeting before switching gears and rushing through it. He does not here say that the "tale is short to tell," but nonetheless makes it so. He even excuses his hero from doing any killing here, shunting that duty off to a follower who, with a minimalist gesture, finishes off what Thiodolf started. All Thiodolf seems to do is box the Roman's ear with his unarmed hand: ironically, the primitive accounts did record this harmless detail. Most interesting, the fatal blow to Thiodolf comes as an afterthought; an expected surprise that signals a certain effect, but without anatomy, without precise detail, and, most of all, without any of the terror and tension and pleasure attending such scenes in Homer. As with the death of Sigurd, though here the kill is not a crime but the moment of highest epic glory, Morris makes it furtive and confused.

MARXIST THEORY VERSUS POET HERO

*Consequently, by discouraging industrial progress, militancy checks the replacing
of ideas of personal agency by ideas of impersonal agency.... History comes to be
made up of the doings of remarkable men; and it is tacitly assumed that societies
have been formed by them. Wholly foreign to the habit of mind as is the thought of
impersonal causation, the course of social evolution is unperceived.... The notion
of a self-regulating social progress is unintelligible.*

—Spencer, *Principles of Sociology*

Thiodolf and Sigurd are war heroes, but they are also culture heroes—
figures of historical legend whom Morris can build up as communal rep-
resentatives of their people's highest hopes. Their significance transcends
their battlefield accomplishments. Morris grows lavish with the details
of their cultural work, much as he skimps on their lethality: Thiodolf is
so uninterested in finishing the Roman Captain, because he is so determined to save the Wolfings' House from fire. But *Sigurd the Volsung* charts
a tragic course away from such communal heroism: Morris's flight to the
past for the primitive energies of epic is disrupted by the lurking effects
of the liberalism that shapes his thinking here too.[16] His epic charts this
decline through a progression of great halls. The poem alters its source to
begin with a loaded description of the "dwelling of King Volsung":

> There was a dwelling of kings ere the world was waxen old;
> Dukes were the door-wards there, and the roofs were thatched with
>   gold;
> Earls were the wrights that wrought it, and silver nailed its doors;
> Earls' wives were the weaving-women, queens' daughters strewed its
>   floors,
> And the masters of the song-craft were the mightiest men that cast
> The sails of the storm of battle adown the bickering blast. (1–6)

Developing his theme of the servants as free heroes and heroines in this
commune, Morris thematizes poetry as a craft like others and simultaneously characterizes poets as war heroes. Such passages resonate with
Morris's own lifelong work in interior design and, more broadly, with his
own self-fashioning as a skilled craftsman (and thus with his own status
as a poet and culture hero). The center of the narrative surrounds the still
heroic but more stratified, less progressive, often ominous city-palace of
the Niblungs. Its tragic conclusion occurs in Atli's great hall at the center of his capital city—"Huge, dim is the hall of Atli" (312)—described,
in contrast to the Volsung hall, as the palace of a greedy, power-hungry

tyrant-king surrounded by servants and slaves, not heroic peers. This progression of symbolic halls matches the theme of "people's praise," which Morris deliberately makes an ambiguous term, hovering between "praise for the people as such" to "praise by the people for their hero(es)." This communal epic notion is associated with the Volsungs, with Sigurd above all, and it declines tragically, "death of the people's praise," with the murder of Sigurd, the fall of the guilt-ridden Niblungs, and the closing supremacy of the isolated tyrant Atli, though the poem ends disastrously for him as well. The conclusion reiterates this decline theme: "Ye have heard of the Cloudy People, and the dimming of the day, / And the latter world's confusion, and Sigurd gone away . . . / All the death of kings and of kindreds and Sorrow of Odin the Goth" (345). "Death of kings and of kindreds" recalls the thematic linking of hero and people, while the precedence of kings underscores how it is the displacement of heroic people that causes the larger decline. The modern world's political and economic progress has spelled disaster for people's heroes and heroic peoples.

The House of the Wolfings intensifies this theme and symbolism, though, as befits Morris's drift toward prose fantasy, it ends more happily. Morris wrote it years later but sets it at an earlier period in the same world. *Sigurd the Volsung* suggests the period of late antiquity around the time of Attila and the Western Empire's collapse: "The mere fact that the famous Germanic epics . . . derive their historical setting from the wild and spacious epoch of the tribal migrations rather than from the solidly established structure of the age of feudalism, gives them breadth and freedom . . . and the human roots . . . go deeper" (Auerbach 111). *The House of the Wolfings* is set nearer the height of the Roman Empire. It represents an earlier stage of Germanic communal heroism: one less aristocratic and more democratic than even the Volsung hall. In contrast, their enemies the Romans are selfish, isolated, class-riven city-dwellers, whose polity has declined from heroic citizenship to corrupt representative government. So, too, Morris opposes Thiodolf in his self-sacrificing heroism (the outcome rests on his willingness to die for his people) to the clever Roman Captain who repeatedly misses chances for Roman victory because of his self-interest: "He had no will to die among the Markmen, either for the sake of the city of Rome, or of any folk whatsoever, but was liefer to live for his own sake. Therefore was he come out to vanquish easily, that by his fame won he might win more riches and dominion in Rome" (133–34). The Roman Captain embodies his city and empire's selfish ideology, through which Morris hints at the condition of England in his own day. Thiodolf gathers to himself the communal hopes symbolized by the people's house. His dying collapse into its high seat in the communal hall, which he had just saved and where his body is later honored by his fellow residents, gathers all Morris's heroic themes into one painterly tableau.

Still, Morris's culture-hero epics, for all their efforts to celebrate the larger life of a heroic and democratic people, remain bound to the individualizing logic of war heroism and depend upon the actions of real heroes in history, however obscured by distance. We are meant to harbor a Carlylean belief in the historical Thiodolf and the historical Sigurd, and this reliance upon an epic ideology of such individual agency and upon the need to trust in it, maybe even to recover it for a modern world in dire straits, looms as an ironic problem at the core of these narratives.[17] For, given the nineteenth-century economic critiques of the very notion of heroism, Morris's epics dramatize that the crisis for the modern world is less the contemporary lack of a real hero (Carlyle's position) and more the continuing belief in that dangerous, because false, hope. The kind of heroic communal life Morris's epics develop with increasing intensity during the 1870s–1880s projects onto the past his own increasingly socialist, even Marxist, worldview. His epics' progression away from the hero contrasts with the steadier Whig views of one of their major influences: Edward Freeman's *History of the Norman Conquest* (1867–76) presents, after *Ivanhoe* (1819), the definitive narrative of heroic Germanic virtue versus militarist Franco-Latin corruption. At its climax the former is defeated at Hastings because of its reliance upon a single leader who dies in a freakish accident. Still Freeman does not question the logic of that reliance, as Morris's epics do individually and, even more clearly, when read together. Marxist ideology does not depend for its agency upon key individuals, but upon the impersonal logic of historical development from aristocratic feudalism to middle-class capitalism to the rule of the proletariat, a process ultimately driven by sheer numbers, not heroes. Despite the scholarly patina of *The House of the Wolfings,* it is not particularly accurate, even by the knowledge available at the time. Then and now the research does not support Morris's vision of communal lodges, of a largely democratic society, or a simple resistance of German natives to Roman conquerors. Herman, the historical German most closely corresponding to Morris's Thiodolf, was an aristocrat, his election hardly democratic, his knowledge of war derived from serving Rome, and his heroic defeat of them, not a simple question of rising up against cruel invaders, but an elaborate matter of plotting, deceiving, betraying, and ambushing. Finally, far from dying heroically in battle for his people, he was assassinated by them years later when he, in turn, had become a tyrant. In short, there is a deeply schizophrenic quality to Morris's epics. I have already mapped the

tension between their foregrounded primitivism and their up-to-date suppression of violence. On the matter of heroic agency, such tension is yet
more taut. Morris's epics knowingly falsify, though in a manner designed
to exude authenticity, the anthropological sketch of the ancient Germans
so as to aggrandize the epic relation of a heroic community and its heroic
leader. Ironically, they do so to project onto the past, and thereby further
in the present, a radicalized liberal Spencerian or Marxist-socialist worldview that has little use for notions of individual heroic agency and whose
vision of communal democracy looks to the future, not the past.

Mackail, his official biographer, emphasized the Morris of romance as
the true Morris, the socialist organizer as an aberration. When he turns to
Morris's politics, Mackail insists that More's *Utopia* meant more to him
than Marx's *Capital*, "which he had been rather dispiritedly ploughing
through" (2:95). For Mackail, even during Morris's headiest commitment
to the socialist agenda, his reading and his imagination remained true
to escapist romance and tales of heroes, ancient and modern: "The rest
were all old and tried friends; *Monte Cristo, The Three Musketeers, Red-
gauntlet, David Copperfield, Great Expectations, Tales of Old Japan,* and on
the last evening of the year his earliest love of all, *The Arabian Nights*" (2:
96). Still, Mackail's virtues as one of the finest practitioners of the Victorian life-and-letters mode of biography result in a portrait that gives real
weight to this socialist side of Morris, rather than merely dismissing it
as so many others in his tradition of the romance Morris do. He documents how Morris's thinking began to question the agency or usefulness
of heroes, especially Carlylean ones: "It has always seemed to me that the
worship of leaders has been a sign of the lifelessness of ordinary Radicalism of late" (2:114). The Marxist historian E. P. Thompson articulated the
most powerful version of this opposing view. His biography casts Morris's
socialist thinking and organizing as the central work of his life. Thompson's emphasis upon this Morris, however, results in sharper insights
into Morris's limitations as a socialist, especially his inability to incorporate socialist thinking successfully into both his imaginative writing and
his sense of himself as a writer for that movement. For though Thompson sometimes asserts a standard Marxist critique of Morris's later turn
back to heroic romances as "pure self-indulgence in pleasurable reverie
or dream, in which neither Morris's intellect nor his deeper feelings are
seriously engaged" (785), at others he sees in these texts, more than in the
earlier epics, evidence that Morris was powerfully imagining the reality of
the collective life of a people, and the agency that could come of that: "His
strength [in *The House of the Wolfings*] is found always in the treatment
of social relations, in the collective life of the folk, in the Hall, at the folk-

mote, in their labour, their battles, their ceremonies" (784). Thompson remains troubled by the romantic dimension of this narrative, however, an emphasis that only grows stronger in the subsequent narratives: "Morris is at his weakest . . . when treating intimate personal relationships" (784). Again it is worth noting the opposing tradition: Northrop Frye holds that all these narratives are best read as personal erotic fantasies, not collective epics.[18]

It is fitting that it is Morris's Marxist *News from Nowhere* (1891) that most fully succeeds in exorcising the heroic ideology that plagues his Victorian liberal epics. In part it does so simply by not being an epic, but a "utopian romance" or "an epoch [not epic] of rest," a socialist end of history, where the last men are not distinguished by race or class or even heroism, but by their communal happiness in work as pleasure. It is also set in the future. Within *News from Nowhere*, however, there is a quasi-epic account of the revolution that ended the capitalist system and set men and women on their way to this utopia. The simple logic of this revolution's success is the solidarity of the mass of working men and women. With no heroes, there are no points of either heroic self-sacrifice or self-aggrandizement. In "How the Change Came," the long central chapter on the war-revolution, agency lies entirely with the tide of history, the ethics of resisting oppression, and the sheer numbers working in unison. It is on the side of the ruling classes and their efforts to resist this inevitable logic that a hero emerges, but Morris's Napoleonic "clever young general" proves powerless before the united masses. Finally, the anti-heroic logic of *News from Nowhere* extends to Morris himself, the hero-poet. He, like his Napoleonic false hero, must fail for the people to succeed.

The narrative is a dream vision of the future state experienced by Morris: he awakes in a better world, sees how it works, and hears how it came to be. It opens with Morris returning home after a night of vain discussion by socialist leaders: "There were six persons present, and consequently six sections of the party were represented, four of which had strong but divergent Anarchist opinions" (43). It concludes with Morris fading out of the future utopia and back into his world: "All along, though those friends were so real to me, I had been feeling as if I had no business amongst them: as though the time would come when they would reject me, and say, as Ellen's last mournful look seemed to say, 'No, it will not do; you cannot be of us'" (228). This opening and closing dramatize Morris's realization of his powerlessness as a socialist leader, his self-conscious abandonment of his role as a hero, and his keen sense that the workers' movement needed to push him and any such inspirational leader aside. Their success would not come because of him or those like him, but only without such vanities. It even seems that he struggles to deny any claim for power for his book *News from Nowhere* to lead to this world. Though the time-travel aspect could have been deployed, in a Shelleyan fashion, to create the future by imagining it, Morris's text refuses to exploit such a paradox to insinuate such a claim. Instead, it tries to deny itself and its writer such Romantic roles. Thus at times the narrative hints at some kind of recognition of Morris by the people of the future, some incipient honoring of a hero from the past. Alternatively, it sometimes seems that the old man who narrates the history of the revolution might turn out to be Morris himself years later, now on the other side, a figure of knowledge and power reflecting to himself on all that he had helped to realize. None of these possibilities is confirmed. Indeed, they all seem to be there only to be rendered vain. The text subverts any possible reading that would give Morris agency as a visionary or writer. Effective heroism is entirely absent from *News from Nowhere,* which is all the more interesting because it is that book that firmly realizes the communal ideal lost or threatened in the earlier epic narratives, which were reliant upon the ideology of the hero. It is a future free of the persistence of epic, of heroes, and thus suffers from no liberal need to hide the murderousness of their agency.

In a fascinating turn, *News from Nowhere* fulfills the daring plot and ideological purpose of Herbert Spencer's aborted epic, "The Rebel": it sees into Spencer's higher ambition and realizes what he could only theorize. Spencer's taste rejected what he saw as the obsolescence of poetry, particularly epic poetry: *The Iliad* ranked lowest in his estimation ("I would rather give a large sum than read to the end" [1:300]); not surprisingly, the radical and nonviolent *Prometheus Unbound* was his favorite long poem ("It is the only poem over which I have ever become enthusiastic" [1:299]). Spencer's own theories, however, led him to doubt Shelley's persistent faith in heroes. Once, while suffering from the "verse-making disorder," he outlined an epic-drama and tellingly centered it upon the inevitable defeat of a hero: " 'The Rebel': the plot of it being not, as the reader may suppose, one exhibiting successful rebellion, but one exhibiting the failure and disappointment of a high-minded hero, consequent on the weakness and baseness of those with whom he acted" (1:260). In his *Autobiography,* Spencer applies this way of thinking, though he assumes the role of the weakly doubting follower, to Ruskin and recounts how he lost all faith in Ruskin's judgment when, in *The Stones of Venice,* he was "called upon to admire a piece of work which seemed to me sheer barbarism" (1:403). Thereafter this radical-liberal condescended to peruse Ruskin's opinions only when excerpted in review articles, though, ironically again, Spencer's epic of failure seems to retell Ruskin's heroic career of isolated rebellion against the dominant culture—followed by abandonment and defeat. Morris's larger evolution also trends away from Ruskin, and toward Spencer's model of collective success grounded in heroic failure. But one should note Spencer's own betrayal of his ideal of impersonal agency: even this arch-theorist of "impersonal agency" falls back into the individualized logic of "self-regulating social progress" (600) and can only envision an epic of heroic failure, not impersonal triumph. Morris's final achievement does just that and marks his long-sought transcendence of liberal modernity and liberal epic, their dubious heroes and shame-faced violence.

ALEXANDER KINGLAKE: MODERN WAR MADE OLD AGAIN

For the combatants on each side at this spot began to hurl against one another some of those loose pieces of rock which there strewed the ground. By some of our officers this Homeric resource was regarded as "unsoldierly," and it seems that their disgust at the sight of such child's play . . .

—Kinglake, *Volume 5—The Battle of Inkerman*

"Homeric resource"! In Kinglake, the most extravagant and devoted of Pope's stylistic epigones, poetic diction at last fashioned Homer's own name into an adjectival element in a bit of elegant obfuscation: "But [Pope's] Iliad—line by line I clasped it to my brain with reverence as well as with love" (*Eothen* 31). In roughly the same span of years that witnessed Morris's poems and stories, his lyrics, romances, and epics, his socialist tracts and speeches, not to mention his carpets, wallpapers, chairs, and beds, Alexander Kinglake laboriously generated one long work, his nine volumes on Victorian England's only major war—*The Invasion of the Crimea* (1863–87). Although Morris and Kinglake shared little politically, socially, or artistically, their contemporary epic efforts strongly exemplify the persistent appeal of Pope for rendering heroic violence, though in them that style has lost much of its anxious disciplining and follows the predominant Victorian pattern of regarding heroic violence as a harmless indulgence for boys or the juvenile in all of us. Both writers also react against the foulness of modern machine warfare by returning to an idealized primitive heroic world—either literally in Morris's case or figuratively in Kinglake's emphasis throughout upon Homeric episodes of childish rock-throwing, Etonian nostalgia, and the like. Kinglake's version, however, reverses Morris's application of Pope to primitive material by deploying him to sanitize and epicize a real war renowned for its messiness and modernity—whether in its causes, justifications, results, or its infamously disastrous logistics that led to the tragic blunder immortalized by Tennyson, the grotesque failures confronted by Florence Nightingale, and the innumerable fiascoes exposed by the *Times* newspaper. A contemporary historian has hyped Kinglake's work as "the greatest military history written in English" (Hibbert iv), but it fell short even of contemporaries, never gaining the influence of Napier's or the sales of Carlyle's. By the time of its completion, more than twenty years after the appearance of the much-acclaimed first volume, it went largely unnoticed and unread.[19]

Still, Hibbert's further description of it as "extravagantly elaborate" and "highly idiosyncratic" finely characterizes this remarkable example of nineteenth-century epic. Its value for my argument lies in how it at once vividly exemplifies up-to-date Victorian contempt for war as economic insanity and political crime, even as it retreats to Pope as its supreme model for popularizing heroic warfare: it is both a liberal denunciation of a bad war trumped up by criminal rulers and public hysteria and a happy indulgence in its sanitized details. Imitating his early influence, Byron, Kinglake traveled to the site of Troy with Pope's *Iliad* in hand to read aloud his boyhood favorite, but Kinglake did not follow Byron's Romantic pattern of further correcting and civilizing Popeian epic to the point of finding all violent heroism repulsive; rather, he insisted that he could see through the sanitizing devices of Pope to the heroic splendor of the Homeric original—and thereby enjoy them safely as a civilized English boy. As an adult, he appealed to Pope's devices as his primary means for retelling the Crimean War in a heroic mode that hid the ugly reality of the war itself and scorned the modern methods—photographs, telegraphs, popular newspapers, and parliamentary blue books—in which its horrors were exposed rather than swathed. For again unlike his early model Byron, the epic history of Kinglake's boyish maturity objected to newspapers not because they jingoistically built up false war heroes, but because they (or one in particular) so eagerly tore his hero Raglan down.

Above all in Kinglake, the higher business of international war is denounced, while the sheer fun of individual combat is embraced. Kinglake's relation to Pope thus epitomizes his relation to the Crimean War. In both cases he turns against the usual liberal strategy of finding redemption in a higher lesson, in some sublimated purpose, while avoiding the ugly details. Instead he scorns the war's larger justifications and plunges into the simple joys of combat: "The way to feel this is not to go casting about and learning from pastors and masters how best to admire it. The impatient child is not grubbing for beauties, but pushing the siege; the women vex him with their delays and talking . . . and on he goes, vengefully thirsting for the best blood of Troy, and never remitting his fierceness" (*Eothen* 32–33). Kinglake does not agree with the officers' dismissal of their men's turn to the "Homeric resource" of throwing rocks; for him "child's play" is not a critique. No such indulgence will be shown to the international great game played by the rulers, whether the Russian Czar, Napoleon III, or the mob of readers of the *Times*.

The Invasion of the Crimea is epic in two senses: one at the level of a self-consciously escapist, primitivist, and childish pleasure in violence; the other at the level of cultural pretension and learned authority—and for both the cultivation of Pope's style is the key. *Eothen* (1844), the Byronic travelogue which established his reputation, documents his early love of Pope's *Iliad*, but also asserts his childish ability to see through Pope to the truth of Homer—"not even a mesh like that can screen an earnest child from the fire of Homer's battles" (31)—and implicitly confesses why its unpretentious immediacy will eschew such refinements for the freshness of Byron. In contrast, as the official biography of the English commander-in-chief, *The Invasion of the Crimea* felt the need to embrace a high style, and Kinglake turned to the one he had absorbed in his youth as the best means of achieving both his history's global and its local epic ambitions. Indeed it is not merely epic, but Iliadic in its deliberate narrative scope. Though nine volumes and nearly four thousand pages long, the story concludes not with the completion of the siege and the end of the war, but with the death and funeral of its hero, Lord Raglan, just before the final storming of the walls. It is also Iliadic in its basic impulse to glorify the names and actions of all the *officers* involved in the various battles and engagements of the war: "I take the liberty of saying that I shall continue to welcome any communications with which I may be honoured respecting the battle of Inkerman, and subsequent events in the Crimea down to the close of June 1855.—A.W.K., 28 Hyde Park Place, London" (4:396n).

Thus ends the fourth volume on Balaclava: even Kinglake's historiography is Homeric, as he relies on oral self-aggrandizement by retired officers at his club and largely ignores the reams of documentary evidence generated by this prototypically modern war. Finally, it is Popeian-Iliadic in Kinglake's deliberate, anomalous (for modern military history), and very Homeric effort to narrate the battles with as much careful attention to individual actions, heroism, killing, and death as possible—but always wrapped in a civilizing Popeian mesh. Thus Inkerman, the most Homeric of all the battles in that the officers of both sides lost control and the battle devolved into a messy series of individual combats, receives a 483–page treatment. Such length arises both from the Homeric detailing and the Popeian periphrases. In contrast, Trevor Royle's lengthy (523 pages) but plain history, *Crimea* (2000), gives it only 15. That is less than 3 percent of his total, while Kinglake's volume on Inkerman is one of his longer ones, making it more like 15 percent of his massive sum. Royle cites a 14–page treatment by ffrench Blake as the "clearest and most concise" version of the battle—revealing his odd lack of interest in the war he has chosen to write about as well as a strange disregard for detail in recounting a battle even he acknowledges was chaotic and therefore, presumably, unfit for clarity and concision.[20]

Kinglake's withdrawal from the unadulterated horrors of Homeric combat into prosaic diction extends to another revealing pattern: his willingness to merge the Homeric theme of epic rage with his own theme of war as adolescent sport. The *Iliad* juxtaposes the rage of combat with the competitiveness of sport through its inclusion of the funeral games, but that is a separate episode, and Homer never regards war and sport as one. Death makes a big difference—not to Kinglake, though, and his linking of battle lust and sportiveness further qualifies and renders eminently Victorian, Thackerayan, and Tom Brownian his punctilious re-creation of full Homeric terror. Throughout his narrative, Kinglake variously comments upon the "warriors by temperament" and their "racial demon of warlike wrath." Even as he dramatizes their ready immersion in the business of slaughter, however, Kinglake repeatedly points to another explanation for the ease with which the English enter into such activity, the old Waterloo myth of "the playing fields of Eton": "General Scarlett's old Eton experience of what used to be called a 'rooge' was perhaps of more worth to him than many a year of toil in the barrack-yard or exercise ground" (4:174); in another instance, Colonel Hodge happily reverts to a maneuver drawn from his crew days—one "expressed by his old Eton word of command . . . 'All Hard Across'" (4:194)—in order to defeat the Russians. His technique makes war less horrible and more stylized, more boyish and amateurish, than does the ever-deadly and ever-professional Homer. In the end, Kinglake's narrative finds not only value in such play but also an analog for the re-creation in his history of his childhood joy in Pope.

His narrative nonetheless retains some of Pope's mature and un-Homeric dismay over his subject matter. Thus, when Kinglake does occasionally strive to show death, not just with his signature detailed fussiness, but as worthy of horror, as in the case of the messenger Nolan vainly striving to redirect the Light Brigade to its correct target and away from its fatal charge, Kinglake overcompensates and makes death so preternatural in its tragic irony that it veers away from a truly Homeric terror and immediacy. Such imaginatively rendered details as the Russian shell not just killing Nolan, but actually tearing "a way into his heart" (4:257), point to an underlying Victorian sentimental recoil before the essential unfairness of death that is deeply un-Homeric: Kinglake literally rends Nolan's heart in order to figuratively rend ours. Here war, combat, and death are no longer objectively exciting, heroic, or brutal, but subjectively tear-jerking.[21] Kinglake's account goes on to explain that, though dead, Nolan, "remaining as yet unreleased still held firm in his saddle" with his arm "still high uplifted in the air," burst forth in "a cry so strange and appalling that the hearer who rode nearest to him always called it 'unearthly'" (4:250). Such tragedy veers into the melodramatic, an elaborate, stagy contrivance by Kinglake to protest against the fact of death when at last compelled to look it in the face.

Lord Raglan's easy heroism and tragic fate sum up the predilections of this idiosyncratic history. Kinglake carefully aggrandizes Raglan's power, before turning to his fall. Generally, Kinglake's protagonist's heroism remains limited to his power of vision and rapid understanding, but on one supreme occasion he places himself on a hill overlooking the battle of Alma. In this exposed position well in advance of the French and English lines, Raglan not only sees, but is seen. The Russian vision of this general and his staff so convinces them (according to Kinglake) of the actual presence of the enemy as to disconcert, then wreck, their heretofore successful maneuvers. Lord Raglan single-handedly wins the battle of Alma:

> Lord Raglan commanded nearly the whole ground destined to be the scene of the English attack. But more, he looked upon that part of the Russian army which confronted ours; he saw ... he saw ... he saw. ... All this—now told with the labour of words—Lord Raglan saw at a glance, and at the same moment he divined the fatal perturbation which would be inflicted upon the enemy by the mere presence of our Headquarter Staff in this part of the field. (2:278–80)

Most historians narrate this event as a series of blunders by the English and the Russians, but in Kinglake Raglan never blunders, and his action becomes a matter of divination and fate—one marked by the heavy anaphora of "he saw." In the remarkable epic logic of this episode, Raglan sees, is seen, and sees the fateful power of thus being seen—and, seizing command of the situation, he controls the outcome of battle as no mere commander of material ever could. Beneath the irresistible gaze and heroic image of Raglan, the Russians cower and scatter, and the victorious English advance to meet their leader.

The battle of Alma, if the allies had followed the advice of Raglan (so says Kinglake), would have resulted in the immediate capture of Sebastopol and rapid victory. But the French refused to follow; the opportunity was lost; and all the horrors of Balaclava, Inkerman, the laborious investiture

of Sebastopol, and the terrible winter on the peninsula resulted. Throughout these ordeals, Kinglake details the interference and double dealing of
Napoleon III, and his consistent efforts to thwart Raglan and delay victory
so as to aggrandize his own glory and that of France. Coolly supported by
French commanders who were receiving secret instructions by telegraph,
Raglan is left wintering in terrible conditions—his men ill-supplied, sick,
and dying—circumstances which he, of course, had long foreseen, but
which the English Parliament, public, and home military authorities had
not prepared for. Kinglake's narrative pins its supreme hero between the
Parisian schemings of Napoleon III and the Trollopean-Olympian editorializing of the *Times*, the two warmongering villains of *The Invasion of
the Crimea*. The narrative ends with his death in order to realize its Iliadic shape, but also because Kinglake has no heart to celebrate the subsequent French-led storming of Sebastopol, wherein Napoleon III reaped
the reward he desired for himself. Thus the most audacious heroicizing
leap of Kinglake's history is to transform the commander-in-chief of a war
famous for the incompetence of its command into its ultimate epic hero
and tragic victim: "On board the Caradoc! The sound, the bare sound of
her name, carried with it a heartrending contrast between the past and
the present. . . . Soon, the Caradoc moved, and was gliding towards the
mouth of the bay, when a flutter appeared at her mast-head which showed
her to be speaking once more. As though in imagined communion with
the honoured freight lying on board, beneath the Flag of the Union, she
flew out the signal—'Farewell'" (9:299–300).

Again, Kinglake descends into tear-jerking melodrama: one is meant
to hear, even feel, a gulping sigh in the dash before "farewell." Curiously,
however, the essential liberalism of this epic resides in this ongoing effort
to defend Raglan, to make the commander, not the men, the principal
victim. In one of the defining moments of liberal epic in the opening of
Don Juan, Byron scornfully turns from any attempt to celebrate one of
the murdering generals offered up as heroes by the gazettes. But in *The
Invasion of the Crimea*, Kinglake conversely undertakes to glorify a general whom the newspapers disparaged as a clumsy murderer. In his epic
history, the two greatest enemies of high-minded liberalism—an ambitious democricide tyrant and a feckless mass public—combine to bring
about a pointless, destructive war, and, as part of this larger crime, manage to thwart, vilify, and destroy the one truly heroic figure involved. One
particular charge by the *Times*—"Raglan and his staff would soon be the
only survivors of the army"—prompted Kinglake to expatiate in one of his
typically elaborate and metaphorical formulations: "At the mere sight of
what he penned, he will writhe like a disinterred worm unwittingly cut by

the spade" (6:273). Raglan's death becomes the fitting, final act in King-lake's epic history, because it enacts the final attitude of liberalism toward war expressed by Byron himself—that it aggrandizes the war-makers, but tramples on the lives of the forgotten men. Kinglake, unlike Byron, did not "want a hero" and engaged in no effort to find one, for he was dealt by Victorian propriety a trump card that Byron never enjoyed—a hero as victim, indeed a noble victim, of both tyrant and mob.

Kinglake's Caradoc finale further ramps up his hero-victim's melo-drama, along with Kinglake's own literary ambitions, by invoking the poet laureate at his sentimental best. *The Idylls of the King* likewise con-cluded with an anguished observer watching the ship bearing Arthur to Avalon fade over the horizon. Recall, too, how Tennyson massaged his sources to render Arthur a Christ-like and "blameless king." Much as the Victorians were shedding the traditional concern about the ill effects of heroic violence (and thus complacently relegating it to adolescent escap-ism), they seemed increasingly prone to seek a semi-divine perfection in their hero-leaders. This drift into eminence was reinforced by the hagio-graphic and cleanly emphases of Victorian biography.[22] Kinglake's history was commissioned and overseen, in a pattern typical of Victorian "life and letters" biography, by Raglan's widow, who expected her husband to be properly glorified, sanitized, and mourned. Such daring concessions to modern literary models and contemporary trends, however, are footnotes to Kinglake's steadfast commitment to history rooted in an epic literary past. The combination of Popeian civilizing humanity and savage Ho-meric delight remains Kinglake's abiding formula and theme. The result-ing overwrought narrative style not only surpasses this study's other epic histories in its detailed facsimile of Homeric terror—it exceeds them in the countereffect of Popeian pity. In the story of Lord Raglan, *The Invasion of the Crimea* thus aggressively extends the liberal penchant for elevating Hector's tragedy over Achilles's triumph.[23] His Raglan gathers, then mag-nifies, all the pity granted by the *Iliad* to its greatest defender and sorriest victim. Kinglake's final achievement is to weave (laboriously) Homeric killing and Popeian death into a massive narrative that is at once a bril-liantly boyish romp through epic's most violent pleasures and an idiosyn-cratic case study in liberalism's angry politics of victimhood.

LIBERAL EPIC BEFORE THE GREAT WAR

HARDY, TREVELYAN, TOLSTOY, AND KEYNES

Lausanne
In Gibbon's Old Garden: 11–12 p.m.
27 June 1897

(The 110th anniversary of the completion
of the 'Decline and Fall' at the same hour and place)

A Spirit seems to pass,
Formal in pose, but grave withal and grand:
He contemplates a volume in his hand,
And far lamps fleck him through the thin acacias,

Anon the book is closed,
With "It is finished!" And at the alley's end
He turns, and when on me his glances bend
As from the Past comes speech—small, muted, yet composed.

—Thomas Hardy

Thomas Hardy's epic-drama *The Dynasts*, published in three parts in 1904, 1906, and 1908, and G. M. Trevelyan's *Garibaldi Trilogy*, published similarly in 1907, 1909, and 1911, represent the self-conscious acme of the liberal epic tradition—one rooted in the stylistic, narrative, and cultural achievement of Gibbon: "The English aristocracy had not one centre but hundreds, scattered all over the country in 'gentlemen's seats' and provincial towns. . . . Patronage had passed into thousands of other hands—though not yet into the hands of millions. Oxford University had done nothing for Gibbon, and royalty had nothing to say to him except, 'Hey, what Mr. Gibbon, scribble, scribble, scribble!' But the reading public of the day was just of the size and quality to give proper recognition to his greatness the moment his first volume appeared (1776)" (Trevelyan, *English Social History* 414). *The Garibaldi Trilogy* and *The Dynasts* foreground this idealized vision of England as a liberal aristocratic nation-state fighting heroically not just in defense of its own freedom, but to further that of Europe, even humankind. The former stands as a particularly strong exemplar insofar as it knowingly inverts Carlyle's reactionary *Frederick the Great*. Trevelyan deeply admired Carlyle, particularly his evocative and poetic early style, as against his "doctrinaire" editorializing of the 1850s, but Trevelyan's history championed the liberal nationalism that Carlyle opposed with a Hegelian-Prussian alternative of patriarchal domination. While laboring over *Frederick,* Carlyle specifically mocked what would become Trevelyan's great theme:

> "Mazzini's presence . . . turned the conversation to Progress and ideal subjects, and Carlyle was fluent in invectives on 'rosewater imbecilities.' Mazzini, after some efforts to remonstrate, became very sad." Mrs. Carlyle said to Mrs. Fuller: "These are but opinions to Carlyle; but to Mazzini, who has given his all, and helped to bring his friends to the scaffold in pursuit of such objects, it is a matter of life and death." All Carlyle's talk that evening (she goes on) was a defence of mere force, success the test of right. If people would not behave well, put collars round their necks. Find a hero, and let them be his slaves. (Froude 1:402)

Republican Italy's subsequent repudiation of its liberal revolution for a Carlylean, imperial, and "successful" model under Mussolini appalled Trevelyan—and further dramatized the tenuous nature of his Edwardian epic history—as, indeed, did the dramatic collapse of the Liberal Party during the course of its composition.[1] Finally, it is worth noting that Carlyle colluded with Ruskin to expose the pretensions of the refined Gibbonian style so admired by Hardy and Trevelyan: "I am . . . reading you, and Gibbon! alternately—on Mahomet! I am going to stigmatize Gibbon's as the worst style of language ever invented by man—its affectation and platitude being both consummate" (Ruskin to Carlyle, June 23, 1878, *Correspondence* 241). In sum, Trevelyan's history further refined liberal epic in the face of influential preexisting attacks on both its theme and its style by an author he much admired—and was itself answered by the liberal disasters of 1911, World War I, and European fascism. Hardy's epic-drama similarly represents the momentary ascendancy in a writer noted for his lyric and novelistic pessimism of an optimistic, progressive ideology: a triumph framed, like Trevelyan's, by ironic negations, here *Jude the Obscure* (1895) and *Time's Laughingstocks* (1909). This chapter thus will survey the Indian summer of this tradition on debacle's verge. But the concluding chapter will take up my last and definitive example of how resilient epic has been in its liberal form—since World War I did not, as often maintained, do away with heroic war narratives in a refined high style. Hardy recanted; Trevelyan despaired; and Mussolini triumphed; yet liberal epic soon found a new, more determined champion in Winston Churchill.

My argument will proceed in four parts: first exploring the surprising affinities between a pessimistic novelist of middle- and working-class tragedy and an aristocratic, country-house, Oxbridge historian dedicated to the Whig thesis of history as a steady march toward ever greater enlightenment and freedom; second contrasting Hardy and Tolstoy, Hardy's closest rival as an epic narrator of the Napoleonic Wars, whom Hardy admired, defended, and ultimately repudiated over this nexus of war, legality, and liberation; third returning to Trevelyan's triumphantly lyrical, well-nigh Shelleyan version of liberal epic; and finally concluding, in the person of Keynes the great economic theorist of governmental action, with how these early twentieth-century epics elucidate the appeal of heroic violence to a liberal ideology increasingly anxious over the problem of agency in the world of the invisible hand.

HARDY AND TREVELYAN'S GENTRIFIED LIBERALISM

The *Garibaldi Trilogy* is an early work by a prolific writer, but it is now commonly regarded as Trevelyan's most significant narrative history.[2] Trevelyan's later, more popular works internalize Trevelyan's preference for epic over the novel, for the cultural dignity attendant upon the former in all its Gibbonian glory. Written during the dire early years of World War II, Trevelyan's *English Social History* (1942) marks a further step in the democratization and professionalization of history by twentieth-century England's leading narrative historian. It simultaneously exudes nostalgia for the amateur, gentlemanly, and country-house world from which Trevelyan emerged. His later years in the very different England of the 1930s–1950s were devoted to the National Trust's efforts to preserve great estates, the symbols of liberal-aristocratic England, from Britain's modern social democracy and its very different economy:[3] neither the great houses, nor their gentlemen readers, nor their liberal epic narratives could thrive in the new machine world powered by anonymous "millions." Despite its ambition, Hardy's epic has not been granted a similarly central status by the critical establishment, much less the reading public. Nonetheless, as with Trevelyan and as the epigraph suggests, Hardy turned to Gibbon at a moment of crisis in his career (this lyric sprang from a visit in 1896 to Gibbon's home in Lausanne, where he famously finished his *Decline and Fall*) as a paradigm of authorial integrity and generic gravitas in the wake of the belittling reviews of *Jude the Obscure*. Hardy was convinced its critics were emboldened by the lower cultural and artistic status of the novel. Thus, the mood of the Lausanne lyric accentuates Hardy's hero worship of Gibbon, his massive history, his critical daring, and his Christ-like iconoclasm: "It is finished" are Christ's, not Gibbon's, last words. The poem concludes by evoking Milton, another epic figure of artistic and moral audacity, and closes with these two lines, which Hardy's autobiography pauses to identify as coming from one of Milton's divorce tracts: "Truth like a bastard comes into the world / Never without ill-fame to him who gives her birth." The poem's larger effect is to link Hardy to Gibbon and Milton, and to underscore his determination to persevere in the dangerous truth-telling of *Jude the Obscure,* but with the cultural dignity of epic.

J. Hillis Miller's 1970s phenomenological work on Hardy demonstrates the imaginative centrality of *The Dynasts* in the larger dynamic of his lyric and novelistic work: "The philosophical passages in *The Dynasts* only make explicit what is implicit in his novels and early poems" (Miller 16). Charles Lock, in more recent historicist studies, complements Miller by stressing Hardy's Vergilian and epic conception of his career, his resistance to Henry James's efforts to elevate the novel, and his lack of interest in James's stylistic sophistication. Lock also argues that Hardy's work on *The Dynasts* and his veneration for the epic were linked to a reconceptualization of his ideal audience in terms of the aristocratic, country-house world of the liberal English aristocracy, a group treated reverentially by his epic-drama.[4] In his autobiography, Hardy tells of grandly arriving at Oxford in a manner his Jude never managed. The day began with a Latin oration by A. D. Godley, which Hardy duly praises as "one of the most felicitous of his many excellent speeches" (407). Godley opens by comparing Hardy to Vergil as masters of pastoral elegance ("Scilicet ut Virgilio nostro") and winds down by referencing *The Dynasts* and "the magnitude of the events it describes" (408). In this record of his ascent to his highest official honor, Hardy stresses how Oxford University mapped him and his career onto the template of the Vergilian progression from pastoral to epic.[5] He then describes how the members of the Oxford Union chose his epic-drama over Shakespeare's patriotic histories for this important production marking this elite club's return to prominence after the hiatus of the war. This chapter serves as the climax of the autobiography's story of triumphant authorial self-fashioning. Thereafter it enters upon a foreshortened account of Hardy's remaining eight years under the rubric "Life's Decline." Miller has similarly shown how Napoleon, the tragic protagonist of *The Dynasts,* resembles and magnifies Jude in his ambition to join an exclusive club of European monarchs—and repeats Jude's failure. But Napoleon and his narrative possess a compelling grandeur denied to the pathetic Jude's downbeat tale. Such cultural splendor bolsters Hardy's confidence in his epic-drama and dramatizes his conviction of having arrived at his highest, securest fame through this work.

Hardy "made minimal claims for the literary or aesthetic value of his novels, or indeed for the novel as a genre"; he "wrote as a ballad-maker would write if a ballad-maker were to have to write novels" (Lock, "Hardy and the Critics" 14, 16). Not only were some of Hardy's earliest poems Napoleonic ballads and battle pieces, but Hardy's autobiography documents his simultaneous work on his first novel and a first, now lost, longer heroic poem on the Napoleonic Wars (*Life* 58). Walter Scott similarly launched his career with ballads, then turned to longer heroic poems made up of shorter balladic units, but his eventual epic was a history, *The Life of Napoleon*. Hardy more fully blended both these complementary impulses—after also following Scott with a long, lucrative detour into the novel—by stitching many short ballad-like scenes into a massive epic-drama of Napoleon, but an epic-drama that harbored a strong historiographical ambition and was thus, like Scott's history, largely a series of paraphrases from historical sources: "as close a paraphrase has been aimed at as was compatible with the form chosen" (preface, viii).[6] Hardy's variation on Scott's influential career—his move from ballads, to pastoral novels, then to his troubled tragic novels, then finally to an historical epic poem—also contained an inner evolving effort to give his narratives a means, here epic machinery, that would allow them to achieve the kind of commentary on the action that James arrived at via elaborating the eminently novelistic device of free indirect discourse. The critical resistance to Hardy's efforts to introduce epic machinery directly into his more ambitious novels finally helped push Hardy to his long-contemplated Napoleon epic: the Oxford visions and Father Time have earned the lion's share of attacks upon *Jude;* his decision to end *Tess* with a reference to an Aeschylean "President of the Immortals" was disparaged as incomprehensible in a novel in a manner that deeply irked him (*Life* 251–52); and his favorite novel, *The Woodlanders,* was planned with higher analytic ambition through the rendering of "visible essences, specters, etc." This higher project had to wait for "the much more appropriate medium of poetry, in the supernatural framework of *The Dynasts*" (*Life* 182).[7] In sum, the shadow of epic constrained Hardy's treatment of the novel, led him to conceive of his novels as both lower than epic and preparatory for it, and eventually resulted in the critical disasters (or what he reacted to as such) of his imperfectly epicized novels that made him, now rich from these works, at last turn to a full-blown epic—a work that both fulfilled, as Miller shows, the inner logic of Hardy's art and dramatized, as Lock

suggests, a lingering cultural dissatisfaction with the novel. For both Trevelyan and Hardy, epic embodied a higher, more certain, more effective
achievement than the popularizing novel that Hardy scoffed at whenever
it sought to be "purposive," and Trevelyan lamented as the preferred form
of a debased mass culture.[8] In their epic narratives, a triumphant liberal
ideology goes hand in hand with powerful conquerors and an authorial
metanarrative of agency absent in Hardy's tragic fictions or Trevelyan's
social history.[9]

HARDY VERSUS TOLSTOY: LIBERAL NATIONALISM
VERSUS CHRISTIAN RADICALISM

*Modern history has rejected the beliefs of the ancients without providing a new
conception to replace them; and the logic of the situation has obliged the historians, after ostensibly repudiating the divine authority of kings and the fatum of
the ancients, to come by another path to the same conclusions: the recognition
(1) that nations are guided by individual men, and (2) that a goal exists toward
which humanity and these nations are moving. These two time-honored, inescapable propositions lie at the base of the works of all modern historians from Gibbon
to Buckle.*

—Tolstoy, *War and Peace*

It is embarrassing that the closest approach to the epic sweep of Tolstoy's
War and Peace among Victorian novels is the largely mock-epic puppetry
of *Vanity Fair*. Hardy's early pastoral novels point toward his later ambitions, but those came in the form of an actual epic, not a grand historical
novel. *The Trumpet-Major* (1880), the novel Hardy wrote and researched
with *The Dynasts* most in mind, is often characterized as the lightest of
his pastoral performances, but it begins and ends with an awareness of
the world of heroic violence that reverses the logic of Homer's epic plots
and similes. Hardy's pastoral comedy glances ominously to the world of
deadly combat his larger narrative trajectory is tending toward, while *The
Iliad* looks in brief similes to the happy pastoral scenes Homer's narratives will reach at *The Odyssey*'s conclusion: "Poor Stanner! In spite of his
satire, he fell at the bloody battle of Albuera a few years after this pleas-
antly spent summer at Weymouth, being mortally wounded and trampled
down by a French Hussar when the brigade was deploying into line under
Beresford" (*Trumpet-Major* 36–37). The novel's final paragraph (its last four
words are "bloody battle-fields of Spain" [301]) exploits the same tension
between pastoral retirement and battlefield death—a classicizing and epic
tension barely evoked, for example, by the influential pastoral novels of
Trollope or Eliot. Hardy's early novels owe much to these two high Victo-

rians: Wessex recalls Barsetshire; *Far from the Madding Crowd* (1874), like Trollope's *Framley Parsonage* (1861), was his breakout novel; both were commissioned by the *Cornhill* on the basis of an earlier, smaller pastoral success with the clear intent to exploit this lesser genre's escapist appeal; early reviewers took that first pastoral, *Under the Greenwood Tree* (1872), to be an Eliot novel under a new pseudonym. But Eliot's georgic-pastoral of work grew into her domestic epic of "business" (Caleb Garth's word for "work") not war, while Trollope's pastoral mock-epic (*The Warden* openly redoes *The Rape of the Lock; Barchester Towers*'s bloodless "War!" [chapter 6] over a pulpit has the same plot as Boileau's *Le Lutrin*) of character led to his Tennysonian and idyllic epic of Plantagenet and Glencora in the *Palliser* series. Eliot's Dorothea and Trollope's Duke ultimately suffer from a similar combination of reformist idealism and lack of effective agency: their peaceful humanity both elevates them as exemplars of liberal morality and diminishes them as heroic agents.[10]

Much as Hardy's relation to pastoral is more epic than Trollope's or Eliot's, so Hardy shares a fascination in Gibbon with two fellow novelists of his prime, George Gissing and H. G. Wells, but Hardy's is consistently more warlike. All three admired, read, and reread Gibbon, and for them his achievement served as a model for rising above their novelistic work. Yet for Gissing and especially Wells, Gibbon also represented a lingering nostalgia for war and the great man, one they sought to transcend in their own more ambitious works inspired by him. Not so Hardy—who on this point strangely resembles Trevelyan both in his admiration for heroic warfare and for the aristocratic country-house world that ruled over England during the heyday of liberal epic and spawned its favorite heroes. Gibbon's vision of modern European civilization was ruled by the liberal logic of progress secured through the balance-of-power dynamism of national competition and self-determination. His idealized competitive model sublimates even the horrors of war into the substance of healthy civilization: "In peace, the progress of knowledge and industry is accelerated by the emulation of so many active rivals: in war, the European forces are exercised by temperate and undecisive contests" (2:513). Such ironically revivifying warfare obeys the rules and avoids the excesses of national conquest and (one is allowed to hope) its individual analog, killing. It functions as the bedrock of both national self-integrity and continental advance. Gibbon's heady combination of liberal nationalism and liberal warfare became for Gissing and Wells a profound error to overcome, while for Hardy (and Trevelyan) it was a heroic solution to adopt and promote. Though Hardy did not follow Gibbon in characterizing wars as "temperate and undecisive" (here he is much closer to Napier, the most respected source for his Peninsular War battles, and the principal model for his many battlefield bird's-eye views[11]), he certainly succumbed to the thrill of "contests." *The Dynasts* exhibits an excited interest in battles fought nobly and according to the rules and upholds the basic liberal justification for war in defense of the self-determining individual and nation-state.

Wells's *Tono-Bungay,* his most autobiographical novel and frequently ranked his best, boasts of him reading *The Decline and Fall* as a young boy in the library of the country house where his mother served: "And, vast book though it was, I really believe I read, in a muzzy sort of way of course, from end to end, and even with some reference now and then to the Atlas, Gibbon—in twelve volumes" (27). Gibbon emerges as the central proponent of one of the novel's primary targets, namely, the persistently aristocratic and landed vision of liberal England, which he labels the Bladesover System, after the name of the fictional mansion (Up Park was its real-life prototype) whose progressivism is consistently perverted by the dead hand of its privileged, rural, and military past. Gissing also proudly recalls, in his own version of a semi-fictional memoir, first encountering Gibbon in boyhood. Where Thackeray's Dobbin received Fénelon as a typical school prize, Gissing's Ryecroft cherished "my Gibbon, for example, my well-bound eight-volume Milman Edition, which I have read and reread and read again for more than thirty years—never do I open it but the scent of the noble page restores to me all the exultant happiness of that moment when I received it as a prize" (29–30). While engaged with this memoir, Gissing was laboring over his last work, *Veranilda* (1904), an unfinished historical novel set in a devastated Italy at the time of the wars between invading Goths and a reemergent Eastern Empire. The novel's thorough indebtedness to Gibbon is the central feature in its limited critical commentary: "It was to have been the offering, so to speak, to the manes of Gibbon, the English author whom Gissing cherished through all the vicissitudes of his life with a kind of idolatrous admiration" (More viii). But this novel possesses none of Gibbon's confidence in the happy nexus of European civilization, the liberal nation-state, and restrained warfare. Gissing's contemporaneous memoir and novel, which both center upon a flight from the capital to a threatened countryside, together reject Gibbon's idealized model of healthy martial competition. They find in war no possibility of redemptive justification or renewal, but only self-destruction and self-defeat, especially for its landed classes and their great houses. Like Gissing and the protagonist of *Tono-Bungay,* Wells himself read and reread Gibbon: he is the most often-cited authority in Wells's *Outline of History,* the epic-length narrative Wells regarded as the defining work of his career. Large chunks of *The Decline and Fall* appear as unadulterated quotations lifted from the source and cemented into Wells's narrative; Gibbon towers as Wells's primary historiographical predecessor, the historian most admired and most emulated. He is also the figure most subject to Wells's corrective rivalry, to his effort to move beyond Gibbon's Bladesoverian values, his nationalist and European parochialism, and his complacent commitment to the wars of great men.

Hardy's higher ambitions, like Wells's, deliberately moved beyond the novel, but also regressed formally in a manner that eschewed, with some of Trevelyan's condescension, any Wellsian effort to make his long-planned lifework one for the masses. *The Dynasts* answers *War and Peace* (1869) as an epic poem and suffers acutely from the condition Tolstoy diagnosed in Gibbon and Buckle. Tolstoy's popular novel, both through its narrative and its philosophical exposition, repudiates the epic idea of decisive warfare under the eye of the hero, while Hardy illustrates more vividly than Gibbon or Buckle that modern history regularly retreated into a fascination with war, heroic violence, and the lives of the illustrious: "Few persons are more martial than I, or like better to write of war in prose & rhyme," as he wrote to a friend in the early stages of composing his prosaic epic poem.[12] In contrast, *The Outline of History* saw itself overcoming Gibbon's country-house Bladesover system and Gibbon's (and Wells's own youthful) nostalgia for war through a work directed at the widest possible array of readers, not the select group assumed by Bladesover, lamented by Trevelyan, and now sought by Hardy. Furthermore, *The Outline of History* aggressively dismisses the career of Napoleon, a career that *The Dynasts* aggrandizes with its epic and tragic treatment: "By that marriage Napoleon was captured for the dynastic system; he might have been the maker of a new world, he preferred to be the son-in-law of the old" (2:365). This passage echoes Hardy's final judgment on Napoleon, but Wells soon turns on Hardy, his nostalgia, and his epic ambitions: "Why, then, is there an enormous cult of Napoleon, an endless writing of books about him, an insatiable collection of relics and documents, a kind of worship of his memory? . . . [Because] he fought to win; when he struck he struck with all his might. And what he wanted, he wanted simply and completely, and got—if he could. There lies his fascination" (2:375). Wells makes it both the narrative and the pedagogical goal of his history to arrive at a world without such fascinations, without such war and war heroes and war poets.

But in *The Dynasts*, for the one and only time as a writer, but at his self-conscious peak, Hardy embraces an ideology of purposeful liberal progress, which comes tightly bound to war narrative and great men, marginal in the novels but central now. His more epic variation upon pastoral and his uncritical admiration of Gibbon anticipated this development, but Hardy's ascent into heroic war narrative, on both large and small scales, is nonetheless surprising—especially when set against his model Tolstoy's version of and attitude toward the same material. At the broadest level, Hardy regularly referred to his epic in terms of the definitive war epic, repeatedly calling it his "Iliad" or describing it as "iliadic." His inevitable sanitization of this Homeric content centers upon the prominence of the "Pities" in his epic's machinery and their Romantic concern for the horrors of battle. Here the "Spirit of the Pities" speaks: *Those who live / Even now advance! I'll see no more. Relate*" (246). Hardy deploys the Pities as the prime critics and commentators on war, but even they often betray their creator's strong interest in its inherent drama and resort to proven techniques for rendering it palatable to themselves and to us. Here the dramatic or staged dimension of *The Dynasts* runs up against its epic or narrated mode. Hardy exploits that tension to highlight liberal epic's vexed relation to heroic violence. The Spirit of the Pities can no longer bear to watch the final French charge at the battle of Talavera, but it still wants to know the result and thus asks to hear about that action's exciting climax. The narration that then follows in iambic pentameter from The Spirit of Rumour closely tracks with its Napierian source and its emphasis upon the Janus face of war. There is marked attention to the admirable bravery of deathless military units, to the heroic energy of both the French and the English, and to a concluding summary of war's horrific toll: "and hurt and slain / Opposed, opposers, in a common plight / Are scorched together on the dusk champaign" (246). This balanced picture of both the glory and the horror of war, which allows us to be both eager and dismayed, is followed by another softening device, in the form of a stage direction: "The fire dies down, and darkness enwraps the scene" (246). Hardy's deft combination of epic narration and the stage variously allows us to join his characters in looking or looking away, in hearing or telling or escaping into silence or darkness, but always the goal is a civilized experience of the always alluring matter of war.

For most of the poem, Hardy's usual irony and pessimism surround the Pities, their lamenting and hopefulness, with undercutting criticism—often from the jaded figure of "Irony," sometimes by the wise "Spirit of the Years." Nonetheless, the patriotism of his narrative (he openly proffered it as an answer to continental histories such as Tolstoy's that downplayed the British contribution) extends to a pervasive effort to show the British commitment to upholding the laws of war.[13] Fox's prominent scene, at the opening of part 2, with a Frenchman offering to assassinate Napoleon, is exemplary: the great Whig aristocrat's humanity and honor lead him angrily to reject the offer, which is made in a flurry of casuistical French rhetoric of how all humanity would benefit from this solitary act, which the Frenchman won't even honestly call assassination, as does Fox: "I care not for names! / A deed's true name is as its purpose is. / The lexicon of Liberty and Peace / Defines not this deed as assassination" (146). Fox pities this man in good liberal terms by lamenting how such schemings "haunt sad brains which brood on despotism / But lack the tools to justly cope therewith!" (147). Fox, of course, is, by implication, "justly" coping, that is, warring with Napoleon. He therefore even considers his ethical obligation to warn the enemy of this unjust threat: "Does strict state-honour ask of me? / . . . that I bare this poppling plot / To the French ruler and our fiercest foe!" (147). The episode ends with the good aristocrat's wish to return to his country estate. In contrast, Hardy accepts the claim that Napoleon connived in a legal assassination of the Duke of Enghien. In a haunting scene before Waterloo, Enghien's ghost parades a dumb show of his war guilt before a sleeping Napoleon: the implication is not only that Napoleon was the more guilty party in these wars but that his final defeat came about because of this guilt, because his reckless disregard for the laws of war finally came back to plague his rest, sap his will, and lead to his just defeat. In effect, Hardy makes liberal guilt the cause of Napoleon's notorious cold to which military historians often ascribe his lethargic failure to crush the Russians at Borodino. Tolstoy famously demolished this favorite example of great-man history, while Hardy augments and moralizes it.

Given these pro-English, pro-liberal, great-man emphases in *The Dynasts,* which climax at Waterloo, the justifications for an optimistic reading of its ambiguous conclusion increase. The Pities once again articulate their vision of an expanding circle of human fellow-feeling, but now their rhetoric becomes more clearly republican, meliorist, epic, even militarist. The potential for Pity to admire what purposeful war, despite its horrors, can achieve had been implicit in their sneaking desire to attend to its heroics when offered up in the kind of stylized sanitization marked above. Now they become eager: "To Thee whose eye all nature owns, / Who hurlest Dynasts from their thrones, / And liftest those of low estate / We sing, with Her men consecrate!" (522).

Here they laud the Immanent Will for its progressive, revolutionary war-making. Here, too, the "Spirit Ironic" at last backs off its constant belittling of the Pities: "For on(c)e I cannot answer" (524).[14] The wise "Spirit of the Years" also strives to embrace the hopefulness it had so often corrected: "You almost charm my long philosophy" (524). These are suggestions, not certainties: irony remains ironic, and wisdom remains cautious, but the pattern of easily mocking or refuting Pity's naiveté has faded, and the final Chorus breaks free of all of Hardy's usual pessimism, doubt, and irony:

> But—a stirring thrills the air
> Like to sounds of joyance there
>> That the rages
>> Of the ages
> Shall be cancelled, and deliverance offered from the darts that were,
> Consciousness the Will informing, till It fashion all things fair! (525)

These are the poem's last lines. Neither Irony's spite nor Year's wisdom is granted a response. There are few more succinct expressions of liberal epic: Homeric rage has evolved into liberal fairness; indeed we are almost in Rawls's liberal paradise ruled by intentional fairness—with the veil lifted; this remarkable achievement has come through legal, just, republican warfare: a Shelleyan goal via compromised un-Shelleyan means, through the kind of heroic warfare rendered casuistically that Godwin and Shelley repudiated—as did Tolstoy.

Beneath this overarching development, much of the most revealing evidence of Hardy's surprising willingness to embrace patriotism and warfare as means of advancing human freedom occurs in the margins and corners of his vast poem. There his troubled relation to Tolstoy helps to highlight the oddity of Hardy becoming a practitioner of liberal epic. In a letter written in 1904 between the publication of its first and second parts, Hardy's ambivalence distills his dilemma: "I am doing the battle of Jena just now—a massacre rather than a battle—in which the combatants were *close* together; so different from modern war, in which distance & cold precision destroy those features which made the old wars throb with enthusiasm & romance. Not that the present war lacks those features, though somehow it seems an anachronism, & to belong to a hundred years ago. I do not read any books about it—only the telegrams in the papers" (3:135). S. L. A. Marshall, perhaps the most influential twentieth-century military historian and theorist, based both his narratives and his theories precisely on this distinction between the Romantic closeness of heroic combat and the scientific coldness of the modern battlefield: Homer versus Kubrick, the plains of Ilium versus the Big Board. Hardy similarly combines a vigorous ethical critique of war as cold massacre with nostalgia for the human thrill of hand-to-hand combat. (In planning his Waterloo, Hardy was excited by "the *nearness* of the French and English lines to each other" [*Life* 292].) Most remarkable is the hint that even the contemporary Boer War, which now figures in military history as an dehumanizing anticipation of trenches and concentration camps, somehow preserved such old-fashioned heroism. The war telegrams Hardy read were most likely Winston Churchill's.[15]

This division in Hardy's response, this tension between up-to-date dismay and nostalgic eagerness, appears best in another marginal instance. Even classical epic had reserved a measure of humane concern for the fate of horses (and occasionally elephants) in battle. Hardy's epic intensified such gestures, and then aggressively extended their humane purpose to rabbits, birds, moles, hedgehogs, even snails and worms: "the mole's tunnelled chambers are crushed by wheels" (483). This Burns-like vision of what the machine of war wreaks upon a series of beings blithely carrying on in their various "households" (483) generously expands the law of war's traditional concern for civilians. It matches Hardy and his wife's campaigning early in the century on behalf of animal rights. His thinking was not, moreover, based on Burns's skills in poetic simile-making nor upon Christian notions of stewardship, but on self-consciously cutting-edge thinking that applies the core liberal concept of individual autonomy to these beings: "Few people seem to perceive fully as yet that the most far-reaching consequence of the establishment of the common origin of all species is ethical; that it logically involved a readjustment of altruistic morals by enlarging as a *necessity of rightness* the application of what has been called 'The Golden Rule' beyond the area of mere mankind to that of the whole animal kingdom. Possibly Darwin himself did not wholly perceive it" (*Life* 359). What has been read as melodramatic anthropomorphizing is thus part of a serious program for asserting evolutionary commonalty that here results in the extension of the law of war to our fellow animal-civilians.

At other times, however, Hardy's concern for animal welfare subtly fades whenever these fellow beasts can be cast as worthy foes, not noncombatants:

> I am not sufficiently acquainted with the many varieties of sport to pronounce which is, quantitatively the most cruel. I can only say generally that the prevalence of those sports which consist in the pleasure of watching a fellow-creature, weaker or less favoured than ourselves, in its struggles, by Nature's poor resources only, to escape the death-agony we mean to inflict by the treacherous contrivances of science, seems one of the many convincing proofs that we have not yet emerged from barbarism. (*Life* 330–31)

This passage is particularly revealing because Hardy interpolates words and phrases into the letter here quoted in his autobiography (or possesses an original unavailable to contemporary editors). These additions (or variants) all tend to highlight that his objection to hunting rests on the loss of a true agon: "by Nature's poor resources only" and "of science" do not appear in the version found in the standard *Collected Letters* edition. Together they reinforce the anticompetitive logic of "weaker or less favoured," and imply an unfair, unsporting oppression of nature by science. There is nothing to admire in pitting an animal on its own against another animal armed with sophisticated technologies.

Hardy thus betrays his longing for the heroic agon that even Tolstoy at times relapses into. Isaiah Berlin notes that Tolstoy reworked the draft versions of Kutuzov, the Russian general in *War and Peace,* to make him more heroic, more antithetical to Napoleon, more spiritually-earthily Russian.[16] Similarly, Aylmer Maude observes that late in his life, when Tolstoy's Christian critique of nationalism and war climaxed in a campaign against Russian military policy, he privately and patriotically "wept" over reports of his country's defeat by the Japanese (2:440). But Tolstoy at least strove to transcend great-man history and to reject all liberal-nationalist defenses of select wars, as here in his brilliant epitome-exposure of epic sanitization: "[Napoleon] conquered everyone everywhere, i.e., killed a great many people because he was a great genius."[17] Tolstoy's heavy use of "kill" in the fuller passage grimly allows no heroic alternatives, even as his equally insistent use of "genius" maintains a bitter irony. Hardy, however, trotted out ambivalence to avoid such efforts and to resist Tolstoy's logical rigor. There is nothing inadvertent about his cultivation of epic; he, much like Fox's Frenchman, cultivates many alternatives to the blunt word "kill," and his studied balancing functions as a rhetorical shield against Tolstoy's insistent purism. This passage immediately follows the condemnation of hunting:

> I should like to be allowed space to express in the fewest words a view of Count Tolstoy's philosophic sermon on war. . . . The sermon may show many of the extravagances of detail to which the world has grown accustomed in Count Tolstoy's later writings. It may exhibit, here and there, incoherence as a moral system. . . . But surely all these objectors should be hushed by his great argument, and every defect in his particular reasonings hidden by the blaze of glory that shines from his masterly general indictment of war as a modern principle, with all its senseless and illogical crimes. (*Life* 331)

This letter in support of Tolstoy's most famous antiwar polemic, *Bethink Yourselves!* (1904), includes faint, but telling, qualifications amid its loud praise.[18] Hardy confines Tolstoy's boundless critique to war as a "modern principle" and to its "senseless and illogical crimes." These phrases harbor serious reservations that allow for war in either older or modern modes: both heroic nostalgia and liberal casuistry.

Tolstoy's theological critique specifically targeted the latter in its effort to undo the turn-of-the-century developments that would result in World War I: "It is in the nature of a government not to submit to others but to exact submission from them, and a government is a government only in so far as it is able to exact submission" (176). A few pages later, Tolstoy approvingly cites another critic who succinctly draws attention to the logic of state power, war, and individual enslavement that together embody a vision of the nation that reverses the liberal myth of the voluntary contract: "'We have ceased to be men and have become the tools of that autocratic abstraction we call the state, which enslaves each of us in the name of the will of all who taken individually would desire the very opposite of what they are forced to do'" (188). Whereas liberalism found a way to defend some wars so long as they follow rules and are fought in defense of liberty and self-determination, Tolstoy asserted that wars or, rather, their very preparations in the form of universal conscription unmasked the deeper reality that all states are founded upon a tyrannous denial of individual autonomy, one that applies to the enemies it kills and to the citizens it forces to kill. *Patriotism and Government* (1901) takes Tolstoy's thinking to its terminus by claiming that it is the goal of governments to oppress, either by killing or by forcing to kill: "The characteristic feature of a Government is that it claims the moral right to inflict physical penalties, and by its decree to make murder a good action" (250); these last five words scathingly impugn the entire "ius in bello" project at the heart of the liberal epic genre, as well as the basic poetic dictional project to soften the vocabulary of violence. Tolstoy applies his logic equally to Eastern European militarist states and Western European republics, that is, to both Hegelian and Lockean polities. Each obeys an essentially anti-liberal paradigm that is ultimately confirmed by their systems for waging war: "The Government, in the widest sense, including the capitalists and the Press, is nothing else than an organization which places the greater part of the people in the power of a smaller part, who dominate them; that smaller part is subject to a yet smaller part, and that again to a yet smaller, and so on, reaching at last a few people, or one single man, who by means of military force has power over all the rest" (251). This statement neatly summarizes in political terms the Achillean ideal of "the last man standing."

Hardy follows Tolstoy's pacifist thinking with insights such as the following: "We call our age an age of Freedom. Yet Freedom, under her incubus of armaments, territorial ambitions smugly disguised as patriotism, superstitions, conventions of every sort, is of such stunted proportions in this her so-called time, that the human race is likely to be extinct before Freedom arrives at maturity" (*Life* 357–58). Still, such reasoning allows for a distinction between a true and a false patriotism that Tolstoy's tighter analysis resists—and Hardy's model implicitly hopes for a realization of true political "Freedom" unavailable within Tolstoy's strict paradigm. While planning for *The Dynasts,* Hardy expressed an approval of patriotism that identified it as a good only qualified by its tragic opposition to another: "Certain things may be both good and mutually antagonistic: e.g., patriotism and universal humanity" (*Life* 290). This pairing recalls the ideological battle of England and France in *The Dynasts* and echoes the tragic resonances of Napier's vivid diptych of these rivals. But Hardy proves far less tragic and conflicted than his source Napier: Hardy ultimately allows England to champion both patriotism and universal humanity. Once again, his relation to a peer dramatizes how patriotic, optimistic, progressive, and epic he insisted upon making his *Dynasts.* Hardy's ambivalence is different from the subtle casuistries of eighteenth-century epic. Instead it maximizes the theme of liberal sympathy or pity for the victims of war, even as it intensifies its patriotic nostalgia in favor of heroic combat. The deep logic of Hardy's *Dynasts* is to portray the English as both superlative heroic fighters and supremely liberal pitiers. The practical result of such an ethical and aesthetic summation of liberal epic's basic paradox is an epic poem rooted in the Romantics, knowledgeable of the most advanced critics of heroic ideology, but determined to persevere in its nostalgic fantasy and the neoclassical devices for realizing it that the Romantics (and Tolstoy) condemned. Trevelyan's *Garibaldi Trilogy* pushes these tendencies to a further extreme of heroic vigor and pitying sympathy, of realism and poetry, and, in so doing, beautifully exemplifies liberal epic in full bloom, even as it further exposes the rot (or emptiness) at its heart.

TREVELYAN'S ETHEREALIZATION OF LIBERAL EPIC

Who blew the breath of life into her frame:
Cavour, Mazzini, Garibaldi: Three:
Her Brain, her Soul, her Sword; and set her free
From ruinous discords, with one lustrous aim.

—Meredith, "The Centenary of Garibaldi"

> *That he might have had the world with him,*
> *But chose to side with suffering men,*
> *And had the world against him when*
> *He came to deliver Italy,*
>   *Emperor*
>   *Evermore.*
>
> —Elizabeth Barrett Browning, "Napoleon III in Italy"

The Garibaldi Trilogy (1907–11) followed immediately upon Trevelyan's enthusiastic book-length study of George Meredith. Meredith played the part
of a patron, sometimes respected and sometimes resented, to Hardy. His
death along with Swinburne's coming just a year after the *The Dynasts*'s
completion left Hardy confident that he had ascended to the position of
England's greatest living author (*Life* 351–58; Millgate 423). *The Poetry and
Philosophy of George Meredith* (1906) reflects cultural valuations similar
to Hardy's by attending much more to Meredith's poetry than his more
famous novels. It overflows with heady observations like the following:
"in the middle of this horror of grave-clothes, of blood, of the plough of
ruin, France is 'still thrilling like a lyre.' To write that line is to understand
the quality which distinguishes the French from the rest of us" (213).[19]
Such a poetical analysis of Meredith's lyrical lament for the armed ascent
of Prussia in "France, December 1870" smoothly extends to Trevelyan's
ecstatic vision of Italian reunification in a history written in poetic prose
to match Hardy's prosaic poetry. Like Hardy, Trevelyan sees his work in
a tradition stretching back through Romantic and Victorian poets to Gibbon and Milton. But like Meredith, Trevelyan will find myriad metaphorical means to suppress the horror of war in favor of its thrilling emotions,
especially sentimental ones. He renounces the Romantics' attentiveness
to war's horrors. His rich, lyrical responses to the sight of battles for liberation set amid a glorious Italian landscape are rendered in the enthusiastic but determinedly evasive manner of Ruskin. But like Hardy's, Trevelyan's version of warfare will come down heavily on the side of the pity of
it all, and that pity will ultimately lead to freedom, human understanding,
and world peace. Yet another point in common is how his interest in this
subject was rooted in childhood fascination with his own family's involve-
ment in his epic's events. Unlike Hardy, however, Trevelyan celebrates a
leader very different from Napoleon. Indeed he will go so far in fashioning his anti-Napoleonic hero into a figure of humane perfection that his
hero's ability to represent historical understanding and agency will come
into question—even for Trevelyan himself. The alternately vivid and wan
result of Trevelyan's etherealization of heroic warfare into lyric thrill amid

the mountains and stars of a tourist's Italy serves as a reminder of terror's necessary role. *The Garibaldi Trilogy* is not just a sanitized, but a purified, version of Homer—and yet in that purity lies an emptiness which another Napoleon fills.

Trevelyan's history of the patriotic Italian struggle against Austrian, Papal, and Neapolitan-Bourbon forces of repression exaggerates the basic contrast of tyranny and freedom. The exuberant historian renders these foes as Gothic monsters from the darkest past (one possesses a castle-prison in Otranto): "The palsied hand was now stretched from beyond the Apennines. . . . Under such a system it was believed then, and is in the highest degree probable, that political and religious reasons were some-times only the cloak for the ruin of individuals who were the victims of personal jealousy, or stood in the way of sinister designs*" (1:59). The footnote (cued by the asterisk) cites Byron as its authority: Trevelyan's oppressors are explicitly painted with the brush of *Childe Harold* and step from the pages of Shelley's *Cenci*. Their heroic opponents, who range from Mazzini to Cavour, are romanticized, aestheticized, humanized, but subordinated in a tale that insistently remains a "Garibaldian epic" (2:6; 2:328).[20] Trevelyan explains the significance of these events in terms of one heroic personality, and not the idealist philosopher or the practical statesman, but the charismatic warrior. Not only does he choose a mili-tary hero as the focus of his history of Italian unification, but, as with Gibbon, Wordsworth, and Byron, Trevelyan dramatizes his search for a properly humane military hero. His book openly surveys other potential candidates around which a suitably progressive epic could be fashioned—Wallace, Tell, and Joan of Arc (all conventional figures of this tradition) form one list; elsewhere he alludes to Cromwell and Washington as rival possibilities—but, for Trevelyan, the "time when Mazzini ruled Rome and Garibaldi defended her walls, sounds like a poet's dream" (1:3), and proves irresistible to his historical, epic, and lyric ambitions. Moreover, unlike these less well-documented rivals, Garibaldi's story provides such com-plete records that, paradoxically, his epic can rise to even more intense heights of idealism: "The records of the Italian national hero and his deeds are detailed to the point of realism," even as his "legendary exploits" are surrounded by an "atmosphere of poetry and high idealism" (2:7). The lat-ter always predominates in Trevelyan's narrative: "Garibaldi had, perhaps, the most romantic life that history records, for it had all the trappings as well as the essence of romance. Though he lived in the nineteenth cen-tury, it was yet his fortune never to take full part in the common prose life of civilized men" (1:23–24). This double gift challenges the intellectual coherence of Trevelyan's history, as his Garibaldi ascends out of "the common prose life of men" and into the heights of Romantic heroism, leaving realistic historiography with its concern to explain through rational processes of cause and effect far behind. In finally rendering poetry and history one, *The Garibaldi Trilogy* risks being neither.[21]

Trevelyan's account, which emphasizes Garibaldi's adventures as a guerrilla fighter and fugitive amid the splendors of the Italian landscape (splendors that Trevelyan piously retraced step by step), abounds with references to and direct quotations from various English Romantics. Garibaldi figures as the historical fulfillment of many a poetic dream, but also (and oddly) "a poet, in all save literary power" (3:296–97). He becomes the ultimate liberal epic hero and poet, leading his men onward with both his stirring acts and his inspiring voice:

> He had all the distinctive qualities of the hero, in their highest possible degree, and in their very simplest form. Courage and endurance without limit; tenderness to man and to all living things, which was never blunted by a life-time of war in two hemispheres among combatants often but half civilised; the power to fill men with ardour by his presence and to stir them by his voice to great deeds; but above all the passion to be striking a blow for the oppressed, a passion which could not be quenched by failure, nor checked by reason, nor sated by success, old age, and the worship of the world. (1:24–25)

He strikes, but only "for," only to champion, never to kill, never against. The rhythms and rhetoric of Trevelyan's evocation of Garibaldi's untouchable, godlike irrepressibility amid the depressing compromises of the real world underscores our epic historian's basic strategy for deflecting any rational political-economic critique by embracing a potent ethical-aesthetic appreciation for Garibaldi. "Ardour" is the key word: it avoids the dismal science and explains his hero's agency through the power of love. In echoing Shelley's equally indomitable skylark, however, Trevelyan's Garibaldi opens himself to the charge of "man thou never wert!"[22] Later in volume 2, Trevelyan returns to this portrait of the humane hero with an epigraph that sees Garibaldi as a better version of an ancient Roman republican—"beyond doubt he is worthy to be compared to the best of the ancient Romans, were it not that in him the sense of humanity was more profound and tender" (2:179). In this vision of Roman heroism humanized we have the ethical essence of liberal epic and its progressive ideal. Ultimately, this progressive and humanizing model joins with a corrective dynamic central to the workings of epic to recast Garibaldi as greater than the greatest of Roman epic heroes. Garibaldi is a better Aeneas, the national liberator, not invading conqueror, of Italy, the expeller of Austrian military dominion and eradicator of papal tyranny, not the oppressor of the native Latin people and founder of a empire.

Such intentions shape Trevelyan's methods of narrating his basic subject matter—warfare. Trevelyan renders Garibaldi's military violence as self-sacrifice, highly sentimentalized pity, and humane beauty, not the terrifying sublime. His volumes highlight Garibaldi's famous battles and sieges, but also meticulously record all his numerous smaller engagements, marches, ambuscades, defeats, and flights. While he acknowledges the tragedy and heroic sacrifice of those who died (Garibaldi's "heroine-wife" Anita in his arms), he avoids gore and rage and foregrounds (even when it's the background) natural beauty and humane pathos. Although Trevelyan claimed to possess an amount of documentation that would allow his "poetic" subject to rise to the detail of "realism," he never deploys that evidence to show realistic killing and death. He never represents the vivid moment of anatomical dissolution, but takes Pope's and Gibbon's basic strategies along with Carlyle's and Meredith's further innovations to their sentimental limit and only shows the aftereffects—the bare fact of death, the funereal body, and the pious lament: "The battle of Varese had cost the mother of the Cairoli the first of those four sons whose lives she gave for Italy. It was Ernesto, a young doctor of law, fighting as a common soldier; he was deeply mourned by Garibaldi, who already knew and loved the Cairoli family, the leaders of patriotic Pavia" (2:95). Thus does liberal epic, at its ripest, mourn for the sacrifices suffered by its heroic aristocracy, and suppress the now of death for the after of mourning.

Even when Trevelyan explicitly identifies the combat as "Homeric—that is, the personal—nature of this combat of June 3, in which so many of these young patricians lost their lives" (1:170), his account, like Carlyle's before it, refuses to follow its own Iliadic cue. Trevelyan stresses movement, advance and retreat, among the walls and streets of Rome: the picturesque locale seduces him into lingering over its many Romantic, historical, and, frankly, touristic features—"this ornate country-house of the Corsini," an "aesthetic fortress." While admitting much death in generalized terms, Trevelyan concentrates what close attention he permits upon two revealing cases. In the first, Enrico Dandolo is quickly "shot dead" in a disastrous charge against a "hidden" French unit. Trevelyan immediately switches to the bravery of his brother Emilio that day, and the pathos of his subsequent discovery: "Many knew of Enrico's death, but none dared tell Emilio. . . . The Colonel . . . took Emilio's hand and said: 'Do not seek your brother any more—it is now too late. I will be a brother to you.' The young man, sick with wounds and grief, fell fainting against Manara, who carried him out of the room in his arms" (1:182). The disproportion between the thinly registered death perpetrated by an invisible foe and the brocaded sentimentality lavished upon the living brother's actions, hopes, realization, and final consolation render Trevelyan's version of Homeric combat utterly un-Homeric, with not a hint left of the joy of killing or dominating. Garibaldi fights only to inspire and console. In the second prominent death, things are little different:

> In the confusion, Masina had been left behind. It is not certain at what spot on the steps or in the garden of the Corsini—at what moment of advance or retreat—he fell; eye-witnesses gave divergent accounts. But his body was left lying in the middle of the slope, sixty paces from the steps up which he so gallantly charged. During the rest of June the Italian bullets from the Vascello, and the French cannon-balls from the Corsini, sang day after day over his whitening bones, which only after Rome had fallen was it possible to seek and bury. (1:185)

Although there were many "eye-witness accounts," he dismisses them all as "divergent." Since "it is uncertain" precisely where or when he fell, no vivid picture is given. Such reticence, fudging, and dismissing is, as with Gibbon, not this historian's normal attitude toward detailed eyewitness accounts. When Trevelyan actually does bring himself to look, he finds the rotting body already in the clean form of "whitening bones" over which the "cannon-balls sang." This is precisely the sort of pastoral-beautiful vision of war that, according to Fussell and others, World War I permanently did away with. Indeed Trevelyan's popular history distilled the essence of nineteenth-century battle conventions so brilliantly that it, not the Georgian Anthology, represents the fullest epitome of all that the World War I poets and their Modernist heirs most despised—for here it is very sweet and beautiful to die for one's country.[23]

Trevelyan clearly has no keenness for the details of lethal combat, but a penchant for soft-focused beautifying, really more neoclassical than Romantic, more Popeian than Shelleyan. Ruskin's similar attraction to heroic warfare, avoidance of death, and swerve into the sublimity of landscape is another relevant model, but then Ruskin learned his lessons from Pope's *Iliad*. In another typical example, involving a battle in which "Garibaldi was to display his peculiar strategical genius at its best," Trevelyan deploys his own peculiar genius to characterize the precise moment of armed encounter. He finds it convenient to rely on a single eyewitness account that, one can now only presume, barely diverged from any others: "Garibaldi gave his orders only by gestures, and our men cast themselves down like a torrent. I am living in a world of poetry" (2:99). The poetry of this epic world is a religious-Romantic poetry of ecstatic self-sacrifice to a higher cause and metaphorical, naturalized death—as their deadly charge morphs into a Shelleyan waterfall flinging its waters into eternity. In one of the most telling instances of Trevelyan's transmogrification of epic combat, he surveys the ground before Palermo, scene of Garibaldi's greatest victory, and describes it as follows:

> The peaks, ridges, and long, deep valleys of the mountains, among which Garibaldi from May 19–26 gradually worked out this supreme military problem of his life, resemble in size, shape, and general character the highest part of the English Lake District. It may give some notion of the character of the ground to imagine the hills between Helvellyn and Scafell with all their water-courses dried up, and instead of an universal and undying plenty of wet grass and moss and bracken spread between one precipice and the next, a sparse and short-lived crop of green herbs and bright-coloured flowers filling the interstices of the grey rocks . . . and in valley bottoms a sudden wealth of olives and fruit-trees in some rocky Eden loud with nightingales. (2:272).

The Lake District without water! Battles without killing! Such is the peculiarity of Trevelyan's Ruskinian imagination, and such is warfare in this most perfect of liberal epic histories, where death, never quite seen, is only self-sacrifice by young heroes and thence the occasions for sentimental mourning by mothers, brothers, friends, and grateful countrymen. Any resemblance to the Iliadic mourning for Hector is misleading: there a doomed city's grief exalts the power of Achilles to kill and destroy; here a rising nation, destined to triumph over imperial tyranny, honors the heroic sacrifices that made this liberal future inevitable.

Trevelyan's indulgence in the details of this landscape precedes the climactic battle of his three-volume history, the capture of Palermo. According to Trevelyan, "The story of Garibaldi and the Thousand," the title of his second volume, "down to the taking of Palermo has an historical and artistic unity" (2:328), and such a claim signals not only the epic ambitions of his narrative (for it is the Aristotelian goal of epic to recast history in artistic proportionality and narrative unity) but also its division between a realistic/historical seriousness and an artistic/Romantic ideality. Once again, this history's determined Romanticism triumphs over its potential realism. As Garibaldi and his troops proceed from their great victory at Calatafimi in the Sicilian heartland toward Palermo on the northern coast, Trevelyan's emphasis on a Romantic—verging on touristic—description of landscape waxes yet fuller. During their advance, we see how on "a starry night . . . Garibaldi gazed at the unwonted brightness of Arcturus," for Garibaldi claimed that "Arcturus was his star, which he had chosen for himself when he was a sailor-lad, and that its splendour foreboded victory" (2:280). Shortly thereafter the tourist-troops, "descending from the higher prairie land, followed one of the most lovely footpaths in Sicily" (2:280). As they approach Palermo, Trevelyan's guidebook mode gestures toward, first, the romantic atmosphere ("it was an enchanted hour that threw its spell on all") and, then, the view of the great edifices that both symbolize and house their oppressive, anti-liberal opponents: "The Cathedral and the Palace, the heart of the enemy's position, rose clear above the city roofs" (2:289).[24] Trevelyan's immediately following description of the army's advance perfectly exemplifies the nature of his narration: "But, whilst he was still gazing upon all this beauty, the soft, green masses below lost shape and colour, the towers and cupolas of Palermo were merged in the undistinguished haze, the rosy tints upon the mountain-tops grew pale, and one by one his own signal fires of war leapt out instead along the circle of the hills, beckoning him to descend into the darkened plain" (2:289). The sharp discrimination typical of the Homeric gaze upon the target city, not to mention the more pedestrian matter of a military commander's responsibilities, fades before an ideal-ized and romanticized psychology that draws Garibaldi into a passionate embrace, not a murderous battle: this paragraph is a fitting microcosm of these three volumes. Its depiction of war echoes the famous scene of city walls, campfires, and stars at the conclusion of *Iliad* 8, which Coleridge and Arnold singled out for opprobrium as an example of Pope's inveter-ate tendency to sublimate Homer's simple, graphic realism into beautiful, high, and vague art. By any measure, Trevelyan's language recalls the "lu-minous haze" of Pope's poetic dictional translation, not Homer's sharp-ness and plainness. Although the imagery of rape frequently governs the language of an epic assault upon a city, as it does in the *Iliad*, in Trevelyan the desires of the liberal hero are given no such disturbing coloration. He appears as a lover beckoned by an intensely feminized landscape into the passionate (and legal) conception of Italian liberty.

When the battle begins, this romantic mood maintains the powerful interdiction against any vivid representation of an agonizing Byronic or Shelleyan death—much less the Homeric joy of killing. Even when Trev-elyan describes a deadly cross fire put up by "the Neapolitan riflemen and their two cannon" and "from the opposite direction a Neapolitan war vessel," his delineation focuses only on the pitiful aftereffects: "Here fell Benedetto Cairoli—yet destined to be the only one of the five brothers to survive the wars of liberation—and Canzio of Genoa, Garibaldi's future son-in-law. Here the brave Hungarian, Tukory, who had led the vanguard, fell wounded to death" (2:300). Two of the three who "fell" did not actually die: metaphorical euphemisms become even more sanitized when made happily literal. Such "death" climaxes in the next paragraph, where one of Garibaldi's fiercest lieutenants is hit: "then the high barricade yielded to the fury of Bixio, undeterred by a bullet in his breast" (2:300). Again death does not result even from such a terrible wound. As long as it is death-less, Trevelyan permits himself to register blood and anatomy: "Bixio was at the moment near fainting with pain and loss of blood, for he had just cut out with his own Spartan hands the bullet that he had received in his breast at the Porta Termini. He had no thought of retiring yet from the fight" (2:302). At this point with such a furious "Spartan" warrior who can cut out the offending bullet, Trevelyan's narrative gets as close to Homeric anatomical terror and rage as it ever will. Thus it is particularly reveal-ing of his deep-seated aversions that soon "Bixio, staggering for loss of blood from his wound, but all in a rage" is removed from the battle. His violent orders and "feverish plan" are "countermanded" by Garibaldi, who "calmed his worthy lieutenant": "Once in bed, Bixio was unable to leave it during the next three days of battle, during which the absence of the dreaded, indefatigable man was a relief alike to friend and foe" (2:305–6)—and our historian.

This mood is confirmed by the reappearance of the calming figure of the true liberal hero. For though the mastermind of the victorious bat-tle, Garibaldi's relation to the killing is a very different one from Bixio's. Immediately upon the removal of the too Achillean lieutenant, Trevelyan describes Garibaldi fixing his headquarters:

> The enemy soon discovered his whereabouts and aimed the bom-bardment specially at the Piazza Pretorio. Although every building on the square and its neighborhood suffered greater or less damage, the Municipality itself was strangely intact. Similarly, though many persons in the square were hit, Garibaldi had his usual luck. The populace cried out on a miracle. At some hazard to themselves they would stand in crowds gazing at him as he sat on the steps, as composed as one of the statues, paying no attention to the shells and abstractedly twirling round and round the string of a little whip which he held in his hand. (2:306)

Trevelyan attempts to foist all the sense of this "miracle" onto the supersti-tion of the Sicilian populace, but his own prose betrays a deep unwilling-ness to enter into a wholly rational explanation. So he turns to phrases such as "strangely intact" and "usual luck," and to an analogy between the living Garibaldi and the statues which, though it logically arises from his abstraction and imperturbability, symbolically identifies his true status as not just a hero, but a saint.[25]

Garibaldi's heroic perfection thus arises from the various liberal, progressive, Romantic, and chivalric reasons detailed so far, but also from the logic of death in Trevelyan's narrative, from the fact of Garibaldi's calm indifference before it, as well as his seeming invulnerability. For, like Trevelyan, his hero, while entering into scenes of epic death, seems easily distracted from war and repeatedly drawn, both literally and figuratively, to live in a world of profoundly un-Homeric poetry:

> While Garibaldi, skillfully avoiding Urban's columns, was winding his way in the darkness by a small track along the slopes of Monte Orfano, he suddenly drew rein and began to listen intently—for the distant sound of horse hoofs or of cannon, as his staff supposed. But, in fact, a nightingale had just broken into song over his head, and in a moment he had been rapt, in that moonlit hour, into another sphere where the inner life of his soul was spent,
>
> 'Some world far from ours,
> Where moonlight and music and feeling
> Are one.'
>
> He sat long motionless, in a trance from which his followers were at last fain to wake him. In the morning they safely entered Brescia, after one of the most hazardous marches of the campaign. (2:104–5)

Hero and historian are as one in their subordination of danger, death, and epic terror to sentimental sympathy, Ruskinian idealism, and an escapist longing to find only the beautiful in a world of violence. Trevelyan implicitly claims that a liberal, progressive cause ideally works this magical charm on the epic matter of war. It is fitting that such a hero, who relentlessly enters into the thick of battle, exposing himself along with his men, is, as if by a miracle, never once wounded. In the same battle in which Trevelyan would not look upon the death of Masina or record any eyewitness accounts, we are treated to this vision of the hero: "The Bersaglieri officers, who came out of the Porta San Pancrazio to announce to him the arrival of their regiment, found him in the thick of the fire, his white mantle riddled with bullets, but himself miraculously untouched, spreading calm and courage wherever he appeared" (1:178). Here not a hero but a saint, with a "white mantle riddled with bullets" to prove by its spotless holiness the authenticity of the miracle, Garibaldi seems to spread "calm and courage," a distinctly liberal epic combination, because Trevelyan can look at him in the full confidence of never seeing rage and death or blood. Garibaldi's saintly confidence spreads first to Trevelyan, thence to the intently gazing soldiers, and, finally, to the reader in a wave of religious-Romantic joy: this is Trevelyan's transformation of the Homeric aristeia, the transcendent fury of the hero has become a transcendental calm.

Such otherworldliness, if it finally secures Garibaldi his status as the perfect heroic ideal of a similarly perfected liberal epic—a liberator from death, not just oppression—finally works against his preeminence in the deeper logic of Trevelyan's history in its (largely repressed) realistic dimension. Eventually, despite the historian-poet's best efforts, some measure of liberalism's intellectual and political-economic critique of heroic warfare returns. It undermines Garibaldi's stature and favors the very different figure of Napoleon III. Garibaldi's lack of a bloody hand renders him useless as a convincing symbol of individual agency, while Napoleon III recalls, however faintly, some of the deadly energy of his greater namesake. In the concluding pages of his history, Trevelyan admits that "there cannot be another revolutionary war precisely of the Garibaldian type in the Europe of the coming era," and that Garibaldi was merely "the right man in the right time and place" (3:296). Far from controlling events and explaining history, Garibaldi emerges as the blessed fool or lucky dupe—a fluke. Trevelyan struggles to justify Garibaldi's centrality by comparing his importance to that of Mazzini and Cavour and finding them wanting, but appearing throughout his narrative there is another figure whom Trevelyan muses over as the exact antithesis to the "simple heroism" of Garibaldi. Napoleon III veers from sending his soldiers to crush Mazzini's Roman Republic in volume 1 to leading his armies against the Austrians at Magenta and Solferino in volume 2, huge bloody battles that more than any of Garibaldi's engagements fatally wounded foreign rule in Italy. He brings about the conditions for Italian unification. These battles, however, were so deadly and ugly that even Napoleon was sickened by them, and, famously, their effect upon Henri Dunant led to the founding of the Red Cross. "This graceful and picturesque town had been transformed . . . into an immense hospital" (Dunant 48): this modern vision reverses the aesthetic propensities of Trevelyan's account, moving away from Romantic and touristic rhetoric and toward technical realities of vast machine-death on the modern battlefield.

Napoleon III cautiously supported a measure of Italian reunification, ironically, on the understanding that Nizza, Garibaldi's Italian place of birth, would by a carefully arranged plebiscite become Nice and French: a novel form of conquest by democracy that enraged Garibaldi. Not only did Napoleon III never desire the full Italian unity that finally resulted from his actions, as if by accident and mischance, but, as Trevelyan's narrative repeatedly confesses, Napoleon III is a mystery, "the doubtful and weak-willed guide of Europe's destiny," who, "if he had been summoned before the throne of Omnipotence to give an account of his intentions, . . . could hardly at any moment of his reign have given a clear and consistent answer. He was at once a selfish and scheming adventurer who murdered liberty in his own country . . . and a romantic idealist who wished to extend the principles of the French Revolution over Europe" (2:74–75). Such conventional but irreconcilable oppositions and such mixing of stereotypes make him a doubly "fascinating and mysterious book" (2:74) for the ever-literary Trevelyan to read and apply to his own effort to cast history in a progressive mold. But this mystery man, not the simple hero, emerges as the truer "guide" to events in Europe and Italy. Yet he is clearly no guide at all, but an enigma who controls, explains, and elucidates little—least of all himself, certainly not history, and not even this epic. Moreover, Napoleon III presents such a bookish enigma, such a complex reality, that none of Trevelyan's off-the-shelf conventions, whether epic or Romantic, gothic or novelistic, can encapsulate or explain him. Napoleon III symbolizes the intellectual failure of Trevelyan's heroic history-biography in which the real "guide" is an utter mystery and the ostensible "hero" rendered as a fluke and saint, one who could quickly confess his sins (zero) before a throne of Liberal Omnipotence, but could never be the explanatory agent of historical events. *The Garibaldi Trilogy* reveals itself as an epic that runs from death and a history that shuns political-economic reality. The very perfection of its realization of liberal epic as a literary historical ambition inevitably exposes the hollowness of its literary attempt to explain history in terms of individual agency—and war—particularly when that agent and that war have been purged of rage and killing. His history's last words give a doctrine not a thesis, a belief not an explanation, a liberal epic prayer for nationalism, freedom, and humanity: "And to us of other lands, and most of all to us Englishmen, Garibaldi will live as the incarnate symbol of two passions not likely soon to die out of the world, the love of country and the love of freedom, kept pure by the one thing that can tame and yet not weaken them, the tenderest humanity for all mankind" (3:297).[26] Three years later Trevelyan began serving in World War I: *he* never wrote this way again, and, as liberal epic migrated into the capable hands of Winston Churchill, it confessed the deeper truth that the thrill (a favorite Churchill word) of killing in battle was a pleasure and a power not to be forsworn, certainly not by the consummate liberal hero of the twentieth century.

KEYNES AS A MODERNIST FÉNELON: THE TRAVAILS
OF ECONOMIC HEROISM

*Before the eighteenth century mankind entertained no false hopes. To lay the illu-
sions which grew popular at that age's latter end, Malthus disclosed a Devil. For half
a century all serious economical writings held that Devil in clear prospect. For the
next half century he was chained up and out of sight. Now perhaps we have loosed
him again. . . . The projects and politics of militarism and imperialism, of racial and
cultural rivalries, of monopolies, restrictions, and exclusion, which were to play the
serpent to this paradise, were little more than the amusements of his daily newspaper, and appeared to exercise almost no influence at all on the ordinary course
of social and economic life, the internationalisation of which was nearly complete
in practice.*

—J. M. Keynes, *Economic Consequences of the Peace*

Keynes was another major figure who, like Churchill, would dominate
the English response to the shortcomings of Trevelyan's rosy brand of
liberalism, heroism, and warfare after 1918. His *Economic Consequences of
the Peace* (1919) articulates the most brilliantly scathing of the postmor-
tems of liberalism's dream world before 1914 that had allowed learned
theorists to claim that no major European war was even possible, that
enabled Trevelyan to compose such a Shelleyan paean in the guise of a
scholarly prose history, and that made even Hardy hopeful. Keynes's preface prominently cites Hardy's *Dynasts* along with Tolstoy's *War and Peace*
in a reverential manner that confirms the novelist's success in achieving
the highest cultural status through devoting himself to an epic project,
but Keynes's ironic purpose is to stress *The Dynasts* as prime evidence of
the absence of heroic agency in the modern world. In so doing he fails
to acknowledge the counterplot this chapter has traced, namely, the rich
brew of Hardy's authorial ambitions, his nostalgia for heroic warfare, and
thus his epic fascination with violent agency. For by removing all traces
of the Homeric celebration of domination and killing from his pure con-
summation of liberal epic (or his purged reduction of Carlylean great-
man history), Trevelyan eviscerated the deeper logic of this paradoxical
modern genre and exposed its ongoing crisis: liberalism required some
vestige of epic's primal scene to imagine its own ideal of individual self-
determination and agency; it needed just a trace of Vico's notion of Homeric "poetic wisdom" to supplement and enliven its far too wan and
rational conception of agency. Arnold's summary judgment of Shelley
encapsulates this dilemma: "a beautiful and ineffectual angel beating in
the void his luminous wings in vain." Arnold was one of poetic diction's
leading critics, especially of its falsification of Homer. Like Coleridge,

however, he missed the civilizing project behind Pope's suppression of Homer's truculent sublimity and graphic realism, but, like Pope, his own requirements for an English translation (particularly his requirement of "nobility") effectively imposed a high-minded liberalizing humanity upon Homer's savage energies. Still, Arnold's authentic learning bears fruit in his comment's suggestive richness: it correctly replaces the sublimity usually associated with epic angels with its Burkean refinement; it links that quality to ineffectuality or loss of power; and its imagery of vain beating dramatizes the emptiness of heroic action without a heroic target.

Keynes is easily the most important twentieth-century heir to the nineteenth-century tradition of neoclassical political economy. Alfred Marshall, Keynes's father's teacher and the influential systematizer of Ricardo and Mill, is not quite so determined as Mill to eliminate warfare from the modern world by the simple rhetorical trick of silently expunging it from his textual analyses, but the opening of his encyclopedic synthesis, *The Principles of Economics* (1890), accomplishes the same goal by openly stating it: "The two great forming agencies of the world's history have been the religious and the economic. Here and there the ardour of the military or the artistic spirit has been for a while predominant: but religious and economic influences have nowhere been displaced from the front rank even for a time; and they have nearly always been more important than all others put together" (1). Marshall's paralleling of heroic ardor and artistic power nods to the eighteenth-century "Homer problem" at my argument's origin. But his solution is a further development of the standard Victorian move to displace such ethical and aesthetic debates over heroic war by a liberal economic paradigm that makes war of secondary, tertiary, or no importance. He pushes that rationalizing answer further than usual by projecting the primacy of hidden economic factors back into all previous historical eras, even into a past where his predecessors such as Smith or Spencer allowed that war and warrior motives still reigned supreme. Marshall also links religious motives, economics' one rival, to the superficial, flash-in-the-pan logic of military agency by seeing it as "more intense" but less pervasive. Marshall fully exemplifies Keynes's claim that the "devil" of warfare was put away in the eighteenth century, reemerged with Malthus, and was then shut up even more securely by the high Victorians.

World War I said goodbye to all that. It overthrew the liberal dreams of Trevelyan and Hardy and demanded Keynes's reevaluation.[27] Indeed it is important to note that Malthus's devil was not precisely war, but the accelerating logic of population growth and the resultant increase in scarcity. Keynes's postwar analysis thus reverses Mill and Marshall's Victorian tendency to suppress war by instead elevating its role in earlier pessimistic paradigms. The epigraph's "serpent" references Malthus's "devil," but now it is war, not scarcity, that shapes Keynes's sense of the threat to liberalism's world order: "militarism," "imperialism," and national "rivalries" introduce and dominate Keynes's analysis, while "the amusements of his daily newspaper" echoes William James's contemporary concern over yellow journalism's exploitative exacerbation of war's appeal. To be sure, both economics and war figure in Keynes's account: scarcity, competition, and underemployment in economies dedicated to laissez-faire policies at home lead nations to compete for markets and thus to return to the mercantilism and the kind of wars first opposed by Fénelon in *Télémaque* at the dawn of the liberal epic era. But Keynes's language renders war the principle demon and its absence from Victorian analyses their most dangerous flaw. War looms over the ignorant dealings of Versailles, and it ultimately determines the "economic consequences." The "peace" of the title hovers as the bastard offspring of one war and the fertile mother of another. Keynes's later *General Theory of Employment, Interest, and Money* (1936) makes "employment" so prominent because it sees in government policies dedicated to maximizing employment the means by which nations might escape the nineteenth-century logic that resulted in competitive imperialism, and then the disaster of 1914–18. This book ends with deep anxiety over another looming European war. Its two final "concluding notes" state that "war has several causes" (381), but stress the fatal linkages between laissez-faire domestic policies, mercantilist imperialism, and the violent results of such competitive rivalry: "Those statesmen were moved by common sense and a correct apprehension of the true course of events, who believed that if a rich, old country were to neglect the struggle for markets its prosperity would droop and fail" (382).

Keynes's "droop and fail" variation upon Gibbon's "decline and fall," however, does not finally accede to the necessity of such policies and such wars, and Keynes refuses Gibbon's formula whereby war becomes a temperate contest among progressive nations, indeed a reinvigorating means of overcoming the logic of decadence. He has not abandoned Fénelon but is striving to renew the great French liberal's key insight, as his follow-up sentence makes clear: "But if nations can learn to provide themselves with full employment by their domestic policy . . . there need be no important economic forces calculated to set the interest of one country against that of its neighbours" (382). Fénelon's internal improvement now recast in the form of full employment becomes the foundation for lasting international peace. Moreover, such policies arise from the work of liberal heroes like Fénelon and Keynes himself, for the very last note begins by wondering if such a world is only a "visionary hope," and answers that "the ideas of economists and political philosophers . . . are more powerful than is commonly understood" (383). "Indeed," Keynes arrogantly continues, "the world is ruled by little else." Evidently, if his ideas can become preeminent, then the world can be saved from the logic of war. What makes this variation upon Shelley's theme of the "unacknowledged legislators of the world" particularly revealing is that Keynes's aspirations for such nonviolent, in both means and results, agency is swathed in rhetoric insinuating his doubts about such evanescent power and how it might actually work. According to Keynes, the rule of ideas acts with vague slowness: "it would be a mistake, I predict, to dispute their potency over a period of time" (383); "not, indeed, immediately, but after a certain interval" (383); "but, soon or late, it is ideas, not vested interests" (384). Lacking the immediate clarity of the great man's violent action, the purported rule of the Shelleyan economist's ideas is asserted in language loaded down with double negatives and dubious denials, with anxious predictions, with uncertain but lengthy stretches of time that together push such ideal powers back in the direction of the invisible hand from which they were struggling to emerge into the flesh.

Even more interesting, these assertions clash with the doctrinaire position of his earlier, more pessimistic work, where agency is explicitly denied to great men of any variety and retained for the usual Malthusian-Smithian suspects: "The great events of history are often due to secular changes in the growth of population and other fundamental economic causes, which, escaping by their gradual character the notice of contemporary observers, are attributed to the follies of statesmen or the fanaticism of atheists. . . . The disruptive powers of excessive national fecundity may have played a greater part in bursting the bonds of convention than either the power of ideas or the errors of autocracy" (12–13). For early Keynes, the gradual is plainly the same as the invisible in contrast to how, for the late Keynes, agency strives to become individual, to rise out of the morass of the gradual into visibility and recognition. The passage's last line even equates the notion that ideas have power with both the crimes and the vainglory of ambitious rulers: no, says the younger Keynes, it is the larger, hidden, impersonal forces of history that rule. This position is reinforced by Keynes's opening citation of *The Dynasts,* with its consistent mockery of epic heroes, to bolster his critique of Wilson and Clemenceau: "One felt most strongly the impression, described by Tolstoy in *War and Peace* or by Hardy in *The Dynasts,* of events marching on to their fated conclusion uninfluenced and unaffected by the cerebrations of Statesmen in Council" (4). Again, the early work links and dismisses the power of ideas (spurned with caustic elevation as "cerebrations") and great men. Keynes then quotes eight lines of typical dialogue from *The Dynasts* in which the realistic "Spirit of the Years" patiently explains to the liberal "Spirit of the Pities" that the Immanent Will acts blindly or "unwittingly," and no leaders possess "wide sight and self-command." The passage also programmatically inverts Achillean agency by describing the "impotent rage" of the "weak." But as this chapter has detailed, it is a mistake to align Hardy and Tolstoy too closely on questions of decisive war, progress, great men, and historical agency. In the end, *The Dynasts* breaks with Tolstoy's theory and reverses dialogues like this one. Its conclusion allows the hopeful Pity to correct the pessimistic wisdom of Years in the wake of what is portrayed as a decisive victory of the legitimately liberal side in war, the legalization and humanization of its practices, and the visionary agency of its heroes. Keynes's later *General Theory* comes closer to *The Dynasts* in this regard than the work that quotes and depends upon Hardy's epic-drama, but there, as we have seen, Keynes grounds his similar hopes in the power of Fénelonian-Shelleyan economists, not Homeric-Napoleonic generals. Inevitably, such wishful thinking peters out, like Arnold's and Eliot's mighty rivers, in tenuous effects and vague stretches of time that, in Keynes's case, meandered from 1935 to 1939 without ever gradually taking effect—Hitler, Stalin, Churchill, and war thus arose, precisely the results his all-powerful ideas of the interwar decades were meant to forestall. His next major work was entitled *How to Pay for the War* (1940).[28]

Keynes's early work exhibits a standard political-economic attitude toward ambitious rulers and statesmen who meddle with the workings of the marketplace: they are fools for thinking they have any real power in the larger sweep of history and against its deeper economic forces, but they can still do great harm simply by interfering. Since so much of *The Dynasts* articulates a similar view of the blind workings of history and the false, but dangerous, recklessness of great men, to label Keynes's citation of Hardy an error, as I have done, is to risk being too severe. Nonetheless, Keynes's failure in 1919 to discern Hardy's subtle but important departures from Tolstoy reappears in his failure in 1935 to realize the inadequacies of Shelleyan agency that *The Dynasts,* for all its heavy debt to that arch-Romantic, abundantly demonstrates by so violently reimagining. Indeed, as early as his obscure fifth novel, *The Hand of Ethelberta* (1876), Hardy suggestively confirms that he saw in epic—but epic with a measure of hard Achillean, not just sweet Promethean, force—evidence of agential power largely absent from the novel and political economy: epic agency necessary to realize liberal ideals. This novel accurately predicts Hardy's career—particularly its attraction to the power of epic. Ethelberta's story speaks of Hardy's own dedication to lyric poetry; his financial success as a novelist along with his increasing scorn as a serious artist for the compromises demanded by this commercial product; and, finally, his turn to epic as a means of transcending the limits of that popular form and its petty critics. Hardy's preeminent biographer Michael Millgate has questioned the common claim that Hardy "must in some sense have been writing an allegory of his own career" (161), but Ethelberta's life as an author obviously tracks Hardy's own. More important here, the novel's obsessive variations upon the imagery and significance of her titular hand confirms Hardy's insight, which looms forth in *The Dynasts,* that the invisible hand of political economy in the world wrought by the novel carries none of the conviction attendant upon the forceful, bloody hand of epic—possessed in abundance by the Napoleonic heroine who bests her numerous foes "single handed" (238) and fittingly concludes her triumphant career by "writing an epic poem" (404). Adam Smith refashioned the Achillean bloody hand into the invisible one—and perhaps hoped thereby to retain what Vico theorized as the power of savage poetic-Homeric thinking for the modern rational world and its too subtle, too rational concept of impersonal agency. But Hardy and Keynes demonstrate, the first positively and the second negatively, what the too sanguine and Shelleyan Trevelyan vainly transcended. Liberalism repeatedly returned to heroic violence, its epics, and bloody wars, because only by thus tinting and thereby embodying the "invisible" hand was it able to see and believe that it had any real power, autonomy, and freedom at all.

SEVEN

FROM LIBERAL EPIC TO EPIC LIBERALISM

CHURCHILL AND WEDGWOOD

I may say that, till this year, I did not know what real vindictive hatred meant. With what horror I used to read in Livy how Fulvius put to death the whole Capuan Senate in the Second Punic War! And with what equanimity I could hear that the whole garrison of Delhi, all the Moulavies and Mussulman Doctors there . . . had been treated in the same way! Is this wrong? Is not the severity which springs from a great sensibility to human suffering a better thing than the lenity which springs from indifference to human suffering? The question may be argued long on both sides.

—G. O. Trevelyan, *Macaulay's Life and Letters*

Here in his journal, Macaulay returns with a vengeance to an almost Achillean rage that liberal epics like his own had set themselves to overcome as they pursued the difficult ideal of "war without hate" in the cause of liberty and humanity. Such raw emotions, however, appear only in these late and private confessions. They exhibit the pressure of England's increasingly assertive imperialism on his earlier high liberalism, but harbor a degree of embarrassment, evident in his need to justify himself even to himself. Churchill's liberal imperialism goes much further, has little pity, and no shame. In his earliest journalistic history of an imperial war, he indulges in the cavalier tone and militarist ideology that will remain in place through to his last writings in defense of constitutional liberty: "One man was found the next morning, whose head had been half blown off by a discharge of case shot from one of the mountain guns. He lay within a yard of the muzzle . . . a victim to that blind credulity and fanaticism now happily passing away from the earth, under the combined influences of Rationalism and machine guns" (*Malakand* 157). Liberal ideals seem untroubled by the empire's violence—indeed they are unproblematically advanced by it. A bit later, the traditional liberal epic emphasis upon pity is knowingly referenced in his attention to the peacefulness of death on the battlefield, but then dismissed in favor of an unabashed interest in the pleasures of killing: "pity was not one of the emotions it aroused. A good many [enemy] fell, subsiding peacefully, and lying quite still. Their fall was greeted by strange little yells of pleasure from the native soldiers" (168). Churchill sanctions the power of scientific war machinery to blast apart even the most heroic efforts of human will—an approval that will come to haunt him and his England in the Great War. That war's manifold disasters, however, Gallipoli included, did not seriously dampen his tendency toward vigorous celebrations of heroic fighting, which remain the exciting focus of his prewar and his postwar best-selling epic histories. Another mythical "end of epic" moment, the muddy trenches and blasted wastelands of the World War I poets, did not stop heroic war narratives or banish their traditional poetic diction—or even their Homeric equation of killing with beauty. Churchill went on to write self-consciously Gibbonian epic histories, which won him the Nobel Prize for Literature, not in spite of World War I, but in order to defend its heroic greatness, liberal necessity, and beautiful lethality.[1]

In contrast, as Vico laid out at the dawn of the liberal critique of epic, the major ethical purpose of modern literature had been to teach humanity and compassion, not cultivate a "truculent and ferocious style," as Homer did in his "bloody battles" (257), and as Churchill did in his imperialist, boosterish, teasing accounts of the "thrill" of combat. By the time Macaulay gets to his last line, he has recovered something of Vico's humanizing agenda. Still he settles upon a defense of oppression in the name of humanity via precisely the kind of casuistry that the Romantic poets of Macaulay's youth had labored eloquently against. Macaulay's evolving reaction to the daily newspaper epic of the Indian Mutiny points to a re-hardening of epic resolve at the expense of liberal idealism, a process this chapter will analyze in its final, climactic phase in Winston Churchill.[2]

Churchill's early histories easily find the interests of England's Asian and African subjects best handled by the British. His later liberal epics also posit a similar alignment between European interests and those of its protector, England. The British ruling classes; the Churchill family; his hero, Marlborough; and implicitly Churchill himself are true to the interests of the world by being true to themselves:

> It would have been more agreeable to the Muse of History if Marlborough had refused all honours and rewards. . . . But then he would not have been the Marlborough who gained the victories. For it is certain that this same matter-of-fact care for his own interests and desire to found a powerful family in an enduring State was an inherent part of his great deeds. He was a builder for England, for posterity, and for himself. No one of these purposes could be removed without impairing

the others, and part of his genius lay in their almost constant harmony.
(*Marlborough* 2:620)

Churchill's scorn of conventional liberal epic idealism (and poetic diction)
in the Muse's quest for the perfect hero matches his credulity in so easily finding "harmony" between a general's greed and his nation's interests. Insofar as Churchill is explicitly one of Marlborough's posterity and
founded his own patriotic career upon a similarly self-serving assumption, the logic is even tighter, more self-interested.

Churchill's histories unironically embody the thesis of Mazower's
Dark Continent (1998) that the Great War exemplified Europeans' willingness to do to themselves what they had long done to non-Europeans.
Though he wrote *The River War* in 1898 long before Europe's imperialist practices were turned back upon itself in the Great War, and though
Churchill suffered a political near death for devising the disaster of Gallipoli to escape from the stalemate of the Western Front, by the year 1930
he could still celebrate Omdurman in ringing tones: "Nothing like the
Battle of Omdurman will ever be seen again. It was the last link in the
long chain of those spectacular conflicts whose vivid and majestic splendour has done so much to invest war with glamour. Everything was visible
to the naked eye" (*Roving* 171). Churchill's nostalgia admits a superficial
change in the beauty of war since 1898. It nonetheless refuses the deeper
ethical and aesthetic insight that the machine-gun slaughter of the charging thousands at Omdurman was no different from what would be visited upon the British by the Germans (and vice versa) in sixteen years.
This striking coupling of an eager desire to look closely with an equally
determined blindness is typical of all of Churchill's epics. Even as he
penned these glowing words, Churchill was immersed in the research for
his greatest epic history, the four-volume heroic biography of his ancestor John Churchill, better known as Marlborough. Amidst the reign of
high modernism's scorn for the vocabulary of glorious war and epic heroism, of which Paul Fussell is the most famous critic-historian and Wilfred
Owen the most famous cynic-poet (indeed at a time when Churchill's own
style had been publicly singled out as the epitome of the kind of false,
overblown, heroic rhetoric that the disasters of World War I had presumably exposed and swept away), Churchill continued to glorify the graphic
details of imperialist warfare and indulge in liberal epic idealisms: "In
the ear of Lytton Strachey and George Orwell, [Churchill's] 'grand manner' just failed to convince" (Cannadine, *Blood, Toil* 8).[3] Churchill's *Marlborough*, finally published in 1938, must be read as a largely successful
apology for World War I and a call to fight such a war again. His history

claims that the bloody battles of a vast European war could be noble, soul-stirring, even beautiful things. That he points to 1702–14 does not hide his deeper interest in 1914–18. Even in 1898, however, measured by the epic writings of Napier, Creasy, Roosevelt, Macaulay, and Gibbon that Churchill knew well, his rhetoric and his attitude exhibited a degree of heroic self-assurance absent in his models.

Thus, with Churchill liberal epic persistence reached its logical end point. Here we have a form of modern epic both committed to liberal ideals and aggressively indifferent to liberal self-doubt, a form whose blindness to its own ironic self-contradictions was brilliantly capped by its far-sighted successes when Churchill, certain of his democratic ideals and on alert for his empire's interests, was among the very first to mark the dual threat posed by Nazi Germany to Britain's freedom and its empire. He then rose to this challenge. A recent commentator has observed that Churchill must always be remembered as "the man who did not lose WWII" (Lukacs 31), but, as John Charmley, one of his few critical biographers, has stressed, Churchill was at least as committed to preserving the British Empire as to defeating Nazi Germany.[4] The first motivated the second, and he failed in his primary ambition. In remembering Churchill's great defense of liberal nationalism against totalitarian conquest, we risk forgetting that he could belittle Gandhi's Indian nationalism as vigorously as he excoriated Hitler's German imperialism with "shocking words . . . that have never been forgotten in India" (Best 135). Various cultural critics have noticed the intensification, despite the efforts of Charmley and a few fellow critics, of Churchill's great-man status in recent years. They have also noted that this hero worship is stronger in liberal imperialist America than Churchill's own chastened nation.[5] My analysis here will forgo yet another biographical treatment of Churchill and look to what his handling of the conventions of liberal epic can tell us.[6] To be blunt, Churchill saw war coming before others and rose to its challenge because Churchill wanted to see that challenge, welcomed the exhilarating violence of war in life and art, and clutched at such heroism and such domination as a leader and a historian.

CHURCHILL AND CREASY

The quality of Churchill's volumes on the Second World War is that of his whole life. His world is built upon the primacy of public over private relationships, upon the supreme value of action, of the battle between simple good and simple evil, between life and death; but, above all, battle.

—Isaiah Berlin, "Winston Churchill in 1940"

Berlin's claim for Churchill's life is true also of his histories: they always center on battle. At the same time, Churchill has emerged as the great liberal defender of the West against totalitarianism, its grandest hero, an increasingly mythical, unquestioned, and unquestionable figure for our troubled time. But was Churchill's imperialist and epic transformation of liberalism an individual idiosyncrasy, an exceptional consequence of his exceptional abilities and circumstances? Or did Churchill merely fulfill the inevitable cultural and historical logic of liberal European nation states developing into liberal empires? Or, finally, did Churchill dramatize some deeper logic of liberalism itself? Did he embody something preprogrammed, the final flowering of the paradox hidden within liberalism's need to believe that the free individual and nation were in fact self-determining? During these years of Churchill's early history writing and rise to political power, the British historian Hobson and then, following him, Lenin were advancing the thesis that, according to the title of one of Lenin's pamphlets, "imperialism [is] the highest stage of capitalism." Politically, Lenin displayed a surprising commitment to the core of liberal epic:

> For almost half a century, the governments and the ruling classes of England, and France, and Germany, and Italy, and Austria, and Russia, pursued a policy of plundering colonies, of oppressing other nations. . . . In China, Persia, India and other dependent countries, on the contrary, we have seen during the past decades a policy of rousing tens and hundreds of millions of people to national life, of liberating them from the oppression of the reactionary "great" powers. A war on such a historical ground can even today be a bourgeois-progressive, national-liberation war. (11)

For Lenin, historical evolution had left the liberal European nation-states no longer capable of supporting such ideals: they were operating in bad faith, their capitalist economies and class systems requiring exploitation and subjugation. My argument does not dispute the obvious validity of Hobson and Lenin's analysis of the historical growth of imperialist capitalism out of the liberal nation-state, but it complicates that picture by insisting that liberalism itself, not capitalism and not imperialism, had something to contribute to the process that culminated in Churchill. His refashioning of liberal epic, when seen in the light of the larger development of that tradition and the associated tradition of theoretical commentary on it that climaxed with Isaiah Berlin, strongly suggests that in the moment of one individual dominating another or one nation conquering another, liberalism possessed the only convincing evidence that the free individual or nation was a self-determining agent at all. Thus Churchill, the greatest liberal statesman, and Berlin, the leading liberal theorist, of the twentieth century, each retained a striking predilection for epic history.

Churchill loved battle, more than any of the historians and poets upon whom he modeled his handling of this core problem of liberal epic: "He mobilized the English language, and sent it into battle" (Cannadine, *Blood, Toil* 11).[7] His loving versions of battle inspired John Keegan, whose own *Face of Battle* has profoundly influenced the contemporary vogue for the ethics of graphic honesty in popular narratives of war. Keegan's biography of Churchill begins with a melodramatic transformation from modernist scoffer to nostalgic hero worshipper. The young Briton, alone in New York in the early days of the Cold War, discovers recordings of Churchill's speeches in the apartment of his American friends. He listens and is reborn: "Three heavy beats—'country,' 'Empire,' 'Allies'—and the dramatic rallentando: 'cause of freedom.' I felt my spine stiffen. . . . Churchill the soldier could not resist recounting the sweep and drama of military maneuver, with brilliant if chilling effect. . . . Finally, there was a promise: 'Conquer we must; conquer we shall'" (5–6). This personal allegory miniaturizes the development of epic liberalism out of liberal epic, as the spineless young internationalist is reborn as a warrior-patriot under the spell of England's ultimate warrior-PM—and, fittingly, goes on to a career as a military historian and theorist whose most famous argument advances the ethical claim that descriptions of battle should be graphically violent—though his description "chilling" liberally obscures the real fear that such violence was, to quote Churchill, actually "thrilling." From Keegan's thesis has grown a reenergized, contemporary, Creasyan decisive history tradition centered on the likes of Max Boot and Victor Davis Hanson, who happily theorizes that the greatness of progressive Western civilization resides in its carnage-based method of war, its insistence upon complete victory over the foe savagely beaten into total surrender.[8] Churchill reworked Creasy and was there long before Hanson. His breathless account of the battle of Omdurman caps his early heroic history of imperial vengeance upon the fanatical Muslims for their earlier victory over and killing of the imperial hero General Gordon. Its deeper rhythm anticipates Keegan's allegory: England recovers from Gladstonian liberalism and reasserts its imperial power over a nation that the prototypical liberal prime minister thought should be left to itself. Churchill's account of Blenheim likewise serves as the climax to his heroic biography of Marlborough, a story of imperial foundations, not revenge, but one that finds as much pleasure in the elimination of the ultra-civilized French as the earlier history found in the slaughter of the ultra-fanatical Sudanese. Leo Strauss, to cite just one influential voice of authoritarian liberalism, enthused that it was "the greatest historical work written in our century."

Churchill's method of composing these histories, particularly the later multivolume extravaganzas, confirms their central thesis and intended effect. Churchill largely left it to others, unnamed if not quite uncredited others, to do the legwork of research, fact checking, outlining, and even drafting.[9] His own contribution took the form of sounding the high notes. His interventions map onto how his leadership in World War II centered upon the poetic symbolism of his stirring speeches and his stubborn public persona. He set the topics and the primary themes; he edited the drafts, sometimes closely but often not; and he personally composed the rhetorical climaxes, the purple passages, where his histories rose to final judgments, crisis points, or grand summations: "A team of research assistants assembled the documents. He composed the text largely by dictation, often from his bed" (Keegan, *Churchill* 174). Keegan assumes too much. We know from other sources that the assistants did more than merely assemble documents: they also tracked down the pertinent facts, outlined the narrative, and then filled in their employer's general ideas.[10] Churchill did far less than dictate the whole, no matter how long he lay abed. In the high points, we find the same ringing emphases, heroic ideology, and historical conviction of England's glorious mission found in his famous speeches. In short, when Isaiah Berlin parallels Churchill's historical narratives with his leadership—"Churchill accepts [that history is what great men do] wholeheartedly. . . . His narrative deals largely in personalities and gives individual genius its full and sometimes more than its full due . . . [, giving] his narrative some of the quality of an epic" (614)—the connection between the two is closer, merely at the level of stylistics, than Berlin's analogy allows. For Churchill's oratorical relation to Parliament, the British people, and the world in his grand addresses of 1940–45 is remarkably close to his relation to his historical narratives, where he occasionally intervenes in set-piece episodes to impose his vision on the actions and thoughts of smaller laborers in the trenches: "The Prime Minister was able to impose his imagination and his will upon his countrymen, and enjoy a Periclean reign, precisely because he appeared to them larger and nobler than life and lifted them to an abnormal height in a moment of crisis" (Berlin, *Proper Study* 620).

Churchill's efforts to slip his heroic self into historical events where he played little or no part demonstrate the intentionality that informed his self-interested version of heroic history. Numerous admiring critics, determined to celebrate him, have proclaimed his indebtedness to the two greatest English historians: "His demands were met by his mother, who sent him expensive books by the crate. . . . The diet was, in its way, as impressive as Kipling's. The mainstay was Gibbon, the greatest of English historians" (Keegan, *Churchill* 38). Such a genealogy is not hard to find, however, since Churchill proclaimed it to the world. His letters record how, on his way to India with history-writing schemes already in his head, he read "fifty pages of Macaulay and twenty-five of Gibbon every day" (38), but his self-fashioned literary heritage is yet more dramatic, more programmatically heroic: "In history I decided to begin [my education] with Gibbon. Someone had told me that my father had read Gibbon with delight; that he knew whole pages of it by heart, and that it had greatly affected his style of speech and writing. So without more ado I set out upon the eight volumes of Dean Milman's edition. . . . I was immediately dominated by both the story and the style. . . . I devoured Gibbon. I rode triumphantly through it from end to end" (*Roving* 111). But this rhetoric of filiopiety, readerly domination, epic tasking, and, finally, readerly triumph claims a closer relationship to Gibbon than my analysis of the actual indebtedness of Churchill's "speech and writing" to Gibbon's far too ironic and skeptical style will ultimately sanction.

Churchill nonetheless sought Gibbon's mantle out of respect for his father, just as his ancestral hero worship eventually provoked him to overstate his rejection of Macaulay, the arch critic of Marlborough. Upon concluding his *Marlborough,* he sent a presentation copy to his king with a reference to his ancestor George III's teasing words to Gibbon— " 'What Mr. Gibbon, another great big volume. Always scribble, scribble, scribble, scribble!' Alas, I fear, Sir, that you might well say the same to me" (Gilbert 5:1157). Such self-comparisons to the gold standard of historiographical achievement had become by then a convention, which in Churchill's case dramatized that Gibbon was the model to be imitated in both length and style. Indeed, in the beginning phases of his labor, Churchill consulted the leading historian Lewis Namier who, after reading volume 1, strongly advised Churchill to play to his strengths with a surer emphasis upon the epic matter of "politics, government, and war," saw a real advantage in the parallels between Churchill and Marlborough, and, finally, returned to Gibbon as the exemplary British historian of war: "You will remember what Gibbon said about [his] experiences as the Captain of the Hampshire Grenadiers and the historian of the Roman Empire" (Gilbert 721). At least one early critic, whom Churchill proudly quoted, declared him "The New Gibbon" (*Roving* 213). These examples reaffirm Gibbon's preeminence for this later text, but Churchill's early histories also "affected a combination of the styles of Macaulay and Gibbon" (*Roving* 211).

His later histories, however, turned against Macaulay and hugged Gibbon closer, even as they quietly left the latter's irony behind for the more ringing, more Macaulayan cadences of imperialist assurance not civilized doubt. I will return to this complicated, paradoxical evolution at the end of this chapter, but will now take up the largely forgotten Creasy regarding whose influence critics and Churchill are silent. His *Marlborough's* first sentence, however, is a quotation—" 'There are few successful commanders,' says Creasy, 'on whom Fame shone so unwillingly as upon John Churchill, Duke of Marlborough' " (1:15)—and this nod is confirmed by Churchill's clear effort to present his battle-focused histories according to the standards of "decisiveness" advanced by Creasy's popular bestseller. Overall, Churchill's *Marlborough* reads like a vastly inflated version of a Creasyan decisive battle narrative, not an exercise in Gibbonian philosophical or Macaulayan people's history. Creasy's emphases upon simple ideological contrasts of progress and regress, often cast in terms of England, the English-speaking, and their cultural ancestors versus all other comers, and dramatically played out in colorful prose and exciting battlefield tests, are what structure Churchill's narratives, not Gibbonian subtleties or Macaulayan experiments.

In contrast to Gibbon, Macaulay, and Creasy, however, Churchill allows, even highlights, the lurid interest shown by the soldiers in the effects of their firepower upon their enemies: "The British infantry stood up on tip-toe to look at the wonderful spectacle of actual war, and at first every shell was eagerly scrutinised and its probable effect discussed" (*River War* 235). Such approving attention to soldiers' pleasure in their craft and its effects is not an aberration. Throughout his histories, Churchill carefully records soldiers' pleasures in observing their own destructive powers. He scorns the "dignity" and humanity of history in favor of the allure of violence: "The account becomes more graphic, if less imposing, more vivid if less judicial. As long as each step down from the 'dignity of history' is accompanied by a corresponding increase of interest, we may pursue without compunction that pleasant, if descending path" (*Malakand* 88). This passage mocks the corrective and disciplinary function of the dignified poetic diction deployed by Pope and Gibbon. It goes beyond Macaulay's appeals for novelistic detail over neoclassical decorum, which nonetheless pauses before such violence. Churchill becomes frankly Homeric, and only sarcastically ethical in the form of scare quotes. Later he dispenses with even the pro forma nod to the immorality of such interest, and finds the technical and anatomical details of killing simply "beautiful": "The result is a wonderful and from the technical point of view a beautiful machine. On striking a bone this causes the bullet to 'set up' or spread out, and it then tears and splinters everything before it, causing wounds which in the body must be generally mortal and in any limb necessitate amputation" (*Malakand* 199). (What struck Churchill as so beautiful is now illegal—"forbidden for use in war by international law, because a soldier hit by an expanding bullet almost always dies" (Larsson 241).)

Churchill dispenses with Burke's subtly evasive sublime: here violence is simply called "beautiful" and depends upon sympathy with the killer. To be sure, Churchill seldom graphically presents to his readers the death of any named person or personalized individual, though he shows himself and his fellow soldiers looking on such with delight. But far from encouraging his readers not to look or enjoy looking, he tantalizes them with scenes of imperial activity, which they, as citizens lazily safe at home, cannot quite taste. Hume's Homer problem is no more. As with his simple defense of the heroic selfishness of the British or his dynasty-founding ancestor, Churchill brushes aside the usual liberal objections to taking delight in such a "wonderful spectacle." Instead he makes it a matter of imperial pride, honest evidence of Britain's civilizing power in the act: "Blind credulity and fanaticism [are] now happily passing away from the earth, under the combined influences of Rationalism and machine guns" (*Malakand* 157).

Such moves run against the well-established codes of liberal epic generally, but *The River War* and *Marlborough*'s knowing, provocative revisionism goes yet further in demonstrating a specific awareness of Creasy's rules for what makes a battle decisive, what makes it worthy of careful narration to modern civilized readers, and how those select battles can be appropriately presented. Churchill then violates these rules to emphasize the pleasures of recording national and personal triumph. He sets forth all the standard liberal rhetoric of humanity and progress and self-determination, but, as with small scenes showing soldiers drawn irresistibly toward the happy evidence of their killing, he implies that he wants to tell of these great battles and his civilized readers want to read of them—and there's nothing wrong with that. His remaining reticence is a kind of lure, a reason to sign up—or to admire those who have. He does not, in contrast to his supposed model Gibbon, signal his care not to show the details of violence as a marker of his readers' civilized blessings. Finally, Churchill does not imply, with the sardonic spite of his older contemporaries Butler and Adams, that his readers are less refined than they presume, more prone to bloodlust than liberal theory supposes. Churchill lets his data and their interest stand as facts that in no way challenge the civilized superiority of his imperial nation and its citizenry: he is impervious to Butler's cynical claim that "English readers" are not interested in

Homer's "more sanguinary parts," because he and his "highly cultivated audience" most certainly are.

Thus, in contrast to Creasy, Churchill acknowledges that the real battle was purely a logistical one. If the railroad to Omdurman could be built through the vast, barren, rugged terrain of the Sudan, then its delivery of trained soldiers and modern equipment to the front would prove unbeatable. Much the same is true for Blenheim, where the real brilliance of Marlborough lay in his ability to supply an army on its long march from the low countries, though the forests of Germany, to surprise the French in Austria and seize the initiative. At the same time as he suggests that the final battles are largely an addendum to these logistical triumphs, he echoes Creasy in conceding that bloody accounts of battles in and of themselves are ethically, intellectually, and aesthetically pointless and, therefore, uninteresting: "It is unlikely that any complete history of these events will ever be written in a form and style which will interest a later generation. . . . One savage army slaughters another. One fierce general cuts his rival's throat. The same features are repeated with wearying monotony" (*River War* 73). This gesture dismissing the drama of vast savage battles echoes Creasy's defining moves in the opening pages of his *Fifteen Decisive Battles of the World,* where the author rejects most battles, all those that were really just foregone conclusions, and particularly those that combine an inevitable result with the barbaric thrill of mass casualties, such as any number of "great" Eastern battles. Omdurman represents a somewhat different variation on mass slaughter, that is, it shows ill-equipped savages against a state-of-the-art imperial force. Even so, Churchill will commit the essential offense of a liberal historian, as defined by Creasy, of retelling a by then well-scripted story of mass bloodshed merely for thrill of it.

Churchill configures his narrative in *The River War* and *Marlborough* to downplay what he himself characterizes as truly "decisive," the logistical matters admitted of the railroad or the "Malbrouck" wagon and to play up the colorful epiphenomena of battle. His histories climax with Omdurman and Blenheim, predetermined bloodbaths, and those events receive narrative space proportionally far outweighing any other event in *The River War* or the entire life of Marlborough. His concluding remarks clearly exhibit his anxiety over this generosity: "Thus ended the battle of Omdurman—the most signal triumph ever gained by the arms of science over barbarians. Within the space of five hours the strongest and best-armed savage army yet arrayed against a modern European Power had been destroyed and dispersed, with hardly any difficulty, comparatively small risk, and insignificant loss to the victors" (*River War* 300).

Churchill's rationale, true to form, confesses both his offense against and his indifference to Creasy's liberal epic standards: "most signal triumph" versus "with hardly any difficulty." Churchill's "most signal" recalls Creasy's standard of "decisive," but he then repudiates Creasy's claim that the battle be hard-fought, a real test. Instead his new criterion turns in the opposite direction—to the ease of victory as a worthy sign of its importance. As with his defense of the selfishness of heroes and nations, Churchill here answers a charge by simply embracing it with a shrug. This pattern is made yet more dramatic when set against Theodore Roosevelt's practices. Given the close similarities between Roosevelt's and Churchill's late Victorian imperialist nationalism, not to mention their parallel literary careers as heroic historians grandstanding with political careers in sight, it is striking that Roosevelt focuses on staying true to Creasy's popularized version of liberal epic, while Churchill knowingly remakes it in a more aggressive manner. Roosevelt breaks his own rules of selection in *The Naval War of 1812* (1882) in order to narrate one land battle, namely, the patriotic victory of the United States over Great Britain at New Orleans. In doing so, Roosevelt is careful to model himself after Creasy. His preliminary dismissal of the land war also derives from Creasyan principles. Roosevelt focused on the key fact that nothing was to be learned from all the other battles: they were mere repetitions of old lessons in the follies of war. Now he makes the case that New Orleans fulfills Creasy's definition of a decisive battle worthy of being narrated to liberal, progressive readers: a supreme test of England's victorious martial aristocracy and America's rising democratic manhood, Wellington's veterans versus Jackson's frontiersmen, a hard-fought battle which nearly went the other way and would then have changed the course of history.[11] (If the Sudanese had won at Omdurman, nothing fundamental would have changed. The British would have just come again at a later date with faster trains and bigger guns.) Judged both in relation to his most relevant model and his closest contemporary, Churchill's handling of the battle piece exhibits a strong move in the direction of making liberalism unapologetically epic—and triumphalist: war narrative for war narrative's thrilling sake.

Finally, Churchill even outdoes himself and breaks his own rules— not, like Roosevelt, to obey a higher liberal principle, but in order to maximize lowly Homeric delights. When excitement calls, he smoothly offends against his own newfound, suspiciously Buckle-like, scientific justification for Omdurman. One might give Churchill the benefit of the doubt and accept his claim that there is a legitimate interest in the details of Omdurman, insofar as it is the supreme demonstration of the ease with which technology can triumph over even the most courageous barbaric army. What, however, can one do when he devotes a significant portion of his account, the portion in which he played the greatest role, to a minute, individualized retelling of the cavalry charge of the 21st Lancers? First, they possess no modern weaponry qualifying as "scientific." In his first history, Churchill waxes lyrical over the cavalrymen's preference for the simple but sure killing effect of the old-fashioned lance: "All admit or assert that the lance is in this warfare the better weapon. It kills with more certainty and convenience" (*Malakand* 202). Here Churchill is eagerly debating the claims of the lance versus the sword. At Omdurman, this sword-and-lance unit engaged in an action that was a throwback to classic cavalry tactics, and was narrated as such by Churchill. His departure can only be understood as an exercise in the beautiful pleasures of Homeric courage and killing: "The general battle was forgotten, as it was unseen. This was a private quarrel. The other might have been a massacre; but here the fight was fair" (*River War* 287). Note that the "ease" justification is now set aside. He revels in the primitive, pure, "fair" scene. Since he was directly involved and knew many who were there, he was able to give numerous detailed accounts of these sporting, hand-to-hand combats: "Then, and not till then, the killing began; and thereafter each man saw the world along his lance, under his guard, or through the back-sight of his pistol; and each had his own strange tale to tell" (286).

Although Churchill cautiously allows readers to discern what other historians have broadcast, namely, that this charge was a distraction, even a mistake, he certainly does not follow them in pointing out that the error turned into a useless, bloody exercise. Despite his "scientific" justifications, he proudly links it to the grandest spectacles from the heroic past: "The 21st Lancers were committed to their first charge in war. . . . The troopers, to shield their faces from the stinging dust, bowed their helmets forward, like the Cuirassiers at Waterloo" (285). The war's official historian compares (to dismiss) this excess to the infamous Charge of the Light Brigade at Balaclava, another embarrassing bit of archaic bravado: "The most futile and inefficient part of the battle was the most extravagantly praised."[12] In sum, it was an obsolete gesture of personal glory amidst the realities of a modern battlefield, but it earned the lion's share of the press because so many upper class officers were able to boast of their exploits in it. Churchill mined that popularity for financial, heroic, and political gain. Both his narration and his historiography slide back toward the clubby, aristocratic, voluble, and deliberately archaic standards of Kinglake, despite Churchill's journalistic credentials and scientific protestations. Such indeed is the status of heroic history throughout *The River*

War. There seems little bad faith in all this: he variously acknowledges the intellectual and moral objections to his battle piece, then proceeds anyway, full bore and with every confidence that he's still being a good historian and a good liberal.

Blenheim, like Omdurman, fulfills the role of the Creasyan "decisive" battle in its long epic history. Indeed, better than Omdurman, it plays that role as one of the fifteen battles in Creasy's history too—and thus allows for a direct comparison. I will, however, forgo a second detailed analysis of how Churchill once again evokes and violates Creasy's rules, then his own. Instead I will merely assert that that is exactly what he does: Blenheim precisely parallels Omdurman, except now it does so after the horrors of and modernist reaction to World War I, and now it does not just celebrate the British Empire at its peak and Churchill's small role in one of its many triumphs, but the victory that Churchill claims founded that empire through the brilliance of the founder of his family. It is grander than Omdurman in every way in its contribution to the progress of civilization, of the British Empire, of the Churchills, and of Winston himself. But it is simultaneously grimmer than Omdurman as an example of inhuman delight in killing and domination: the liberal progressivism of this ultimate decisive battle seems to require its violent extremes. Churchill openly admits Marlborough's atrocities and offenses against the new Grotius-inspired laws of war. As just one example, Marlborough illegally devastated Bavaria and collectively punished its civilians in order to disadvantage the French before the coming battle. Churchill defends him on the grounds of necessity, and praises Marlborough for, for once, looking past his personal self-interest: "His military needs conquered both his avarice and his humanity" (1:808). Winston is not criticizing, and the metaphor of conquest reveals the nature of the necessity here, as always, to win, to defeat the French, is the only thing that counts. This attitude leads him repeatedly to comment upon and appeal to readerly delight over the lurid results: "England, though startled by the casualties, was proud of the victory and thrilled by the prowess of her troops" (1:806–7). He both teases and lingers over the realistic details of combat: "There is no moment in war more thrilling than a surprise attack at dawn" (950); "Of course, when we read of troops being 'cut to pieces' we may be sure that the greater number usually escape somehow. But these poor soldiers of France behaved so bravely that the positions they had held could be plainly seen the next day upon the battlefield by their corpses lying in ranks" (862). The point here rests in Churchill's surprised lack of disappointment, his joy in the clear evidence that they really were "cut to pieces," his partly modernist, partly Homeric pleasure that this cliché was for once refreshingly literal.

In the end, his hero remains good for mankind; his Blenheim altered history for the better; his always bloody, sometimes criminal means were fully excused by their glorious results; his cultivated readers, finally, could and should savor the graphic details of his supreme skill—without any risk to their humanity. Indeed it has become an important part of their educations as good citizens of their progressive empire, whose power, all for the best, was as solidly founded at Blenheim as it was later confirmed at Omdurman.

CHURCHILL AND WEDGWOOD

It seems best to march from Creasy, Churchill's principal Victorian model, past Strachey, his brilliant but lightweight modernist peer, to a comparison with the most relevant narrative history by Churchill's leading contemporary rival as a serious epic and military historian, Cecily Veronica Wedgwood: "The greatest narrative historian of the twentieth century ... *The Thirty Years War* shows her at her epic best" (Grafton xi).[13] Wedgwood never won a Nobel Prize, but she had a long career as a popular and critically acclaimed historian working outside of the academy, and earned a living as well as several major honors: the James Tait Black Memorial Prize, Dame of the British Empire, and British Order of Merit.[14] Wedgwood dramatizes what Creasy cannot, that Churchill was glorifying war in the ways he did at a time in literary and cultural history when even such highly qualified, deeply anxious heroic narratives as Creasy's had fallen into severe disfavor—and when even such popular and ambitious historians as Wedgwood refused to celebrate war. Of course, Creasy was an eminent Victorian, but Churchill was unironically outdoing them. Perhaps it is best to regard him as the most eminent Victorian of all, and this in the very teeth of the active, debunking work of Lytton Strachey et al. He trotted out the full heroic rhetoric of admiration so common in the Victorian age and presented his historical figures (and himself) as heroic agents, even as the modernists were making the rejection of heroic Victorianism a hallmark of their literary program. And though Churchill sometimes affected an un-Victorian bluntness, he could be very pious, too. Fussell has singled out the rejection of the specialized Victorian chivalric language of war as the surest, simplest sign of the modernist revolution. Though Churchill often cultivated a plain style, his grand impulses easily found room for almost all the obsolete words in Fussell's list—and in all seriousness (Fussell 21–22). With his popularity and prominence, Churchill was the leading 1920s–1930s writer to resist the turn against heroic warfare. His resistance to the new mode was also an active defense of the old, even a promotion of it, and not just of a style, but of the ideal-ized concept of heroic warfare itself—in literature, politics, state policy, history, and historiography.

Consider how his account of the Blenheim campaign heavily stresses Marlborough's diplomatic and strategic debates with the Dutch allies, who were determined to keep their armies and their focus on the war in the west, the war along the heavily fortified and largely immobile front in Belgium, where the French were firmly entrenched in fortified cities they seized early in the conflict. Marlborough, in contrast, advocated seizing the initiative by striking boldly far to the east, in Bavaria. He won this ar-gument, and the experiment was tried. According to Churchill, such bold thinking saved the Allies, saved many lives in the long run, and ultimately won the war. Churchill constructs a transparent analogy-apology for his own Gallipoli campaign, its failure notwithstanding. What's more, the *Marlborough*, written during the darkening 1930s and finally published in 1938 on the eve of another terrible war most were dreading, implicitly defends such a war along with the Great War itself. The disasters and horrors of the Great War are seen as local failures, as symptoms of insuf-ficiently heroic action and insufficiently visionary planning. Churchill's cultivation of a supposedly outdated heroic style and outdated epic genre was his preferred means to campaign for England to rethink its grim at-titude toward war and re-embrace the possibility of glorious victory.

Wedgwood represents Churchill's closest rival as an epic historian, yet her epic is prototypically modernist. *The Thirty Years War* (1938), pub-lished in the same year as the *Marlborough* and similarly poised with one eye toward World War I and one toward its looming return, is best de-scribed as an anti-epic. Certainly, its goal is to reject the greatness of war, unless the sheer amount of horror counts as greatness, to question the idea that war determines history in ways transcending death and ruin-ation, and to belittle the agency of all hero-killers. Still, it is a big book about a big war—clocking in at 506 dense pages in my recently published edition. Both were also avowed disciples of Gibbon, and thus their re-casting of his style reveals much about their differing purposes. Whereas Churchill inflated Gibbon's progressive rhetoric and retained the state-liness of his periodic sentences, while largely dispensing with their sting of ironic, probing doubt, Wedgwood intensified those skeptical qualities into a kind of neoclassical modernism of elegantly ironic darkness and despair, a case study in how to write about chaos and confusion with a crystalline stateliness that never quite pierces through to the heart of its horrific subject—and thereby makes its darkness painfully visible. Such limitation seems purposeful: Wedgwood's narrative is a masterly presentation of a horrendous disaster, one that is not interested in pretending to make it all finally make sense.

Churchill chose a war that could reasonably be refashioned to champion the epic ideal of a great and worthy war in the cause of freedom and progress, one with a hero who could plausibly demand our admiration. Wedgwood sought to enforce the dark, modernist view of World War I, and indirectly to appeal against any new descent into the trenches. She selected a long, disastrous, tortuous, and pointless war that ravaged Germany's cities, lands, and peoples, and sent it back politically, economically, and culturally almost into Gibbon's dark ages. Her seventeenth-century Germany becomes a transparent model for twentieth-century Europe mindlessly ripping itself apart. Unlike Churchill's, her narrative, though filled with battles and campaigns, stresses the destruction and horror of war, not its thrills and heroic challenges:

> The imperialists had slaughtered children in the cellars, thrown the women out of the upper windows of houses and boiled a housewife in her own cauldron. The Swedes had sprinkled gunpowder on their prisoners and set fire to their clothes, the Bavarians under Werth had shut the citizens into Calw, fired the walls, trained guns on the gates and shot the people as they tried to escape the flames. The stories were exaggerations but based on the increasing and now general barbarity of the war. (398)

Wedgwood first presents exaggerations as facts only to turn the tables once again by exposing, then accepting, them as valid evidence of a deeper, uglier truth. Out of the expansive array of evidence that she puts on display, the notorious catastrophe of Madgeburg best symbolizes her view of the entire war, and how it figured as both a deliberate horror and a tragic mistake: "One thing, however, was clear to Tilly and Pappenheim, as they looked at the sulphurous ruin and watched the dreary train of wagons that for fourteen days carried the charred bodies to the river—Madgeburg could no longer feed and shelter either friend or foe" (279). Wedgwood's artistry here appears best in her subtle construction of an allegory for the war as a whole, but also in her ironic use of that eminently enlightened word "clear": only when it's too late do the great leaders understand, and what they learn is painfully self-evident, clear to the rankest fool—after the fact.

On the matter of military heroes and what they do in battle, when they are not mistakenly or deliberately torching cities and massacring noncombatants, Wedgwood's war proffered a more likely candidate than even Churchill's Marlborough. Gustavus Adolphus, the conquering king of

Sweden, who entered the war to rescue the scattered Protestants of Germany from the oppressions of the Catholic Imperialists and won several brilliant victories to make good his promise, had long sparkled in history with little of the tarnish that so disfigured Marlborough's tin star. Wedgwood slowly chips away at his traditional status, an ironic process that culminates in her final judgment upon him as essentially a war maker: "The apologists of Gustavus, if such a word may be used for the admirers of an accepted hero of European history, argue that he would have made a strong and lasting peace had he lived. The case must stand on private conviction and not on evidence. . . . Gustavus was one of those born conquerors to whom peace is an ideal state, always for excellent reasons unattainable" (322). The epic assumption of heroic agency is marked as an irrational belief. The only lesson she allows is again self-evident: military heroes thrive upon war and embrace it as the best, often only, way of achieving desirable ends. Indeed she implies that a state of war is their desired end. In this light, this passage might well remind us of Churchill's strong wish to continue World War II with an immediate attack upon Soviet Russia. Even his theoretical admirer Isaiah Berlin expressed private dismay over his hero's eagerness for more of that drug. Wedgwood completely reverses the traditional logic of epic by disqualifying Gustavus precisely because of his greatness in war and his readiness to see in it the best solution for any problem. She also uses this hero's fate to reinforce her portrait of the horror of war. She focuses upon the World War I–like detail of the discovery of his body on the day after battle: "They found him at last; he had been shot between the ear and the right eye, the wound that killed him, but he had other wounds, a dagger thrust and a shot in the side, two bullets in the arm and one—which caused great rumour of treachery—in the back. He lay on what had been the enemy's side of the contested ditch, naked, under a heap of dead" (318).

Wedgwood's history abounds with concerted efforts to undermine the notion of heroic warfare in both its epic-artistic dimension and its assumption of historical agency and importance. Furthermore, her narrative specifically targets the ideal of liberal warfare, of rules in war, which focuses upon distinguishing between soldier and civilian, and strives to restrict war's activities as much as possible to the former. In her accounting, the opposite ruled the day—"The virulent hatred between soldiers and civilians, rising almost to a frenzy, increased the horrors of war" (249). *The Thirty Years War* tells many stories of soldiers slaughtering civilians, and vice versa. It becomes an epic historical expansion of the mood and imagery of the World War I poets, or of T. S. Eliot's *The Waste Land* (1922) and David Jones's *In Parenthesis* (1937): "Even in Bavaria starved bodies lay unburied on the roads. The harvest of 1627 on the banks of the Havel had promised well, but retreating Danes and pursuing imperialists destroyed it" (248). Churchill emphasizes the "thrill" of war and its supreme value for settling differences and solving crises. His narrative makes only limited gestures to its horrors and its costs—especially given that those were often paid to his great ancestor as profits and to himself in the form of royalties. Wedgwood shows little interest in hunting for the thrills, but serious dedication to cataloging and explaining the criminality and chaos wrought by all the self-deceived "agents" amid the events that spun out of their control. The sheer amount of evidence, however, raises methodological problems: it is possible to hunt down examples in Churchill of the meaningless horror of war, and, in Wedgwood, of effective heroic action and glory (and she exhibits a surprising fondness for Richelieu, though mainly due to his skill in ironic self-deprecation). Such counterexamples do not, however, outweigh the preponderance of evidence on each side. Thus I will conclude with two instances plucked from all the thousands of pages: first, their summary judgments on the single greatest battle in each of their narratives; and second, their elaborate Gibbonian perorations. These examples fairly represent their respective intentions and efforts. Blenheim, of course, plays that role in the *Marlborough*. Churchill cannot resist having two conclusions—one for the battle itself and one for the larger campaign surrounding it. Rocroy has that status in *The Thirty Years War*. The fearsome reputation of the French army was reduced at Blenheim, but it was first earned at Rocroy, where it destroyed the once equally fearsome reputation of the Spanish. Within their respective epic histories, these battles stand at the forefront of many great battles, the ones with the best claim to the status of "decisive." In each case the historian provides the conventional summary judgment required by this Creasyan subgenre of liberal epic.

Wedgwood stresses the plight and the cost for the defeated, while Churchill focuses upon the hard work and glorious achievements of the victors, above all, their great commander. More subtly, Wedgwood suggests a theme of heroic vanity—for winners and losers alike, while Churchill generously grants glory to both. The hero of Rocroy, the future Great Condé, is powerless, in her account, to restrain his men from a cruel slaughter: "In vain, Enghien shouted to his men to give quarter"; "on the following day he entered Rocroy in triumph, a fact recorded to this day on the gates of the little town" (444). The first passage highlights Wedgwood's ongoing interest in the criminality and horror of war (the "furious" soldiers slaughter most of the enemy); the second insinuates an ironic judgment upon epic fame: the shock of noticing a placard commemorating a largely forgotten decisive victory on the gates of a tiny town. Churchill, in contrast, builds up his hero, his power, his meaningful achievements, and their worthy memorials. Marlborough discerns his larger goal beyond his glittering victory. He, unlike Enghien, compels his men, who are eager to rest and celebrate, to obey him and his vision of the larger cause: "This winter effort of Marlborough's will-power deserves admiration. . . . But Marlborough was deaf to all appeals. . . . He yielded to neither success nor exhaustion" (1:905). Here we have a touchstone of epic—heroic agency that demands glory from us. Unlike Wedgwood's hero helpless before his men, Marlborough's men are helpless before his determination. The final sentence reaches a higher pitch but hits the same note: "It is these moral and soldierly virtues which made Marlborough the greatest servant, who remained a servant, of any sovereign in history" (1:905). Here his excellence becomes superlative, and even that harbors a further illiberal threat or wish. Marlborough's liberal credentials lie in his morality and his self-limiting obedience to nation and sovereign, but Churchill hints—and his final page will go further—that with more power, England would have been yet better "served." The republican ideal here teeters dangerously before the epic impulse toward domination. Finally, Churchill has little to say about the defeated, and what he does mention remains thoroughly positive in its epic resonance: he praises their heroic spirit, stressing the "grief and fury" of the "unbeaten troops" forced to surrender. Wedgwood looks to all the dead Spanish and what that ultimately meant for Spain: "It was the end of the Spanish army. . . . They had not lost their reputation at Rocroy . . . but they had died to keep it. The veterans were gone, the tradition broken, and no one was left. . . . In the centre of their position on the fields before Rocroy there stands today a little modern monument, an unassuming grey monolith, the gravestone of the Spanish army; almost, one might say, the gravestone of Spanish greatness" (444). Wedgwood is clearly drawn to the defining, unheroic word "little" throughout her judgment, and, strikingly, it elevates the ominous monument of Spanish disaster over the minor memorial of French victory. Her logic of tragic diminution gives the crown of this anti-epic to Spain. To the extent that war really does or means anything, it is more about death and ruin than victory and fame. One should note as well that the field in question lies in Belgium, near many scenes of death and slaughter in the Great War, and this "modern" monument to an old defeat is intended to have an unsettling contemporary relevance.

These patterns are elevated and reinforced in the summaries of these histories as wholes. Churchill is upbeat and triumphant about the war and his hero. He calls to England to remain true to its (and his) glorious past and to strive to repeat such victories in the future. Wedgwood dwells with dismay not only upon the pointlessness of the Thirty Years War, but on the fact that the participants seemed to learn nothing from it. The implication is clear for her sense of both the Great War and the "greater" one looming. Each historian concludes with a doublet of paragraphs, a short pithy statement of themes that is then fleshed out in the lengthier peroration. I will quote the two shorter ones in full:

> After her death, in accordance with her wish, Marlborough's body was removed from King Henry VII's Chapel in Westminster Abbey to the tomb she had built at Blenheim. There they lie side by side in victorious peace. (*Marlborough* 2:1040)

> After the expenditure of so much life to so little purpose, men might have grasped the essential futility of putting the beliefs of the mind to the judgment of the sword. Instead, they rejected religion as an object to fight for and found others. (Wedgwood 506)

Wedgwood goes on in her final paragraph to a denunciation of war centering on the simple assertions that "the war solved no problem" and "it is the outstanding example in European history of meaningless conflict" (506); but the last sentence of this preliminary paragraph is more effective in its nuanced reworking of Gibbon's periodic irony with the final sting of "and found others." The darkness and despair are palpable. Her narrative has no use for the glory of wars, the power of visionary leaders, or the lessons of history—its own included: "They wanted peace and they fought for thirty years to be sure of it. They did not learn then, and have not since, that war breeds only war" (506). Her bitter rejection of the final liberal justification of war—"the war to end all wars"—comes to fruition in her last image of its hellish logic of rebirth. Wedgwood draws upon Gibbon for these stylistic flourishes, but where his irony builds a wall between the ignorance and criminality and disasters of history and the enlightened wisdom of his own eminently civilized present, Wedgwood deploys his style only to show that it and she and her world cannot control and civilize those forces, that they have been and will be overwhelmed.

How very different is Churchill's grand vision of "victorious peace"! His scene of heroic memorialization concludes with that phrase, and one can here discern a triumphant fulfillment of the genre—"liberal epic" is as much of an oxymoron as "victorious peace," though Churchill's phrase is more emphatic in so closely combining the defeat and killing of the enemy lurking in "victorious" with the progressive and humane resonance of "peace." This intensification plays out in his final paragraph, where all is emphatic, upbeat, positive. The war was good for England and the world; the hero was good and made it all happen: "He had proved himself the 'good Englishman' he aspired to be" (2:1040). Here the scare quotes do not signal sarcasm, but the anti-Byronic cant of a resurrected cliché. The last sentence follows the troubled logic of "victorious peace" to an even more vivid claim: "History may declare that if he had had more power his country would have had more strength and happiness, and Europe a surer progress" (2:1040). History becomes prophecy, and gone now is the previous qualification of "servant." Only a wish for more power remains at the end. On the one hand, Churchill's statement seems eminently liberal in terms of its rhetoric of happiness and progress for all, though one is left wondering about France. On the other, the logic of power, of more and more power concentrated in the hands of one dominant man at the head of one dominant nation, itself the center of a global empire, directly contradicts all that Lockean liberalism holds dear. In this one sentence the sneaking paradoxes and crises of liberal epic and victorious peace seem to reach their climax or nadir, except that Churchill intends nothing of the sort. There is no irony and no doubt and no second-guessing in his forceful assertions of what he offers as simple, certain truths.

CHURCHILL AND MACAULAY, GIBBON AND NAPIER: HELPLESS IRONY

Indeed, not only are they not ironic, but, to borrow a brilliant formulation by Napier that sums up the uselessness of any ironic critique of imperialist self-justification, irony is helpless before them: "To this proof of moderation and disinterestedness, the humbled Ameers, bending in submission and fear, replied with helpless irony, that their eyes were opened. They had found it difficult to overcome the prejudice and apprehension of their tribes, who had always been led to think the only object of the British was to extend their dominion. Now they had been taught by experience English strength and good faith" (*Conquest* 80–81). Here the vanity of Churchill's efforts to claim Gibbon as his literary father becomes fully transparent. Wedgwood writes of the common phenomenon of historians' false use of Gibbon's style. She could have had Churchill in mind: "[Gibbon's style] is also a dangerous style to copy and he has suffered badly from imitators who aped his mannerisms without understanding their purpose" (31). Wedgwood emphasizes how Gibbon's stateliness, which often makes use of apparent repetition, is always meant to slow the reader's pace for the purpose of making him or her think. Such is not the effect of Churchill's prose with its unreflective reiteration and intensification: "We will fight them on X, Y, Z." In her own case, she certainly blackens and thickens the self-satisfied original to an unpleasant pitch. She then applies it to herself and her world as well as to the past, while Gibbon had, in another example of liberal epic illogic, striven brilliantly to relegate the grimmer implications of epic savagery for others and keep only its invigorating virtues for his enlightened European present: "In war, the European forces are exercised by temperate and undecisive contests" (2:513). This is a fitting description, one with a soupçon of both poetic diction and the law of war, of one liberal epic ideal: no winners, no domination, no death apparently, only rule-bound competition, the enlivening effects and peaceable values of the marketplace smoothly translated to the battlefield. One can hear in it the beginnings of the triumphant paeans Creasy would sing over the Crystal Palace's peaceful competitions, perhaps the high-water mark of liberal hopes that war had been left firmly behind. But whether Gibbon's language fits the Seven Years' War is open to question, and the Crimean War soon came to spoil the headier dreams of 1851.[15] Still Wedgwood stays true to the purposes of his style, arguably making them even truer than Gibbon himself with his occasional blind spots. Churchill's departures, however, are not occasional, but endemic, and they trend against all that Gibbon represents. Superficially, one can detect numerous signs of his efforts to imitate Gibbon's phrasings, his triplets, his vocabulary, his stateliness, and so on, but, at the level of meaning or of worldview, Churchill's triumphant, unquestioning embrace of a heroic logic of more and still more is utterly un-Gibbonian. His wars are certainly not "temperate and undecisive contests." Churchill wants clear winners and will pay the price in blood—and enjoy doing so. His periods do not promote careful thought or consideration; they renounce civilized self-doubt and self-restraint for the steady march of imperial, national, familial, and personal gain without end.

Ironically, the logic of Churchill's prose is much closer to Macaulay's patriotic exuberance than Gibbon's coy French sophistication. Indeed, they logically extend Macaulay's own efforts to get past neoclassical poetic diction to the plain, popularizing language of the novel. Gibbon originally planned to write his history in French, and with over 90 percent of the modern scholarship backing it up French, it is important to acknowledge how thoroughly Gallic Gibbon's English remains. Such civilized, philosophical, erudite, enlightened, and rationalizing Parisian roots certainly nourished the softness of the violence his history primarily derived from Pope, whose own coy violence was equally indebted to Fénelon's and Dacier's French restraint, humanism, and legality. Churchill and Macaulay, on the other hand, are self-consciously English and Anglo-Saxon. For all

their differences over the particular question of Marlborough's criminality, to which I will return below, they cultivate a style of patriotism, pride,
and unquestioning approval that points away from liberal discipline and
its universally humanizing doubts. From yet another perspective, Namier
observed that Churchill's "pre-occupation with Macaulay" so disfigured
his own portrait of his hero that he recommended removing the argument to an appendix: Macaulay's vision and style were in effect too deeply
coloring Churchill's own. The *Marlborough* is a late work and one in which
Churchill's differences with Macaulay are on such prominent display that
they obscure his deeper, long-standing indebtedness. His earliest history,
however, *The Story of the Malakand Field Force,* shows him openly praising
Macaulay as well as Gibbon, and meticulously imitating the former in a
more fundamental manner than the latter. In a series of letters complaining to his mother about the publisher's careless treatment of his manuscript, he begins by referring to "Lord Macaulay's essay on Mr Robert
Montgomery's poems" (Randolph Churchill 1:895) as the best analogy
for his own anger and disappointment.[16] In a specific complaint about
one annoying alteration, he claims that his original "is modelled directly
on Gibbon's famous remark" (899), but the clear pattern points more
securely to Macaulay in terms of Churchill's sense that the publisher had
repeatedly altered his prose out of "an aversion to simple language" (896)
or "horror of plain English" (899).

Churchill follows and extends to violent killing Macaulay's efforts to
render epic history more plainly: "Another instance of this aversion to
simple language which finds support in the best authors—*Macaulay* particularly (in one passage in his history he speaks of a statesmen who
adopted a piddling policy)" (896). Gibbon colors Churchill's penchant for
elaborate and moralistic phrasing, but Macaulay is his touchstone for
graphic simplicity. As we have seen, however, Macaulay himself reverts to
Gibbonian neoclassicism when depicting heroic violence. It is thus especially important that Churchill's turn to the plain style is most closely
associated with his desire to show the reality of warfare: "The contrast is
destroyed—and the whole para becomes pointless. More than this the
idea of my line was to show that however much you might gild death by
glory—it remained an ugly naked fact. This too perishes" (897). This
complaint is part of a clear pattern that begins with Churchill comment-
ing on how the publisher altered his preface's simple declaration of the
overriding desire to "show the reader *what it looked like*" (896), where "it"
refers to war and combat, into an elaborate and poetic cliché—"to show
the reader *the theatre of our operations*" (896). Churchill concludes "this is
a vy typical alteration." His comment points to a basic clash between tra-

ditional liberal epic depictions of warfare, which Gibbon helped establish and Macaulay unsuccessfully resisted, and Churchill's own determination to change all that. Churchill's publisher systematically reimposed poetic diction upon the plain style of his novice author's violence, and the young Churchill vented to his mother. With Churchill, liberal epic has been turned around in both its ideology and its style: self-determination is largely dismissed and graphic violence eagerly cultivated, but, particularly in his first book, he had to fight hard against the entrenched traditions of sanitization.

Thus by some relevant measures, Churchill has little in common with the great Victorian proponent of the plain style. Macaulay's famous rapidity is either beyond Churchill's abilities or of no interest to him. The Victorian's ongoing effort to introduce a measure of novelistic detail to his grand history is also opposed by Churchill's determination to remain focused upon war and high politics with a fitting oratorical presentation. More pointedly, though Churchill began his career with deep respect for Macaulay, by the time he got to his *Marlborough,* Macaulay had become the enemy, the writer most responsible (more than Swift or Thackeray) for ruining the reputation of his dynasty's founder.[17] In the preface, Churchill tells a story meant to justify his conflict with Macaulay. He introduces a literary agon between Macaulay and himself that will continue subtextually, with occasional explicit eruptions, for the next two thousand pages. Churchill had long aspired to write on Marlborough, but having been convinced by *The History of England* that Marlborough had secretly betrayed his country and sent hundreds of its soldiers and sailors to their deaths for French money and to ruin a rival officer, he could not rise to the challenge of making such a villain the hero he required. Then one day—

> Lord Rosebery said, "Surely you must write *Duke John* [as he always called him]: he was a tremendous fellow." I said that I had from my childhood read everything I came across about him, but that Macaulay's story of the betrayal of the expedition against Brest was an obstacle I could not face. The aged and crippled statesman arose from the luncheon table, and, with great difficulty but sure knowledge, made his away along the passages of The Durdans to the exact nook in his capacious working library where "Paget's Examen" reposed. "There," he said, taking down the unknown, out-of-print masterpiece, "is the answer to Macaulay." (1:18)

This touching scene extends to the whole of Churchill's pious history: "A very obvious mistake of *Marlborough* is Churchill's excessive and vindictive campaign against Macaulay—a strange and unusual exception to Churchill's usual magnanimity and to his willingness to forget past wrongs" (Lukacs 115). This judgment assumes a Churchill ruled by the epic virtue of magnanimity, but, as we have seen, he was much drawn to the Homeric ideal of domination, even destruction, of the foe—and in literary terms that is Macaulay's sorry role.[18]

Still, Lukacs's critique has considerable merit. The Paget's *Examen* story is suspiciously overdone and seems contrived to justify Churchill's familial vengeance, a motive that years earlier had inspired a similar biography of his father. Furthermore, this pamphlet was hardly "unknown," and not only to be found by ancestral wisdom. The basic argument had been summarized by J. Cotter Morison: "Mr. Paget, in his *New Examen*, has proved beyond question that, with regard to Marlborough and Penn, Macaulay has been guilty of gross inaccuracy, nay, even perversions of the truth" (157). Morison's account continues for a couple of pages, more than enough to free Churchill's mind of the burden of Macaulay's attack. It appears in the handy volume on *Macaulay* in the ubiquitous *English Men of Letters* series published by MacMillan. This slim, readily accessible, biography-based study first appeared in 1882, and was reprinted in 1884, 1885, 1889, 1896, 1902 (twice), 1903, and 1909. It came from the closest thing in its day to a popular series of critical overviews. Maybe Churchill had never encountered this text, though it is difficult to believe that his numerous research minions were equally oblivious, but it certainly undermines his archival romance of the unearthing of a unique magical talisman by an ancient lord and patron.

Churchill has constructed this vignette to aggrandize his pious epic undertaking and, following a metaliterary convention, to personalize his epic contest with Macaulay—"Upon this issue I join battle [with Macaulay]" (*Marlborough* 1:18). He stages a literary parallel to the heroic struggle taking place within the *Marlborough*'s main narrative. As this chapter's opening pages suggested, however, there is more than a little overlap between the embarrassed illiberal imperialism of the late Macaulay and the aggressive heroic histories of empire by the early Churchill. Even between such seeming opposites as Macaulay's *History of England* and Churchill's *Marlborough* there are profound thematic and stylistic similarities. On the face of things, Churchill's declaration of war with Macaulay seems to hold true: the two histories cover roughly the same period and center on England's great struggle with Louis XIV's France; each seeks to cast that era and its events as definitive for the shaping of modern England, indeed the modern world; but Macaulay turns to the Glorious Revolution, to the emergence of a modern nation centered on parliamentary government, the growth of commercial power, and the rise of the middle classes, whereas Churchill retorts with an emphasis on defeating France for European hegemony, on securing the foundations of empire, and upon the rise of his own family, a sign of the still aristocratic logic of England's greatness. To be sure, each focuses on a particular hero who happens to be a noble male warrior of the received type. Macaulay's William III, however, is an odd Dutch duck who loses most of his battles with Louis's armies and whose idiosyncrasies and authoritarianism at home ironically lead to parliamentarian and commercial ends he never really sought. Churchill's Marlborough, in contrast, is simpler, wholly unironic in his intentions and his achievements: in short, a hero who wins all his battles, sees and gains what he wants, and makes England great not by mischance, but by willpower and vision. Clearly, Churchill is not only a more vigorous imperialist, but possesses a more straightforwardly epic imagination as well.

Still, for all his waverings, there is a fundamental logic of epic domination in Macaulay that eventually overpowers his liberal qualms and points directly toward Churchill, and thus to an inner logic of liberalism. His history sees the triumph of Western civilization in the triumph of one nation, England, not in the balance of power or the competitive national self-determination lauded by Gibbon and Hume, by Fénelon and Voltaire. Macaulay's own epic rivalry with Hume's *History of England* centers upon his relatively simple Whiggery, and desire for that party to triumph over its Tory rival, in contrast to Hume's balanced appreciation for the claims of both parties. Like Churchill, Macaulay wants a clear winner and a loser. Both Churchill and Macaulay, moreoever, see themselves as winners. Both are marked by a supreme self-confidence and a pronounced contempt for their intellectual, political, and military foes. More to the point, each is confident that his progressive theories trump hard little facts. Both possess an assurance that overrides fussiness over details.[19] In Churchill's case, this appears in his champagne and bed-ridden compositional technique: his imposition of broad outlines and purple passages upon a larger narrative that was mainly assembled by a team of lowly workers, who were expected to make the facts fit that vision, not find data that would trouble its surfaces. Macaulay is much the same, though in his case, his famously prodigious memory allowed him to dispense with the assistants. That memory, which remains a legendary fact for many modern historians, was not everything it was cracked up to be. Macaulay's willingness to dismiss Paget's *Examen*, which destroyed the factual basis for his destruction of the heroic claims of Marlborough, is one example of this tendency. (And here it is worth noting that Macaulay's dismissal is little different from Churchill's aggrandizement: both responses are dictated by the needs of their epic confabulations.) It also appears in boasts—

such as the one about his ability to recoup all Shakespeare out of his head should some disaster destroy all the written copies. Claims of this sort underwrote his compositional technique and ideological fact-checking in his great history: he wrote with extreme fluency because he was sure he remembered.

One final vignette, appropriately in reference to *Paradise Lost,* will sum up the problem. Regarding a particular research trip to Ireland for book 12 of *The History of England,* the epic climax of his larger history with its focus on the Homeric siege of Londonderry (the "research" was really an effort to gather local color, to see in person the great sites of the war he planned to celebrate), Macaulay had the following recollection: "We sailed. . . . As I could not read, I used an excellent substitute for reading. I went through *Paradise Lost* in my head. I could still repeat half of it, and that the best half. I never enjoyed it so much" (G. O. Trevelyan 2:172). Contemporary admirers of Macaulay still cite the myth of his total recall of *Paradise Lost.*[20] But Macaulay did not remember all of it, even by his own admission, and his assertion of remembering even half seems dubious in this light. What's more, his proud insistence that the part he did recall was the "best half," and his self-satisfaction in asserting that he'd "never enjoyed it [half] so much," together suggest that Macaulay's pleasures might well have been founded upon his suppression, as he journeyed back toward his own celebration of conquest and oppression in the name of god and country, of all those portions of Milton that mock the pretensions of war epic's national heroes.

Macaulay and Churchill thus exhibit a hearty ability to neglect counterevidence, to make much of what they do know and to regret, wanly, what they do not. Stylistically, this tendency appears in the driving rhythms of their prose, its logic of simple emphasis without qualification on unquestioned themes. That stylistic logic of more and more, which appears in the last sentence of Churchill's *Marlborough,* imposes on the world and on the reader the liberal triumph of one nation and one ideology. At the same time, both evince a belief in their cultivation of realism, in outlook and in style, but neither ever succeeds in applying it to the violent actions of the alternately parliamentary or imperial England he celebrates. Macaulay proclaims his transcendence of neoclassical propriety, but quietly reassumes it for his epic warfare; Churchill goes further by embracing the Homeric pleasure of terror that liberalism struggled to suppress, but then only points to that pleasurable end while largely suppressing its graphic means. Macaulay and Churchill's hardening of liberal epic into epic liberalism succeeds through their gradual evacuation of liberal epic's original intent to repress. Both claim to be recovering something that had been lost and fail to realize that it had in fact been carefully put away. Irony indeed seems helpless against their aggressive project, but one might be forgiven for desiring an inverted Freudian return of the enlightened repression once wrought by liberal epic—by Gibbon and Napier—and then gradually unraveled by its greatest Victorian and modern hero-practitioners whose civilized self-certainties found irony decidedly unhelpful.[21]

EPILOGUE

THE WARM AND VISIBLE HAND
OF LIBERAL EPIC

War had been the severest test of political and social character, laying bare whatever was feeble, and calling out whatever was strong; and the effect of removing such a test was an untried problem.

    —Henry Adams, *History of the United States of America*

And I detect that most men who serve in armies recruited in liberal states are disturbed by the inconsistencies of defending a free society by an institution that is its ideological antithesis—dictatorial, unrepresentative, and often extremely unjust.

    —John Keegan, "The Historian and Battle"

This study's focus on the persistence of epic makes it logical to conclude before the cultural change wrought by World War II, the so-called Best War Ever, which reenergized the belief in war as a positive solution and war leaders as powerful agents.[1] Since my argument has demonstrated how effectively epic survived despite the cultural and historical forces arrayed against it in 1688, 1815, 1851, or 1914–18, it seems superfluous to continue the argument once 1939–45 rendered epic's task so much easier. Nonetheless, beneath this story of the confident revival of epic history in the bright light of World War II (from which was born, decades later, the History [alias Hitler] Channel with its unflinching view of history as war) bubbles a counterplot of doubting the heroic and, worse yet, fearing that this greatest of liberal victories encoded the deepest self-betrayal. For, it was dreaded, maybe the West prevailed precisely because it was more coolly scientific, less likely to surrender itself to the warm embrace of some martial hero, and more prone to rely on the productivity of its vast factories in Detroit. A survey of key figures from the three liberal nations central to this study—France, America, and England—will grant final insight into the price liberalism willingly paid, in its intellectual coherence and sympathetic humanity, to remain heroically agential.

In 1946 H. G. Wells died convinced by the return of war (and unmoved by final victory) that his high hopes for scientific history to educate the world's citizens to see beyond their borders, beyond liberal nationalism and its inevitable descents into competitive warfare, had failed. (Contrast the heady 1922 conclusion to his shortened *Outline of History* ["Can we doubt that presently our race . . . will achieve unity and peace"] to his "Adapt or Perish"—with strong emphasis on the latter—conclusion to the 1945 edition.)[2] Before suffering this personal, authorial, and racial tragedy, however, Wells, with his more usual upbeat confidence, had often best summed up my study's key themes: "Winston Churchill [and] George Trevelyan . . . remained puerile in their political outlook because of its [war fantasy's] persistence" (*Experiment in Autobiography* 76). In the larger passage, Wells restates the liberal anxieties of Milton, Locke, Vico, and Rousseau from which this study commenced: "I think there is no natural bias toward bloodshed in imaginative youngsters, but the only vivid and inspiring things that history fed me with were campaigns and conquests" (75). Such a late reiteration of a long-standing article of liberal faith dramatizes the fundamental liberal epic paradox. If there is no natural pleasure in such matter, why did liberal societies and individuals for so long prove unwilling to forgo it? Why did they continue to devote some of their best energies to producing and consuming new versions of it from Pope and Gibbon to Macaulay and Churchill? Indeed why did Wells take till 1914, when his fictional uncle Edward Ponderevo was able to articulate so pithily the basic objection in 1908: "He became in those days the terror of eminent historians. 'Don't want your drum and trumpet history, no fear'" (*Tono-Bungay* 214)? Finally, why did liberalism so eagerly interpret the lessons of World War II to rejuvenate war history?

In his 1908 novel, six years before the Great War, and in his 1934 memoir, six years before the greater one, Wells mocks his own adolescent pleasures in imagining battle and his dreams of heroic agency. He then extends that mockery to Hitler—and Churchill. Within a decade, however, Churchill's triumphs had exploded such sarcastic equivalencies. His leadership and his histories had dramatically redeemed wars, heroes, and their agency. In the early twenty-first century, Niall Ferguson, once in *The Pity of War* (1999) a historian of the horrific consequences of military solutions, became an ardent disciple of Churchillian resolve—and adventurism. In *Colossus* (2003), he campaigned for America to take up, with renewed determination, the civilizing burden of the British Empire, for its president to model himself upon the indomitable prime minister, and for its citizens to act decisively under such leadership in the real world of war. Later he began his *War of the World* (2006) by evoking Wells's turn-of-the-century novel as the definitive model for twentieth-century history: "Published on the eve of the twentieth century, H. G. Wells's *The War of the Worlds* (1898) is much more than just a seminal work of science fiction. It is also a kind of Darwinian morality tale, and at the same time a work of singular prescience" (xxxiii). But Wells regarded his true career as a prophet and a historian of the transcendence of war, as an heir to Gibbon, but one ambitious to correct his lingering militarism, and a more successful, more popular follower of Adams and Buckle. Indeed, Wells followed his first extended effort in scientific historiography, *The Outline of History* (1920), with an equally massive biology textbook, *The Science of Life* (1929), wherein he argues that scientific history will itself evolve into the yet higher form of the history of science, and that along with that trend will come the inevitable "Supersession of War" (1464–65): "supersession"!—a hazy (Coleridge's judgment) or luminous (Craddock's) Gibbonian dream word coyly signifying victory. Even in his moment of fulfillment, Wells ached, though with appropriately Bladesoverian decorum, for what he deplored.

Still, World War II did not inspire Wells to turn from his failed intellectual endeavors back to his youthful heroic dreamings. But it did do something much like that for Fernand Braudel. Braudel published his first history the year Wells died. At least initially, the war seemed to drive him further into cultivating a Wellsian scientific historiography that downplayed war's eventfulness in favor of deeper, more lasting, less flashy forces. But victory and the revival of republican France under its hero de Gaulle led to his transformation of this innovative project back into a kind of heroic history even Voltaire once mocked. Certainly, the sophisticated historiographical experiments of Marc Bloch's Annales School far surpassed the amateur insouciance of Wells. It produced as its first masterpiece Braudel's *The Mediterranean and the Mediterranean World in the Age of Philip II* (1946), a brilliant work of scholarship and art that begins with a revealing apology: "I hope too that I shall not be reproached for my excessive ambitions, for my desire and need to see on a grand scale" (1: 21–22). Given his bold intention to be both scientific and epic, Braudel, like the similarly conflicted Henry Adams, struggled more than most historians with the historiographical challenge of war and its "great man" paradigm: "For war, as we know, is not an arena governed purely by individual responsibilities" (1:21). Ultimately, however, Braudel's work abandoned this halting demur and exhibited little of Adams's statistical innovations for comprehending war apart from the heroic.[3] He re-embraced the simple, powerful tool of the individual hero and his heavy burdens. While his history incorporates a wide array of scientific and social scientific analyses, it nonetheless offers itself as the answer to a prayer for "great history" rather than yet another learned monograph: "It is fear of great history which has killed great history," wrote Edmond Faral, in 1942. "May it live again!"

(qtd. in Braudel 1:22). Its epic scope allows for Braudel's slow march back toward an explicitly heroic narrative. His theory of *la longue durée* initially functions as a scientific consolation, written as it was in a German POW camp, a means of hoping for the recovery of his beloved France, for seeing the debacle Bloch examined in *Strange Defeat* (1940) as merely a short-term setback of "event" history.[4] Even so, Braudel's finally triumphant narrative tellingly reverses his master's sequence. Bloch moves from events to culture to environment, while Braudel organizes his narrative the other way—part 1: The Role of the Environment; part 2: Collective Destinies and General Trends; part 3: Events, Politics, and People. Braudel's progression allows his history to climax with a decisive battle. At Lepanto, Don John of Austria pushes aside the cautious advice of his counselors, who echo Hallam's comments on the dangers of thinking in "decisive" terms. Like Creasy ignoring his master, Braudel and Don John ignore theirs and come to believe in the possibility of great victory. Such courage gains a signal triumph, one that determines, like Herodotus's Marathon and Vergil's Actium, the subsequent Western-dominated history of the Mediterranean. Braudel memorializes this victory in prototypically epic language and finds himself explicitly defending his assertions against another venerable master of French historiography, Voltaire, and implicitly against Bloch himself: "There is no doubt Don John was the instrument of destiny. . . . Before joining Voltaire in his ironic comments on Lepanto, we would do well to measure the immediate impact of the victory—which was breathtaking" (2:1103–4). His history thus circles back to the exciting matter of war, explains its results in terms of individual determination, finds it a "breathtaking" matter of "destiny," and "no doubt" cringes before Voltaire's lash.

World War II England played a more glorious role and possessed a greater savior than France, so it is hardly surprising that English historians returned to advocating epic history even more vigorously—and with less anxiety about what their fathers might think. Chapter 3, however, highlighted Trevor-Roper's conflicted deployment of World War II to castigate scientific history for its neglect of great men before spinning about to clobber Carlylean historiography, with the same weapon, for its Hitlerian spawn. Utilizing Trevor-Roper's heroic World War II, Isaiah Berlin, the preeminent postwar philosopher of liberalism and a wartime emissary for Churchill, writes with unusual forcefulness (and less obvious self-contradiction) against the impersonal aspirations of scientific history and in defense of Churchill as both a historian and an exemplar of greatness. His World War II–based writing on these matters sports a clear-cut certainty absent from his subtle meditations on the same debate in

Tolstoy's notorious historiographical speculations. Once again 1939–45 decided matters in favor of epic, but a closer look reveals embarrassments amid all the hoopla—for Berlin's rhetoric suggests his knowing exaggeration of the historiographical value of Churchill's works. Gibbon was at the forefront of historical research in his day, and Macaulay participated in the emerging phenomenon of "people's history." Theodor Mommsen, the only historian besides Churchill to win the Nobel Prize for Literature, was nineteenth-century Germany's (and thus the world's) leading textual scholar in addition to being a best-selling narrative artist. But Churchill contributed little more than his heroic self to his historiography. It is thus inevitable that the chief virtue, according to Berlin, of his epic volumes is to fight on the shore against the rising tide of a dehumanizing scientific historiography:

> History, we are told by Aristotle, is "what Alcibiades did and suffered." This notion, despite all the efforts of the social sciences to overthrow it, remains a good deal more valid than rival hypotheses, provided that history is defined as that which historians actually do. At any rate Churchill accepts it wholeheartedly, and takes full advantage of his opportunities. And because his narrative deals largely with personalities and gives individual genius its full and sometimes more than its full due, the appearance of the great wartime protagonists in his pages gives his narrative some of the quality of an epic. (*Proper Study* 614)

Here Berlin spends lavishly to get back to epic. His argument resembles Creasy's in its glancing acknowledgment of problems followed by its quick suppression of doubts. Surely, the authority of Aristotle and the evidence of what some "historians actually do" followed by an "at any rate" inspire little confidence in Berlin's incisiveness here. His retreat into what Churchill himself did "wholeheartedly" suggests Berlin's own half-heartedness. He then plunges into the most circular of circular argumentation: Churchill's epic practice proves his epic theory. Churchill recalls Buckle in becoming the prime evidence for the thesis of his own histories—but, whereas that self-aggrandizement earned Buckle the dripping contempt of Acton and Berlin, now the liberal critic approves of his hero's taking "full advantage" of "individual genius," even if that means giving it "more than its full due." Berlin privately lamented his chosen hero's penchant to see war as the first solution, but publicly dreaded a world ruled by impersonal statistics. Indeed, he goes so far as to write appreciatively of Joseph de Maistre's ultra-violent and reactionary theory: "Battles are won psychologically, battles are won by acts of faith. Above all, what happens happens as a result of some kind of mysterious inner force which is certainly not rational calculation or the careful application of a textbook set of rules, some kind of elaborate rational calculation or plan which wins or loses battles" (*Considerations on France* xx). Scientific rationalism has its excesses, but here the mystic obscurantism, which Berlin exposes and accepts, is patent, even painful. He proceeds to theorize de Maistre's influence over Tolstoy's antiliberal views of war, particularly as it is expressed in his Battle of Borodino in *War and Peace*. He thus attacks not only scientific history, but even liberalism's more modest efforts to rationalize and regulate warfare. When confronted by the soullessness of scientific history, one of the leading theorist-apologists of modern freedom drifts back into admiring the will to power and the will to win over the well-established efforts to embody his own negative liberty in enlightened practices (and representations) of legalized warfare.

Most fascinating among these post–World War II liberal historians and theorists is S. L. A. Marshall. America triumphed most spectacularly of all in this war, but in Marshall that victory for American values generated a response that intensified the pattern found in Braudel and Berlin: at once newly confident in the virtue of heroic liberalism, anxious about the deeper reality of an impersonal scientific advance, and truly disturbing in its more than Churchillian (or even Homeric) remedy. Marshall, the first to apply sociological research techniques to the study of combat, was highly controversial for his splendidly humane thesis that the vast majority of American soldiers were not shooting to kill—even in the thick of battle, and even to save their own lives. The still lively debates over Marshall's thesis have ignored how much it owes to Marshall's literary roots in liberal epic.[5] Whatever one makes of the strengths and weaknesses of his post-combat interviewing, his causal explanation for the results he claimed was the self-same disciplinary regimen promoted by Vico and Locke and enacted by Pope and Gibbon: "He [the American soldier] is what his home, his religion, his schooling, and the moral code and ideals of his society have made him. . . . He comes from a civilization in which aggression connected with the taking of human life is prohibited and unacceptable. The teaching and the ideals of that civilization are against killing, against taking advantage" (78). For this, his theory's linchpin, Marshall provides not a shred of evidence. It is an article of faith—or generic convention. Another crucial feature of Marshall's thesis, one similarly neglected by the critics of his techniques and results, is his motive. Once again, though famous for his attentiveness to soldiers' actual experiences through his immediate post-combat interviews, this deeper dimension of Marshall's theory derives from the literary tradition of liberal epic, but now its violent side. Marshall, as another worker in the Best War Ever, both rejoiced in the victory of the liberal allies and worried that liberalism had won by compromising with the logic of scientific totalitarianism, with the kind of central planning that was systematically reducing warriors to cogs in a vast military machine.

In *Men against Fire* (1947), Marshall's thesis, that most American soldiers were not firing, was driven by his fears that the American military establishment was determined to conceptualize war as a scientific exercise. Military planners increasingly sought to cast the battlefield as an industrial zone, and the soldier as a mere worker within its intricate churnings: "My answer to this fundamental proposition in traditional military logic is that it is absolutely false. The heart of the matter is to relate the man to his fellow soldier. . . . Only when the human, rather than the material, aspects are put uppermost" (38). He insists that so long as the military treats the human as a cog, that cog will fail to act. Only by treating the soldier as a human-hero can his ability to act be restored. That action is to fire lethally upon a fellow human being. (His title is thus brilliantly, triply ironic: it is not, as one first thinks, about men facing fire; it is about the crisis of men refusing to fire—they are "against" it; but its goal is to restore their full humanity and thus make them heroes capable of gladly firing—for only mere "men" are against it.) Marshall labels this machine scenario "The Illusion of Power" in relation to the planner and "Combat Isolation" from the perspective of the soldier. It has precipitated the crisis Marshall seeks to resolve by claiming that war must be understood in heroic terms: "The great victories of the United States have pivoted on the acts of courage and intelligence of a very few individuals" (208). And here he means individuals fighting in the front lines, not individual strategists in the rear. Above all he rejects the impersonal "Detroit" thesis: "Being from Detroit, I am accustomed to hearing it said publicly that Detroit industry won the war" (209). The question becomes, how can the soldier-agent escape from the factories of Detroit and return to the plains of Ilium? The answer is to restore contact with a human opponent. Unfortunately, the bedrock reality of the modern battlefield is one of little or no contact with a personalized, human enemy. What can be done?

For Marshall the only possibility left is to put him in contact with his fellow-soldier, the buddy. The common explanation for this move is that the liberal subject, who refuses to kill to save himself, will fight to avoid being shamed in front of his comrades and will kill to save a friend, a beloved, the buddy in the larger "band of brothers." His heroism is restored by that human contact. Unfortunately, this rosy scenario presupposes that the buddy makes three—the hero, the friend, the enemy—but in Marshall's version there is no such crowd. There are still only two when the buddy is there. He is there precisely to get to two, to end the isolation in the only way possible. Thus, more ominously, the epic or heroic explanation is that it is the buddy who plays the part of the human rival in the reconstituted primal scene. The presence of the friend is the one means to recover the necessary agential drama of agon and triumph. Only this scenario can reestablish human individuality and agency as against the machine, but it comes at the very steep price of asking for the triumph to be over a friend, a fellow soldier, the only kind of human the modern battlefield will allow him to see and know and surpass. Invisible enemies, like invisible hands, just don't cut it: "I hold it to be one of the simplest truths of war that the thing which enables an infantry soldier to keep going with his weapon is the near presence or presumed presence of a comrade. The warmth which derives from human companionship is as essential to his employment of the arms with which he fights as is the finger with which he pulls the trigger or the eye with which he aligns his sights" (42). Human warmth is a trigger finger or an aiming eye. And what or whom is it aiming at? Certainly not the comrade in any literal sense, but metaphorically that figure, his presence, is what restores the heroic scene. The buddy by dying (and doesn't Buddy always die?) allows once again for visceral victory, tangible superiority over another human being. Marshall recovers agency by restoring epic's core—even a friend, because only a friend, can now play that part, and this friend is not Patroclus, but Hector. Stephen Ambrose's popular military histories such as *Citizen Soldiers* (1997) and *Band of Brothers* (1992) (along with their adaptations by Steven Spielberg) are deeply indebted to Marshall's theories for their basic democratic and "buddy" theory of heroism. Ambrose and, of course, Steven thoroughly sentimentalize Marshall's disturbing thesis: *Saving Private Ryan* (1998) indeed.

Epic survived or persisted or flourished in the modern liberal world and in spite of liberalism's profound ethical and intellectual objections, because liberalism needed and still needs its horrific or sublime, offensive or beautiful drama of domination. To survey a range of leading liberal thinkers rejecting the very thought of scientific history and clinging to a history of war and war heroes is to enjoy evidence that something more than compromise or bad faith is at play. Tolstoy on the failure to transcend the hero, Adams on the various failures to transcend war, late Wells on his successful transcendence of his puerile war-fantasizing early self versus Ferguson's liberal preference for the early Wells of war, Acton and Berlin on Buckle, Berlin on Churchill, Churchill on Marlborough (and himself), Trevor-Roper on Hitler—and Churchill, Braudel on Don John, Marshall on the hero-soldier—all declare the need of the good nineteenth- and

twentieth-century liberal to cling to the one literary genre supremely dedicated to convincingly representing human agency. In the end, liberalism
cannot and will not divorce itself from epic, and epic has not yet begun to
decline. To rework the words of the creator of *Doom*, an early example of
contemporary culture's most lucrative art form, it seems that to be self-
respecting liberal agents, "we must kill each other!" And so we do.

NOTES

PROLOGUE

1. See Benedetto Croce's *History as the Story of Liberty* (1941) and Colling-wood's translation of Guido de Ruggiero's *History of European Liberalism* (1927). Davidson, 13–18, explores the tension between Keynes's liberal politics and his attack, in the name of governmental agency, upon traditional liberal laissez-faire policies and the invisible hand. This study looks to the politics of Keynes—and his efforts to make liberal economics act directly. Overall, my use of *liberal* refers to the cultural ideology that advocates national self-determination, rejects wars of conquests, favors constitutional systems based upon an expanding definition of citizenship, and defends the principal of granting individual rights and autonomy as generously as possible.

2. The epilogue will return to this basic dilemma.

3. Green's larger argument with the academic establishment and its neglect of the "adventure tale" overlaps with mine here. Green blames snobbish sophistication for the disregard of violent adventure narratives. My study's texts have not been thus treated individually: many of them still rank very high in the canon. Rather, their enormous length is a strong constraint upon how often they can be taught and has thwarted the ability of scholars to see them as a self-conscious tradition.

INTRODUCTION

1. Leo Braudy's *From Chivalry to Terrorism* (2003) is the most detailed recent study to restate the conventional view of a modern trend away from a heroic culture of war. Robert Adams's *Better Part of Valor* (1962) is an older but valuable study of the same. Edmund Wilson's classic *Patriotic Gore* (1962) is close to my own in its perspective and its combination of history and poetry. Nonetheless, Wilson appeals to the standard hypocrisy thesis in critiquing liberalism's attachment to heroic warfare, while I argue for a more fundamental connection between the two. Freud remains the most famous advocate for the view that human nature is naturally drawn to aggressiveness in a way that liberal humanism cannot hope to overcome.

2. See Pocock 2:72–162 for Locke's influence upon Voltaire.

3. For Michelet and Vico and the transformation they together effected upon the writing of history, see Fisch 72–80 and Monod 1:30–43.

4. Mack provides the fullest background history of Pope's unprecedented earnings from his *Iliad*. Mack also represents an authoritative restatement of the traditional neoclassical Pope. For a different view, see Helen Deutsch's *Resemblance and Disgrace* (1996), which looks past the usual Pope of elegance, order, and sanitization to a set of categories summed up in the word "deformity."

5. See Guillory 124–33 for an alternative account of poetic diction, its relation to prose, and its roots in pastoral. Donald Davie's *Purity of Diction* (1952) and Geoffrey Tillotson's "Eighteenth-Century Poetic Diction (II)" (*Essays* 63–85) are influential accounts that similarly emphasize pastoral as the major genre for this phenomenon. Tillotson, 68–69, observes that Coleridge's special object of critique in Pope's Homer has distinctly pastoral features, but this insight slights the unpastoral siege elements: one implication of my argument is that Pope tends to emphasize the pastoral elements of the epic, but that effort remains part of the larger dilemma surrounding heroic violence.

6. See Michael Walzer's *Obligations* (1970) and Yael Tamir's "Nationalism, Liberalism, and the State," 231–32, in McKim and McMahan 227–44 for examples of the well-discussed problem of contractarian liberalism and self-sacrifice. This crisis centers on the question of why an individual who has become part of a liberal society so as to secure life and livelihood could be expected to willingly sacrifice his or her life in war for that society. Hobbes's theory goes so far as to assert the individual cannot be expected to make that sacrifice.

7. See Annabel Patterson's *Nobody's Perfect* (2002) for Milton's importance to early liberal thinking, particularly in America.

8. John Grenier's *First Way of War* (2005) challenges the view that American culture was one of the first to embrace the law of war and an antiwar position generally.

9. See Bordwell 8 for Grotius's flight from the Thirty Years' War to Homer's more humane violence.

10. The Nazi-era German political scientist Carl Schmitt critiques this liberal penchant for euphemism and self-justification: "A new and essentially pacifist vocabulary has been invented. War is condemned. . . . The adversary is no longer called an enemy but a disturber of the peace and is thereby designated to be an outlaw of humanity" (79). Schmitt also notes the fundamental paradox for liberal self-determination and national warfare, namely, the necessity for liberal states to force their citizens to fight, kill, and die in their wars: "In case of need, the political entity must demand the sacrifice of life. Such a demand is in no way justifiable by the individualism of liberal thought" (71).

11. See Tillyard 488–509 for the strongest claims that Pope's *Iliad* should be regarded as the eighteenth century's most representative "original" epic. Lord Chesterfield preferred Voltaire's *La Henriade* to Homer and Vergil.

12. See Leigh 152–53 for Voltaire's ennui before Homer's violence.

13. See the *OED* entry on "transpierce."

14. M. S. Anderson's *War and Society in Europe of the Old Regime* (1988) provides the fullest documentation of the cultural shift away from the celebration of war—a process that centers on the same years as Dryden's career.

15. Howard's *War and the Liberal Conscience*, 13–30, emphasizes how the French were at the forefront of developing and implementing the law of war in

the 1700s. Foucault's *Discipline and Punish* (1977), especially 135–41, presents an analysis of Louis XIV's regime's imposition of Cartesian order on the definition of a soldier and the internal workings of his army—but a similar attempt was made to impose regularity upon its external activities in war.

16. Harth, 141–45, discusses Grotius's influence upon Dryden, but he focuses on religious toleration, not war.

17. Other instances of Dryden's introducing variants of the words "just" or "unjust" into combat, where the original had no direct Latin equivalent, are the following: 7.152–53, 322; 8.118, 147–49, 395; 10.532; 11.113, 232, 361–62; 12.187, 798.

18. Weinbrot, 237, notes another revealing interpolation of liberal hopefulness into Vergil's illiberal empire: "To tame the proud, the fetter'd slave to free" (6.1176).

19. See Green, *Seven Types* 50–51, on Rousseau's championing of Defoe. Weinbrot, 230–32, sees this epic's violence as "Christianized" rather than liberalized.

20. Siebart, 369–72, notices similar ironies in Hume's heroic account of Montrose, but Alfred is both more primitive and more humane.

21. Katie Trumpener's *Bardic Nationalism* (1997) is the authoritative treatment of this larger phenomenon of self-consciously primitive heroic poetry produced in and by modern liberal cultures. See also Quint's discussion of Ossian, 343–68.

22. Voltaire's *Essay on Epic Poetry* disqualifies *Télémaque* from full epic status not because it is in prose, but because of its long pedagogical and instructional asides.

23. Howard and Cherel survey Fénelon's influence over eighteenth-century legal and economic critiques of war. See Vattel's preface, vii–xvii, for his understanding of his theory's relationship to the work of Hobbes, Grotius, and Pufendorf. For Fénelon's clearest statements on the republic of nations, the equality of power, and the critique of war, see the *Examen*, in *Oeuvres* 989–1003, and the *Supplement*, in *Oeuvres* 1003–9. This work ties Fénelon's understanding of Grotius and Pufendorf and the modern *ius in bello* to his practice of epic in *Télémaque*.

24. See Cherel 314–21 and 393–400 for Fénelon's influence upon Rousseau's educational theory. Cherel's study documents Fénelon's influence in a range of eighteenth-century French movements: education, antiwar, agriculture and economics, politics, and narrative.

25. See Leslie A. Chilton's introduction to Fénelon's *The Adventures of Telemachus* (Athens: U of Georgia P, 1997) for the critical debate over the authenticity of Smollett's translation (xxiv–xxvii).

26. See Campbell's essay on the paradox of war and liberal benevolence in Godwin's writings, especially 343–44.

27. This is the reading of the last, the 1796 edition—in contrast to the "chambermaid, wife, mother" reading of 1793. The 1796 version serves my epic purposes, as the 1793 serves those of the readers of *Caleb Williams* (1794). See Fludernik 857–61 and Radcliffe 529–36 for analyses of his novel through this Fénelon episode. Carnall, 26–27, observes Robert Southey's reading of Godwin on Fénelon and casuistry.

28. See Radcliffe 533–34 and Epstein 9.

29. Compare H. G. Wells's depiction of serious fighting versus gentlemanly

boxing among boys in *Tono-Bungay:* "I was used to inflicting and enduring savage hurting" (40).

30. See Chandos's *Boys Together* for critical attention to the relation between the ethos of the schoolyard and the Victorian attitude toward war.

31. Holt, however, notes the slow early sales (134).

32. See Crotty and Segal on mutilation in Homer.

1. THE ETHICAL-AESTHETIC CHALLENGE TO EPIC

1. See Bakhtin's "Epic and the Novel" in *Dialogic Imagination* 13–19, or Wilkie 3–4, for this pervasive thesis.

2. Charles Taylor's discussion in *Sources of the Self* of the ancient value system of "dignity" (16) in contrast to modern liberal sense of the moral self fails to capture the aggressive edge of Homeric values that Hume's term "courage" does.

3. Marshall's analysis of Hume's essay is particularly insightful regarding Hume's cultivation of analogies that he pushes toward paradox. See especially 337–38.

4. See Weinbrot 194–236 for a broader cultural account of this "Homer Problem."

5. Segal's *The Theme of the Mutilation* demonstrates that there is an ethical judgment upon the mutilation of dead bodies, but this is crucially different from the skill and beauty displayed by a hero killing an active enemy. Scarry's parallelism between killing in combat and torture makes this same mistake. Bourke's *Dismembering the Male,* particularly 31–75, presents a more skeptical history of this phenomenon.

6. See Ram, 3–27, for a useful overview of the history of and scholarship on the sublime.

7. Des Pres complements my analysis, but he passes over the key point—that Burke's tense relation to Homeric epic was determined by his effort to recast terror in terms of the reader feeling sympathetic fear, not sympathizing with the Achillean terrorizer.

8. Lynch, 7, notes Pope's excess here, though as part of a different argument. Here Pope earns the contemporary's judgment that Lynch took for her title, "vile forgery."

9. Townsend's "Lockean Aesthetics" lends valuable insight into the interpenetration of liberal political and aesthetic theory that is present practically in Fénelon, is doubted and ironized by Hume, and is powerfully restated by Kant. See especially 349–52.

10. See Cleere and Macarthur.

11. Pocock has devoted four learned volumes (so far) of *Barbarism and Religion* to the context surrounding Gibbon's quip and influential thesis.

12. See Hepp 629–60, Williams 49–52, and Weinbrot 198–201 for critical treatments of Homer, Dacier, and Pope.

13. See Williams, chapters 3–6, and Thomas, 15–16, for discussions of the relationship between Pope's women readers and his *Iliad.*

14. Technically, Pope describes the second piece as "Observations," not an "Essay," but it interrupts the flow from books 18 to 19, as the former does from books 4 to 5.

15. See Shankman 120–28 for a succinct comparison of Pope's and Chapman's translations.

16. Pocock's *Barbarism and Religion,* 307–418, is a full and detailed treatment of the ironies besetting Gibbon's liberal and enlightened history of ancient tyranny and violence.

17. See Grafton's *The Footnote,* which makes Gibbon the key early protagonist of this form.

18. Indeed, Bury simply (and inaccurately) says, "Gibbon has reproduced the account of Ammianus, and you may conveniently read it in his pages" (*Invasion* 58–59).

19. Georg Lukacs's *The Historical Novel* (1937) and Jameson's *Political Unconscious* (1981) detail the negative effect of Flaubert's style upon novelistic realism, but fail to see what Flaubert does to epic grandeur. Rawson's *Satire and Sentiment,* 32 and 71–72, has the most insightful reading of *Salammbo*'s relation to the epic tradition of graphic violence. Rawson's "Gibbon, Swift, and Irony," especially 188–91, notes some exceptions to the sanitizing pattern traced here. Badian's "Gibbon on War" follows Keegan's now standard thesis when he claims that it is a result of Gibbon's ignorance of war—and squeamishness. See Womersley's analysis, 170–75, of Gibbon's debt to Ammianus and strategies for softening his excesses—but Womersley's analysis has a different purpose.

20. See Barbero 282–85 for the most up-to-date account of the fate of the Old Guard.

21. Alexander Welsh's *The Hero of the Waverley Novels* (1963) still articulates the most useful account of the Scott passive hero.

22. See Macarthur 135–39 on Ruskin, disgust, and the sublime.

2. ROMANTIC LIBERAL EPIC

1. Keegan, *Face of Battle* 37–40, skillfully analyzes a Napier battle piece, but fails to note this deliberate, artistic double-sidedness, much as his larger thesis falls short in not realizing the poetical and fictional origins of the traditional battle piece.

2. See Tucker, *Epic* 231, for a more straightforward view of Byron's scorn for heroic cant.

3. See Gooch 286 for "the extensive literature provoked" by Napier's history.

4. Timko, 91–93, condenses several decades of Carlyle's contempt for Tennyson's poetry qua poetry.

5. Thus I will use the last, more accessible edition. Tucker, *Epic* 77, points to Southey's admiration for Spenser.

6. Raymond and Pratt elucidate early Southey and revolution. Simpkins is especially valuable on Southey's prefaces.

7. See Speck 42–82.

8. Here I disagree with Christopher Smith on its being dedicated to "some idea of the Universal Family" (85) and Tucker on its "political neutrality" (*Epic* 79). It is shaped by the logic of liberal nationalism.

9. See Bainbridge 17–20 on the Romantics' rewriting of their opposition to Napoleon and the French Revolution.

10. Tucker, *Epic* 76–80, focuses his reading around the poem's surprising neglect of her later trial and tragedy.

11. For a helpful reading of Coleridge's relation to Southey's *Joan of Arc,* see Sternbach. For Southey's patriotism and his poetic language, see Eastwood, especially 266–67.

12. Compare a recent and similarly dubious attempt to deal with Nelson's war criminality in Vincent's heroic biography: "Nothing else can explain the inspired phraseology of the letter and the pains he took to present it properly" (426). Henry Adams's account of the War of 1812 has the most meticulous narrative of British (and French) violations of the law of war at sea. See 2:478–92 for his analysis of British exceptionalism.

13. See Bainbridge 119–25 for Southey's use of Old Testament imagery in his portrayal of the French; alternatively, see Bainbridge 137–38 for the typical Whig defense and admiration of Napoleon.

14. Southey's Wellington adheres to Keegan's thesis in *Mask of Command,* 92–163.

15. See Tucker, *Epic* 231–32, for a brief but insightful discussion of the interplay of cant and rhyming in *Don Juan.*

16. See McGann, *Don Juan* 85, for the largely elegiac style of the siege cantos, which I see in terms of the "relief," the moment after death, in the pastoral similes in Pope's *Iliad.*

17. See Stabler 121–35.

18. Southey's *Peninsular Wars* account of this siege, which he similarly aggrandizes ("never were brave men exposed to slaughter under more frightful circumstances" [3.1:422]), confirms Napier's strengths. Southey is thinner in his details, and his evocation of anatomical reality in battle frequently sacrifices realism for silly bravado: "[Girsewald] severed his antagonist's head from his shoulders" (424).

19. See Bruce's biography of Napier, especially chapters 12 and 13, for the fullest presentation of his political opinions and experiences.

20. See Morse Stephens's definitive article on Napier in the ninth edition of the *Encyclopedia Britannica.* He emphasizes Napier's debt to and rivalry with Thucydides.

21. See Keegan's final judgment on Wellington in *The Mask of Command* for just how heroic a modern and critical treatment of Wellington can still be.

22. Bruce notes the common view of contemporaries that Napier too greatly admired Napoleon's genius. See Bruce 1:502–4 and 2:337–43.

23. See Schell 64–72 for the theory of People's War and the central place of Spain's revolt against Napoleon in this tradition. Schell relies on the French general Jomini's account but pays no regard to Napier, who also served in Spain and wrote the definitive contemporary account of the war, but who consistently dismissed the Spanish claims.

24. Napier's history was conceived largely in opposition to Southey's vehemently anti-French and pro-Spanish account. See Bathurst's entire article or Speck 191–92 for simple assertions.

25. See Bruce 2:47 and 337–43 on Napier and Plutarch.

26. See *Face of Battle* 37–40.

27. See Hughes 259–319.

28. The collection of letters edited by Bathurst is filled with outbursts against Southey—and all bad history of the war is made Southeyan: "Southey is raving and rabid" (741) and "his work is full of the grossest abuse . . . [,] quite as bad as Southey himself" (744).

3. EPIC HISTORY, THE NOVEL, AND WAR IN THE 1850S

1. See Mary Poovey's *Uneven Developments* (1988) and Ian Duncan's *Modern Romance and Transformations of the Novel* (1992). Beyond attending closely to his famous style and realism, Thackeray scholarship largely falls into two groups— one exploring his canonical rise and fall, the other looking to the ephemeral superficiality of his key themes. Barbara Hardy's *The Exposure of Luxury* (1972), Andrew Miller's *Novels behind Glass,* and Dames's "Brushes with Fame" exemplify the latter, as Tillotson's *Thackeray the Novelist,* Carlisle's *Sense of an Audience,* and, most of all, Trollope's study of a novelist he nonetheless greatly admired represent the former. Both traditions look to the contrast with Dickens, his securer fame, greater self-confidence, and magnificent theme of London. My argument combines both approaches.

2. See Harden 38–40 and 102–5 for Thackeray's pattern of moving from literary historical to fictional works.

3. Phillipps's chapter titled "The Language of Henry Esmond" presents the most searching analysis of Thackeray's Augustan pastiche.

4. See Tillotson, *Thackeray* 41–46.

5. See Harden 66–69 for a list of the Vergil parallels and references.

6. For a differently inflected analysis of Macaulay's interest, see Horn.

7. Phillipps observes the difficulty, for Thackeray's Victorian imitation of eighteenth-century prose, "to render the speech of an outspoken age in the vocabulary of a prudish one" (174).

8. But Leigh, ix–xi, neatly presents the difference between the epic and letter-writing Voltaire on this battle.

9. Thackeray highlights this challenge by having one of his protagonists write and stage a historical heroic play. Sadly, Douglas observes, "The evidence of the sources places Thackeray's display of historical learning in an unfavourable light" (166).

10. "Another contributor to the *Foreign Quarterly Review* [in 1843] . . . commented on the French 'historic mania' of the time, with reference to the fame enjoyed by Guizot" (Douglas 167). Thackeray was just then seeking this journal's editorship.

11. See J. Hillis Miller's "Trollope's Thackeray" on the continuing value of this early retrospect.

12. See my longer article version of this reading of Macaulay with its extensive notes and bibliography (172–74).

13. Pincus's *1688* (2009) sees the Glorious Revolution as far more violent than Macaulay's influential version. This possibility complements my thesis: Macaulay systematically downplayed the military aspect in his people's history's first two volumes and intentionally increased it in the more heroic later ones.

14. Woolf and Forster register Macaulay's canonical status—and the beginning of its decline with the Modernists, especially in contrast to Gibbon.

15. See Duncan for the displacement of epic poets by novelists in the nineteenth century. Rosenberg's *Carlyle and the Burden of History,* 29–53, surveys the theoretical and literary historical issues surrounding the notion of a modern epic in prose. Mark Cumming's *Disimprison'd Epic* (1988) provides the fullest discussion.

16. Tucker's *Epic,* 190–233, showcases several epics published from 1815 to 1820 that retained the kind of neoclassical conventions Macaulay's essay mocks.

17. As with his use of Saint-Simon's *Memoirs* for his accounts of continental warfare, Macaulay's reliance on a dubious source for his epic narrative is more extensive than his notes admit.

18. See Levine 79–163, but especially 162–63, for a complementary reading of Macaulay's career as one marked by "progress" then "retreat."

19. For a broader treatment of Carlyle's tense relation to the modern, of his paradoxical combination of eager prescience and heroic resistance, see LaValley.

4. UTILITARIANISM AND THE INTELLECTUAL CRITIQUE OF WAR

1. Edmund Silberner's *The Problem of War in Nineteenth-Century Economic Thought* (1946) is a valuable overview of the basics of this Victorian debate. Niall Ferguson's *The Cash Nexus* (2001) is a contemporary restatement, with a Carlylean title, of the issue and possesses an excellent bibliography. Most interesting is the work of Stephen Jay Gould, particularly in *Time's Arrow, Time's Cycle* (1987), on Charles Lyell. Gould emphasizes the intensity of the Victorian debate over historical agency. Lyell best stated the basic problem and was a key influence on both Creasy and Buckle—not to mention Tennyson and Darwin. His famous *Principles of Geology* (1830–33) opens with a contrast of battle history and natural history—and thus the contest between spectacular heroic causes and unnoticed ones pervades his argument.

2. Richard Burton's late and unfinished *Book of the Sword* (1884) represents an idiosyncratic effort to counter the trend toward Spencerian industrial-impersonal agency with a picturesquely heroic-nostalgic paradigm, while Thorstein Veblen's *Theory of the Leisure Class* (1899) presents an intensified version of Spencer's "impersonal" model in the form of a brilliant satire upon Burton's brand of nostalgic heroic thinking.

3. Carlyle's *Past and Present* and Tennyson's *Maud* are the two best examples of this conservative Victorian pattern of seeing open heroic warfare as preferable to the disguised warfare of capitalism. Mill deplores the latter, looks forward to progressing beyond it, but seems to find nothing to admire in the former.

4. Walzer, *Just and Unjust Wars* 87–96, has the most informed brief analysis of Mill's theory of intervention, but he minimizes the conflicts between Mill's political economics and his liberal interventionism and pays no attention to the rhetorical contrasts between the former's skeptical restraint and the latter's heroic exuberance. For a valuable critique of Mill's rhetoric, see Hamburger 203–24. Hamburger notes Mill's "method of silence, of misleading by avoiding the occasion to address an issue" (218), which appears in his silence on the subject of war.

5. See Noam Chomsky's *Failed States* (2006) and Sullivan 610–17.

6. See Keegan, *Face of Battle* 57–61.

7. Throughout this book, "scientific history" designates the Cartesian effort to elevate history into a natural science, which is what Buckle is trying to do (and later Adams) and which Creasy rejects. The term can cause confusion. Collingwood, the influential philosopher of history, attacks this notion of history as a science, but uses the term to indicate a humanist endeavor, in the anti-Cartesian tradition of Vico that, under the guidance of German textual scholarship, was learning to treat its documents more "scientifically." See W. Jan Van Der Dussen's *History as a Science* (1981) for the most thorough exploration of Collingwood's version.

8. See Parker on English historians' resistance to positivism generally and see Beirne: "Quetelet's writings on crime exerted a great influence on work as diverse in content and separated in time as Henry Buckle's *History of Civilization in England* (1860) and Charles Goring's celebrated *The English Convict* (1913)" (1162). Quetelet applied his methods primarily to criminals, and that emphasis colored Buckle's dim view of historical heroes.

9. Diamond, 405–25, has an authoritative overview of the effort to turn history into a science. Hanson, 359–61, sums up his version of Creasyan "decisive battle" history and discusses his debates with Diamond: they epitomize the persistence of this contest.

10. See Quint.

11. See Pocock's analyses of Voltaire's histories (2:72–162).

12. See Semmel.

13. G. A. Wells notes that Acton was the earliest and fiercest critic.

14. See Parker 125–26 for another analysis of Acton's critique.

15. See Beirne 1161–66 on the critics of Quetelet.

5. POPEIAN STRATEGIES IN PRIMITIVE AND MODERN WAR EPIC

1. See Wohlgemut on Southey, Macaulay, and picturesque history. Cleere and Macarthur helpfully discuss sanitization and the sublime in Ruskin.

2. Gladstone finds a prototype of England's Parliament and cabinet in the Homeric assemblies and councils (3:94–144), but no parallel in the Trojan practices (3:206–49).

3. See Burrow's *History of Histories*, 154–228, for an in-depth treatment of English history, Whig politics, and the Germanic *witenagemot;* and Culler 154–55 for a much briefer survey of claims regarding the same.

4. Alternatively, Harrison, 1–13, presents a suggestive Vico-based commentary on Roman enmity toward, fear of, and likeness to the Germans as a function of a deeper love-hate relation to the forest from which their city rose and into which it would decline: the Germans, in Morris's *House of the Wolfings*, are similarly rising as they clear the forests, but the urban-palatial end of this progress will be their doom.

5. See Best for the mid-nineteenth-century developments for treatment of prisoners, civilians, etc., that established practices that Morris's barbarians follow. See Best 150–52 for the first Geneva Convention meeting of 1864.

6. Riddlehough, 338–46, argues that Morris has deliberately translated Vergil to make him more "barbaric."

7. See Spatt 361 and 366 for Morris and Carlyle on Odin as a kind of God-Man.

8. "A Visit to an Old Bachelor" in Gaskell's *Cranford* (1851) dramatizes the re-pute of Tennyson's sharp eye.

9. As with Southey, there is a long-standing critical tradition of wrangling over whether to see his narrative poems as romances or epics.

10. See Green, *Seven Types* 179–83, for a Haggard-inflected reading of this heroic narrative. My approach, which emphasizes its historical and epic dimen-sions—and its portions in verse, sees it in light of culturally privileged categories that link it to *Sigurd the Volsung* and Tacitus.

11. See the end page of Longman's 1903 edition.

12. Peter Wells, 191–92, presents the most up-to-date scholarship on German atrocities, but Tacitus recorded the essential horrors.

13. Rosenberg's *Fall of Camelot*, 66–73, discusses the morality of battle in Ten-nyson and its relation to moral and visual clarity.

14. "A German archaeologist wrote to Morris asking him what new sources of information he used in writing *The House of the Wolfings*" (Thompson 784). Green, *Seven Types* 179–83, also emphasizes this anthropological dimension.

15. See Mackail 1:340–43 for the best example of the common assertion of a distinctly Homeric quality to *Sigurd the Volsung*.

16. Tucker's thesis is meant to rescue Morris from the frequent complaints, then and now, about his archaisms.

17. In *On Heroes,* Carlyle insisted that such heroes be real, not allegorical.

18. Frye, *Secular Scripture* 6–8.

19. "Kinglake's voluminous 'History of the Crimean War,' once so eagerly read, is now almost forgotten" (Gooch 375).

20. The most popular account is Cecil Woodham-Smith's *The Reason Why* (1954). It details the war's most well-known feature—the criminal incompetence of the authorities overseeing it. Kinglake's grandeur contrasts with all this war's dominant memes.

21. Ulrich Keller's *Ultimate Spectacle* (2001) thoroughly documents all the modernities of the Crimean War.

22. Richard Altick's *Life and Letters* (1969) is the definitive study of family propriety's influence over conventional Victorian biography. Royle, 509–11, gives the background for Raglan's family's relation to Kinglake's project.

23. See Crotty for an excellent scholarly example or Hollywood's *Troy* (2004) for a popular one.

6. LIBERAL EPIC BEFORE THE GREAT WAR

1. See George Dangerfield's *Strange Death of Liberal England* (1961) for the Liberal Party's triumph of 1907 and disaster of 1911. See Hernon 73–75 for the relationship of Trevelyan's history to this fall.

2. See Cannadine, *Trevelyan* 66. Hernon, 84, presents Trevelyan's own judg-ment to this effect.

3. Cannadine 153–79 explores Trevelyan's preservationist activities.

4. See Lock's "Hardy Promises," 87–89, for his liberal and imperialist aristo-cratic socializing while engaged on *The Dynasts.*

5. See Lock, "Hardy Promises" 98–111, for a detailed account of the deepening Vergilian logic of Hardy's evolving editions of *The Dynasts*.

6. Clifford, 160–61, details Hardy's efforts to make his epic-drama as historically accurate as possible—even to rendering much of its verse distinctly prosaic.

7. For his grand plans for *The Woodlanders* delayed and saved for his epic, see *Life* 182; for his response to the critic who seemed bewildered by his novel *Tess*, presuming to reference the machinery of Greek tragedy, see *Life* 251–52.

8. Hardy's autobiography regularly discounts the belief that a novel could have the power to achieve any social reform in the tradition of Dickens or Zola. See *Life* 280 and 288 for two examples among many of this pattern. Hardy usually puts the term " 'purpose' novel" in dismissive scare quotes.

9. For the larger context for this reading of Trevelyan's stance, see Jann in particular, her claim that Trevelyan is the key transitional figure (142).

10. See Tracy 92–97 for a suggestive analysis of the parallels between Tennyson's and Trollope's weak heroes.

11. See Wright 177–78 for Hardy's use of Napier—especially his numerous maps that Hardy carefully marked up in his personal edition. These battlefield maps and Napier's rich evocations of the landscapes largely explain the often-asserted "filmic" qualities of this epic-drama's battles.

12. Thomas Hardy to Mrs. Henniker, Oct. 11, 1899 (*Letters* 2:232).

13. Whitehead notes the lack of critical attention to Tolstoy's influence on Hardy; he sees more in common in their views on war, but stresses Hardy's patriotism.

14. "One" is the correct reading. (Spirit Ironic's "As once . . ." four lines later seems to preclude the possibility of an unnoted error convenient for me here.) Furthermore, this passage directly and ironically answers a more immediate question. Nonetheless, the larger mood of this conclusion has irony on the rare defensive and pity feeling confident in the manner described.

15. See Jenkins, 47–63, for Churchill's adventure with the Boers and his popular telegraph reporting.

16. See Berlin, *Proper Study* 457–58.

17. Berlin, *Proper Study* 452. His translation of *War and Peace*'s epilogue emphasizes Tolstoy's heavy, self-conscious use of "kill."

18. See Green's *Origins of Nonviolence*, 209–19, for the relentless attacks, often by liberals, upon Tolstoy for his vigorous campaigning for nonviolence from 1894 to 1910.

19. Hernon, 75–76, discusses Trevelyan's joy over the victory of the Dreyfusards in France in and his deep admiration for Zola's literary heroism. He speculates that only his resistance to writing contemporary history prevented him from writing a major work on heroic liberal France.

20. Scirocco, x–xi, lists various contemporary demands for an epic on Garibaldi, since his career seemed to demand such treatment. Riall, 13–14, discusses how well Garibaldi fit Trevelyan's need for a perfect heroic-historical morality tale.

21. Hernon's comment on Trevelyan's "weaknesses in failing to explore the economic and social causes of Italian nationalism" (73) echoes the major note of criticism in contemporary reviews.

22. See "Shelley's Skylark" for Hardy's more normal grimly ironic lyrical mode.

23. Fussell and Modris Eksteins's *Rites of Spring* (1989) have the fullest accounts of the opposing modernist convention of disgust over the death of youth in battle.

24. See Burrow's *Liberal Descent*, 174–84, for the urban, archeological, and geological historiography of Edward Freeman. Freeman was the most important Victorian historian to write on Sicily before Trevelyan, and it is striking to contrast Freeman's innovative and scientific attention to landscape to the later historian's romantic and touristic emphases.

25. Riall, 272–305, provides a detailed analysis of the Garibaldian legend's flirtation with sainthood—and its effect on Trevelyan.

26. For an overview of the political debates surrounding Trevelyan's easy linkage of nationalism and freedom, see Butterfield for the classic account of Whig optimism and Schleffer in McKim and McMahan, 191–208, for more skeptical analyses.

27. Davidson, 10–12, briefly explains how war made this good liberal into the radical economist that the rest of his book defends.

28. It profoundly reshaped British policy through 1945, but his postwar efforts crafting a world economic system to preclude war were largely frustrated by the new Pax Americana. See Moggridge 627–48 and Davidson 116–25.

7. FROM LIBERAL EPIC TO EPIC LIBERALISM

1. Churchill both conforms to Eksteins's thesis that World War I decisively pushed modernism to an aesthetic of youth-sacrifice and challenges it by embodying an older, pre-liberal, Homeric variation.

2. See Sullivan.

3. See Cannadine, *Blood, Toil* 1–11, Fussell 18–29, and Berlin, *Proper Study* 605.

4. See John Charmley's aptly titled *Churchill: The End of Glory* (1993) and its basic thesis of the imperialist basis of Churchill's liberalism.

5. See Martin Gilbert's *Churchill in America* (2005).

6. See Valiunas's citations for an example of how most literary criticism of Churchill's histories depends entirely upon a biographical approach.

7. Qtd. in Cannadine, *Blood, Toil* 11.

8. Hanson unironically appeals both to violent domination (carnage) and heroic agency to explain Western cultural superiority.

9. His most important assistant was John Ashley, who is not credited in the *Marlborough* volumes. Namier, whom Churchill asked to read and critique volume 1, gives stylistic, rhetorical, and thematic praise and criticism, but points out that on matters of fact, he is separately corresponding with Ashley: "With the petty detail I do not mean to trouble you—corrections which I have to suggest on that nature I have communicated to Ashley" (Gilbert's companion to volume 5, part 2, page 720).

10. All the biographies treat Churchill's pleasures in historical composition in bed. See Ashley's *Churchill's Method of Writing History*, 22–37, for the most intimate account. See Ignatieff 125 for Isaiah Berlin's reactions.

11. See Roosevelt's *The Naval War of 1812:* "Napier possessed to a very eminent degree the virtue of being plain-spoken" (265).

12. This observation from the official history of the British Cavalry is quoted by Jenkins 40–41.

13. Grafton's judgment excuses my exclusion of another rival here, Trevelyan, who during the 1930s was composing an epic trilogy, one comparable to his earlier *Garibaldi Trilogy*, on the same period. He colorfully narrates the same Marlborough battles. Trevelyan, however, is a weak compromise figure here: not as gung-ho as Churchill, and constantly worried—"I have been terrified by the fear of its becoming 'drum and trumpet history,' especially in these anti-war times" (qtd. in Hernon 85)—that he was being outstripped by the likes of Wedgwood.

14. See Soffer on the professionalization of history in Oxbridge historians.

15. Ferguson's statistical tables documents the Seven Years' War's very high costs in lives and capital (xxxv).

16. The citation and the ones following are from companion volume 2 to volume 1 of this huge biography.

17. Though Trevelyan's history of the same period largely shares Churchill's more admiring view of Marlborough, the literary logic of epic rivalry and filiopiety led him to publicly critique the intensity of Churchill's attack on his great-uncle Macaulay (Hernon 85).

18. Namier objected, "My first criticism concerns your pre-occupation with Macaulay" (720).

19. See my article on Macaulay for a fuller treatment of his literary ambitions and rhetoric (145–58).

20. See Plumb 257, where Macaulay recalls the "bulk" of the poem "without fault."

21. In *Nationalism and Irony* (2004), Yoon Sun Lee has elegantly teased out their entanglements in the writings of Burke, Scott, and Carlyle. I see irony as essential not so much to the nation as to the liberal nation. Irony is certainly an essential feature of liberal epic narratives in celebration of national self-determination, as it is of the elaborate, evasive poetic diction that first enabled them. But the gradual eradication of irony and its elegant diction seems a prerequisite for the rise and growth of liberal imperialism or what I am calling epic liberalism. Certainly, such eager disciples of Churchill as Hanson and Boot recognize the shock value of their titles—*Culture and Carnage* and *The Savage Wars of Peace*, respectively—but are committed to explaining the irony away. (Boot goes so far as to borrow his title from the deliberately ironic and anti-imperialist *A Savage War of Peace* 1977 by Alistair Horne on the Algerian War: American-Churchillian liberal imperialists allow no irony.) The point is to learn that Western warfare is not beset by paradox, but is honest and ultimately humane. Tacitus, the pithiest historian, who is "one of the few great writers who are utterly without hope" (Trilling 194) manages to impugn, in a single clause, both the lies of elegant diction and of manly honesty: "solitudinem faciunt, pacem appellant" ("they make a wasteland and call it peace" [*Agricola* 30])—helpless and hopeless.

EPILOGUE

1. Michael Adams's *The Best War Ever* (1993) documents this phenomenon. Nicholson Baker's *Human Smoke: The Beginnings of World War II, the End of Civilization* (2008) eloquently objects.

2. David Smith, 476–77, maps Wells's complicated final additions to this version of his central work.

3. Wills notes Adams's innovations in assessing war's action by means of financial and industrial analyses, but does not realize that, for Adams, this result represented a larger failure for Jefferson's America—and his history.

4. Richard Mayne in his introduction to Braudel's *A History of Civilizations* (1993) provides the biographical data and notes this patriotic motive behind long duration. This later work, removed from the pull of World War II, also finds Braudel back at scientific history where war comes to be seen not through epic lenses but through "polemology."

5. Bourke, *Intimate History* 63–76, provides a critical overview of the debate. Keegan, "Historian and Battle" 145–47, assesses Marshall's "genius" and "greatness."

WORKS CITED

Acton, Lord. *Essays in the Liberal Interpretation of History.* Chicago: U of Chicago P, 1967.

Adams, Edward. "Macaulay's History of England and the Dilemmas of Liberal Epic." *Nineteenth-Century Prose* 33 (2006): 149–74.

Adams, Henry. *History of the United States of America.* 2 vols. New York: Library of America, 1986.

Aickin, Joseph. *Londerias.* Dublin, 1699.

Ammianus Marcellinus. *Histories.* Trans. J. C. Rolfe. 3 vols. Cambridge, MA: Harvard UP, 1935.

Arnold, Matthew. *The Poems of Matthew Arnold.* London: Longman's, 1965.

Ashley, Maurice. *Churchill as Historian.* New York: Charles Scribner's, 1968.

Auerbach, Erich. *Mimesis.* Trans. Willard Trask. Princeton, NJ: Princeton UP, 2003.

Badian, E. "Gibbon on War." *Gibbon et Rome.* Ed. Pierre Ducrey. Geneve: Drox, 1977. 103–36.

Bainbridge, Simon. *Napoleon and English Romanticism.* Cambridge: Cambridge UP, 1995.

Bakhtin, M. M. *The Dialogic Imagination.* Trans. Caryl Emerson and Michael Holquist. Austin: U of Texas P, 1981.

Barbero, Alessandro. *The Battle: A New History of Waterloo.* Trans. John Cullen. New York: Walker, 2003.

Barlow, Joel. *The Columbiad.* Washington, DC: Milligan, 1825.

Bathhurst, James, ed. "Letters from Colonel William Napier to Sir John Colborne." *English Historical Review* 18 (1903): 725–53.

Beirne, Piers. "Adolphe Quetelet and the Origins of Positivist Criminology." *American Journal of Sociology* 92 (1987): 1140–69.

Berlin, Isaiah. Introduction. *Considerations on France.* By Joseph de Maistre. Trans. Richard Lebrun. Cambridge: Cambridge UP, 1994.

———. *The Proper Study of Mankind.* New York: Farrar, Strauss & Giroux, 1998.

Best, Geoffrey. *Humanity in Warfare.* New York: Columbia UP, 1980.

Bigelow, John. *William Cullen Bryant.* New York: Chelsea House, 1980.

Blake, William. "On Homer's Poetry." *Blake's Poetry and Designs.* Ed. Mary Lynn Johnson and John E. Grant. New York: Norton, 1979. 428.

Bolingbroke, Lord. *The Works of Lord Bolingbroke.* 4 vols. London: Bohn, 1844.

Boot, Max. *The Savage Wars of Peace.* New York: Basic Books, 2002.

Bordwell, Percy. *The Law of War between Belligerents.* Littleton, CO: F. B. Rothman, 1994.

Bourke, Joanna. *Dismembering the Male.* Chicago: U of Chicago P, 1996.

———. *An Intimate History of Killing.* New York: Basic Books, 1999.

Brailsford, H. N. *Shelley, Godwin, and Their Circle.* London: Oxford UP, 1913.

Braudel, Fernand. *The Mediterranean and the Mediterranean World.* 2 vols. Trans. Sian Reynolds. New York: Harper & Row, 1972.

Bruce, H. A. *Life of General Sir William Napier.* 2 vols. London: Murray, 1864.

Buckle, Henry Thomas. *History of Civilization in England.* 3 vols. Oxford: Oxford UP, 1903.

Burke, Edmund. *A Philosophical Enquiry into the Origin of Our Ideas of the Sublime and the Beautiful.* Oxford: World's Classics, 1990.

Burrow, J. W. *A History of Histories.* New York: Knopf, 2008.

———. *A Liberal Descent.* Cambridge: Cambridge UP, 1981.

Bury, J. B., ed. *The Decline and Fall of the Roman Empire.* By Edward Gibbon. 7 vols. London: Metheun, 1896.

———. *The Invasion of Europe by the Barbarians.* New York: W. W. Norton, 1967.

Butler, Samuel, trans. *The Iliad.* Mineola, NY: Dover, 1999.

Byron, George Gordon (Lord). *Don Juan.* Ed. T. G. Steffan, E. Steffan, and W. W. Pratt. London: Penguin, 1973.

———. *Selected Poems.* Ed. Susan J. Wolfson and Peter J. Manning. London: Penguin, 1996.

Campbell, Timothy. "'The Business of War': William Godwin, Enmity, and Historical Representation." *ELH* 76 (2009): 343–69.

Cannadine, David, ed. *Blood, Toil, Tears, and Sweat.* Boston: Houghton Mifflin, 1989.

———. *G. M. Trevelyan.* New York: W. W. Norton, 1992.

Carlisle, Janice. *The Sense of an Audience.* Athens: U of Georgia P, 1981.

Carlyle, Thomas. *History of Friedrich II of Prussia Called Frederick the Great.* 8 vols. London: Chapman & Hall, 1897.

———. *On Heroes and Hero-Worship.* Lincoln: U of Nebraska P, 1966.

Carnall, Geoffrey. *Robert Southey and His Age.* Oxford: Oxford UP, 1960.

Chandos, John. *Boys Together: English Public Schools, 1800–64.* New Haven, CT: Yale UP, 1984.

Cherel, Albert. *Fénelon au XVIIIe siècle en France.* Paris: Hachette, 1917.

Churchill, Randolph. *Winston S. Churchill.* Vols. 1–2. Boston: Houghton & Mifflin, 1966–83.

Churchill, Winston. *Marlborough.* 2 vols. Chicago: U of Chicago P, 2002.

———. *The River War.* New York: Carroll & Graf, 2000.

———. *A Roving Commission.* New York: Scribner's, 1930.

———. *The Story of the Malakand Field Force.* Brooklyn: 29 Books, 2004.

Cleere, Eileen. "Dirty Pictures: John Ruskin, 'Modern Painters,' and the Victorian Sanitation of Fine Art." *Representations* 78 (2002): 116–39.

Clifford, Emma. "Thomas Hardy and the Historians." *Studies in Philology* 56.4 (1959): 654–58.

Coleridge, Samuel Taylor. *Biographia Literaria. The Major Works.* Ed. H. J. Jackson. Oxford: Oxford UP, 1985. 135–482.

————. *Table Talk*. 2 vols. London: Routledge, 1990.

Collingwood, R. G. *Autobiography*. Oxford: Oxford UP, 1939.

Craddock, Patricia. *Edward Gibbon: Luminous Historian*. Baltimore: Johns Hopkins UP, 1989.

Creasy, Edward. *The Fifteen Decisive Battles of World History*. London: Dent, 1908.

————. *First Platform of International Law*. London: Voorst, 1876.

Crotty, Kevin. *Poetics of Supplication*. Ithaca, NY: Cornell UP, 1994.

Cullen, A. Dwight. *The Victorian Mirror of History*. New Haven, CT: Yale UP, 1985.

Dames, Nicholas. "Thackeray and the Work of Celebrity." *Nineteenth-Century Literature* 56.1 (2001): 23–51.

Davidson, Paul. *John Maynard Keynes*. New York: Palgrave, 2007.

Defoe, Daniel. *Robinson Crusoe*. London: Penguin, 2001.

Des Pres, Terence. "Terror and the Sublime." *Human Rights Quarterly* 5 (1983): 135–46.

Diamond, Jared. *Guns, Germs, and Steel*. New York: Norton, 1997.

Douglas, Dennis. "Thackeray and the Uses of History." *Yearbook of English Studies* 5 (1975): 164–77.

Dryden, John. *Poems and Fables*. Oxford: Oxford UP, 1970.

————, trans. *Virgil's Aeneid*. Harmondsworth, UK: Penguin, 1997.

Dunant, Henri. *A Memory of Solferino*. Washington, DC: American National Red Cross, 1959.

Duncan, Ian. *Scott's Shadow*. Princeton, NJ: Princeton UP, 2007.

Eastwood, David. "Robert Southey and the Intellectual Origins of Romantic Conservatism." *English Historical Review* 104 (1989): 308–31.

Eisler, Benita. *Byron*. New York: Knopf, 1999.

Eliot, George. *Middlemarch*. London: Penguin, 1995.

Epstein, James. *Radical Expression: Political Language, Ritual, and Symbol in England, 1790–1850*. Oxford: Oxford UP, 1994.

Fénelon, François. *Adventures of Telemachus*. Trans. Tobias Smollett. Athens: U of Georgia P, 1997.

————. *Oeuvres*. Vol. 2. Paris: Gallimard, 1997.

Ferguson, Niall. *The War of the World*. New York: Penguin, 2006.

Fisch, Max Harold. Introduction to *The Autobiography of Giambattista Vico*. Ithaca, NY: Cornell UP, 1944. 1–107.

Flaubert, Gustave. *Salammbo*. Trans. A. J. Krailsheimer. Harmondsworth: Penguin, 1977.

Fludernik, Monika. "William Godwin's *Caleb Williams:* The Tarnishing of the Sublime." *ELH* 68 (2001): 857–96.

Foucault, Michel. *Discipline and Punish*. Trans. Alan Sheridan. New York: Vintage, 1991.

————. *"Society Must Be Defended": Lectures at the Collège de France, 1975–76*. Trans. David Macey. New York: Picador, 1997.

Froude, James Anthony. *Thomas Carlyle: A History of His Life in London*. 2 vols. London: Longman's, 1884.

Frye, Northrup. *Secular Scripture*. Cambridge, MA: Harvard UP, 1975.

Fussell, Paul. *The Great War and Modern Memory*. Oxford: Oxford UP, 1975.

Gallagher, Catherine. *Nobody's Story*. Berkeley: U of California, P, 1994.

Gibbon, Edward. *The Decline and Fall of the Roman Empire*. 3 vols. Harmondsworth, UK: Penguin, 1994.

———. *Memoirs*. Harmondsworth, UK: Penguin, 1990.

Gilbert, Martin. *Winston S. Churchill*. Vols. 3–8. Boston: Houghton & Mifflin, 1966–83.

Gissing, George. *Private Papers of Henry Ryecroft*. Bibliobazaar, 2007.

Gladstone, William. *Studies on Homer and the Homeric Age*. 3 vols. Oxford: Oxford UP, 1858.

Godwin, William. *Enquiry concerning Political Justice*. 2 vols. Toronto: U of Toronto P, 1946.

Gooch, G. P. *History and Historians in the Nineteenth Century*. Boston: Beacon Press, 1959.

Grafton, Anthony. *The Footnote*. Cambridge, MA: Harvard UP, 1997.

Green, Martin. *The Origins of Nonviolence*. University Park: Pennsylvania State UP, 1986.

———. *Seven Types of Adventure Tale*. University Park: Pennsylvania State UP, 1991.

Grotius, Hugo. *De Jure Belli et Pacis*. Washington, DC: Carnegie Institute, 1913.

———. *The Rights of War and Peace*. Trans. A. Campbell. Washington, DC: Dunne, 1901.

Guillory, John. *Cultural Capital*. Chicago: U of Chicago P, 1993.

Hallam, Henry. *History of Europe during the Middle Ages*. 2 vols. New York: Colonial Press, 1899.

Hamburger, Joseph. *John Stuart Mill on Liberty and Control*. Princeton, NJ: Princeton UP, 1999.

Hanson, Victor Davis. *Carnage and Culture*. New York: Anchor, 2001.

Harden, Edgar. *Thackeray the Writer*. New York: St. Martin's, 2000.

Hardy, Thomas. *Collected Letters*. 7 vols. Ed. Richard Little Purdy and Michael Millgate. Oxford: Oxford UP, 1978–88.

———. *The Dynasts*. London: MacMillan, 1925.

———. *The Hand of Ethelberta*. London: Penguin, 1997.

———. *The Life of Thomas Hardy*. Ware, UK: Wordsworth Editions, 2007.

———. *The Trumpet-Major*. Harmondsworth, UK: Penguin, 1997.

Harrison, Robert Pogue. *Forests: The Shadow of Civilization*. U of Chicago P, 1992.

Harth, Phillip. *Contexts of Dryden's Thought*. Chicago: Chicago UP, 1968.

Hayley, William. *An Essay on Epic Poetry*. Gainesville, FL: Scholars Facsimiles, 1968.

Hepp, Naomi. *Homère en France au XVIIe siècle*. Paris: Klincksieck, 1968.

Hernon, Joseph M., Jr. "The Last Whig Historian and Consensus History." *American Historical Review* 81.1 (1976): 66–67.

Hobbes, Thomas, trans. *The Iliads and Odysseys of Homer*. London: Crook, 1677.

———, trans. *Peloponnesian War*. By Thucydides. Chicago: U of Chicago P, 1989.

Holt, Lee. *Samuel Butler*. New York: Grosset & Dunlap, 1964.

Horkheimer, Max, and Theodor Adorno. *Dialectic of Enlightenment*. Trans. Edmund Jephcott. Stanford, CA: Stanford UP, 2002.

Horn, Robert. "Addison's Campaign and Macaulay." *PMLA* 63 (1948): 886–902.

Howard, Michael. Foreword. *The Shield of Achilles.* By Philip Bobbitt. New York: Anchor, 2002. xv–xix.

——. *War and the Liberal Conscience.* New Brunswick, NJ: Rutgers UP, 1978.

Hughes, Robert. *Goya.* New York: Knopf, 2003.

Hume, David. *Enquiries concerning Human Understanding and concerning the Principles of Morals.* Oxford: Oxford UP, 1975.

——. *Essays.* Indianapolis: Liberty Fund, 1985.

——. *History of England.* 6 vols. Indianapolis: Liberty Fund, 1983.

Ignatieff, Michael. *Isaiah Berlin.* New York: Metropolitan Books, 1998.

Irving, Washington. *A History of New York.* New York: Library of America, 1983.

James, William. "The Moral Equivalent of War." *War.* Ed. Leon Bramson. New York: Basic Books, 1964. 21–31.

——. *A Pluralistic Universe.* Lincoln: U of Nebraska P, 1996.

Jann, Rosemary. "From Amateur to Professional." *Journal of British Studies* 22 (1983): 122–47.

Jenkins, Roy. *Churchill.* New York: Plume, 2002.

Joll, James. *The Anarchists.* London: Eyre & Spottiswoode, 1964.

Johnson, Samuel. *Lives of the Most Eminent English Poets.* 3 vols. London: Murray, 1854.

Keegan, John. *The Face of Battle.* New York: Viking, 1976.

——. *The Mask of Command.* Harmondsworth, UK: Penguin, 1987.

——. *Winston Churchill.* New York: Penguin, 2002.

Keynes, J. M. *The Economic Consequences of the Peace.* London: Macmillan, 1919.

——. *The General Theory of Employment Interest and Money.* New York: Harcourt, Brace, 1936.

Kinglake, Alexander William. *Eothen.* Evanston, IL: Marlboro Press, 1992.

——. *The Invasion of the Crimea.* 9 vols. Edinburgh: Blackwood, 1863–87.

Knapp, Lewis. "Smollett's Translation of Fénelon's *Télémaque.*" *Philological Quarterly* 44 (1964): 390–416.

Kushner, David. *Masters of Doom.* New York: Random House, 2003.

Lanza, Conrad. "War and Peace through History." *American Journal of Economics and Sociology* 16 (1957): 433–38.

Larsson, Stieg. *The Girl Who Played with Fire.* Trans. Reg Keeland. New York: Vintage, 2009.

LaValley, Albert. *Carlyle and the Idea of the Modern.* New Haven, CT: Yale UP, 1968.

Lecky, William. *History of European Morals from Augustus to Charlemagne.* 2 vols. London: Longman's, Green, 1913.

Leigh, John. *Voltaire: A Sense of History.* Oxford: Voltaire Foundation, 2004.

Lenin, V. I. *Imperialism, the Highest Stage of Capitalism.* Peking: Foreign Languages Press, 1973.

Levine, George. *The Boundaries of Fiction.* Princeton, NJ: Princeton UP, 1968.

Lock, Charles. "Hardy and the Critics." *Thomas Hardy Studies.* Ed. Phillipp Mallett. New York: Palgrave, 2004. 14–37.

——. "Hardy Promises: *The Dynasts* and the Epic of Imperialism." *Reading Thomas Hardy.* Ed. Charles Pettit. New York: St. Martin's, 1998. 83–116.

Locke, John. *Some Thoughts concerning Education.* Oxford: Oxford UP, 1989.

Lockhart, J. G. *Life of Sir Walter Scott.* 2 vols. Philadelphia: Blanchard, 1838.

Lukacs, John. *Churchill: Visionary, Statesman, Historian.* New Haven, CT: Yale UP, 2002.

Lynch, Kathryn. "Homer's *Iliad* and Pope's Vile Forgery." *Comparative Literature* 34 (1982): 1–15.

Lyotard, Jean-François. *The Postmodern Condition.* Trans. Geoff Bennington and Brian Massumi. Minneapolis: U of Minnesota P, 1984.

Macarthur, John. "The Heartlessness of the Picturesque." *Assemblage* 32 (1997): 126–41.

Macaulay, Thomas Babington. *The History of England.* 5 vols. New York: Harper & Brothers, 1877.

———. *Miscellaneous Essays and Poems.* 3 vols. Boston: Houghton Mifflin, 1901.

Mack, Maynard. *Alexander Pope.* New York: W. W. Norton, 1985.

Mackail, J. W. *The Life of William Morris.* 2 vols. London: Longmans, Green, 1922.

Marshall, David. "Arguing by Analogy: Hume's Standard of Taste." *Eighteenth-Century Studies* 28 (1995): 323–43.

Marshall, S. L. A. *Men against Fire.* Washington, DC: Infantry Journal, 1947.

Maude, Alymer. *The Life of Tolstoy.* Oxford: Oxford UP, 1987.

Mazower, Mark. *Dark Continent.* New York: Vintage, 2000.

McGann, Jerome. *Byron and Romanticism.* Cambridge: Cambridge UP, 2002.

———. *Don Juan in Context.* Chicago: U of Chicago P, 1976.

McKim, Robert, and Jeff McMahan, eds. *The Morality of Nationalism.* New York: Oxford UP, 1997.

Mill, John Stuart. *Autobiography.* Boston: Houghton Mifflin, 1969.

———. *Dissertations and Discussions.* Vol. 3. New York: Henry Holt, 1874.

———. *Principles of Political Economy.* 2 vols. New York: Appleton, 1882.

Miller, Andrew. *Novels behind Glass.* Cambridge: Cambridge UP, 1995.

Miller, J. Hillis. *Thomas Hardy: Distance and Desire.* Cambridge, MA: Harvard UP, 1970.

———. "Trollope's Thackeray." *Nineteenth-Century Fiction* 37 (1982): 350–57.

Milton, John. *History of Britain.* New York: Columbia UP, 1932.

Moggridge, D. E. *Maynard Keynes.* London: Routledge, 1992.

Monod, Gabriel. *Vie et Pensée de Jules Michelet.* 2 vols. Paris: E. Chompion, 1923.

More, Paul. Introduction. *Private Papers of Henry Rycroft.* By George Gissing. London: Boni & Liveright, 1918. iii–xii.

Moretti, Franco. *Modern Epic.* London: Verso, 1996.

Morison, J. Cotter. *Macaulay.* London: Macmillan, 1909.

Morris, William. *House of the Wolfings.* New York: Russell & Russell, 1966.

———. *News from Nowhere and Other Writings.* Ed. Clive Wilmer. London: Penguin, 1994.

———. *Sigurd the Volsung.* London: Longman's, Green, 1903.

———. *Works.* 24 vols. New York: Russell & Russell, 1966.

Napier, W. F. *Conquest of Scinde.* London: Boone, 1845.

———. *The History of the War in the Peninsula.* 5 vols. New York: Widdleton, 1863.

Nuttall, A. D. *Why Does Tragedy Give Pleasure?* Oxford: Oxford UP, 1996.

Parker, Christopher. "English Historians and the Opposition to Positivism." *History and Theory* 22.2 (1983): 120–45.

Phillipps, K. C. *The Language of Thackeray.* London: Andre Deutsch, 1978.

Plumb, J. H. *The Making of an Historian.* Athens: U of Georgia P, 1988.

Pocock, J. G. A. *Barbarism and Religion.* 4 vols. Cambridge: Cambridge UP, 1999.

Pope, Alexander, trans. *The Iliad of Homer.* Harmondsworth, UK: Penguin, 1996.

Prothero, Roland, ed. *The Works of Lord Byron.* 6 vols. London: Murray, 1922–24.

Pufendorf, Samuel. *De Jure Naturae et Gentium.* Oxford: Oxford UP, 1934.

Quinault, Roland. "Winston Churchill and Gibbon." *Edward Gibbon and Empire.* Ed. Rosamond McKitterick. Cambridge: Cambridge UP, 1997. 317–32.

Quint, David. *Epic and Empire.* Princeton, NJ: Princeton UP, 1993.

Radcliffe, Evan. "Godwin from 'Metaphysician' to Novelist." *Modern Philology* 97 (2000): 528–53.

Ram, Harsha. *The Imperial Sublime.* Madison: U of Wisconsin P, 2003.

Rawls, John. *Political Liberalism.* New York: Columbia UP, 1996.

Rawson, Claude. "Gibbon, Swift, and Irony." *Edward Gibbon, Bicentenary Essays.* Ed. David Womersley. Oxford: Voltaire Foundation, 1997. 179–202.

———. *Satire and Sentiment.* New Haven, CT: Yale UP, 2000.

Riall, Lucy. *Garibaldi: The Invention of a Hero.* New Haven, CT: Yale UP, 2007.

Ricardo, David. *On the Principles of Political Economy and Taxation.* London: Murray, 1821.

Riddlehough, Geoffrey. "William Morris's Translation of the *Aeneid.*" *Journal of English and Germanic Philology* 30 (1937): 338–46.

Ridenour, George. *The Style of Don Juan.* New Haven, CT: Yale UP, 1960.

Robertson, John Mackinnon. *Buckle and His Critics.* London: Swan Sonnenschein, 1895.

Roosevelt, Theodore. *The Naval War of 1812.* New York: Modern Library, 1996.

Rosenberg, John D. *Carlyle and the Burden of History.* Cambridge, MA: Harvard UP, 1985.

———. *The Fall of Camelot.* Cambridge, MA: Harvard UP, 1973.

Rothschild, Emma. *Economic Sentiments.* Cambridge, MA: Harvard UP, 2001.

Royle, Trevor. *Crimea.* New York: Palgrave, 2000.

Ruskin, John. *The Correspondence of Thomas Carlyle and John Ruskin.* Ed. George Allan Cate. Stanford, CA: Stanford UP, 1982.

———. *Works.* 39 vols. London: George Allen, 1903.

Scarry, Elaine. *The Body in Pain.* New York: Oxford UP, 1985.

Schell, Jonathan. *The Unconquerable World.* New York: Henry Holt, 2003.

Schmitt, Carl. *The Concept of the Political.* Trans. George Schwab. Chicago: U of Chicago P, 1996.

Scirocco, Alfonso. *Garibaldi.* Princeton, NJ: Princeton UP, 2007.

Scott, Sir Walter. *Ivanhoe.* Oxford: Oxford UP, 1996.

———. *Life of Napoleon.* 9 vols. Edinburgh: Caddell, 1834.

———. *The Poems and Plays.* Vol. 1. London: Dent, 1900.

———. *The Tale of Old Mortality.* Harmondsworth, UK: Penguin, 1999.

Segal, Charles. *The Theme of the Mutilation of the Corpse in the "Iliad."* Lugduni Batavorum: E. J. Brill, 1971.

Semmel, Bernard. "H. T. Buckle: The Liberal Faith and the Science of History." *British Journal of Sociology* 27 (1976): 370–86.

Shankman, Steven. *Pope's "Iliad."* Princeton, NJ: Princeton UP, 1983.

Shelley, Percy Bysshe. *Poetical Works*. Ed. Thomas Hutchinson. London: Oxford UP, 1970.

Shillingsburg, Peter. *Pegasus in Harness*. Charlottesville: U of Virginia P, 1992.

Showalter, Dennis. "Of Decisive Battles and Intellectual Fashions." *Military Affairs* 52 (1988): 206–8.

Siebart, Donald. "The Sentimental Sublime in Hume's History of England." *Review of English Studies* 40 (1989): 352–72.

Smith, Adam. *An Inquiry in the Nature and Causes of the Wealth of Nations*. 2 vols. Indianapolis: Liberty Fund, 1981.

Smith, Christopher. *A Quest for Home*. Liverpool: Liverpool UP, 1997.

Smith, David. *H. G. Wells*. New Haven, CT: Yale UP, 1986.

Soffer, Reba. "Nation, Duty, Character and Confidence: History at Oxford, 1850–1914." *Historical Journal* 30.1 (1987): 77–104.

Southey, Charles Cuthbert. *Life and Correspondence of Robert Southey*. New York: Harper, 1851.

Southey, Robert. *Joan of Arc*. Boston: Houghton Mifflin, 1895.

———. *The Life of Admiral Nelson*. New York: Burt, 1902.

———. *Life of Wellington*. Dublin: Mullens, 1816.

Spatt, Hartley. "Morrissaga: Sigurd the Volsung." *ELH* 22 (1977): 355–75.

Speck, W. A. *Robert Southey*. New Haven, CT: Yale UP, 2006.

Spencer, Herbert. *An Autobiography*. 2 vols. New York: Appleton, 1904.

———. *Principles of Ethics*. 2 vols. New York: Appleton, 1904.

———. *Principles of Sociology*. 3 vols. New York: Appleton, 1897.

St. Aubyn, Giles. *A Victorian Eminence*. London: Barrie Books, 1958.

Stabler, Jane. *Byron, Poetics and History*. Cambridge: Cambridge UP, 2002.

Stephen, Leslie, and Sidney Lee. *Dictionary of National Biography*. Vol. 14. Oxford: Oxford UP, 1917.

Sternbach, Robert. "Coleridge, Joan of Arc, and the Idea of Progress." *ELH* 46 (1979): 248–61.

Storey, Mark. *Robert Southey*. Oxford: Oxford UP, 1997.

Strauss, David Friedrich. *The Life of Jesus Critically Examined*. Trans. George Eliot. Ramsay, NJ: Sigler, 1972.

Sullivan, Eileen. "Liberalism and Imperialism." *Journal of the History of Ideas* 44 (1983): 599–617.

Thackeray, William Makepeace. *Barry Lyndon*. Oxford: Oxford UP, 1984.

———. *English Humorists of the Eighteenth Century*. Boston: Ginn, 1911.

———. *Henry Esmond*. Harmondsworth, UK: Penguin, 1985.

———. *Selected Letters*. Ed. Edgar Harden. New York: New York UP, 1996.

———. *Vanity Fair*. Oxford: Oxford UP, 1983.

———. *The Virginians*. 2 vols. London: Dent, 1961.

Thomas, Claudia. *Alexander Pope and His Eighteenth-Century Women Readers*. Carbondale: Southern Illinois UP, 1994.

Thompson, E. P. *William Morris: Romantic to Revolutionary*. New York: Monthly Review, 1961.

Tillotson, Geoffrey. *Essays in Criticism and Research*. Cambridge: Cambridge UP, 1942.

———. *Thackeray the Novelist*. Cambridge: Cambridge UP, 1964.

Tillyard, E. M. W. *The English Epic and Its Background*. New York: Oxford UP, 1954.

Timko, Michael. *Carlyle and Tennyson*. Iowa City: U of Iowa P, 1987.

Tolstoy, Leo. *Essays and Letters*. Trans. Aylmer Maude. Freeport, NY: Books for Libraries Press, 1909.

———. *The Kingdom of God and Peace Essays*. Trans. Aylmer Maude. London: Oxford UP, 1936.

———. *War and Peace*. Trans. Ann Dunnigan. New York: Signet, 1968.

Townsend, Dabney. "Lockean Aesthetics." *Journal of Aesthetics* 49 (1991): 349–61.

Tracy, Robert. *Trollope's Later Novels*. Berkeley: University of California Press, 1978.

Trevelyan, G. M. *English Social History*. Harmondsworth, UK: Pelican, 1964.

———. *The Garibaldi Trilogy*. 3 vols. London: Longmans, Green, 1912.

———. *Poetry and Philosophy of George Meredith*. New York: Scribner, 1912.

Trevelyan, G. O. *Life and Letters of Lord Macaulay*. Detroit: Belford Brothers, 1876.

Trevor-Roper, Hugh. *The Last Days of Hitler*. New York: MacMillan, 1947.

Trilling, Lionel. *The Liberal Imagination*. Garden City, NY: Anchor, 1953.

Trollope, Anthony. *Thackeray*. London: Trollope Society, 1997.

Tucker, Herbert. "All for the Tale: The Epic Macropoetics of Morris's *Sigurd the Volsung*." *Victorian Poetry* 34 (1996): 372–94.

———. *Epic: Britain's Heroic Muse, 1790–1910*. Oxford: Oxford UP, 2008.

———. "Southey the Epic-Headed." *Romanticism on the Net* 32–33 (2003–4).

Valiunas, Algis. *Churchill's Military Histories: A Rhetorical Study*. Lanham, MD: Rowan & Littlefield, 2002.

Vattel, Emmerich de. *The Law of Nations*. Trans. Joseph Chitty. Philadelphia: Johnson, 1863.

Vico, Giambattista. *New Science*. Trans. David Marsh. New York: Penguin, 1999.

Vincent, Edgar. *Nelson: Love and Glory*. New Haven, CT: Yale UP, 2003.

Voltaire. *The Age of Louis XIV*. 2 vols. Trans. William Fleming. Paris: E. R. Dumont, 1901.

———. *History of Charles XII*. Trans. Tobias Smollett. Paris: E. R. Dumont, 1901.

———. *La Henriade*. Charlestown, MA: Rodenburgh, 1836.

Walzer, Michael. *Just and Unjust Wars*. New York: Basic Books, 2000.

Wedgwood, C. V. *Edward Gibbon*. London: Longmans, Green, 1969.

———. *The Thirty Years War*. New York: NYRB, 2005.

Weil, Simone. *The "Iliad," or the Poem of Force*. Wallingford, PA: Pendle Hill, 1956.

Weinbrot, Howard. *Britannia's Issue*. Cambridge: Cambridge UP, 1993.

Wells, G. A. "The Critics of Buckle." *Past and Present* 9 (April 1956): 75–89.

Wells, H. G. *An Experiment in Autobiography*. New York: Macmillan, 1934.

———. *Outline of History*. 2 vols. New York: Macmillan, 1924.

———. *Tono-Bungay*. London: Penguin, 1909.

Wells, Peter. *The Battle That Stopped Rome*. New York: W. W. Norton, 2003.

Whitehead, James. "Hardy and Englishness." *Thomas Hardy Studies*. Ed. Phillip Mallett. New York: Palgrave, 2004.

Wilkie, Brian. *Romantic Poets and Epic Tradition*. Madison: U of Wisconsin P, 1965.

Willcock, M. *"The Iliad" of Homer, I–XII.* London: St. Martin's, 1978.

Williams, Carolyn. *Pope, Homer, and Manliness.* London: Routledge, 1993.

Wills, Garry. *Henry Adams.* Boston: Houghton Mifflin, 2005.

Wohlmegut, Esther. "Southey, Macaulay, and the Idea of a Picturesque History." *Romanticism on the Net* 32–33 (November 2003). http://www.erudit.org/revue/ron/2003/v/n32–33/009261ar.html.

Womersley, David. *The Transformation of "The Decline and Fall of the Roman Empire."* Cambridge: Cambridge UP, 1988.

Wright, Walter. *The Shaping of the Dynasts.* Lincoln: University of Nebraska Press, 1967.

INDEX

Recent Books in the Victorian Literature and Culture Series

Barbara J. Black
On Exhibit: Victorians and Their Museums

Annette R. Federico
Idol of Suburbia: Marie Corelli and Late-Victorian Literary Culture

Talia Schaffer
The Forgotten Female Aesthetes: Literary Culture in Late-Victorian England

Julia F. Saville
A Queer Chivalry: The Homoerotic Asceticism of Gerard Manley Hopkins

Victor Shea and William Whitla, Editors
"Essays and Reviews": The 1860 Text and Its Reading

Marlene Tromp
The Private Rod: Marital Violence, Sensation, and the Law in Victorian Britain

Dorice Williams Elliott
The Angel out of the House: Philanthropy and Gender in Nineteenth-Century England

Richard Maxwell, Editor
The Victorian Illustrated Book

Vineta Colby
Vernon Lee: A Literary Biography

E. Warwick Slinn
Victorian Poetry as Cultural Critique: The Politics of Performative Language

Simon Joyce
Capital Offenses: Geographies of Class and Crime in Victorian London

Caroline Levine
The Serious Pleasures of Suspense: Victorian Realism and Narrative Doubts

Emily Davies
Emily Davies: Collected Letters, 1861–1875
EDITED BY ANN B. MURPHY AND DEIRDRE RAFTERY

Joseph Bizup
Manufacturing Culture: Vindications of Early Victorian Industry

Lynn M. Voskuil
Acting Naturally: Victorian Theatricality and Authenticity

Sally Mitchell
Frances Power Cobbe: Victorian Feminist, Journalist, Reformer

Constance W. Hassett
Christina Rossetti: The Patience of Style

Brenda Assael
The Circus and Victorian Society

Judith Wilt
Behind Her Times: Transition England in the Novels of Mary Arnold Ward

Daniel Hack
The Material Interests of the Victorian Novel

Frankie Morris
Artist of Wonderland: The Life, Political Cartoons, and Illustrations of Tenniel

William R. McKelvy
The English Cult of Literature: Devoted Readers, 1774–1880

Linda M. Austin
Nostalgia in Transition, 1780–1917

James Buzard, Joseph W. Childers, and Eileen Gillooly, Editors
Victorian Prism: Refractions of the Crystal Palace

Michael Field
The Fowl and the Pussycat: Love Letters of Michael Field, 1876–1909
EDITED BY SHARON BICKLE

Dallas Liddle
The Dynamics of Genre: Journalism and the Practice of Literature in Mid-Victorian Britain

Christine L. Krueger
Reading for the Law: British Literary History and Gender Advocacy

Marjorie Wheeler-Barclay
The Science of Religion in Britain, 1860–1915

Carolyn Betensky
Feeling for the Poor: Bourgeois Compassion, Social Action, and the Victorian Novel

John O. Jordan
Supposing "Bleak House"

Edward Adams
Liberal Epic: The Victorian Practice of History from Gibbon to Churchill